Rebalancing Economies in Financially Integrating East Asia

Since the Asian Financial Crisis (AFC) of 1997–98, large current account surpluses have accumulated in the countries of Asia and the Pacific with corresponding deficits elsewhere. The sharp plunge in global trade volumes during the global financial crisis has highlighted the need for 'rebalancing' – focussing more on domestic sources of economic growth than on exports in some Asian economies. One key objective of the book is to elucidate the economic structures and policies that give rise to current account surpluses and imbalances and consider what policy adjustments could change them. Another objective is to show the link between financial systems, financial integration and the transmission of economic shocks between countries.

The book offers new dimensions to understand rebalancing and provides alternative and arguably more fundamental solutions to address imbalances. Rather than focussing on exchange rate misalignment, this book begins with the premise that the imbalances are a macroeconomic problem that reflects a mismatch between savings and investment in the surplus countries. Then, it examines exchange rate policies adopted by countries in the region and finds that part of the explanation for their currency strategy lies in their perceived need to build foreign exchange reserves to provide a buffer in case of instabilities. The book examines whether there are other possibilities for countries to insure against economic volatility by more actively and openly engaging with international capital markets. The studies show that closer financial integration, involving more open financial markets, with well-chosen partners, would be welfare improving and should reduce the need for the counter-productive, self-insurance policies that result in foreign exchange accumulation.

Jenny Corbett is Professor of Economics, Australian National University and Pro Vice-Chancellor (Research and Research Training), Australian National University. She is also Reader in the Economy of Japan, University of Oxford; a Research Associate of the Centre for Applied Macroeconomic Analysis (CAMA); and a Research Fellow at the Centre for Economic Policy Research (CEPR), London.

Ying Xu is Lecturer in the Crawford School of Public Policy, Australian National University. She is also Research Associate at the Centre for Applied Macroeconomic Analysis (CAMA), Australian National University.

Routledge-ERIA Studies in Development Economics

1 **Economic Consequences of Globalization**
Evidence from East Asia
Edited by Shujiro Urata, Chin Hee Hahn and Dionisius Narjoko

2 **Real and Financial Integration in Asia**
Edited by Shandre Mugan Thangavelu and Aekapol Chongvilaivan

3 **Energy Market Integration in East Asia**
Deepening understanding and moving forward
Edited by Yanrui Wu, Fukunari Kimura and Xunpeng Shi

4 **Rebalancing Economies in Financially Integrating East Asia**
Edited by Jenny Corbett and Ying Xu

Rebalancing Economies in Financially Integrating East Asia

Edited by Jenny Corbett and Ying Xu

Routledge
Taylor & Francis Group
LONDON AND NEW YORK

ERIA

First published 2015
by Routledge
2 Park Square, Milton Park, Abingdon, Oxon OX14 4RN

and by Routledge
711 Third Avenue, New York, NY 10017

Routledge is an imprint of the Taylor & Francis Group, an informa business

British Library Cataloguing in Publication Data
A catalogue record for this book is available from the British Library

Library of Congress Cataloging-in-Publication Data
Rebalancing economies in financially integrating East Asia / edited by Jenny Corbett, Xu Ying.
pages cm. — (Routledge-ERIA studies in development economics ; 4)
Includes bibliographical references and index.
1. East Asia—Economic policy. 2. Finance—East Asia. 3. International finance—East Asia. 4. Investments, Foreign—East Asia. 5. Banks and banking—East Asia. I. Corbett, Jenny, editor of compilation. II. Ying, Xu, editor of compilation.
HC460.5.R4297 2015
332′.042095—dc23
2014018214

ISBN: 978-0-415-85936-3 (hbk)
ISBN: 978-1-315-74581-7 (ebk)

Typeset in Galliard
by Apex CoVantage, LLC

Contents

List of tables vii
List of figures xi
List of boxes xv
List of contributors xvii

1 Macroeconomic rebalancing and financial integration in East Asia: overview 1
JENNY CORBETT AND YING XU

2 Growth rebalancing and investment in Asia and the Pacific 10
PETER WARR

3 Corporate savings, investment and financial structure in East Asia: micro-evidence 25
JENNY CORBETT AND GARRY TWITE

4 China's exchange rates or other factors in global rebalancing? 53
SHANG-JIN WEI

5 Do Asian countries fear appreciation against the renminbi? 75
VICTOR PONTINES AND REZA SIREGAR

6 What drives some countries to hoard foreign reserves? 102
DYNA HENG AND JENNY CORBETT

7 Defining openness and economic interconnection in East and Southeast Asia 129
TONY CAVOLI

8 Choosing the best partners for risk-sharing integration 149
ACHMAD MAULANA, WEI FENG AND JENNY CORBETT

9 The influences of international and domestic shocks on East Asia 181
MARDI DUNGEY AND M. TUGRUL VEHBI

10 International bank claims to East Asian economies: stabilizers or destabilizers? 217
VICTOR PONTINES AND REZA SIREGAR

11 The rise of Asian-owned foreign banks and credit stability in Asia 240
YING XU

Index 261

Tables

2.1	Cumulative current account balance and components, 1996–2009 (constant 2009 US$ millions)	14
2.2	Cumulative current account balance and components, 1996–2009 (constant 2009 US$, percentage of total)	15
3.1	Mean leverage	29
3.2	Asset accumulation	37
3.3	Explaining total savings	40
3.4	Explaining capital expenditure	43
3.A1	Sample size	49
3.A2	Definitions and data sources of country-level variables	50
3.A3	Industry groups	51
4.1a	Current account persistence by country sample, by regime	55
4.1b	Current account persistence by country sample, by regime	56
4.2	Current account persistence, by country sample	57
4.3a	Current account persistence, by country sample, by Reinhart–Rogoff regime	59
4.3b	Current account persistence, by country sample, by Reinhart–Rogoff regime	59
4.4	Real exchange rate persistence, by country sample	60
4.5	Chinese corporate gross savings (as a share of assets)	63
4.6	Ln(real exchange rate) and the sex ratio, using private credit to GDP ratio as the measure of financial development	70
4.7	Ln(real exchange rate) and the sex ratio, using financial system sophistication as the measure of financial development	72
4.8	Real exchange rate undervaluation and excess current account: the case of China	74
5.1	Threshold values (per cent)	81
5.2	People's Bank of China's swap agreements with Asian central banks	86
5.B1a	Estimation results of LSTR2 models for East Asian currencies vis-à-vis the US dollar (pre-GFC sample period, weekly data, January 2000–December 2006)	92

5.B1b	Estimation results of LSTR2 models for East Asian currencies vis-à-vis the US dollar (GFC sample period, weekly data, January 2007–July 2009)	93
5.B1c	Estimation results of LSTR2 models for East Asian currencies vis-à-vis the US dollar (post-GFC sample period, weekly data, August 2009–March 2011)	94
5.B2a	Estimation results of LSTR2 models for East Asian currencies vis-à-vis the Chinese renminbi (pre-GFC sample period, weekly data, January 2000–December 2006)	94
5.B2b	Estimation results of LSTR2 models for East Asian currencies vis-à-vis the Chinese renminbi (GFC sample period, weekly data, January 2007–July 2009)	95
5.B2c	Estimation results of LSTR2 models for East Asian currencies vis-à-vis the Chinese renminbi (post-GFC sample period, weekly data, August 2009–March 2011)	96
6.1	Regression result with log (foreign reserves/GDP) as dependent variable	116
6.2	Robustness check with access to international market (external access)	118
6.B1	List of variables, definition and data source	127
6.B2	Summary statistics	128
7.1a	Business cycle synchronisation	137
7.1b	Relative PPP deviations	138
7.1c	UIP deviations	138
7.1d	Trade openness	139
7.2	Average regional integration by measure	140
7.3	Top 5 interconnections by measure	142
7.4	Normalized overall integration using all four measures (min = 0, max = 4)	144
7.5	Normalized overall integration Top 5	145
8.1	Coefficients of variation of GDP growth rates	154
8.2	Correlations with global consumption and output	154
8.3	Optimal pool for each country	164
8.4	Impacts on welfare gain for China with different risk-aversion	165
8.5	Impacts on welfare gain with different theta for China	165
8.A1	Ideal risk-sharing partners for ASEAN5 countries	169
8.A2	Ideal risk-sharing partners for non-ASEAN5 countries	170
8.C1	Ideal risk-sharing partners for non-ASEAN5 countries (gamma = 3)	177
8.C2	Ideal risk-sharing partners for non-ASEAN5 countries (gamma = 7)	178
8.C3	Ideal risk-sharing partners for non-ASEAN5 countries (theta = 4)	179
8.C4	Ideal risk-sharing partners for non-ASEAN5 countries (theta = 10)	180

9.1 Augmented Dickey Fuller unit root test 188
10.1 Annual average growth of international bank claims in major East and Southeast Asian economies 221
10.2 Average share of Japanese, UK and US banks in foreign bank lending to major East and Southeast Asian economies 223
10.3 Dynamic panel estimation results of determinants of changes in international total bank claims, 2000Q1–2010Q3 228
10.4 Dynamic panel estimation results of determinants of changes in cross-border bank claims, 2000Q1–2010Q3 230
10.5 Cross-border banks in South East Asian Central Bank (SEACEN) economies 233
11.1 Foreign banks in Asia and the Pacific 243
11.2 The average growth rate of foreign bank lending pre-GFC and during the GFC: Asian-owned versus global foreign banks 244
11.3 Comparing Asian-owned and non-Asian foreign banks in Asia: 2000–09 247
11.4 Variable definitions and data sources 248
11.5 The China sample 249
11.6 The five economies that have Asian-owned foreign banks 250
11.7 The four economies without Asian-owned foreign banks 251
11.8 Money market transmission of credit instability 253
11.A1 The relationship of foreign bank lending and local credit stability 258

Figures

2.1 Annual current account balance: 12 Asian Pacific countries (constant 2000 US$) 13
2.2 Cumulative current account balances: 12 Asian Pacific countries 16
2.3 Savings and investment shares of GDP: China (per cent) 17
2.4 Savings and investment shares of GDP: India (per cent) 17
2.5 Savings and investment shares of GDP: Indonesia, Korea, Malaysia, the Philippines and Thailand (per cent) 18
2.6 Savings and investment shares of GDP: Australia and New Zealand (per cent) 18
2.7 Savings and investment shares of GDP: all 12 countries (per cent) 19
2.8 Change in savings share of GDP, 1990–96 to 1999–2009 (per cent) 19
2.9 Change in investment share of GDP, 1990–96 to 1999–2009 (per cent) 20
2.10 A loanable funds model of global imbalances 21
3.1 External financing/total financing by year 27
3.2 External financing/total financing by country (1989–2010) 27
3.3 Sources of financing by year 28
3.4 Sources of financing by country (1989–2010) 28
3.5 External sources of finance by year 29
3.6 External sources of finance by country (1989–2010) 30
3.7 Financing sources by year 31
3.8 Cash holdings by year 32
3.9 Cash holdings by country (1989–2010) 33
3.10 Fixed assets by year 33
3.11 Fixed assets by country (1989–2010) 34
3.12 Retained earnings by year 34
3.13 Retained earnings by country (1989–2010) 35
3.14 Dividend payout by country (1989–2010) 35
3.15 Dividend payout by year 36

4.1	Individual auto-regressive coefficients (no trend) for LYS categories (higher indicates more fixity)	58
4.2	Individual auto-regressive coefficients (with trend) for LYS categories (higher indicates more fixity)	58
4.3	Initial sex ratios and growth rates of private firms, 1995–2004	64
4.4	Sex ratios and saving rates	66
5.1	Exchange market pressure index	78
5.C1	Indonesia trade	97
5.C2	Indonesia–Japan–China trade	97
5.C3	Korea–China–US trade	98
5.C4	Korea–China–Japan trade	98
5.C5	The Philippines–China–US trade	99
5.C6	The Philippines–China–Japan trade	99
5.C7	Thailand–China–US trade	100
5.C8	Thailand–China–Japan trade	100
5.C9	Singapore–China–US trade	101
5.C10	Singapore–China–Japan trade	101
6.1	Top 10 reserve-accumulating economies: 1995–2010 (in USD trillion)	104
6.2	Reserves/GDP in 2010	105
6.3	Reserves to imports	105
6.4	Reserves to imports	106
6.5	Reserves to imports	106
6.6	Reserves to short-term debt (Greenspan–Guidotti rule)	107
6.7	Reserves to M2	107
6.8	Reserves to M8	108
7.1	Trade openness	131
7.2	Capital flows/GDP	132
7.3	Chinn–Ito index	133
7.4	Total regional overall integration	141
8.1	GDP growth across ASEAN5 countries, 1981–2011	153
8.2	GDP growth across non-ASEAN5 countries, 1981–2011	153
8.3	Dynamics of Indonesia's optimal pool	159
8.4	Dynamics of Australia's optimal pool	160
8.5	Maximum welfare gain of each country	162
8.6	Welfare implication of different pooling size	163
8.B1	Dynamics of China's optimal pool	171
8.B2	Dynamics of Japan's optimal pool	172
8.B3	Dynamics of Korea's optimal pool	172
8.B4	Dynamics of Malaysia's optimal pool	173
8.B5	Dynamics of the Philippines's optimal pool	173
8.B6	Dynamics of Singapore's optimal pool	174
8.B7	Dynamics of Thailand's optimal pool	174

8.B8	Dynamics of the United States' optimal pool	175
8.B9	Dynamics of the United Kingdom's optimal pool	175
9.1	Impulse response functions (foreign output shock)	190
9.2	Impulse response functions (domestic output shock)	191
9.3	Historical decomposition of output	192
9.4	Historical decomposition of inflation	193
9.5	Impulse response functions (foreign output shock)	194
9.6	Impulse response functions (domestic output shock)	195
9.7	Historical decomposition of output	196
9.8	Historical decomposition of inflation	196
9.9	Impulse response functions (foreign output shock)	197
9.10	Impulse response functions (domestic output shock)	198
9.11	Historical decomposition of output	199
9.12	Historical decomposition of inflation	199
9.13	Impulse response functions (foreign output shock)	200
9.14	Impulse response functions (domestic output shock)	201
9.15	Historical decomposition of output	201
9.16	Historical decomposition of inflation	202
9.17	Impulse response functions (foreign output shock)	203
9.18	Impulse response functions (domestic output shock)	203
9.19	Historical decomposition of output	204
9.20	Historical decomposition of inflation	204
9.21	Domestic output responses to a US output shock (solid line)	205
9.22	Inflation responses to a US output shock	206
9.23	Interest rate responses to a US output shock	207
9.24	Real exchange rate responses to a US output shock	207
9.25	Domestic output responses to a Chinese output shock (solid line)	208
9.26	Inflation responses to a Chinese output shock	209
9.27	Interest rate responses to a Chinese output shock	209
9.28	Real exchange rate responses to a Chinese output shock	210
9.A1	Singapore's variable plots	213
9.A2	Thailand's variable plots	214
9.A3	The Philippines' variable plots	214
9.A4	Indonesia's variable plots	215
9.A5	Malaysia's variable plots	215
10.1	Average annual growth rate of foreign and local bank claims in major East and Southeast Asian economies	219
11.1	Upper limits on foreign bank ownership (left) and asset shares of foreign banks (right) in Asian countries	243

Boxes

6.1 Traditional indicators for reserve adequacy 108
6.2 List of explanatory variables for reserve build-up 111

Contributors

Tony Cavoli is Senior Lecturer in the School of Commerce, University of South Australia and Deputy Director of the Australian Centre for Asian Business, University of South Australia. He is also Senior Research Fellow at the Centre for Emerging Markets Policies, George Mason University.

Jenny Corbett is Professor of Economics, Australian National University and Pro Vice-Chancellor (Research and Research Training), Australian National University. She is also Reader in the Economy of Japan, University of Oxford; a Research Associate of Centre for Applied Macroeconomic Analysis (CAMA) and a Research Fellow at Centre for Economic Policy Research (CEPR), London.

Mardi Dungey is Professor of Economics and Finance, University of Tasmania. She is also Senior Research Associate at the Centre for Financial Analysis and Policy, University of Cambridge and Adjunct Professor at the Centre for Applied Macroeconomic Analysis (CAMA), Australian National University.

Wei Feng was a postgraduate student at the Crawford School of Public Policy, Australian National University at the time her research was done.

Dyna Heng is President of the Cambodian Economic Association, Cambodia. He was a PhD student at the Crawford School of Public Policy, Australian National University at the time his research was done.

Achmad Maulana is a PhD candidate at the University of California, Santa Cruz. He is also Researcher at the Centre for Economics and Development Studies, Padjadjaran University, Indonesia. He was a postgraduate student at the Crawford School of Public Policy, Australian National University at the time his research was done.

Victor Pontines is Research Fellow at the Asian Development Bank Institute (ADBI), Japan. He is also Research Associate at the Centre for Applied Macroeconomic Analysis (CAMA), Australian National University.

Reza Siregar is Lead Economist and Group Head for the ASEAN+3 Macroeconomic Research Office (AMRO), Singapore.

Garry Twite is Visiting Professor of Finance at McCombs School of Business, University of Texas at Austin. He was Professor of Finance at the Australian National University when the research was done.

M. Tugrul Vehbi is Senior Analyst at the New Zealand Treasury and Research Associate at the Centre for Financial Analysis and Policy, University of Cambridge and the Centre for Applied Macroeconomic Analysis (CAMA), Australian National University.

Peter Warr is John Crawford Professor of Agricultural Economics and Director of the Poverty Research Centre in the Arndt-Corden Department of Economics at the Crawford School of Public Policy at the Australian National University. He is also the President of the Australian Agricultural and Resource Economics Society (AARES).

Shang-Jin Wei is N.T. Wang Professor of Chinese Business and Economy, Columbia University, Professor of Finance and Economics (Business School), Columbia University and Professor of International and Public Affairs (SIPA), Columbia University. He is also Research Associate of the National Bureau of Economic Research and Non-resident Fellow of Brookings Institute.

Ying Xu is Lecturer in the Crawford School of Public Policy, Australian National University. She is also Research Associate at the Centre for Applied Macroeconomic Analysis (CAMA), Australian National University.

1 Macroeconomic rebalancing and financial integration in East Asia

Overview

Jenny Corbett and Ying Xu

1. Introduction

After the Asian Financial Crisis (AFC) of 1997–98, large current account surpluses accumulated in the countries of Asia and the Pacific with corresponding deficits elsewhere. These surpluses were the result of a complex mix of factors that resulted from rapid economic growth with an increasing dependence on export-oriented industries in the countries of the region. Past experience of global external imbalances teaches that they may be sustainable for extended periods as long as the matching financial flows do not strain the international financial system but, eventually, if they do not unwind naturally, the pattern is unsustainable. Deficit countries have to adjust their macroeconomic policies and reduce consumption, while surplus countries must also adjust policies or allow inflation to erode the competitive advantage that underpins export performance. They will also face changes to the structure of their economies as resources are shifted from externally oriented sectors (traded) to domestically oriented ones (including non-traded). Deliberate and managed "rebalancing" can reduce the vulnerability to the high cost of sudden reversals.

The studies in this volume consider the East Asian side of the equation. We look at the economic structures and policies that gave rise to current account surpluses and consider what policy adjustments could change them. While the biggest imbalances of the first decade of the 21st century were largely unwound through differences in growth rates between surplus and deficit countries, the underlying drivers have not yet disappeared and still warrant research. The problems lay not only in Asia. History makes abundantly clear that behaviour, policy and economic structure on both sides of global imbalances need to adjust. The great disruptions to the global economic system, such as the collapse of the Bretton Woods system of managed exchange rates in the 1970s, occur when adjustment is asymmetric and postponed to the point of explosion. The focus on Asia also derives from the recognition that the surplus countries have important interests in reducing the imbalances just as much as the deficit countries. From the perspective of the East Asian countries, the interest in growth rebalancing is motivated by several concerns. First, there is the possibility of being forced to turn current account surpluses (positive flows) into deficits (negative flows) at short notice, leading to social disruption and other adjustment costs. Second, there is the fear that the stock of debt owed to them, which represents the accumulated surpluses and is largely held in dollar denominated government bonds, might become so high that repayment becomes impossible. Third is the possibility that, in the absence of a managed process, uncontainable pressure builds in either the foreign exchange markets or the domestic money markets. In the former case, sudden changes to currency values could result in capital losses on the foreign assets held, while in the latter, domestic inflation could become difficult to control.

The studies draw a more nuanced picture than is usually available in discussing imbalances. We begin from the observation that the imbalances are a macroeconomic problem that reflects a mismatch between savings and investment in the surplus countries. Causality is difficult to establish, but it is clear that either or both of high savings and low investment will give rise to a savings gap that must be matched either by domestic government consumption (fiscal deficits) or by external surpluses. To understand the origins of the mismatch, we consider what policies impacted on the incentives to save and invest in the Asian surplus economies. We consider whether the macroeconomic and microeconomic evidence supports the idea that corporate savings, in particular, are the source of the imbalance in China (which is such a large part of the story) or in the other countries of the region, and draw attention to reasons to doubt one current conventional view.

Since causation can also run from the large export surplus back to domestic excess savings, we also look for evidence of policies that distort resource allocation towards "excessive" focus on export sectors or outward orientation of the economies. Much policy debate (too much in our view) focuses on the role of prices (i.e. exchange rate misalignment) in encouraging exports. This focus implies that changing relative prices, by revaluing Asian currencies, will be the key to correcting imbalances. We consider whether, and why, Asian economies might resist foreign pressure for revaluation, as the Chinese have. Part of the explanation for their currency strategy lies in their perceived need to build war chests of foreign exchange reserves to provide a buffer in case of instabilities similar to those of the Asian and recent global financial crises. The excessive reliance on exports is as much a consequence of these other reasons for keeping exchange rates low and accumulating reserves as it is a cause. We therefore consider whether countries are able to take advantage of other possibilities for insuring against economic volatility by more actively and openly engaging with international capital markets. In different studies in the volume, we establish elements of an argument that the perceived need for self-insurance is indeed a driver of exchange rate policy but that closer financial integration, involving more open financial markets, with well-chosen partners, would be welfare-improving and should reduce the need for the counter-productive self-insurance policies that result in managed exchange rates and foreign exchange accumulation.

The measurement of integration, in both financial and trade spheres, is not easy, so it is useful to set out some stylized facts about which countries are most closely integrated with which others in the region. A new method for measuring integration reveals some surprises about which partners are currently most closely linked. Often these are not those that profess the greatest desire for linkage. Importantly, they are also often not the most beneficial partners. We show which countries would be the best partners for financial integration based on economic welfare considerations rather than the historical and political ones that typically give rise to the current arrangements. Again there are patterns that challenge understandings of the status quo: countries are rarely engaging with those that would be their best partners. The policy message is not, however, to unpick existing arrangements, but that there are still further gains to be derived from more integration and openness, often with specifically selected partners, and that these gains come because openness reduces rather than increases volatility.

Much of this analysis leads to the conclusion that financial market liberalization and reform, greater openness and more flexible exchange rates will be important policy tools to enable the structural changes that support a gradual reduction of surpluses and a redirection of resources to the non-traded sector that will absorb employment and allow an orderly rebalancing. What are the risks? Governments in the region still worry that moving in this direction will bring greater rather than less economic volatility, so we examine how financial integration is linked to the transmission of economic shocks to the real economy and between economies to demonstrate the costs as well as the benefits.

To address that concern, we look at the transmission mechanisms of real sector volatility and whether the countries in the region have become decoupled from global business cycles. These studies establish that business cycle volatility is still largely transmitted from the United States and that the region is not decoupled from the rest of the world. There are many channels for the transmission of shocks, but we focus on one that was a key to the Global Financial Crisis (GFC) – banks. Two chapters look closely at the role of banks in transmitting financial shocks and compare the role of cross-border bank flows with the activities of multinational banks within countries. The behaviour of regionally owned banks is seen to differ from multinationals and was a stabilising influence in the most recent episode of financial crisis.

2. Economics of savings, investment and currency misalignments

While almost all countries in the region (except Australia and New Zealand) were running large current account surpluses until slower growth took hold from 2010, Warr (Chapter 2) notes that China accounted for over half the total during the height of the imbalance period; the countries that were most affected by the Asian crisis accounted for a much smaller part of the region's surplus. Unpacking the matching savings-investment imbalance, Warr notes that in the crisis-affected countries (Indonesia, Korea, Malaysia, the Philippines, Thailand and Vietnam) there was a large but not overwhelming increase in private savings. In the group of countries not affected by the Asian crisis (Australia, New Zealand,

China and Japan), on the other hand, the total current account surplus was due primarily to a massive increase in private saving. Chinese private savings were the largest but were almost matched by Japanese private saving. With public sector savings added, Japan's aggregate savings were even larger than China's. Overall, there is a significant increase in savings for all countries but large declines in investments in the affected countries and smaller investment declines in the other countries. There is evidence that the imbalances are as much driven by investment behaviour as by savings. While the decline in investment was partly a correction of the overinvestment boom before the crisis, both the savings increase and the investment declines appear to have been driven by rising uncertainty in Asia. Warr's policy conclusion is that improvements to the investment climate and the provision of social safety nets will go some way to solving these problems. Restoring confidence in household income growth would reduce the need for households' precautionary savings (the low share of household income in China has been noted by the International Monetary Fund (2010) as a cause of relatively high savings there). On balance, it is more important to focus on policies that increase investment than on those that reduce savings since the former will promote growth, which will, in turn, allow consumption growth. Warr points out that if the bulk of adjustment comes from reduction in Asian savings, global interest rates will rise. This is an important reason why an increase in savings in the deficit countries will be a significant element of the global solution.

The macroeconomic analysis in Warr's chapter already raises questions about a conventional view that excess savings in Asia is the major source of the imbalances. Corbett and Twite (Chapter 3) and Wei (Chapter 4) further argue that the microeconomic evidence from listed-company accounting data also do not indicate a problem with excessively high company savings. Companies in the region do not have excessively high retentions nor are their dividend payouts unusually low. When they do build up accumulations of liquid assets (i.e. holding their accumulated profits as cash or in financial assets), these are quickly applied to capital expenditure, with the result that the share of fixed assets (plant and equipment) in total assets is high. Available data do not cover the entire corporate sector, excluding small and medium firms that are not listed, but the listed company sector is now quite large in most of the region's economies, so the picture is representative of an important part of most of these economies. Furthermore, several of China's state-owned enterprises are now partially privatized and have some shares listed, so they are included in the analysis.

Corbett and Twite, and Wei also conclude that the imbalance between savings and investment seems to be the result of constraints on the investment side rather than incentives to build up excessive savings. A policy focus on the drivers, determinants and impediments to investment will be a more productive way to respond to global imbalances than a narrow focus on corporate savings. Preliminary results suggest that financial constraints are an impediment to investment for many firms, providing further support for the need for financial sector reform. Further research on elements of the broad, country-level policy variables used in this study (legal systems, corporate and shareholders rights, indicators on corruption and financial market openness) would help to identify particular policy actions.

Wei (Chapter 4) additionally presents two further important arguments about global rebalancing and the case of China. First, he doubts there is a strong link between exchange rate regimes and current account imbalance. Wei reiterates the results of his own earlier empirical studies showing that shifting to flexible exchange rates in China might not lead to a fast adjustment of the current account. Second, he argues that China's unusually high national saving rates is a more fundamental factor than its exchange rate regime in explaining China's current account surplus. As noted above, he emphasizes that Chinese national savings are driven by household savings, not by corporate behaviour and argues that the best explanation for high household savings is demographic. As a result of the one-child policy and the resultant gender imbalance that arose, there is a competition for marriage partners, which leads to savings for wealth accumulation. The policy responses that are normally proposed to change savings behaviour will not redress this balance, and there is no benefit to the commonly proposed policies to change exchange regimes or to focus on corporate savings behaviour.

The exchange rate argument is also crucial to an understanding of the other surplus countries in the region. Pontines and Siregar (Chapter 5) draw attention to the importance of the response by Asian countries to revaluation of the Chinese renminbi (also the subject of Chapter 6). They show evidence of a general fear of appreciation, not just during crisis periods, but also over long periods not associated with crisis, for major Asian countries including (but not only) China. Their smooth transition auto-regressive (STAR) model finds that five countries (Indonesia, Korea, the Philippines, Thailand and Singapore) show clear aversion to currency appreciations during the pre-GFC period of 2000–06 and a stronger aversion to appreciation against the Chinese renminbi than against the US dollar. Under crisis conditions, there is a general tendency to manage exchange rates and avoid currency movements in either direction. This finding confirms the view that movements in the Chinese currency have a special role within the region, even though they are not the major cause of imbalances between China and the United States. Heng and Corbett extend the understanding of the region's currency management by showing that there are multiple reasons why countries manage exchange rates so as to accumulate foreign exchange reserves from current account surpluses. In addition to any "mercantilist" desire to preserve exchange rates for competitiveness, a dominating motivation is self-insurance: countries are accumulating reserves beyond what would be needed just to meet private sector demands and keep the exchange rate stable. Governments are doing more than just "leaning against the wind" to stabilize currencies and are helping to keep them undervalued to build war chests of reserves. Understanding this motivation gives rise to policy recommendations. Since the concern is about instability rather than competitiveness, policies to improve access to international financial support in times of crisis (including explicit international and regional cooperation) would reduce this pressure. The Chiang Mai initiative, appropriately expanded and multilateralized, could be one useful element in the policy arsenal.

3. Economic integration, welfare gains and the transmission of shocks

While open financial markets are often considered conducive to the efficient allocation of resources and also beneficial for growth rebalancing, a valid policy concern is whether they bring greater vulnerability to shocks. This is the question addressed by the remaining chapters in this volume, which focus on the major transmission mechanisms of shocks, the degree of external decoupling and the role of banks in shock transmission, against the background of an increasingly liberalized but still incompletely integrated Asian financial system.

Economic integration in Asia is an ongoing, dynamic and multifaceted process. Compared to North America and Western Europe, it is commonly understood that economic integration in Asia is in its early stage and confined to a few sectors of a few countries in the region. However, since the aftermath of the AFC, economic liberalization and integration in Asia have gained momentum. Integration has become more far-reaching, and interactions among Asian economies in trade and financial sectors have become more complex than a decade ago. The chapters by Cavoli (Chapter 7) and Maulana, Feng and Corbett (Chapter 8) provide fresh perspectives on the increasingly complex, dynamic nature of the integration process in Asia and shed light on a number of important policy agendas.

There is no single measure that sufficiently captures all salient characteristics of integration between economies. Cavoli employs various measures of real and financial elements to capture the extent of economic integration in East and Southeast Asia. He also uses a principal components analysis to create a measure of "overall" integration and finds that the original Association of South-East Asian Nations (ASEAN) (Indonesia, Malaysia, the Philippines, Singapore and Thailand) are more integrated with the rest of Asia than other groups (new ASEAN, CJK, ASEAN+3) in terms of both real and financial integration. They also tend to be well integrated with each other. The newer ASEAN members are the least integrated across all measures. Japan, Korea and China are highly integrated when measuring both trade intensity and foreign direct investment (FDI) and portfolio intensity but less so in finance. The measures indicate that there are quite well-defined clusters, or sub-regions, in terms of integration. While the larger economies are quite well integrated with the smaller ones, they are not as well integrated with each other. The policy implications for the design of trade or investment accords need to be further examined, but the results suggest that the region as a whole does not yet meet the criteria for close integration.

Cavoli's results leave open the question of whether variable levels of integration matter and why. Maulana et al. consider the benefits of integration and examine welfare gains in the East Asian region from greater use of the risk-sharing opportunities provided by financial integration with countries that have different patterns of income variation. They identify which partnerships provide the biggest gains from more integration and estimate the scale of the welfare gains. The calculations suggest significant welfare gains of up to 5 per cent of annual consumption for some countries. Under certain assumptions, the best pair for most of the Asian countries studied is a developed country with a different business-cycle pattern, such as Australia. The best overall group for many countries includes about five partners with a mixture of developed and developing countries both inside and outside the region. Geographically defined groups, such as the current ASEAN5 grouping, are not optimal in terms of risk reduction, nor is there much welfare gain from an integrated grouping of China–Japan–Korea. For policy makers, the welfare benefits of risk-sharing are large enough that they should form an additional part of the policy dialogue on regional integration. The results of such discussions might change the perspective about which partners should begin the process of closer financial cooperation. Since that process can be difficult, it may be easier to begin with particular partners, where integration will provide the largest benefits, and subsequently add extra partners.

Despite the potential welfare gains from regional integration, there is bound to be concern about any increased potential for volatility resulting from the process of liberalization and integration. The severe damage imposed by the recent GFC makes it imperative to understand the transmission mechanism of shocks to the region and the spread of the shock in the region. Dungey and Vehbi's study (Chapter 9) provides such an analysis by focusing on the contribution of international and domestic shocks to macroeconomic outcomes in selected Asian countries. They model five East Asian economies (Singapore, Thailand, the Philippines, Malaysia and Indonesia) in a small, open economy Vector Error Correction Model (VECM) and investigate the historical evolution of domestic responses to domestic and external output shocks. The external output shocks mainly originate in the United States and China during the period 1986–2009. Despite the rapid growth of China's importance in the region, their study suggests that the United States remains much more important than China as a source of external influences. The result delivers an important policy message that the economic situation in the United States remains *the key factor* to be considered for understanding external sources of business cycle shocks and that, despite rapid growth and increasing regional integration, the region has not yet decoupled from the United States.

What are the mechanisms for the transmission of shocks? It is commonly agreed that Asian financial markets are still dominated by banks. Total bank assets in Asia in 2012 exceeded 185 per cent of GDP, compared to 93 per cent in the United States. A critical question that follows is what role banks play in the transmission of shocks, and especially financial shocks to the region. Pontines and Siregar (Chapter 10) examine cross-border bank loans from the United Kingdom, the United States and Japan to five major Southeast Asian economies and Korea. They examine evidence on the push-and-pull factors of cross-border bank loans and show that global banks indeed act as a channel of financial shock transmission from the global financial markets to the regional economy. Policy reaction will require cross-border banking supervision and cross-country supervisory cooperation to overcome information asymmetry on cross-country risk exposure, and they recommend the establishment of a college of supervisors to facilitate cross-border policy cooperation. Meanwhile, national policies to reduce the complexity of global banks, and their banking business would also help to reduce volatility.

Since the 1997–98 AFC, Asian economies have gradually opened their financial markets. An increasing number of foreign banks have been allowed to enter and expand their presence in the region. Xu (Chapter 11) focuses on foreign banks' local lending and provides fresh evidence that the country of origin of foreign banks explains variations in lending behaviour and has distinctive effects on credit stability in Asia. Asian-owned foreign banks behaved quite differently from non-Asian-owned banks during the GFC. The former showed the mildest change in credit growth in times of stress, contributing to credit stabilization, whereas the latter cut-off credits sharply from the Asian periphery, undermining credit stability in the region. An important reason for the sudden withdrawal of credit from non-Asian-owned banks lay in the meltdown of the global wholesale funding market, where many of these banks source their funding to finance local lending. The Asian-owned banks relied more for their funding on their more stable deposit base, developed out of increasing savings within the region. Policies to encourage Asian banks' entry to the local financial markets may, therefore, be useful to enhance stability. More precisely, diversification of ownership of foreign banking, facilitated by greater regional financial integration, may be crucial in building a stable regional financial system and therefore a robust Asian economy. Here, and in the recognition of the significance of the US economic cycle in the cyclical behaviour of the region, we provide the elements of an argument in favour of the regional element in integration, which needs to be considered alongside the observation that welfare-enhancing financial integration requires a wider, extra-regional and more inclusive focus.

4. Conclusion

The world economy is an increasingly interconnected and integrated entity with economies constantly influencing one another. "Decoupling" is probably a myth[1]. Asia, once a passive outsider, is now an active component of the entity. On the one hand, through its massive and rapidly growing activities in international trade and financial markets, Asia is integrated with the global economy on an unprecedented scale and is at the centre of the quest for rebalancing the world economy. On the other hand, Asian economies unavoidably expose themselves to more trade and financial turmoil from the outside world than ever before, so the desire for a strengthened regional response is understandable. The studies in this volume provide the missing pieces in understanding both the conventional economics of growth rebalancing and a different perspective on the contribution made by closer financial linkages. Both add to the regional integration debates and uncover the missing link between the two.

The evidence from the studies in this volume seems to challenge the conventional wisdom on growth rebalancing in the following two ways. First, lower investment rather than higher saving is the main ingredient of the Asian part of the imbalance problem. Although there is no evidence of corporates in the region hoarding savings, the growth of investment is much slower than that of saving, creating a large saving-investment gap. Second, the fear of external capital reversal rather than a desire for export gain has been the main driver of the region's currency strategies, which contributed to a substantial accumulation of foreign reserves.

These findings challenge the conventional prescriptions for growth rebalancing. An excessive emphasis on consumption and exchange rate revaluation would not resolve the imbalances effectively unless the fundamental causes of low investment and vulnerability to external financial turmoil are taken into account. The bottleneck for investment in many Asian firms lies in their financial constraints. Concern for macroeconomic vulnerability also derives from financial sector underdevelopment. Counter-intuitively, there are significant gains to be achieved in both regional stability and welfare from greater financial openness and closer integration, but this requires careful consideration of the role for regional partners, and the important contribution of extra-regional involvement. The regional approach should be able to provide a part, if not the whole, solution to the rebalancing challenge and to developing more robust financial systems when combined with appropriate regulatory and policy coordination.

Note

1 The term was used in a remark made by Christine Lagarde, director of the International Monetary Fund, in *The Economist* (online version) <http://www.economist.com/blogs/freeexchange/2011/08/world-economy> (28 August 2011).

Reference

International Monetary Fund (IMF) (2010) *Regional Economic Outlook Asia and Pacific*, April, Washington: IMF.

2 Growth rebalancing and investment in Asia and the Pacific

Peter Warr

1. Introduction

Since the Asian Financial Crisis (AFC) of 1997–98, the countries of Asia and the Pacific have, in aggregate, run huge annual current account surpluses. Much the same has been true of the oil-exporting countries of the Middle East. The counterpart of these surpluses has been correspondingly huge current account deficits in the rest of the world, including Europe and, most especially, the United States. Over the decade and a half that this process has continued, huge stocks of debt have accumulated. Much of this is US Government debt owed to the central banks of the East Asian countries. About half of it is held by China. It is, of course, expected that the debt will eventually be repaid, and this implies that the surpluses must eventually turn into deficits, and vice versa. Indefinite accumulation of debt is unsustainable.

Many observers regard the process described above as unsustainable, even in the short-run, implying that its cessation will occur sooner rather than later. First, East Asian countries might be unwilling to continue to accumulate US debt and might even wish to reduce the stock they hold already. Second, the United States might be unwilling to allow this accumulation of indebtedness to continue and might indeed wish to reduce the stock of debt it currently owes. The two outcomes are not mutually exclusive and could even happen at the same time. They both rest on the fear that the burden of debt servicing might suddenly become intolerable for the debtors – notably, the United States. The emphasis is on "suddenly", meaning that an unexpectedly rapid adjustment becomes necessary.

There is some possibility that East Asia's current account surpluses might have to decline, and even turn into deficits, very quickly. Of course, this must happen eventually. The question is *when*. If the answer is "gradually and predictably", there is not necessarily any problem. But if it is "soon", at an unexpectedly rapid rate, there could be a serious adjustment problem involved. By anticipating this potential problem, it might be possible to avoid the large-scale unemployment and other social costs that would otherwise result from an unanticipated economic crisis. To put it mildly, these events are uncertain. "Growth rebalancing" is essentially a problem of risk management.

From the perspective of the Asian Pacific countries, the interest in growth rebalancing is motivated by two concerns. First, there is the possibility that current account surpluses (positive flows) will have to turn into deficits (negative flows) at short notice, leading to social disruption and other adjustment costs. Second, there is the fear that the stock of debt owed to them might become so high that repayment becomes impossible. The first concern is more immediate.

The essence of the "growth balancing" literature is the insight that macroeconomic balances, in particular the magnitude of the current account balance (the difference between aggregate savings and investment), are related to economic structure. Consider, on the one hand, the difference between aggregate savings and aggregate investment and, on the other, the difference between the total production and consumption of traded commodities. The key point is that these two magnitudes must be the same because both are equal to the current account balance.

The principal adjustment mechanism involved in changing the balance between total production and consumption of traded commodities is changes in the real exchange rate. Consider the production possibilities frontier, specifying the maximum possible production of (i) commodities and services traded that are internationally traded (tradables) and (ii) commodities and services destined only for the domestic market (non-tradables). The position and shape of the production possibilities frontier depends on the resources and technologies available within the domestic economy. Where the economy produces along this frontier (assuming full employment for now) depends on the real exchange rate – the prices of tradables relative to non-tradables.

For example, a real depreciation (an increase in the prices of tradables relative to non-tradables) induces a shift in production around the production possibilities frontier towards tradables and away from non-tradables. The proportions in which these two sets of commodities are consumed moves in the opposite direction. The current account balance – the difference between the production and consumption of tradables – increases. Real appreciations do the opposite.

It follows from all this that a change in the balance between savings and investment must have its exact counterpart in the balance between the production and consumption of tradables. An increase (decline) in the current account balance must mean *both* an increase (reduction) in (a) the difference between aggregate saving and investment and (b) the difference between production and consumption of internationally traded commodities. But the latter involves economic structure, in particular the balance of production between goods destined for international markets and goods and services destined for the domestic market. That is, it involves changes in the allocation of resources between industries. In the short run, "resources" means labour in particular, but also some capital. Global rebalancing involves more than just changes in macroeconomic aggregates like savings and investment. It also involves changes in the allocation of labour and capital between industries – and this implies adjustment costs.

For Asia, the 1997–98 AFC was a watershed. Since then, the countries of Asia have, to varying extents, refocused their production structures increasingly towards exports. Resources have moved away from production for the domestic market and towards production of traded goods and services destined for external markets. Hence, the current account surpluses. If these current account surpluses are now to be reduced significantly, or even reversed, and if massive unemployment is to be avoided, resources must be reallocated in the reverse direction – away from production for the export market and towards production for the domestic market. The alternative is that as the gap between production and consumption of tradables declines, the resources (particularly labour) released from tradables production will simply become idle, with devastating social consequences.

For the deficit countries (notably the United States), the danger is almost exactly the reverse. For them, the greatest concern is that resources released from non-tradables production will not soon find employment in the production of tradables.

Growth rebalancing is the term that has been applied to describe this process. The policy imperative is similar in both cases: to avoid the disruption, especially the unemployment, that could result from a required rate of adjustment that is too rapid. In the current global environment, Asia's position is precarious in that it is vulnerable to such an adjustment problem arising at short notice and in a way that Asia cannot predict, let alone control. The suggestion is that some policy-induced rebalancing now – away from reliance on external demand and towards domestic demand – can lessen this vulnerability by reducing Asia's export dependence.

This chapter is structured as follows: the next section presents an overview of global imbalances, followed by a discussion in Section 3 of saving and investment balances in Asia. Section 4 presents a loanable funds model of global imbalances, followed by a summary of results from empirical studies undertaken by the International Monetary Fund (IMF) on determinants of investment. Section 6 concludes with policy implications.

2. Global imbalances

Current account imbalances are not necessarily a problem. They reflect what Obstfeld and Rogoff (1997) and Corden (2007, 2011) call international inter-temporal trade. One country (the surplus country) is exchanging current goods and services for financial assets that are claims on goods and services in the future. The other country (the deficit country) is doing the reverse. Mutual gains from trade can arise from these transactions because the initial circumstances of the countries involved are not the same. For some countries, it makes sense to save more now in order to consume and invest more later. For others, the reverse applies. In this respect, inter-temporal trade is not fundamentally different from contemporaneous trade in goods and services. But basic differences do exist. The time dimension can mean that the individuals obliged to

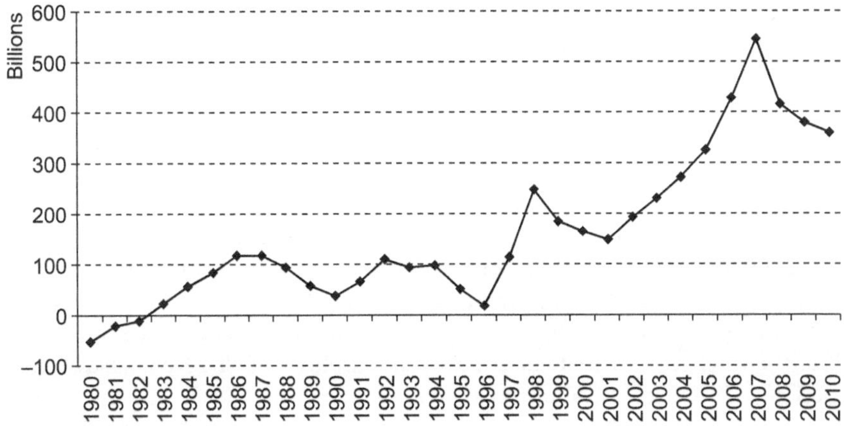

Figure 2.1 Annual current account balance: 12 Asian Pacific countries (constant 2000 US$)

Source: IMF, CEI

repay a debt might not be the same as those who incurred it. The outcomes chosen by this generation of Americans, for example, can create an unwelcome problem for the next generation.[1]

Since the 1997 AFC, Asia has run large current account surpluses, and the rest of the world (especially the United States) has run correspondingly large deficits. Figure 2.1 summarizes the annual magnitude of these current account balances added over the 12 countries:

Group I: Crisis affected

- Indonesia
- Korea
- Malaysia
- The Philippines
- Thailand
- Vietnam

Group II: Not crisis affected

- Australia
- China
- India
- Japan
- New Zealand
- Singapore

For reasons that will become clear from the subsequent discussion, the 12 countries are grouped above according to those significantly affected by the 1997–98 AFC (Group I) and those not significantly affected (Group II).

3. Saving and investment balances in Asia

The first column of Table 2.1 summarizes the cumulative current account surpluses of the 12 Asian Pacific countries listed above, added across the years 1996–2009 inclusive. Here we use cumulative surpluses because this is the counterpart of the stock of outstanding debt. The calculations are performed in US dollars, expressed in constant 2009 prices. China accounts for just over half of the total accumulated current account surpluses of all 12 countries. The Group I (AFC-affected) countries represent about one-quarter of the total. The remaining four columns draw upon the familiar macroeconomic identity that the current account balance is equal to the difference between aggregate saving and aggregate investment. Aggregate saving can be further divided into public saving (the government's budgetary balance) and private saving

Table 2.1 Cumulative current account balance and components, 1996–2009 (constant 2009 US$ millions)

	Cumulative current account balance	*Cumulative public saving*	*Cumulative private saving*	*Cumulative public investment*	*Cumulative private investment*
Australia	–127,094	180,211	2,307,637	303,765	2,311,177
China	1,917,468	–576,539	17,858,557	9,973,138	5,391,411
India	–328,925	–484,810	3,657,512	927,000	2,574,628
Indonesia	275,526	–46,787	1,751,369	225,660	1,203,397
Japan	837,139	1,027,368	16,740,204	4,079,948	12,850,485
Korea	230,140	230,589	2,791,411	492,722	2,299,137
Malaysia	395,659	62,272	846,944	236,611	276,946
New Zealand	1,060	67,583	263,332	69,911	259,945
The Philippines	–46,364	–45,096	301,299	63,290	239,278
Singapore	412,850	128,917	802,324	89,233	429,158
Thailand	170,338	–36,944	1,014,089	235,017	571,791
Vietnam	–73,287	–44,174	260,012	140,079	149,045
Total	**3,664,511**	**462,592**	**48,594,690**	**16,836,374**	**28,556,397**
Group I	**952,013**	**119,861**	**6,965,124**	**1,393,379**	**4,739,593**
Group II	**2,712,498**	**342,730**	**41,629,566**	**15,442,994**	**23,816,804**

Note: Group I = Indonesia, Korea, Malaysia, the Philippines, Thailand, Vietnam; Group II = Australia, China, India, Japan, New Zealand, Singapore.

(household plus corporate), and aggregate investment can be similarly subdivided into public and private, giving

$$CAB = S - I = S_{PUB} + S_{PRIV} - I_{PUB} - I_{PRIV}. \quad (1)$$

In the Group I countries, there was a large increase in private savings accompanied by a somewhat smaller increase in private investment. Public investment increased by slightly more than public savings, offsetting about half of the difference between private savings and investment. In the Group II countries, the total current account surplus was due primarily to a massive increase in private savings. Chinese private savings were the largest but were almost matched by Japanese private savings. When public sector savings are taken into account, Japan's aggregate savings were larger than China's. In addition, there was a very large increase in both private and public investment in the Group II countries. A large, positive gap remained between the increase in private investment and private savings. Again, public investment increased more than public savings, offsetting a little over half the private savings-investment gap. Table 2.2 presents

Table 2.2 Cumulative current account balance and components, 1996–2009 (constant 2009 US$, percentage of total)

	Cumulative current account balance	*Cumulative public saving*	*Cumulative private saving*	*Cumulative public investment*	*Cumulative private investment*
Australia	–3.47	38.96	4.75	1.80	8.09
China	52.33	–124.63	36.75	59.24	18.88
India	–8.98	–104.80	7.53	5.51	9.02
Indonesia	7.52	–10.11	3.60	1.34	4.21
Japan	22.84	222.09	34.45	24.23	45.00
Korea	6.28	49.85	5.74	2.93	8.05
Malaysia	10.80	13.46	1.74	1.41	0.97
New Zealand	0.03	14.61	0.54	0.42	0.91
The Philippines	–1.27	–9.75	0.62	0.38	0.84
Singapore	11.27	27.87	1.65	0.53	1.50
Thailand	4.65	–7.99	2.09	1.40	2.00
Vietnam	–2.00	–9.55	0.54	0.83	0.52
Total	**100**	**100**	**100**	**100**	**100**
Group I	**25.98**	**25.91**	**14.33**	**8.28**	**16.60**
Group II	**74.02**	**74.09**	**85.67**	**91.72**	**8.40**

Note: Group I = Indonesia, Korea, Malaysia, the Philippines, Thailand, Vietnam; Group II = Australia, China, India, Japan, New Zealand, Singapore.

these data as shares of the total current account surplus of all 12 countries. Figure 2.2 shows this graphically.

Figures 2.3–2.7 examine these data by looking at aggregate savings and investment over time, expressed as shares of GDP. In China (Figure 2.3), the aggregate savings share increased dramatically after 2000. The investment share also increased, but not as much, hence the huge surplus. In India (Figure 2.4), both savings and investment shares increased significantly, but by similar amounts. In the group of countries seriously affected by the AFC (Indonesia, Korea, Malaysia, the Philippines and Thailand) (Figure 2.5), both savings and investment shares declined following the AFC, but the decline in investment shares was larger, leading to a substantial current account surplus. Table 2.1 makes it clear that private investment is the principal source of this decline. Even though the absolute level of private investment increased, it declined significantly as a share of GDP. Figure 2.6 shows similar information for Australia and New Zealand, confirming small current account deficits. Finally, from Figure 2.7, it is clear that when the data for all 12 countries are added, the share of savings in aggregate GDP increased from about 2002, but the share of investment increased even further.

Figures 2.8 and 2.9 compare the average GDP shares of savings and investment, respectively, between two periods: the pre-AFC period of 1990–96 and the post-crisis decade of 1999–2009. This comparison is made for all 12 countries. China's increase in savings was huge in total, but as a share of GDP it was by no means the largest. India, Malaysia, the Philippines, Singapore and Vietnam all increased their savings shares by larger proportions. Figure 2.9 shows that the post-crisis increase in China's investment share was smaller than India's. The figure also shows the dramatic difference between the

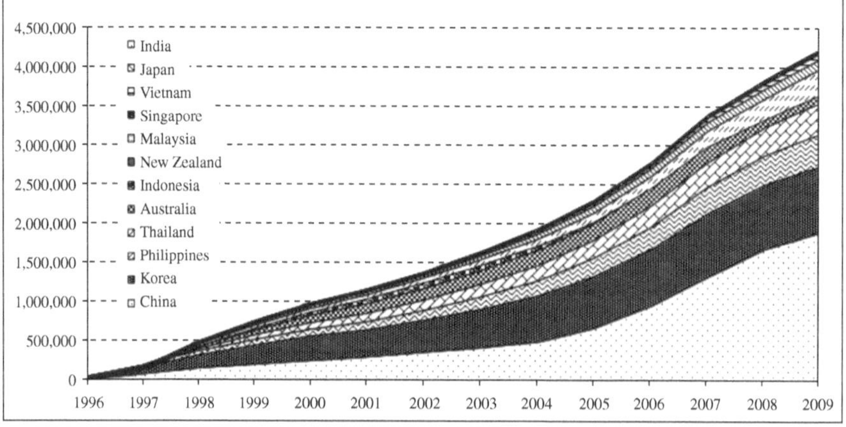

Figure 2.2 Cumulative current account balances: 12 Asian Pacific countries

Source: IMF, CEIC

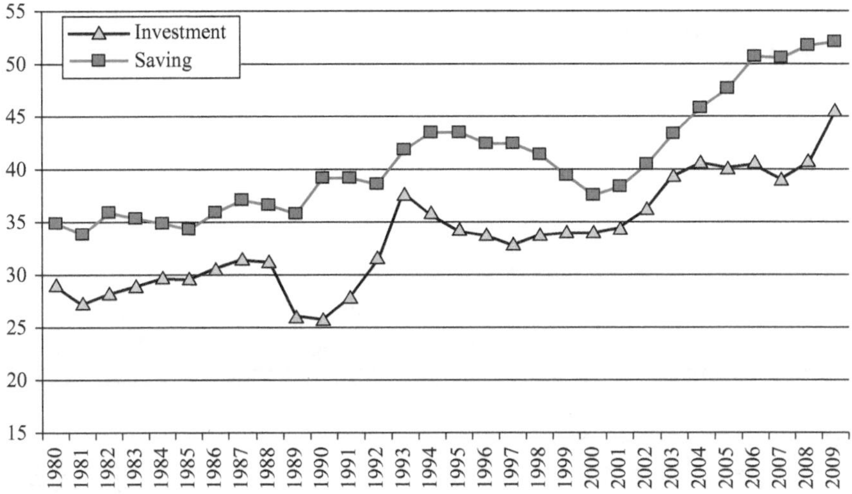

Figure 2.3 Savings and investment shares of GDP: China (per cent)

Source: IMF, CEIC.

Note: Investment = gross fixed capital formation; saving = gross domestic savings.

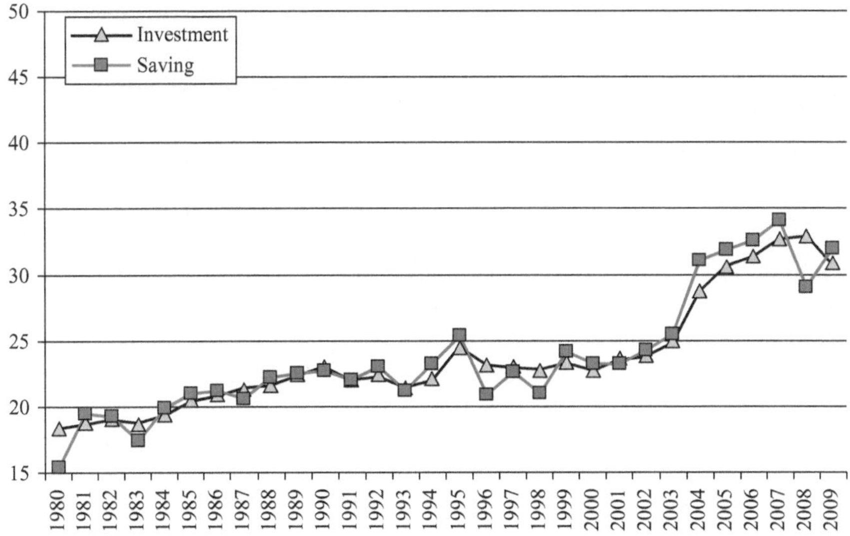

Figure 2.4 Savings and investment shares of GDP: India (per cent)

Source and note: See Figure 2.3.

Group I and Group II countries with respect to investment. Investment shares contracted in all of the countries affected by the AFC except Vietnam and increased in all other countries except Japan. The contractions in Malaysia and Thailand were especially large. Indonesia is an interesting outlier. Although

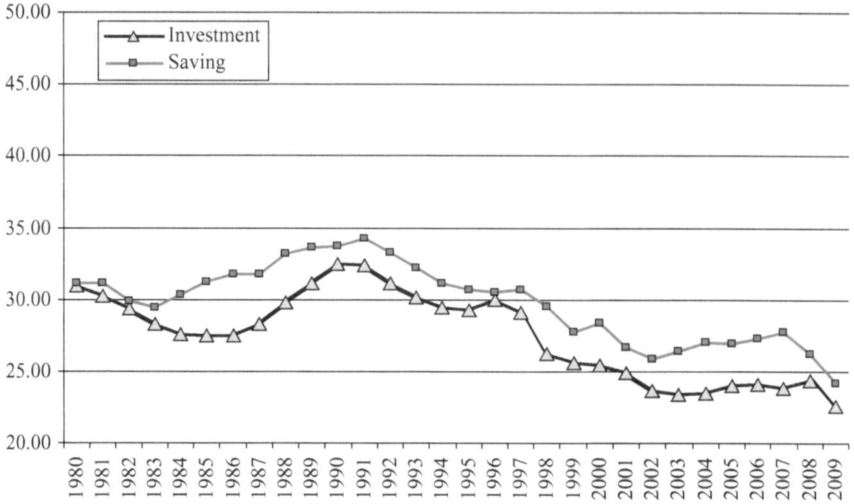

Figure 2.5 Savings and investment shares of GDP: Indonesia, Korea, Malaysia, the Philippines and Thailand (per cent)

Source and note: See Figure 2.3.

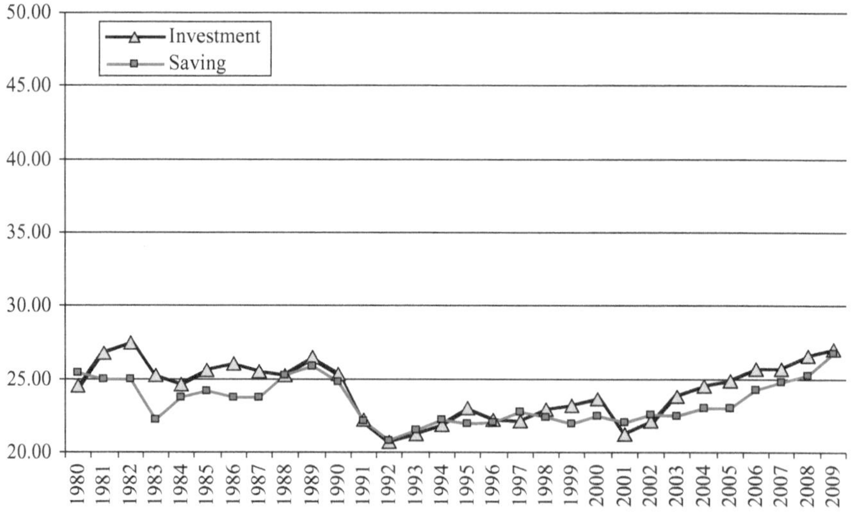

Figure 2.6 Savings and investment shares of GDP: Australia and New Zealand (per cent)

Source and note: See Figure 2.3.

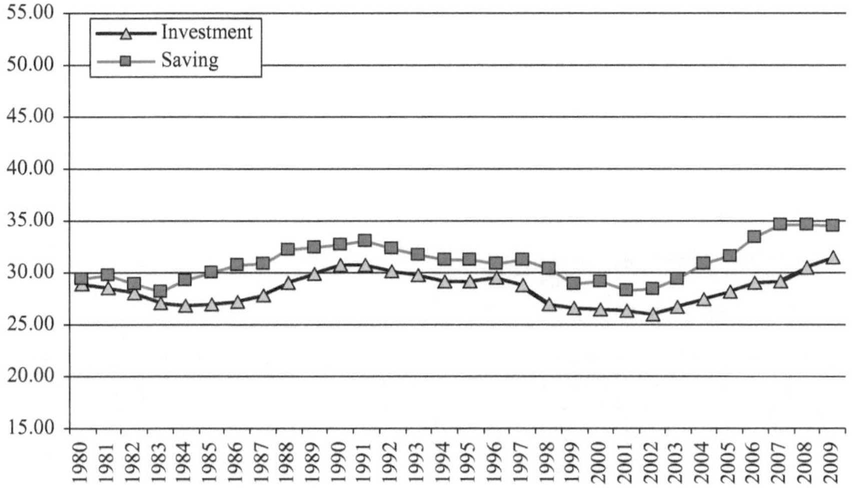

Figure 2.7 Savings and investment shares of GDP: all 12 countries (per cent)

Source and note: See Figure 2.3.

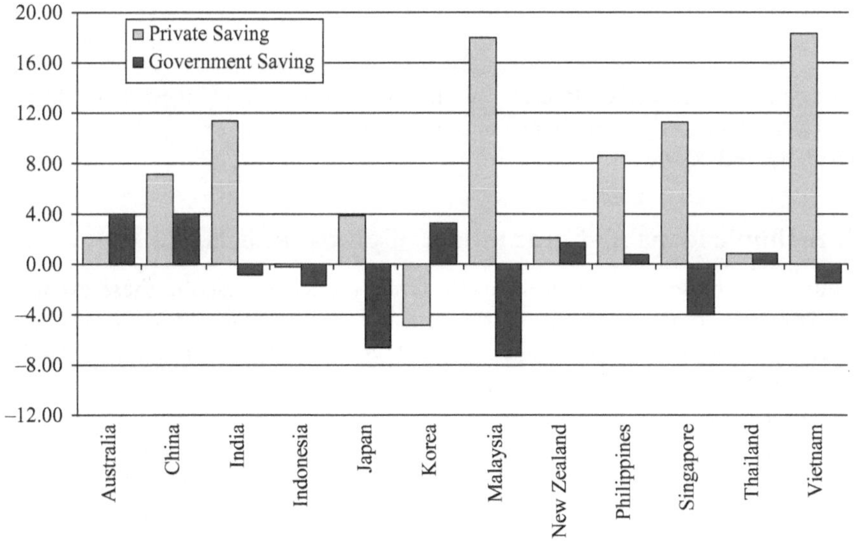

Figure 2.8 Change in savings share of GDP, 1990–96 to 1999–2009 (per cent)

Source: World Bank, IMF, CEIC.

Note: Pre-crisis average calculated over 1990–96, and post-crisis average calculated over 1999–2009; change in savings share of GDP = post-crisis share – pre-crisis share.

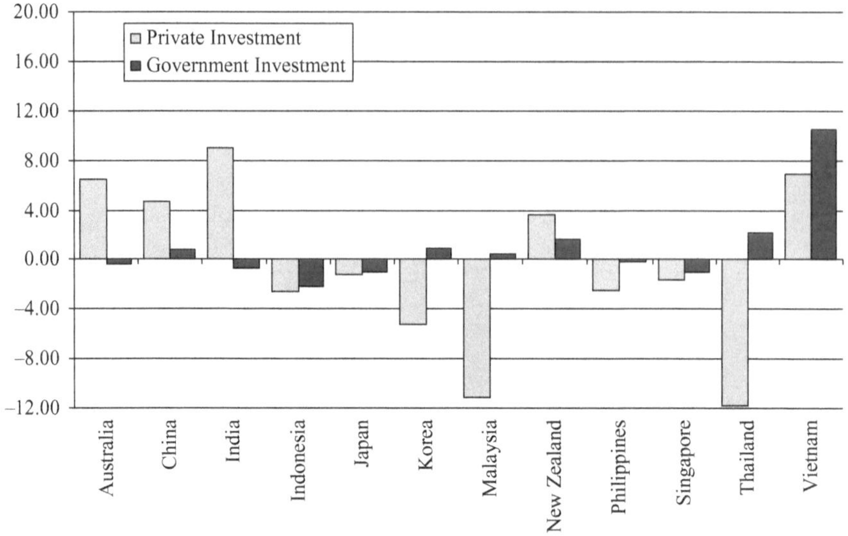

Figure 2.9 Change in investment share of GDP, 1990–96 to 1999–2009 (per cent)

Source: World Bank, IMF, CEIC.

Note: Pre-crisis average calculated over 1990–96, and post-crisis average calculated over 1999–2009; change in savings share of GDP = post-crisis share – pre-crisis share.

Indonesia was severely affected by the AFC, its private investment share contracted post-crisis much more moderately than, for example, Malaysia, Thailand and Korea.

4. A simple loanable funds model of global imbalances

Figure 2.10 presents a simple loanable funds model to describe these events. Investment is represented by the demand for loanable funds and savings are represented by their supply. Consider panels A and B first, representing "Asia" (panel A) and the "rest of the world" (panel B), respectively. These two panels represent the global market for loanable funds. They determine the equilibrium world interest rate at the level where Asia's current account surplus (or deficit) is equal to the rest of the world's deficit (or surplus). For convenience, it is assumed that both Asia and the rest of the world are in current account balance in the initial period (period 0), roughly representing the late 1990s. The world interest rate is r_0.

The second period (period 1) represents roughly 2009. For simplicity, the supply and demand for loanable funds in the rest of the world are each assumed to remain stationary, as is assumed in the well-known Bernanke "savings-glut" interpretation of global imbalances (Bernanke, 2005). The action takes place initially in Asia. There is a huge shift to the right in Asia's supply of loanable

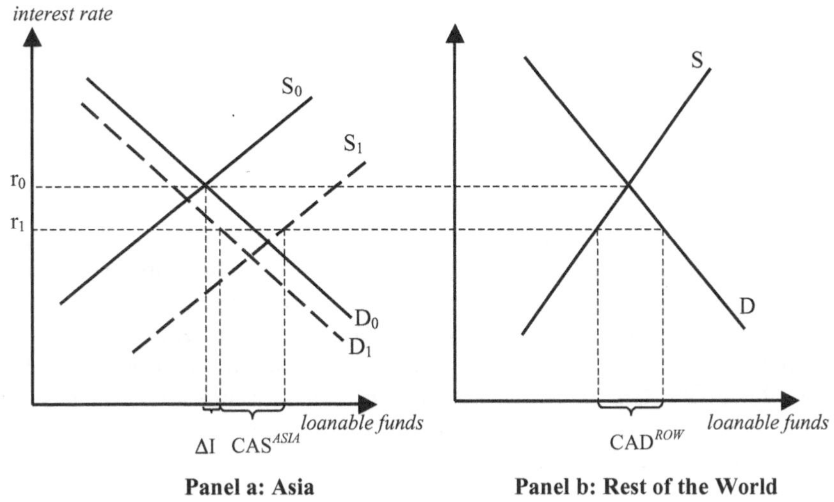

Figure 2.10 A loanable funds model of global imbalances

funds (savings), from S_0 to S_1, and a smaller shift to the left in the demand (investment), from I_0 to I_1. The world interest rate declines from r_0 to r_1. In the rest of the world, the fall in interest rates induces a movement along both the supply and the demand schedules for loanable funds, inducing a contraction of savings and an expansion of investment, producing a large current account deficit, CAD^{ROW}. In Asia there were both (i) the *shifts* in the supply and demand schedules described above and (ii) a movement *along* the new schedules as interest rates fell. The result was a huge increase in aggregate savings and a small increase in aggregate investment. Investment increased in spite of the net leftward shift in Asia's investment demand schedule because of the large decline in interest rates. Asia's current account moved to a large surplus – the difference between Asia's savings and investment at the lower interest rate, where $CAS^{ASIA} = CAD^{ROW}$.

What caused the shift in Asia's savings and investment schedules? In the Group I countries, confidence was negatively affected by the devastation of the AFC. The demand for loanable funds (investment) shifted to the left as firms became much more pessimistic about future prospects. Growth rates declined significantly compared with the pre-crisis decade of 1986–96. In the Group II (not crisis-affected) countries, there was an export-led economic boom. Savings increased as a share of GDP in response to the income growth.

Figure 2.10 can be used to make one further point. If the "rest of the world" – principally the United States – wishes to reduce its current account deficit, the question arises as to whether it is better to make the adjustment itself or to attempt to induce Asia to adjust? If the United States adjusts, either by shifting its demand for loanable funds to the left or by shifting its supply to the right, its excess demand for loanable funds contracts, the equilibrium level of its current account deficit declines and world interest rates fall. If Asia contracts its excess supply of loanable funds, the same combination of current account balances might result, but with an *increase* in world interest rates. Given the huge level of its stock of debt, the United States has a strong interest in low world interest rates. It is therefore in the United States' own interest to do the adjusting itself and not to berate Asia to reduce its current account surpluses.

Asia's current account surpluses can be lowered either by reducing savings (by increasing consumption) or by increasing investment. In the Group I (crisis-affected) countries, both are possible strategies. Fiscal expansion can reduce public sector savings by increasing social expenditures on education, health and other public services. The same can be done in the Group II countries – notably China. But in the Group I countries, policies that raise investment will have the dual benefit of reducing current account surpluses and raising growth rates. We shall therefore focus on this option.

5. Should Asia's rate of investment rise?

What is likely to happen to investment levels in Asia, and indeed what should happen? Is export-dependent Asia investing too little? One way of approaching this question is to compare actual investment shares in GDP with steady-state shares calculated from a neo-classical growth model (Islam, 1995). The purpose of this exercise is to attempt to predict the changes in investment behaviour that are likely in Asia, if it is to sustain satisfactory rates of economic growth.

Abstracting from population growth for simplicity, the required steady-state level of investment i^* is given by

$$i^* = k^* (g + d) / (1 + g), \quad (2)$$

where k^* denotes the steady-state capital–output ratio, d denotes the rate of depreciation and g denotes the potential rate of growth of output. For a given value of d, k^* is found as the mean value of the capital–output ratio over a long period (1950–2008). An International Monetary Fund study (IMF, 2005) derived the potential rate of output growth from medium-term projections from the IMF *World Economic Outlook*. It found that application of this simple neo-classical framework leads to three conclusions concerning the emerging countries of Asia other than China:

i. In the years preceding the AFC, actual investment shares exceeded steady-state shares, suggesting over-investment.
ii. In the years immediately following the crisis, actual investment shares were below steady-state shares, as firms moved to eliminate excess capacity.
iii. Actual shares still remain below the steady-state shares required to sustain real GDP growth rates above 5 per cent (IMF, 2010). That is, emerging Asia (except China) is under-investing. If growth rates of 5 per cent are to be maintained, actual investment shares need to increase (for example, by

5 per cent of GDP in Thailand and by 3 per cent in Malaysia and the Philippines).

This analysis suggests investment to output ratios for most Association of South-East Asian Nations (ASEAN) economies below their required levels. For most ASEAN countries, achievement of the IMF growth projections requires investment as a share of GDP to increase by an average of about 5 percentage points.

An econometric study of the determinants of investment (IMF, 2009) suggests three conclusions. First, GDP growth slowed since the AFC, lowering the rate of return to investment, and this reduced investment spending relative to GDP by an average of 2.5 percentage points. Second, macroeconomic uncertainty caused firms to hold back on investment plans and this greater uncertainty since the AFC reduced the investment share of GDP by about 1 percentage point. Third, a deterioration in investors' perceptions of the investment climate – including application of the rule of law, creditor rights and transparency of government operations – has reduced the investment to GDP share by just less than 1 percentage point. Some progress has occurred in most of these areas since the AFC, but investors' perceptions have been slow to catch up.

6. Policy conclusions

This chapter has attempted to develop an understanding of the relationship between the payments imbalances between Asia and the rest of the world (principally the United States) and economic structure in these two regions. In this context, "economic structure" means the balance of resource allocation between the production of goods destined for international markets and goods destined for the domestic market.

Accumulated current account surpluses in Asia and corresponding deficits in the United States have produced an accumulation of debt owed by citizens and institutions of the United States to those of Asia. It is generally agreed that this continued accumulation of debt is ultimately unsustainable. A rebalancing will occur. The trading imbalance must stop and must ultimately be reversed. This adjustment must imply a reallocation of resources within Asia away from goods destined for export markets and towards goods destined for the home market. The opposite must happen in the United States. The question is not *whether* but *when* this rebalancing and consequent economic adjustment will happen. When it does, adjustment problems are inevitable in both Asia and the United States. The faster the rebalancing required, the greater the adjustment costs.

So far as Asia is concerned, the growth rebalancing literature has suggested that some "rebalancing" now – away from reliance on external demand and towards domestic demand – can reduce vulnerability to the possibility of large and sudden adjustment costs. Policies designed to increase investment within Asia are one way of doing this. Increasing investment in Asia should not be seen as an objective in itself. It is desirable in part as an instrument of growth rebalancing, but only if it is productive. Research from the IMF has suggested that to maintain satisfactory rates of growth, Asian countries other than China do need to raise the share of investment in GDP, especially those countries that were affected negatively by the 1997–98 AFC. The effects of that crisis on investor confidence are still apparent.

Four means of increasing levels of private and public investment in Asia seemingly warrant consideration. The first is increased public sector infrastructure investment. A higher level of private investment requires infrastructure improvements. Greater use of public–private partnership models can assist in financing this investment. The second is fostering improvement in the private sector investment climate. This includes governance issues, including more consistent application of the rule of law, creditor rights and transparency of government operations, including procurement. It also includes further reform to enhance the competitiveness of output and labour markets.

A third issue is promoting better private sector access to finance. This can include development of a domestic corporate bond market and reform of collateral laws to enable a wider range of securitization beyond real estate and other fixed assets. Finally, credit risk can be reduced by promoting corporate restructuring. Creating a market for distressed corporate debt by the purchase of non-performing loans (NPLs) from banks and repackaging them for subsequent sale to the private sector can reduce the negative effect that NPLs have on financial institutions' willingness to lend.

Note

1 This phenomenon is already being recognized politically in the United States under the label "intergenerational theft".

References

Bernanke, B.S. (2005) *The Global Savings Glut and the US Current Account Deficit*, Washington, DC: Federal Reserve Board. Online. Available at <http://www.federalreserve.gov/boarddocs/speeches/ 2005/200503102/default.htm>.

Corden, W.M. (2007) 'Those current account imbalances: a sceptical view', *The World Economy*, 30: 363–82.

———. (2011, April) 'Global imbalances and the paradox of thrift', *Policy Insight*, 54, Centre for Economic Policy Research.

International Monetary Fund (IMF) (2005) *World Economic Outlook*, September, Washington, DC: IMF.

———. (2009) *Asian Economic Outlook*, September, Washington, DC: IMF.

———. (2010) *Asian Economic Outlook*, September, Washington, DC: IMF.

Islam, N. (1995) 'Growth empirics: a panel data approach', *Quarterly Journal of Economics*, 110: 1127–70.

Obstfeld, M. and Rogoff, K.S. (1997) *Foundations of International Macroeconomics*, Cambridge, Mass.: MIT Press.

3 Corporate savings, investment and financial structure in East Asia

Micro-evidence

Jenny Corbett and Garry Twite

1. Introduction

Global current account imbalances are widely acknowledged to reflect internal savings–investment imbalances. Yet it is not always clear which side of the savings–investment ledger is out of line, and a failure to analyze this clearly can lead to mistaken policy advice. Even if correctly identified, it can be quite difficult to explain why those savings imbalances arise. Indeed, it is not even straightforward to measure the domestic components of the imbalances and to allocate them accurately between household and corporate sectors, though the effort is important for policy analysis, as demonstrated by Bayoumi et al. (2010).

This chapter draws attention to the role of finance for the listed corporate sector as a key part of the economic structure that underlies global macroeconomic imbalances. If listed companies are amassing large savings balances, there will be some economic reason for that behaviour. Either firms are building savings in order to invest, or they are accumulating excess savings because they are unable (or unwilling) to invest. The first pattern of behaviour suggests that firms might be unable to raise funds for investment when needed from the financial system and are forced to rely on their own savings. The second would arise when firms earn profits that they cannot apply to investment projects and that accumulate inside the firm, or are used for the acquisition of financial assets rather than physical capital expenditure. Each of these stories would give rise to distinctive patterns in corporate financial structure.

Our purpose in this chapter is to examine and clarify claims that recent macroeconomic imbalances are largely caused by excessive corporate savings and that these are driven by inadequacies in financial systems. This claim has been made in many quarters, including by the International Monetary Fund (IMF, 2009) and is primarily based on macroeconomic data from national income accounts. We use micro-data from company accounts of listed firms to shed light on these problems.[1] If the claims from the macro-data are correct, they should also be reflected in companies' financial accounts. We examine the evidence of the patterns of retained earnings, dividend payouts and the accumulation of assets and find little support for the idea that there is a build-up of excessive finance in the listed company sector. Not only do firms not retain earnings to an unusual degree or build-up war chests of cash and liquid assets, but the internal and external finance available is being used primarily to finance real asset creation. The micro-evidence does not support the macro-claims, but it does support the alternative hypothesis that more investment could be undertaken with different policy settings and possibly greater development of financial systems.

The structure of the chapter is as follows. First, we consider how firms raise their finance (that is, in what form) and what they do with the funds raised. We then use the micro-data to see whether they support claims that corporate savings are a large part of the "excess savings" story. Both sides of this coin are important for policy responses to understanding financial needs and to addressing imbalances. Our data bring a micro-perspective to the question of whether the financial system is contributing to a build-up of corporate savings or to low levels of investment, or both. We examine whether firms are financially constrained in investment and what characteristics explain different patterns of retention or accumulation of liquid assets.

Section 2 demonstrates that Asian firms are somewhat unusual in raising a large part of their funds externally (not from retained earnings). Although there has been a steady increase in retained earnings for some firms, there are others with negative earnings that have no retention and are entirely dependent on external finance for survival. Amongst the sources of external finance, there has been an increasing role for equity financing. This is unusual in an international context and challenges the conventional view that companies in East Asia are excessively dependent on debt. Furthermore, there have been significant changes around crisis events.

We then turn the data around to ask whether firms use their finance for investing in real physical assets or for accumulating cash or other financial assets. Since the previous data show only where funds come from and not what they are used for, this section gives an important perspective on whether finance is used to create the real assets that are the source of countries' productive capacity and growth.

From the data in Section 2, we can clarify the role of firms' own funds (retentions from profit) in the creation of real assets and increase the understanding of whether the pattern and scale of corporate savings are unusual in Asia and whether there is a problem of corporations withholding their savings from productive investment. This leads, in Section 3, to a discussion of whether the micro-data are consistent with the macro-evidence on corporate savings reported in other studies.

Section 4 presents regression results to explain the link between savings and investment and to examine the extent of financial constraints on investment. We link these results to the earlier discussion of whether accumulated assets are being hoarded by firms. Section 5 draws conclusions and policy implications.

2. Sources of finance: where do firms get their funds?

Corbett and Twite (2010) noted several unusual features of corporate finance in the Asian region – in particular, the relatively high dependence on external finance and, within that, a rather large role for equity finance as a source. Figures 3.1–3.6 show that these features have become even more pronounced in the recent period of global financial turmoil.

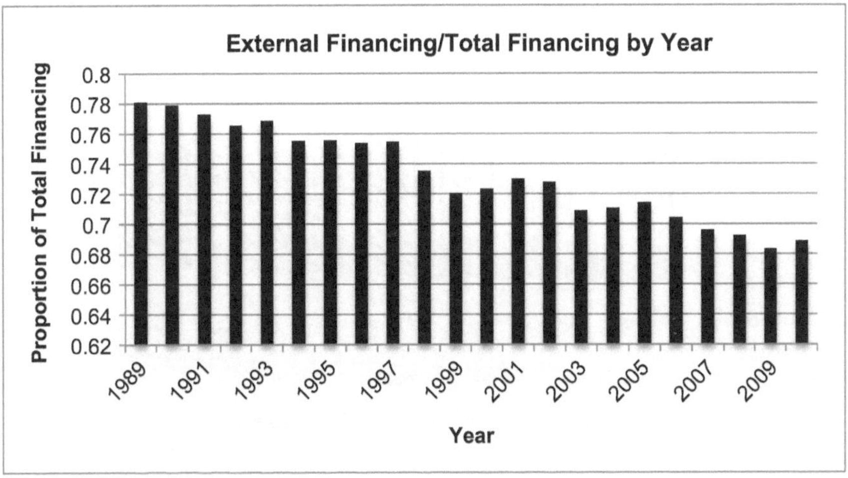

Figure 3.1 External financing/total financing by year

Note: We use book values and drop firms with negative earnings for which the concept of internal finance is not meaningful. This applies to Figures 3.1–3.6.

Source: Refer to the Appendix for data source.

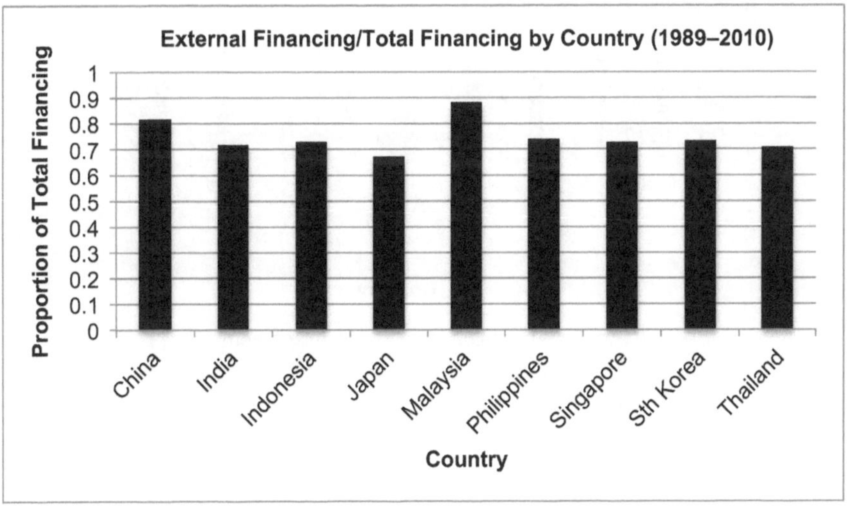

Figure 3.2 External financing/total financing by country (1989–2010)

Source: Refer to the Appendix for data source.

While the share of external sources in total finance fell after the Asian Financial Crisis (AFC) of 1997–98, and has continued to fall, it is still about 70 per cent for the nine countries considered (Figures 3.1 and 3.2). As Figure 3.3 shows, debt began to decrease significantly as a share of financing after the AFC, while issues of both common stock and the use of retained earnings rose. Countries vary significantly in their use of debt versus equity (Figure 3.4), with China,

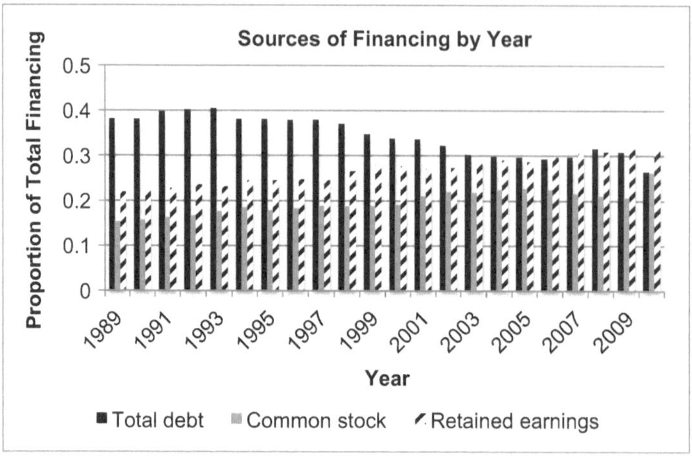

Figure 3.3 Sources of financing by year

Source: Refer to the Appendix for data source.

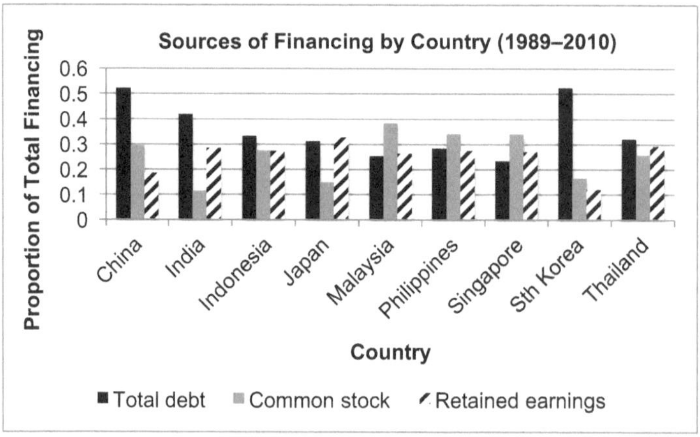

Figure 3.4 Sources of financing by country (1989–2010)

Source: Refer to the Appendix for data source.

India and Korea the high-debt users (at 40 per cent to 50 per cent of total financing sources), followed by Indonesia and Thailand (at more than 30 per cent). Japan also uses considerable debt but differs from the other high-debt countries in using more retained earnings than either separate source of external finance.[2]

Another striking feature is the substantial use of common stock by several countries. For Malaysia, the Philippines and Singapore, common stock issues have been the largest source of finance, accounting for more than either debt or retained earnings. In Thailand, Indonesia and China, they have accounted for more than 25 per cent. This might seem surprising given the conventional view that corporate sectors in Asia are heavily bank dependent,[3] but it is consistent with data showing that the listed firms in the region are not dramatically different from global averages in the debt/equity structure of their finance. The average leverage ratio (total debt/book value of firm) for all countries covered by Compustat data is 31 per cent; the United Kingdom is 28 per cent and Australia 21 per cent. Table 3.1 shows the average for our sample against relevant comparators.

Breaking down external sources into more detailed components, Figures 3.5 and 3.6 also show the growing share of equity and the decline in both long and short-term debt after the AFC. Amongst debt instruments, the most important is now trade credit between companies. Data for individual countries show the consistently important role of trade credit and short-term debt (presumed to be bank debt), but again the striking role of equity issues. Long-term debt has been a generally smaller share and no doubt reflects the underdeveloped corporate bond markets.

Table 3.1 Mean leverage

	Mean leverage
Our sample	0.4555
Total other countries in Compustat	0.3028
Developed countries	0.3247
Developing countries	0.3092

Note: Leverage is defined as total debt over (total debt + book value of common stock + book value of preferred stock), where total debt is long-term + short-term debt.

Source: Refer to the Appendix for data source.

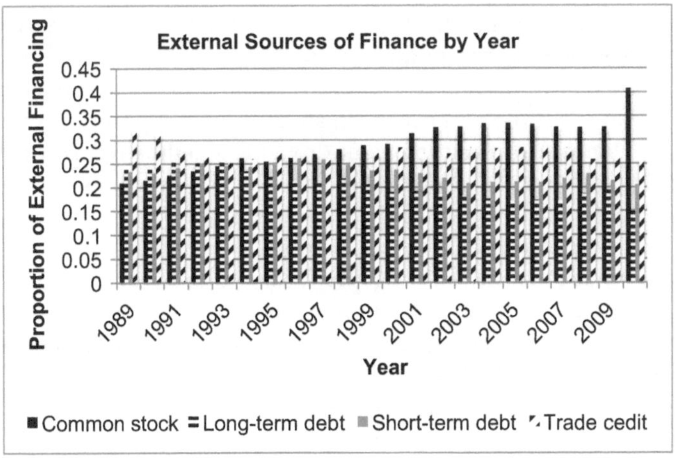

Figure 3.5 External sources of finance by year

Source: Refer to the Appendix for data source.

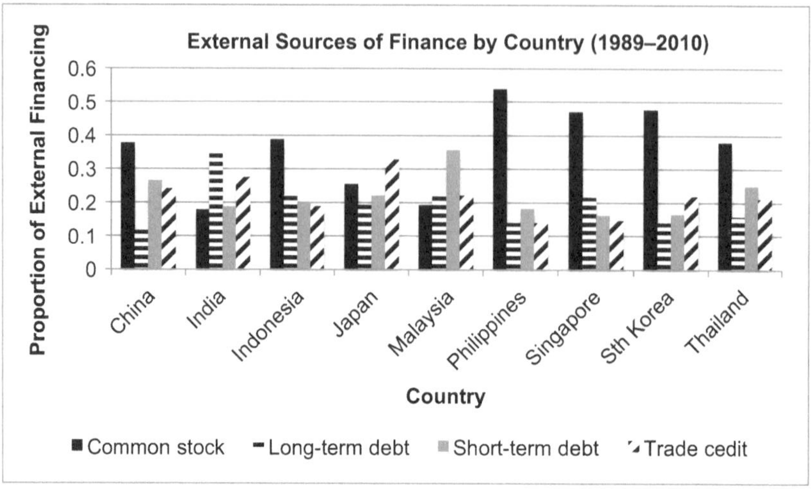

Figure 3.6 External sources of finance by country (1989–2010)

Source: Refer to the Appendix for data source.

Figures 3.3 and 3.4 also indicate the steady increase over time in the role of retained earnings in financing, albeit at fairly low levels. Across countries, retentions generally vary between 20 per cent and 30 per cent as a share, with the remainder of financing coming from external sources. This finding contrasts with a widely held view in corporate finance that retained earnings are generally a larger source of finance than external sources. Even in Japan – the country in our sample with the largest share for retentions – external sources combined are a larger share of total financing. China – contrary to the view that companies are building up large savings (further discussed below) – is much more dependent on external sources than internal ones.

For the sample of companies with positive earnings, we conclude that at the time of the AFC, as external finance began to drop, retentions were used to keep the total amount of financing from dropping significantly. This trend has continued, bringing these firms closer to international norms in their reduced dependence on external finance. In some countries, they have increasingly used equity as the larger source of external financing.

Once we include the firms with negative earnings, however, the role of retentions is quite different, with large negatives recorded since 2000 and an increasing share of equity finance offsetting falling internal sources (with particularly large declines in retentions in 2002 and 2005) (Figure 3.7). For the corporate sector as a whole, therefore, external finance has remained very important.

While this implies that, on the positive side, some external finance is available to act as a buffer when corporate profits plunge, it also means that as a result of crisis periods the corporate sector becomes more dependent on external finance at the margin. If these changes in the finance mix could be achieved rapidly at

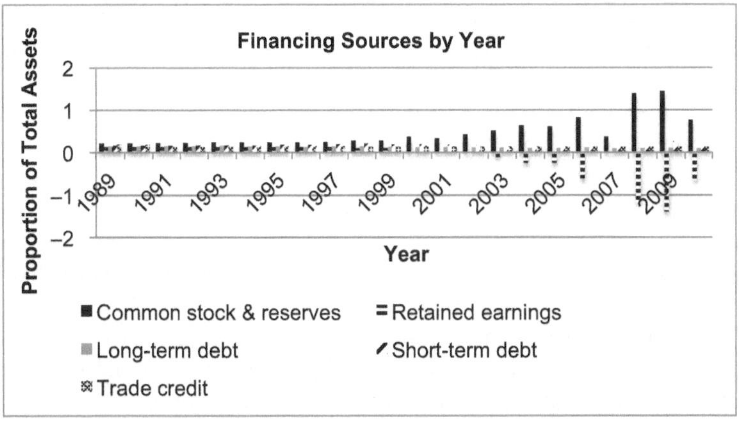

Figure 3.7 Financing sources by year

Source: Refer to the Appendix for data source.

times of crisis, without a large drop in the overall quantity of finance, the impact of crisis on capital expenditure (investment) would be less than if finance were not available, and this is an important function of the financial sector.

The puzzle identified by Corbett and Twite (2010) – that there is no impact from the mix of financial sources on investment – might be partly tempered by the emerging picture. Given the patterns described, we might not expect to observe a close contemporaneous correlation between the mix of finance and the creation of real assets. Yet, at times of crisis, the ability to source new finance does matter, and it might result in significant changes in the mix, as firms replace difficult sources with more readily available ones. An inability to replace declining sources of finance with alternative sources would have an impact on the amount of investment carried out. The question to ask is not whether having more debt or more equity allows firms to invest more, but whether the ability to change the funding mix reduces constraints on investment.

Another perspective on the role of different types of finance and their ability to acquire assets comes from focussing on the uses of firms' finance rather than the sources.

2.1 The uses of funds

If firms are uncertain about the reliability of external financing sources, we might observe a build-up of cash and other liquid assets because firms want a war chest from which to fund planned investment in the future, or because they become more conservative generally and want to hoard cash against future financing shortages, even if they have no plans for investment. In the former case, we should observe that, even if cash holdings are large, or rise at times of crisis, they will be used for capital expenditure. In the latter case, we might see large cash build-ups that do not result in the formation of assets. To understand this behaviour, we look at the share of different types of asset acquisition in the total assets of firms.

A pattern of acquisition of accumulated cash and liquid asset sources could help to explain earlier results (Corbett and Twite, 2010) showing the irrelevance of financial structure to investment (with only country characteristics mattering for investment performance). While consistent with other studies, it seemed a surprising result for Asia since it appeared to imply that improving access to particular types of finance (for example, strengthening the corporate bond market or the stock market) would have little effect on companies' investment behaviour. This seemed to mean that increasing the breadth and depth of financial markets would not increase investment, though macroeconomic studies typically show that financial depth improves investment and growth. It seems more likely that the financial mix does affect the investment behaviour of firms, but that econometric exercises might not detect the effect because of the ability to disconnect current investment from current financing by using accumulations of liquid assets.[4] If markets worked perfectly, this behaviour would not be necessary: if some types of finance were not available, firms would be able to substitute them with others and would not have to cut investment, but in the presence of financial friction firms might build up cash reserves to protect investment plans.

We find, in fact, that cash holdings (and cash plus equivalent liquid assets) at less than 20 per cent as a share of assets are not particularly large in any of the countries (Figures 3.8 and 3.9), though there is cross-sectional variation. There had been a steady decline in the lead-up to the AFC and liquid holdings stayed low after the crisis until countries began to build them up again from 2002–03. It appears that during and immediately after the AFC, even though profits fell, firms raised more finance despite the poor economic situation and

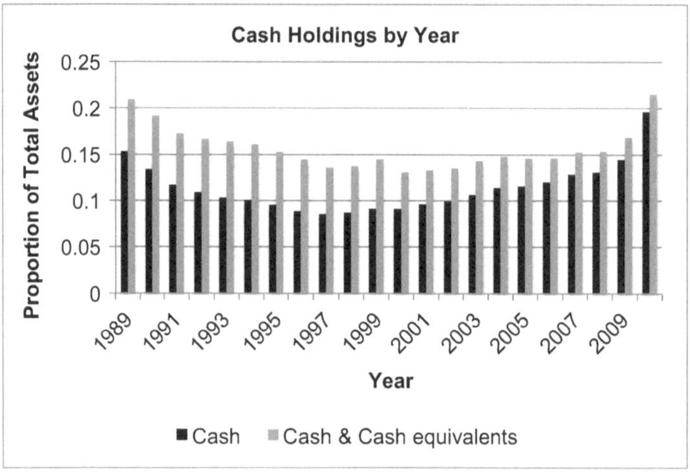

Figure 3.8 Cash holdings by year

Source: Refer to the Appendix for data source.

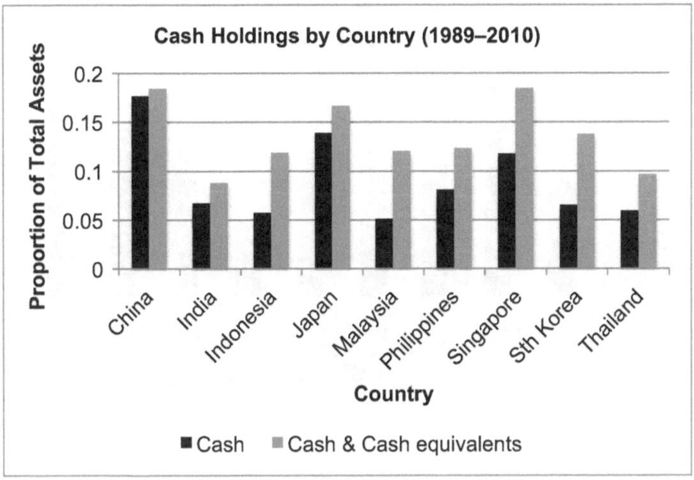

Figure 3.9 Cash holdings by country (1989–2010)

Source: Refer to the Appendix for data source.

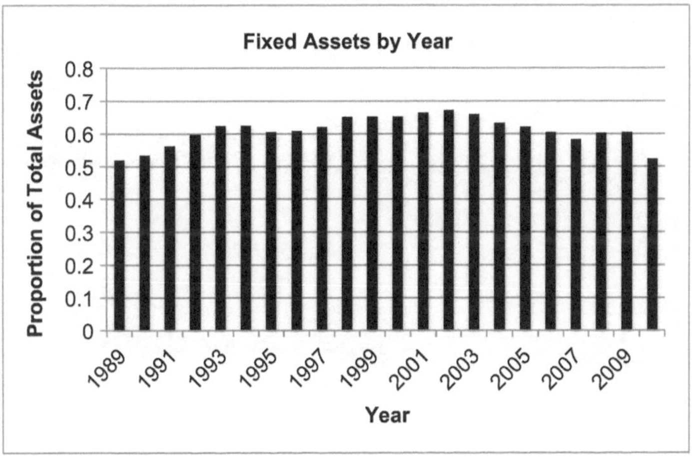

Figure 3.10 Fixed assets by year

Source: Refer to the Appendix for data source.

ran down their own liquid assets, with the result that fixed assets stayed at a fairly stable share of total assets (Figures 3.10 and 3.11).

An alternative to managing liquid assets for firms facing financial constraints is to manage retentions. Firms with poor access to external financial markets, but with productive investment opportunities, could cut dividends to provide more retained earnings. Shareholders might be willing to accept this in the short-term if longer-term investment returns are positive. The effect in company accounts would be a rise in the share of retentions relative to assets (given that

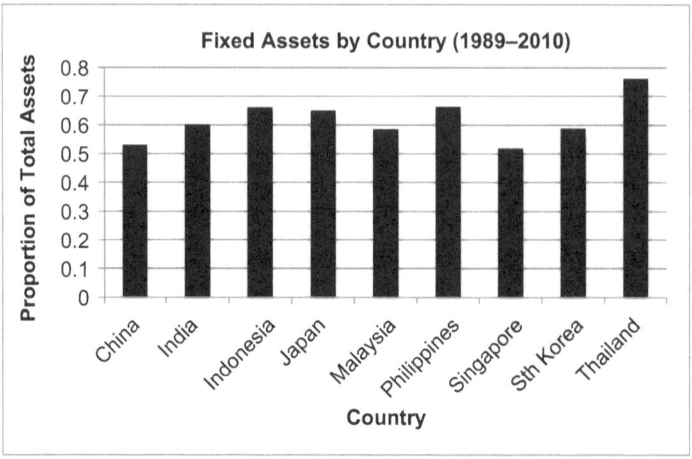

Figure 3.11 Fixed assets by country (1989–2010)

Source: Refer to the Appendix for data source.

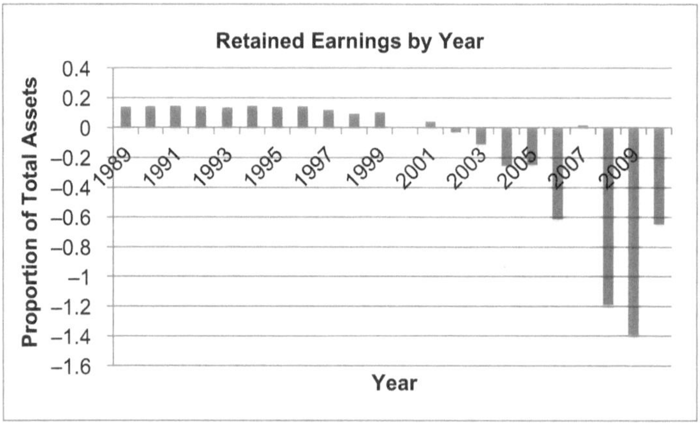

Figure 3.12 Retained earnings by year

Source: Refer to the Appendix for data source.

dispersing retentions into fixed assets cannot take place immediately), and this would, in effect, be a temporary deferral of acquisition of current real assets for future ones.

Figures 3.12 and 3.13 show no evidence of large accumulations of retained earnings. In fact, as noted above, despite the increase in retentions for some firms, when all firms are included (even those with negative earnings) retentions have declined since the AFC, and in some years have become heavily negative. This is not the result of large dividend payouts: Figures 3.14 and 3.15 show payout ratios across countries and over time that are not significantly different from international standards (at about 0.6).[5] Rates have fallen since 2000, but this is also true across the world.

There is little evidence, therefore, that cash accumulations or retained earnings were hoarded rather than used for real asset creation. Figures 3.10 and 3.11 show that even the lowest countries have a high proportion of fixed assets in total assets, at 50 per cent to 70 per cent. Even during the crisis years, the proportion of fixed assets remained high. From 2003 onwards, these shares have fallen – consistent with other evidence that investment has slowed in most of these countries (possibly in response to "excess" investment in the pre-AFC

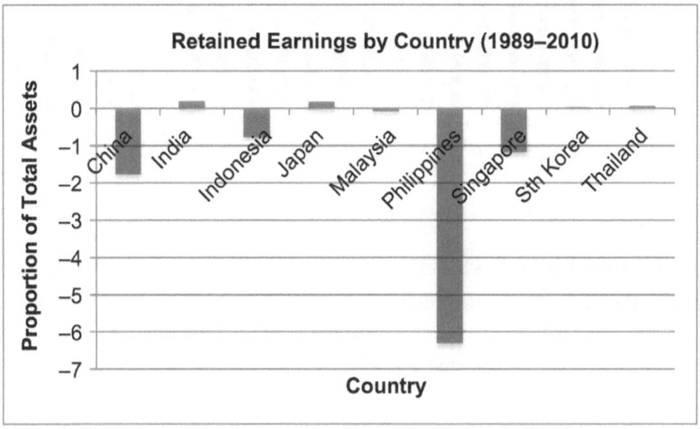

Figure 3.13 Retained earnings by country (1989–2010)

Source: Refer to the Appendix for data source.

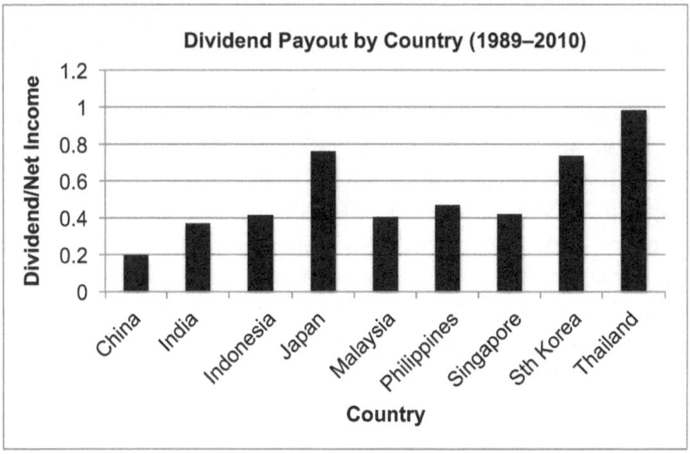

Figure 3.14 Dividend payout by country (1989–2010)

Source: Refer to the Appendix for data source.

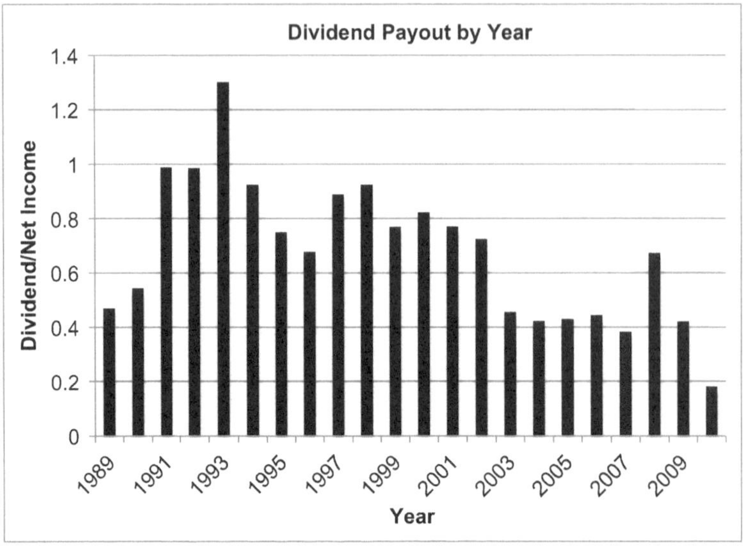

Figure 3.15 Dividend payout by year

Source: Refer to the Appendix for data source.

years), but even at their lowest level in 2010, fixed assets represented 50 per cent of total assets.

We can exploit the variation in the pattern of retentions and accumulation of liquid assets to look more closely at the main drivers of asset-accumulation behaviour. Table 3.2 presents a set of regression results that shows the significant effects of country-level policy and institutional factors on firms' allocation of funds between different uses (retained earnings, liquid assets and fixed assets). These are the results of two-stage regressions that give the country-specific factors affecting the acquisition of different types of assets, after accounting for firm and year effects, which we argue provide the appropriately corrected standard errors on the country-level variables.[6] The two-stage procedure regresses the dependent variable on firm characteristics (listed in the data appendix), then uses the error terms from those regressions as dependent variables in the second stage. The first-stage dependent variables are (i) cash and cash equivalents over total assets; (ii) retained earnings over total assets; and (iii) fixed assets over total assets.

The picture that emerges is that firms in common-law systems retain less and also accumulate lower proportions of cash. This result is consistent with common-law systems providing better investor protection, and enabling investors to "demand" higher dividend payments and more frequent monitoring via external financing. The observation that common-law systems are associated with lower levels of fixed assets is consistent with better property rights protection facilitating the investment in intangible assets. Interestingly, firms in countries with high corruption levels have lower cash and higher retentions. As expected, the higher retentions result in an increase in fixed assets rather than an accumulation

Table 3.2 Asset accumulation

Dependent variables (error terms from first-stage regressions):	*Cash & cash equivalents/ total assets*	*Retained earnings/ total assets*	*Fixed assets/ total assets*
Independent variables:			
Country factors:			
Common law	–0.0795	–2.6953	–0.3694
	(–12.81)***	(–3.05)***	(–7.93)***
Corruption	–0.0060	0.5289	0.0547
	(–2.04)**	(2.60)***	(2.44)***
Creditor rights	0.0138	–0.8143	–0.0971
	(3.31)***	(–2.49)***	(–2.74)***
Shareholder rights	–0.0001	0.6541	0.1401
	(–0.02)	(2.39)***	(10.58)***
State-owned bank	0.0489	1.6164	0.3065
	(4.15)***	(1.92)*	(3.97)***
Tax evasion	0.0105	1.8507	0.2056
	(1.38)	(2.97)***	(3.47)***
Openness	0.0038	–0.6970	–0.0010
	(1.21)	(–2.61)***	(–0.08)
AFC	–0.0224	0.4202	–0.0243
	(–4.25)***	(1.04)	(–1.10)
Industry:			
Non-durables	0.0033	0.0609	0.0643
	(0.58)	(0.37)	(1.96)*
Durables	0.0300	0.1678	0.0593
	(4.11)***	(1.33)	(0.97)
Manufacturing	0.0011	–0.7551	0.0686
	(0.30)	(–0.71)	(2.49)**
Energy	0.0198	–0.2167	0.1901
	(1.84)*	(–0.76)	(3.60)***
High-tech	0.0918	0.3931	–0.3659
	(7.88)***	(2.11)***	(–9.48)***
Telecommunications	0.0616	0.4748	0.0506
	(5.60)***	(3.27)***	(0.64)
Shops	–0.001	0.1629	–0.1930
	(–0.30)	(1.24)	(–9.55)***
Health services	0.0179	0.2689	0.1266
	(1.47)	(1.16)	(0.78)
Number of observations	75,883	76,790	76,216
R-squared	0.1357	0.0002	0.1901

Note: Two-stage regression of dependent variable on country-level variables, controlling for firm and industry. Standard errors are robust to clustering within country over time. T-statistics are given in parentheses. Significance levels: * 10 %; ** 5 %; *** 1 %.

of cash. This is consistent with higher corruption levels implying less ability to protect property and enforce non-defined contracts, giving a disadvantage to holding cash and an advantage to investing in fixed (non-discretionary) assets. This might result in over-investment in inefficient physical projects. Stronger creditor rights are normally associated with the use of more debt, allowing lower retained earnings, as we find. In our results, the puzzle is that this leads to higher accumulation of cash rather than investment in fixed assets. As expected, stronger shareholder rights are associated with higher levels of retained earnings and fixed assets because shareholders' confidence in their ability to exercise their property rights gives them the confidence to allow firms to retain earnings. Recent criticism of the indices that we and many others use to capture investors' rights raises issues about the interpretations of the results and is discussed in more detail in the conclusion.

An important finding for the region is that the more open the economy, the stronger the reliance on external financing and the lower the level of retained earnings, though openness has no effect on the allocation between cash and fixed assets. Finally, the AFC seems to have had little impact on either the level of retention or the accumulation of fixed assets, but certainly did result in a decline in cash holdings, suggesting that at least part of the firms' investment during that period was financed by a depletion of cash holdings rather than the use of external financing.

This closer consideration of the accumulation of retentions also helps to make the link we seek between corporate savings behaviour and investment. What can we conclude about the hypothesis that the region suffers from excess corporate savings, given the evidence of the declining role for retentions and a growing need for external sources of finance?

3. Do East Asian firms save a lot or a little?

As noted in the introduction, we are interested in the sources and uses of financing, not only for what they tell us about the way in which access to finance might impact on the formation of productive assets, and as a means to understand the transmission of financial shocks to real investment, but also because they provide another lens through which to understand the development of corporate savings. Our evidence on retained earnings so far does not suggest that these are unusually high, or that dividend payouts are out of line with international norms. Furthermore, it appears that retentions have been managed along with total financing and the acquisition of assets so as to keep the share of fixed assets quite high. There is little support for the idea of unproductive hoarding of corporate earnings. Yet the idea that excess corporate savings is an important source of global imbalances has been prevalent.

Two recent IMF studies give rather different pictures of the contribution of corporate savings to global imbalances. The IMF (2009) claims that corporate savings have increased in Asia since the turn of the century, that they have driven up national savings rates because households have not reduced their savings to compensate and that they now account for a rising share of global savings. The data to support these claims are not easy to verify as many countries in the region do not report corporate savings in their national income accounts, and the source of the IMF study data is not given. The study argues that a combination of stagnant investment and household consumption plus rising corporate savings creates the global imbalances. They attribute rising corporate savings to governance structures and financial institutions that give rise to high retained earnings (IMF, 2009:57). In an argument paralleling ours above, they note that limited market financing options and low shareholder pressure to pay dividends *could* give rise to an "excessive" build-up of retentions. They claim their micro-data-based study, using 20,000 firms from 60 countries, shows that a lack of financial development leads to an external finance premium forcing Asian firms to save (defining savings as after-tax earnings net of dividends divided by sales). Full details of the study are not available, but those that are reported in fact show that an interaction term between financial liberalization and an Asian region dummy has a significant, and large, negative coefficient, implying that financial liberalization in Asia has reduced corporate savings by even more than in other regions (see pp. 69–70). This can be interpreted as showing that financial liberalization has an even greater effect in Asia than elsewhere, but it does not, directly, allow the interpretation that there is an external finance premium. Furthermore, the results as reported do not provide evidence of whether Asian firms' savings differ from the average, much less whether they are unusually high, so the interpretation that financial liberalization would "improve" the results depends on other evidence that Asian corporate savings are above average. That evidence comes from a regression on aggregate corporate savings in national income accounts data in which Asia post-2000 does seem to be larger than the mean of other countries. It is not clear, however, which Asian countries have been included or whether the definitions of corporate savings are comparable (see our discussion below about the problem of depreciation in the data).

The authors conclude that though improvements in both governance and financial markets have occurred in Asia, reducing the need for corporations to "amass a large war chest of savings" (IMF 2009:57), these effects have been "offset" by rising corporate savings. They draw the policy conclusion that more of the same governance and finance reforms are needed to further reduce savings.

An alternative interpretation is proposed in IMF (2010) and in Bayoumi et al. (2010) (see also the chapter by Wei in this volume). Both papers argue that corporate savings are not a particular problem in Asia generally, or even in the most likely case of China, and that the problem is high, though stable, household savings, low household incomes and low corporate investment. The important difference of emphasis has policy significance. If corporate savings are not the main problem, then policy attention should be focussed on the investment side of the corporate equation. It might still be that the improvement of financial markets plays a role here, but, as we show below (and as is borne out in many other studies), a focus on the general investment and legal climate is likely to be critical. If these policies have an effect, it will come about by increasing investment, not by reducing savings.

We have already shown that retention ratios are not particularly high relative to assets, nor are dividends unusually low. Furthermore, even companies with positive earnings are accessing external finance, implying that they are creating fixed assets beyond their own resources (that is, that their investment exceeds their savings).

To consider what factors influence the accumulation of corporate savings, Table 3.3 reports regressions of gross savings (over total assets) and gross savings adjusted for dividends (over total assets) on firm and country-level variables, controlling for industry. The firm-level characteristics are firm size (natural logarithm of sales), leverage (book value of total debt over book value of total debt plus book value of common stock plus book value of preferred stock), asset tangibility (fixed assets over total assets) and profitability (net income over total assets) lagged one period to allow for contemporaneous correlation between profitability and gross savings. As expected, we find that the larger the firm, the higher are gross savings and the higher is the investment in fixed assets, while leverage is lower (that is, the less use is made of external finance). These results are consistent with other literature and indicate that firms with higher investment needs will accumulate high savings. As we have shown from the descriptive data, there is evidence that these savings are used for investment rather than being hoarded.

The country variables, which are of particular interest, show (somewhat puzzlingly) that the level of gross savings is higher under strong legal environments – namely, where there is a common-law system, lower corruption and less tax evasion. This result could be consistent with better legal systems allowing for the

Table 3.3 Explaining total savings

Dependent variables:	*Gross savings/total assets*	*Gross savings dividend adjusted/total assets*
Independent variables:		
Firm factors:		
Size	0.0140	0.0071
	(6.22)***	(3.20)***
Leverage	–0.0096	–0.0184
	(–3.13)***	(–2.32)**
Asset tangibility	0.0118	0.0279
	(0.72)	(3.72)***
Profitability(t-1)	0.0409	0.0462
	(1.26)	(1.90)*
Country factors:		
Common law	0.1450	0.0795
	(6.44)***	(3.21)***

Dependent variables:	*Gross savings/total assets*	*Gross savings dividend adjusted/total assets*
Corruption	–0.0070	–0.0093
	(–2.44)***	(–1.76)*
Creditor rights	–0.0036	0.0064
	(–1.20)	(1.44)
Shareholder rights	–0.0366	–0.0191
	(–5.38)***	(–2.76)***
State-owned bank	–0.0751	–0.0388
	(–3.87)***	(–2.47)***
Tax evasion	–0.0402	–0.0396
	(–3.99)***	(–3.68)***
Openness	0.0037	0.00630
	(1.67)*	(1.94)*
AFC	–0.0105	–0.0079
	(–0.95)	(–1.21)
Industry:		
Non-durables	0.0090	–0.0083
	(1.86)*	(–0.59)
Durables	0.0097	0.0104
	(1.53)	(1.99)**
Manufacturing	0.0110	0.0068
	(2.47)***	(2.56)***
Energy	0.0125	0.0133
	(1.03)	(1.02)
High-tech	0.0027	0.0100
	(0.28)	(1.61)
Telecommunications	0.0185	0.0337
	(2.00)**	(6.08)***
Shops	–0.0058	–0.0027
	(–0.59)	(–0.51)
Health services	0.0096	0.0080
	(1.52)	(0.79)
Number of observations	81,546	57,807
R-squared	0.0711	0.0103

Note: Regression of gross savings (over total assets) and gross savings adjusted for dividends (over total assets) on firm and country-level variables controlling for industry. Standard errors are robust to clustering within firm and country over time. T-statistics are given in parentheses. Significance levels: * 10 %; ** 5 %; *** 1 %.

enforcement of non-defined contracts and permitting the retention of funds within the firm. The observation that stronger shareholder rights are associated with lower levels of gross savings would imply that, with better shareholder protection, shareholders "demand" the distribution of earnings and more frequent monitoring via external financing, but this is not consistent with the result on the legal system. Curiously, the results suggest that firms in countries characterized by state ownership of banks have lower levels of gross savings, suggesting that bank financing might in fact substitute for corporate savings in these countries.

While we do not include a variable for financial reform (as in IMF, 2009), our variable for financial openness is only marginally significant, so there is no strong evidence that companies hoard savings as economies liberalize. The AFC dummy is insignificant, so the apparent crisis-induced increase in savings in the raw data does not survive once controls for other effects are included. We have some doubts about the reliability of regressions such as these, for reasons noted in the conclusions below, and put more weight on the results reported in Table 3.2, which cast a different light on savings behaviour. Since the savings variable used in Table 3.3 is the same as that in IMF (2009), their results might also require care in interpretation.

4. Savings and investment

We have previously described how firms allocate their financial resources to different types of assets (liquid versus fixed) and found little evidence that they hoard cash and liquid assets, but they do appear to use them for fixed asset formation. We can consider more directly the hypothesis that firms' investment activity is dependent on their accumulated cash balances or their contemporaneous cash flow (for example, when they cannot access external finance) to see whether there is evidence of an incentive to build war chests. To examine this, we can exploit the variation in the sensitivity of firms' investment to cash flow. High cash flow sensitivity would suggest that firms use cash flow and cash holding as sources of funding for investments. We can, furthermore, look for direct evidence of whether this sensitivity is stronger for financially constrained firms that face limits to the use of external financing.

We present results in Table 3.4 showing a regression of capital expenditure (normalized by total assets) on cash and cash equivalent (over total assets) lagged one period to allow for contemporaneous correlation between cash holdings and capital expenditure, and cash flow (over total assets). We also include market-to-book ratios (Tobin's Q) and control for country-level factors and industry effects. The three firm-level variables are interacted with a financial constraint dummy (FC). The financial constraint dummy takes a value of 1 if the firm has above median dividend payout and leverage (total debt/[total debt + book value of common stock + book value of preferred stock]) and 0 otherwise.

While we find no general relationship between cash flow and investment, we find a positive and significant relationship between cash flow and capital expenditure for financially constrained firms, suggesting that investment by firms faced

Table 3.4 Explaining capital expenditure

Dependent variables:	*Capital expenditure/ total assets*
Independent variables:	
Firm factors:	
Cash & cash equivalents(t-1)/total assets	0.0023
	(0.14)
Cash flow/total assets	0.0002
	(1.60)
Market-to-book	0.0001
	(1.88)*
FC*Cash & cash equivalents(t-1)/total assets	–0.0096
	(–0.89)
FC*Cash flow/total assets	0.1677
	(11.19)***
FC*Market-to-book	0.0001
	(0.06)
Country factors:	
Common law	0.0055
	(2.81)***
Corruption	–0.0032
	(–6.66)***
Creditor rights	0.0044
	(2.06)**
Shareholder rights	0.0024
	(2.74)***
State-owned bank	0.0212
	(9.23)***
Tax evasion	–0.0123
	(–8.79)***
Openness	0.0011
	(0.84)
AFC	0.0110
	(3.58)***
Industry:	
Non-durables	–0.0025
	(–0.74)
Durables	0.0094
	(1.17)

(*Continued*)

Table 3.4 (Continued)

Dependent variables:	*Capital expenditure/ total assets*
Manufacturing	0.0002
	(0.09)
Energy	0.0111
	(1.13)
High-tech	−0.0109
	(−3.00)
Telecommunications	0.0160
	(1.83)*
Shops	−0.0078
	(−1.81)*
Health services	0.0147
	(2.01)**
Number of observations	60,632
R-squared	0.0815

Note: Regression of investment (capital expenditure) sensitivity to cash and cash equivalent (over total assets) lagged one period, cash flow (over total assets) and market-to-book (Q) controlling for country-level factors and industry. In addition, these three variables are interacted with a FC (financial constraint) dummy. The dummy takes a value of 1 if the firm has above median dividend payout and leverage (total debt/[total debt + book value of common stock + book value of preferred stock]) and 0 otherwise. Standard errors are robust to clustering within firm and country over time. T-statistics are given in parentheses. Significance levels: * 10 %; ** 5 %; *** 1 %.

with constrained access to external financing is sensitive to the availability of the firms' own cash and cash flows. This has fairly immediate and obvious policy implications – developed below.

In addition, we find that capital expenditure is higher under a strong legal environment – namely, a common-law system – with better shareholder and creditor protection, lower corruption and less tax evasion. Interestingly, the results suggest that firms in countries characterized by state ownership of banks invest more in fixed assets. These results provide more unambiguous evidence that improving the legal environment increases firms' willingness to invest compared with the more tentative results on the effect on fixed assets as a share of total assets.

5. Conclusions

We have shown that the financial patterns that emerged in Corbett and Twite (2010) have continued to be the predominant pattern for Asian firms despite the Global Financial Crisis. Although retained earnings have risen as a source of finance, companies are generally heavily dependent on external sources of funds and are increasingly using common stock issuance as the means of raising finance. This implies that even the strongest firms in these economies – those with positive net earnings and with access to the stock market – are net borrowers rather than net savers. These firms do not have abnormally low dividend payouts and do not accumulate very large cash and liquid asset balances. Their assets are dominated by fixed assets (that is, physical investment in plant and equipment), and the share of fixed assets has been maintained during periods of crisis.

The choice of how to allocate finance to different asset classes – that is, whether to hoard it in liquid assets or to use it for fixed asset formation – is influenced by the presence of common-law systems providing better investor protection, by the absence of corruption, by shareholder and debtor rights, and by openness. The AFC also had an effect. Common-law systems that are usually regarded as giving higher protection for property rights have a different effect from the direct effect of stronger shareholder rights. The former results in lower retentions and lower fixed asset shares (and possibly higher intangibles, though we did not explicitly consider this), while the latter are associated with higher retentions and higher fixed assets. Higher corruption increases retentions and fixed assets, perhaps because these are less likely to be expropriated or subject to fraud than cash and liquid assets. This might result in over-investment in inefficient physical projects. Stronger creditor rights are linked with lower retentions. These do not give rise to higher fixed assets but to higher cash accumulations. Since the basis of legal systems (common versus civil) is hardly likely to be changed, a policy focus on strengthening shareholders' rights and reducing corruption is more likely to be useful in reducing the incentives for firms to hold on to retained earnings. Stronger creditor rights will enable greater access to debt finance and reduce the need for retentions.

An important finding for the region is that the more open the economy, the stronger is the reliance on external financing and the lower is the level of retained earnings, though openness has no direct effect on the allocation between cash and fixed assets.

Our regressions on savings are somewhat different from the findings on retentions. The level of gross savings seems to be higher under strong legal environments – namely, where there is a common-law system, lower corruption and less tax evasion. This result might be interpreted as meaning that better legal systems allow for the enforcement of non-defined contracts and thus allow for the retention of funds within the firm, though that is not what we found when regressing retentions directly on these variables. The savings data, by necessity, include amounts that firms retain for depreciation and we believe that this introduces a bias into the evidence on savings. The result is that when comparing countries, we are picking up any variation in the depreciation practices as if they were differences in savings. In a country such as China, where the main growth in fixed assets has been quite recent, the amount of depreciation is likely to be small, while in countries that have had a long history of fixed asset investment, these amounts will be large. In addition, if there are differences or changes in accounting practices that lead to different depreciation amounts, these will also confound the results. Since we have confidence in the retention regressions reported earlier (which are not subject to this problem), we prefer those results. This also means that other studies that have drawn conclusions about savings behaviour using similar variables to those in our savings regressions might be unreliable.

Finally, our investment regression shows that financial constraints do hold back investment so that, in addition to improving the general support of investors and creditors rights, policies that remove financial constraints would impact on investment.

Clear policy recommendations require further research and would benefit from an extension to other country policy variables that are of specific interest in the region, particularly a more fine-grained analysis of the elements of openness, financial sector reform and accounting changes that impact on company strategies and on data. We note also that there has been much careful criticism of the La Porta et al. (1998) indices on investors' rights and the legal systems. As Spamann (2010) notes, the classification of countries into civil or common law has led to corrections in the classifications that are significant enough to undermine previously accepted research results. Spamann's correlation between the corrected and original values is only 0.53, and he points out that many empirical results established using the original index might not be replicable with corrected values. This will also apply to the work done here, and it remains an open question as to whether countries need to be reclassified and what impact that would have on the results. One particularly important aspect of this is that Spamann's newer results fail to support the notion that shareholder protection is higher in common than in civil-law countries. This has implications for our interpretations of our regression analysis.

We conclude by returning to a point made at the outset. There is little evidence that listed firms in the region are hoarding savings. The savings in the corporate sector are being used for investment purposes. Thus, while it might be true that there is some accumulation of assets in retentions or in liquid form, this seems to be in the group of firms that behave as if financially constrained. A further policy focus on the drivers, determinants and impediments to investment will be a more productive way to respond to global imbalances than a narrow focus on corporate savings.

Notes

1 While the unlisted company sector may be important in some countries, there is little data on their finances. We discuss the implications of this for our analysis in Appendix A.
2 This replicates the finding in Corbett and Jenkinson (1997) that Japan used a "balance" of sources of financing across retentions, equity and debt.
3 It might be partly explained by the fact that we are considering the listed company sector and do not have data for the small and medium firms that are not

listed, and which might be more debt financed. As we have argued in the discussion of our data, the listed firm sector is now a significant part of the region's economies and cannot be dismissed as unrepresentative or unimportant, though it is likely true that its financial structure is different from family-owned and small and medium firms.

4 Note that if liquid assets are parked somewhere (for example, bank deposits) then running these down becomes a source of finance, but it shows up as a change in assets (reduction), not a change in liabilities. The "net sources" approach of Mayer (1988) might miss this effect by deducting the change in assets holdings from the change in similar liabilities, but would pick it up if there is no change in the matching liability (or if the change in assets is larger than the change in liability, so adding to the total source from, for example, banks). The only way to fully capture this is to show the assets side, which is what we do in the next section.

5 The Mean Dividend Payout Ratio for all countries in the Compustat data is 0.600011; all countries excluding the United States have 0.608032; the United States has 0.23906; all countries with payout <1 have 0.414713; developing countries have 0.405512; developed countries have 0.794509.

6 We recognize that since the regression residuals are heteroskedastic and correlated across both firm and country-level observations, ignoring this error structure will bias downward the estimated standard errors. To account for this potential problem we employ a two-stage regression procedure that should provide more conservative standard errors. In the first stage, we estimate firm-level determinants accounting for heteroskedastic and correlation across firm-level observations. In the second stage, we cluster by country and year. In adopting this two-stage approach, we ignore the possibility that the firm-level variables may be correlated with the country-level explanatory variables used in the second stage. To the extent that an association between firm-level variables and country-level factors exists, it will bias downwards our estimated second stage coefficients. Hence, by adopting a two-stage procedure, we generate conservative estimates of the country-level effects.

References

Bayoumi, T., Tong, H. and Wei, S-J. (2010) 'The Chinese corporate savings puzzle: a firm level cross-country perspective', *IMF Working Paper* WP/10/275.

Caprio, G., Laeven, L. and Levine, R. (2005) 'Governance and bank valuation', *Working Paper,* World Bank and University of Minnesota.

Chinn, M.D. and Ito, H. (2008) 'A new measure of financial openness', *Journal of Comparative Policy Analysis: Research and Practice*, 10: 309–22.

Corbett, J. and Jenkinson, T. (1997) 'How is investment financed: a study of Germany, Japan, UK and US', *The Manchester School, Papers in Money, Macroeconomics and Finance,* 65: 69–93.

Corbett, J. and Twite, G. (2010) 'Capital structure of firms and real financial linkages in East Asia', in C. Findlay, F. Parulian and J. Corbett (eds), *Real and Financial Linkages in East Asia*, 153–95, Jakarta: ERIA.

Djankov, S., Ganser, T., McLiesh, C., Ramalho, R. and Shleifer, A. (2010) 'The effect of corporate taxes on investment and entrepreneurship', *American Economic Journal: Macroeconomics*, 2: 31–64.

Djankov, S., La Porta, R., Lopez-de-Silanes, F. and Shleifer, A. (2003) 'Courts', *Quarterly Journal of Economics*, 118: 453–517.

———. (2008) 'The law and economics of self-dealing', *Journal of Financial Economics*, 88: 430–65.
Djankov, S., McLiesh, C. and Shleifer, A. (2007) 'Private credit in 129 countries', *Journal of Financial Economics*, 84: 299–329.
International Monetary Fund (IMF) *International Financial Statistics*, Washington, DC: IMF.
International Monetary Fund (IMF) (2009) *Regional Economic Outlook Asia and Pacific*, October, Washington, DC: IMF.
International Monetary Fund (IMF) (2010) *Regional Economic Outlook Asia and Pacific*, April, Washington, DC: IMF.
La Porta, R., Lopez-de-Silanes, F., Shleifer, A. and Vishny, R. (1998) 'Law and finance', *Journal of Political Economy*, 106:113–55.
Mayer, C. (1988) 'New issues in corporate finance', *European Economic Review*, 32:1167–1189.
Spamann, H. (2010) 'The "antidirector rights index" revisited', *Review of Financial Studies*, 23: 467–86.
Transparency International (n.d.) *Corruption Perception Index*, London: Transparency International.
Treisman, D. (2000) 'The causes of corruption: a cross-national study', *Journal of Public Economics*, 76: 399–457.
World Bank, (various years) *World Development Indicators*, Washington, DC: The World Bank.

Appendix A
Data

We use firm-level data from the *Compustat Global Database* from 1989–2010. We include data for China, Indonesia, India, Japan, Korea, Malaysia, the Philippines, Singapore and Thailand. Table 3.A1 shows the number of observations in total and by country. As can be seen from the last two columns of Table 3.A1, the use of the listed firm sample results in different numbers of observations across countries. Country differences in market capitalization reflect both the size and importance of unlisted firms within the country and the uneven coverage of firms across the countries by Compustat. For most of the economies, the market capitalization of the listed firm sector represents more than 40 per cent of GDP, but because we are using listed company data, we are not able to draw conclusions about the whole corporate sector. Unlisted small and medium enterprises (SMEs) and non-listed firms, such as family firms, are not covered. This sample bias could explain the low levels of cash holdings together with the weak relationship between cash flow and investment in our results if cash is held in the unlisted parts of the enterprise. Furthermore, by excluding

Table 3.A1 Sample size

Country	*Number of firms*	*Total firm-year observations*	*Mean stock market captialization to GDP (%)*
China	2,234	13,256	40.5731
India	2,354	14,420	41.0818
Indonesia	469	5,060	21.7931
Japan	4,893	67,045	79.5645
Malaysia	1,193	13,339	51.8070
Philippines	261	2,898	151.4674
Singapore	835	7,748	45.6541
South Korea	2,336	19,652	157.0782
Thailand	766	8,278	52.1391
Total	15,341	151,696	71.8142

Source: World Bank, (various years) *World Development Indicators*

unlisted firms that are more likely to use internal sources of finance or, if external, to rely on debt, we may be exaggerating the role of external equity finance. This does not, however, alter the fact that our results show a marked difference in the use by listed firms of external equity financing sources, particularly post-AFC, compared to listed companies in developed countries.

Definitions of variables

In the regressions reported in the text, the firm-level variables are fixed assets or asset tangibility (fixed assets over total assets), profitability (net income over total assets), firm size (natural logarithm of sales), the market-to-book ratio (market value of equity over book value of equity), dividend payout (total dividend over net income), leverage (total debt/[total debt + book value of common stock + book value of preferred stock]), cash (cash over total assets), cash and cash equivalents (cash and cash equivalents over total assets), cash flow (cash flow over total assets), and a financial constraint dummy that takes a value of 1 if the firm has above median dividend payout and leverage and 0 otherwise. The country-level variables cover several institutional features: the legal system (common law versus civil law dummy), a corruption index, an indicator of whether the banking system is state-owned, a tax-compliance variable, variables for creditors' and shareholders' rights and the degree of openness of the financial system. We also include an indicator for the AFC that takes a value of 1 for 1997 and 1998 and 0 otherwise. The definition and sources for these country-level variables are given in Table 3.A2. Finally, we have adopted a 10-industry classification. The industry classifications are given in Table 3.A3.

Table 3.A2 Definitions and data sources of country-level variables

Variable	*Description*	*Source*
Common law	A 0 or 1 dummy variable indicating whether a country adopts the common-law system.	Treisman (2000) and La Porta et al. (1998)
Corruption index	An index ranging from 0 to 10, with larger value indicating more severe corruption.	Corruption Perception Index (Transparency International, n.d.)
Creditor rights	An index aggregating creditor rights – restrictions for a debtor to file for reorganization; secured creditors are able to seize their collateral after the reorganization petition is approved; secured creditors are paid first out of the proceeds of liquidating a bankrupt firm; management does not retain administration of its property pending the resolution of the reorganization. The index ranges from 0 (weak creditor rights) to 4 (strong creditor rights).	Djankov et al. (2007)

Variable	*Description*	*Source*
Tax evasion	Executives' assessment of how important tax evasion is in their country (the lower the measure, the more rampant is tax evasion).	Djankov et al. (2009)
Shareholder rights	Aggregate index of shareholder rights. The index is formed by summing (1) vote by mail; (2) shares not deposited; (3) cumulative voting; (4) oppressed minority; (5) pre-emptive rights; and (6) capital to call a meeting.	Djankov et al. (2003, 2008)
State control	An index measuring the proportion of a country's banks that are state controlled, where a bank is defined to be state controlled if the state–s voting rights exceed 10 per cent.	Caprio et al. (2005)
Openness	An index that measures the extent of openness in capital account transactions. Higher values represent more open economies.	Chinn and Ito (2008)

Table 3.A3 Industry groups

Industry	*Four-digit SIC code*
Non-durables: Consumer non-durables – food, tobacco, textiles, apparel, leather, toys	0100–0999, 2000–2399, 2700–2749, 2770–2799, 3100–3199, 3940–3989
Durables: Consumer durables – cars, TVs, furniture, household appliances	2590–2599, 3630–3659, 3710–3711, 3714–3714, 3716–3716, 3750–3751, 3792–3792, 3900–3939, 3990–3999
Manufacturing: Manufacturing – machinery, trucks, planes, chemicals, office furniture, paper, com. printing	2520–2589, 2600–2699, 2750–2769, 2800–2829, 2840–2899, 3000–3099, 3200–3569, 3580–3629, 3700–3709, 3712–3713, 3715–3715, 3717–3749, 3752–3791, 3793–3799, 3830–3839, 3860–3899
Energy: Oil, gas, and coal extraction and products	1200–1399, 2900–2999

(*Continued*)

Table 3.A3 (Continued)

Industry	*Four-digit SIC code*
High-tech:	3570–3579, 3622–3622, 3660–3692, 3694–3699, 3810–3839, 7370–7372, 7373, 7374, 7375, 7376, 7377, 7378, 7379, 7391, 8730–8734
Business equipment – computers, software, and electronic equipment, industrial controls; services – computer programming and data processing; computer-integrated systems design; services – computer processing, data prep.; services – information retrieval services; services – computer facilities management services; services – computer rental and leasing; services – computer maintenance and repair; services – computer-related services; services – research and development labs; services – research, development, testing labs	
Telecommunications:	4800–4899
Telephone and television transmission	
Shops:	5000–5999, 7200–7299, 7600–7699
Wholesale, retail and some services (laundries, repair shops)	
Health services:	2830–2839, 3693–3693, 3840–3859, 8000–8099
Health care, medical equipment and drugs	
Utilities:	4900–4949
Electric, gas and sanitary services, natural gas transmission and distribution, electric and other services combined, gas and other services combined, water supply	
Other:	
Other–mines, construction, building materials, transport, hotels, bus services, entertainment, finance	

4 China's exchange rates or other factors in global rebalancing?[1]

Shang-Jin Wei

1. Introduction

One of the seemingly intractable problems in the world economy in recent years has been the global current account imbalance. China and a few other countries have been running large current account surpluses since the beginning of this century, which are matched by persistently large current account deficits in a group of other countries – most notably, the United States. The problem has been identified as a root cause of, or a contributing factor to, the 2007–09 Global Financial Crisis (GFC), and possibly a ticking time bomb that could lead to a future world economic crisis.

Very commonly, the fixed exchange rate regime of certain surplus countries is understood to be a key cause of the current account imbalance problem. Both official statements and opinion pieces in news media have reinforced such a view. For example, a communiqué of G20 finance ministers and central bankers declared that "an orderly unwinding of global imbalances, while sustaining global growth, is a shared responsibility involving . . . greater exchange rate flexibility".[2]

These statements are not, however, founded on systematic analysis of actual country experiences. Indeed, it is not difficult to find counter-examples. While Egypt has a relatively rigid exchange rate regime, it has a relatively fast current account convergence. On the other hand, while Japan has a flexible exchange rate regime, it does not have a fast convergence speed. Of course, there is a limit to how much we can learn from individual examples.

This chapter is structured as follows: the next section reviews empirical results regarding the relationship between exchange rate regimes and current account adjustment. Section 3 presents the hidden source of China's surplus problem and highlights the sex ratio imbalance as a factor underlying the exchange rate. Section 4 concludes with discussion of the risks of a misdiagnosis of the global current account imbalance.

2. Exchange rate regimes and current account adjustment

Chinn and Wei (forthcoming) sought to address this deficiency by systematically investigating the data for all International Monetary Fund (IMF) member countries. After examining the data in many different ways, we found no support for the notion that countries on a more flexible exchange rate regime robustly exhibit a faster convergence of their current account to the long-run equilibrium.

We estimated variations of the following specification for 170 countries over the period 1971–2005

$$ca_{it} = \rho_0 + \rho_1 ca_{it-1} + \theta_{0j} \sum_{j=0}^{k} regime_{jit} + \theta_{1j}(ca_{it-1} \times \sum_{j=0}^{k} regime_{jit}) + v_{it}, \qquad (1)$$

where ca_{it} is the current account to GDP ratio for country i in year t, and the variable *regime* is the de facto exchange rate measure, proposed by either Levy-Yeyati and Sturzenegger (2005) or Reinhart and Rogoff (2004).[3] As is standard in the international finance literature, the speed of current account convergence can be inferred from the AR(1) coefficients.[4] (As an extension, we allow for both country fixed effects and year fixed effects; this does not alter the basic conclusion of this chapter.)

In Tables 4.1a and 4.1b, we separate countries into different groups based on a combination of two criteria: a country's stage of economic development (income) and its nominal exchange rate regime. The nominal exchange rate regime classification is per Levy-Yeyati and Sturzenegger (2005). The most salient feature is the lack of a clear sign that more flexible regimes provide faster current account adjustment. In Table 4.2, we pool all countries together. The same conclusion emerges.

To make sure that our result is not driven by a few outliers, Figure 4.1 plots the distribution of the AR(1) coefficients by country groups, where a country's group affiliation is defined by its nominal exchange rate regime. It is clear from the graph that there is no strong or systematic association between the nominal exchange rate and the speed of current account adjustment.

Additional regressions include more controls that might affect current account adjustment. We also deal with the possible endogeneity of a country's nominal exchange rate regime by using instrumental variables proposed by Levy-Yeyati and Sturzenegger (2005). The basic conclusion is the same.

We also replicate the analysis with the Reinhart and Rogoff (2004) classification of exchange rate regimes. The results are reported in Tables 4.3a and 4.3b. The qualitative results are the same: there is no robust support for the view that more exchange rate flexibility yields faster current account adjustment.

To understand why this is a sensible result, we have to realize that the current account responds to the real exchange rate, not the nominal exchange rate. A large body of empirical research in international finance shows that the real exchange rate tends to be stationary and converges to the steady state in the long run. The question is whether its convergence speed is connected to a country's nominal exchange rate regime. In Table 4.4, we examine this connection systematically by following a specification that is similar to the current account regressions. The evidence is clear that the convergence speed of the real exchange rate is not systematically related to a country's nominal exchange rate regime.

Table 4.1a Current account persistence by country sample, by regime

	(1)	*(2)*	*(3)*	*(4)*	*(5)*	*(6)*	*(7)*	*(8)*
	All				*Industrial countries*			
	Floating	*Dirty float*	*Dirty/crwl*	*Fixed*	*Floating*	*Dirty float*	*Dirty/crwl*	*Fixed*
CA(-1)	0.630	0.762	0.788	0.735	0.867	1.060	0.893	0.929
	(0.111)***	(0.068)***	(0.065)***	(0.030)***	(0.044)***	(0.066)***	(0.120)***	(0.033)***
Constant	–0.010	0.002	–0.006	–0.012	–0.001	0.003	–0.001	0.000
	(0.004)***	(0.003)	(0.003)**	(0.002)***	(0.001)	(0.003)	(0.004)	(0.001)
Observations	769	278	388	2,125	209	50	35	279
Adjusted R^2	0.38	0.55	0.64	0.58	0.71	0.88	0.8	0.78

Note: Robust standard errors in parentheses. Significance levels: * 10 %; ** 5 %; *** 1 %. Dependent variable = CA; exchange rate regimes are based on Levy-Yeyati and Sturzenegger (2005) definitions.

Table 4.1b Current account persistence by country sample, by regime

	(9)	*(10)*	*(11)*	*(12)*	*(13)*	*(14)*	*(15)*	*(16)*
	Non-industrial countries				*Non-industrial countries ex-oil*			
	Floating	*Dirty float*	*Dirty/crwl*	*Fixed*	*Floating*	*Dirty float*	*Dirty/crwl*	*Fixed*
CA(-1)	0.596	0.726	0.781	0.728	0.564	0.717	0.797	0.701
	(0.122)***	(0.078)***	(0.068)***	(0.031)***	(0.133)***	(0.071)***	(0.072)***	(0.039)***
Constant	–0.014	0.000	–0.007	–0.014	–0.016	–0.001	–0.006	–0.020
	(0.005)***	(0.004)	(0.004)*	(0.002)***	(0.006)***	(0.004)	(0.004)	(0.003)***
Observations	560	228	353	1,846	529	209	331	1,579
Adjusted R^2	0.34	0.5	0.62	0.57	0.33	0.49	0.65	0.51

Source: Chinn and Wei (forthcoming), RESTAT.

Note: Robust standard errors in parentheses. Significance levels: * 10 %; ** 5 %; *** 1 %. Dependent variable = CA; exchange rate regimes are based on Levy-Yeyati and Sturzenegger definitions

Table 4.2 Current account persistence, by country sample

	(1)	*(2)*	*(3)*	*(4)*
	All	*Industrial countries*	*Non-industrial countries*	*Non-industrial countries ex-oil*
CA(-1)	0.630	0.867	0.596	0.564
	(0.111)***	(0.044)***	(0.122)***	(0.133)***
CA(-1) x LYS1	0.132	0.193	0.131	0.153
	(0.130)	(0.079)**	(0.145)	(0.151)
CA(-1) x LYS2	0.158	0.026	0.185	0.233
	(0.128)	(0.125)	(0.140)	(0.152)
CA(-1) x LYS3	0.105	0.062	0.132	0.137
	(0.115)	(0.055)	(0.126)	(0.139)
LYS1	0.012	0.003	0.014	0.016
	(0.005)**	(0.003)	(0.007)**	(0.007)**
LYS2	0.004	–0.001	0.007	0.011
	(0.005)	(0.004)	(0.006)	(0.007)
LYS3	–0.002	0.001	0.000	–0.003
	(0.004)	(0.002)	(0.006)	(0.006)
Constant	–0.010	–0.001	–0.014	–0.016
	(0.004)***	(0.001)	(0.005)***	(0.006)***
Observations	3,560	573	2,987	2,648
Adjusted R^2	0.57	0.79	0.56	0.52

Source: Chinn and Wei (forthcoming), RESTAT.

Note: Robust standard errors in parentheses. Significance levels: * 10 %; ** 5 %; *** 1 %. Dependent variable = CA; LYS1 is a dummy variable for a dirty-float regime; LYS2 is a dummy variable for a dirty float/crawling peg; LYS3 is a dummy variable for fixed.

In short, the proposition that flexible exchange rates give you a faster adjustment of current accounts is wishful thinking and is not supported by a systematic data analysis.

3. The hidden source of China's surplus problem

The debate on exchange rate flexibility is driven largely by a desire to get China to let go of its exchange rate management. Our discussion would not be complete if we did not dissect the red dragon in the room – namely, the role of the renminbi (RMB) exchange rate in the country's current account surplus.

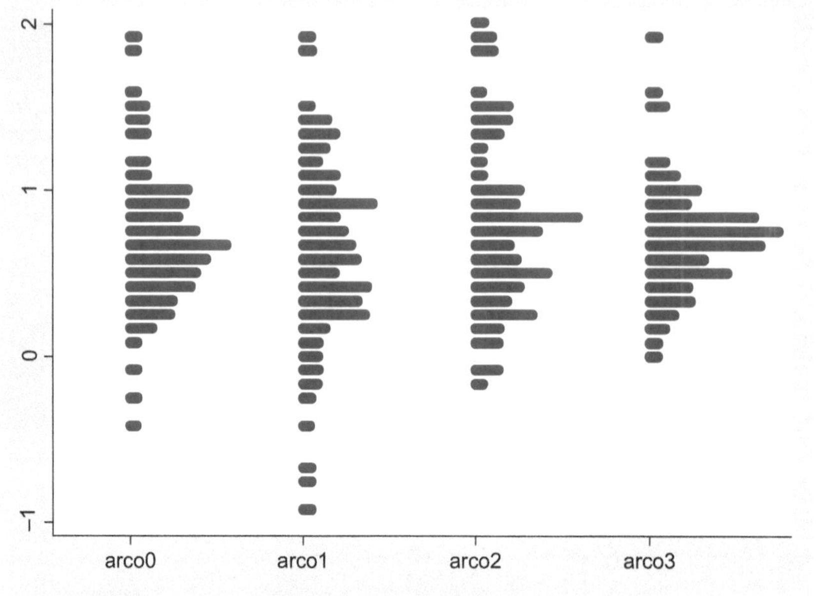

Figure 4.1 Individual auto-regressive coefficients (no trend) for LYS categories (higher indicates more fixity)

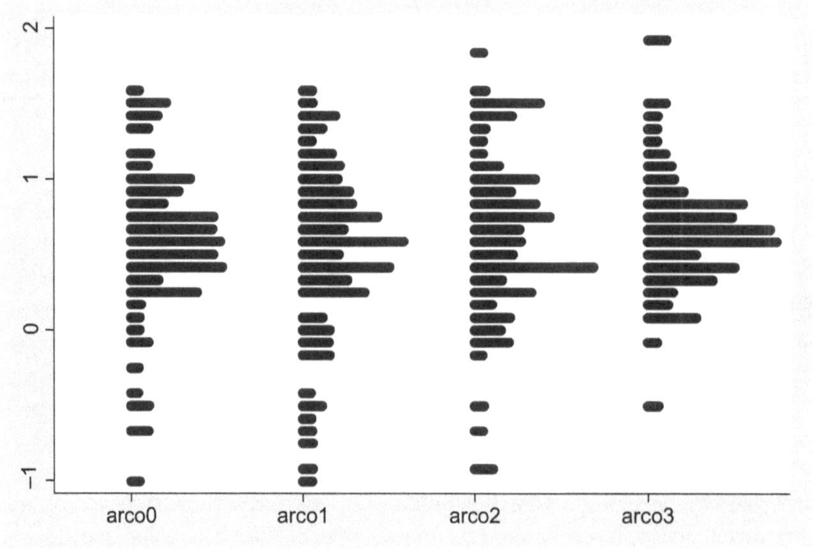

Figure 4.2 Individual auto-regressive coefficients (with trend) for LYS categories (higher indicates more fixity)

Source: Chinn and Wei (forthcoming).

Table 4.3a Current account persistence, by country sample, by Reinhart–Rogoff regime

	(1)	*(2)*	*(3)*	*(4)*	*(5)*	*(6)*
	All			*Industrial countries*		
	Floating	*Band/crwl*	*Fixed*	*Floating*	*Band/crwl*	*Fixed*
CA(-1)	0.663***	0.799***	0.719***	0.925***	0.840***	0.946***
	(0.0639)	(0.0595)	(0.0455)	(0.0427)	(0.0424)	(0.0417)
Constant	–0.005*	–0.005**	–0.015***	–0.000	–0.001	0.001
	(0.003)	(0.002)	(0.003)	(0.001)	(0.002)	(0.001)
Observations	619	1,275	1,179	204	307	200
Adjusted R^2	0.442	0.666	0.51	0.784	0.663	0.84

Note: Robust standard errors in parentheses. Significance levels: * 10 %; ** 5 %; *** 1 %. Dependent variable = CA; exchange rate regimes are based on Reinhart–Rogoff definitions; "free fall" regime observations omitted.

Table 4.3b Current account persistence, by country sample, by Reinhart–Rogoff regime

	(7)	*(8)*	*(9)*	*(10)*	*(11)*	*(12)*
	Non-industrial countries			*Non-industrial countries ex-oil*		
	Floating	*Band/crwl*	*Fixed*	*Floating*	*Band/crwl*	*Fixed*
CA(-1)	0.621***	0.795***	0.688***	0.656***	0.800***	0.655***
	(0.071)	(0.063)	(0.048)	(0.084)	(0.066)	(0.054)
Constant	–0.007**	–0.006**	–0.021***	–0.009**	–0.007**	–0.026***
	(0.004)	(0.003)	(0.003)	(0.005)	(0.003)	(0.004)
Observations	415	968	979	348	921	905
Adjusted R^2	0.391	0.662	0.47	0.445	0.673	0.431

Source: Chinn and Wei (forthcoming), RESTAT.

Note: Robust standard errors in parentheses. Significance levels: * 10 %; ** 5 %; *** 1 %. Dependent variable = CA; exchange rate regimes are based on Reinhart-Rogoff definitions; "free fall" regime observations omitted.

The Chinese real exchange rate is widely believed to be substantially undervalued. The standard narrative one often hears goes as follows. The Chinese nominal exchange rate is undervalued largely through deliberate and massive government intervention in the currency market. The rapid accumulation of the country's foreign exchange reserve is prima facie evidence that the authorities have engaged in massive currency-market interventions. The undervalued

Table 4.4 Real exchange rate persistence, by country sample

	(1)	(2)	(3)	(4)	(5)	(6)	(7)	(8)	(9)	(10)	(11)	(12)
	All			*Industrial*			*Non-industrial*			*Non-industrial ex-oil*		
REER(-1)	0.797	0.782	0.785	0.624	0.579	0.704	0.803	0.814	0.832	0.779	0.733	0.728
	(0.024)***	(0.056)***	(0.053)***	(0.055)***	(0.103)***	(0.102)***	(0.024)***	(0.054)***	(0.060)***	(0.030)***	(0.043)***	(0.066)***
REER(-1) x LYS1		–0.042	–0.029		0.035	–0.119		–0.063	–0.034		0.001	0.019
		(0.075)	(0.072)		(0.159)	(0.141)		(0.077)	(0.074)		(0.083)	(0.083)
REER(-1) x LYS2		–0.101	–0.115		–0.124	–0.107		–0.120	–0.125		–0.033	–0.068
		(0.111)	(0.106)		(0.152)	(0.159)		(0.110)	(0.106)		(0.095)	(0.096)
REER(-1) x LYS3		0.064	0.093		0.075	0.022		0.032	0.074		0.097	0.126
		(0.083)	(0.073)		(0.104)	(0.095)		(0.084)	(0.076)		(0.099)	(0.094)
LYS1		0.181	0.121		–0.171	0.546		0.280	0.136		–0.002	–0.092
		(0.349)	(0.340)		(0.732)	(0.647)		(0.360)	(0.353)		(0.394)	(0.403)
LYS2		0.450	0.517		0.611	0.518		0.529	0.557		0.140	0.307
		(0.507)	(0.487)		(0.701)	(0.729)		(0.503)	(0.483)		(0.444)	(0.449)
LYS3		–0.248	–0.377		–0.351	–0.106		–0.073	–0.270		–0.366	–0.500
		(0.386)	(0.339)		(0.490)	(0.445)		(0.390)	(0.352)		(0.471)	(0.450)

	(1)	(2)	(3)	(4)	(5)	(6)	(7)	(8)	(9)	(10)	(11)	(12)
	All			*Industrial*			*Non-industrial*			*Non-industrial ex-oil*		
REER(-1) x												
Trade openness			–0.115			–0.122			–0.130			–0.134
			(0.052)**			-0.135			(0.056)**			(0.057)**
REER(-1) x												
Financial openness			–0.029			–0.055			–0.007			–0.036
			(0.024)			(0.037)			(0.029)			(0.044)
Trade openness			0.359			0.408			0.423			0.410
			(0.212)*			(0.602)			(0.233)*			(0.242)*
Financial openness			0.129			0.267			0.025			0.148
			(0.112)			(0.171)			(0.139)			(0.206)
Constant	0.956	1.001	1.129	1.749	1.957	1.454	0.932	0.840	0.918	1.037	1.205	1.420
	(0.111)***	(0.258)***	(0.255)***	(0.256)***	(0.481)***	(0.462)***	(0.112)***	(0.245)***	(0.295)***	(0.139)***	(0.205)***	(0.333)***
Observations	2,489	1,936	1,728	687	571	515	1,802	1,365	1,213	1,587	1,176	1,024
Number of cn	92	90	88	24	23	22	92	67	66	92	59	58
R-squared	0.64	0.63	0.66	0.46	0.47	0.49	0.65	0.64	0.67	0.61	0.59	0.64

Source: Chinn and Wei (forthcoming), RESTAT.

Note: Robust standard errors in parentheses. Significance levels: * 10 %; ** 5 %; *** 1 %. Dependent variable = REER; LYS1 is a dummy variable for a dirty-float regime; LYS2 is a dummy variable for dirty float/crawling peg; LYS3 is a dummy variable for fixed.

currency has in turn created both a growing current account surplus and an increasing departure from purchasing power parity.

3.1 An alternative perspective

This narrative is not, however, the only way to piece together the real exchange rate, the current account and the foreign exchange reserve. Du and Wei (2011) investigated an alternative perspective. Technology and policy shocks might have triggered a race to raise savings and to work longer and harder. These developments led to a simultaneous decline in the value of the real exchange rate and a rise in the current account (even though the exchange rate is not the cause of the current account surplus). Once the current account is put into a surplus gear, foreign exchange reserve accumulation happens largely passively, as a result of the country's capital control regime, which – as with capital control regimes in many other countries – requires mandatory surrender of foreign exchange earnings by firms and households.

The initial technology shock in the new narrative was the spread of ultrasound B machines in China in the 1980s, which allowed expectant parents to easily detect the gender of their fetus. The initial policy shock was the implementation of a strict version of the family planning policy. By interacting with a long-existing parental preference for sons, the combination of the two shocks started to produce an unnaturally high ratio of boys to girls at birth from the early 1980s. In about 2003, the first cohort born with an excess number of males was entering the marriage market. The competition for a marriage partner by young men has become progressively more intense since then. In 2007, the sex ratio for the pre-marital age cohort (5 to 20) was about 115 young men per 100 young women. This implies that about one out of every nine young men cannot get married, mathematically speaking.

Why would a rise in the sex ratio imbalance trigger a significant increase in savings rates? The short answer is that family wealth is a key status indicator in the marriage market (other things being equal). As the competition for brides intensifies, young men and their parents raise their savings rate in order to improve their relative standing in the marriage market. If the biological desire to have a female partner is strong, the response of the savings rate to a rise in the sex ratio can also be quantitatively large.

I would contend that the increased sex ratio has significantly raised both the corporate and the household savings rates in China, and might have indirectly contributed to an increase in government savings as well.

3.2 How does a higher sex ratio raise the corporate savings rate?

While it is commonly claimed that the primary driver for China's high corporate savings is the misgovernance of state-owned firms (that they do not pay enough dividends to their shareholders), this is an incomplete story. Bayoumi *et al.* (2010) examined a sample of Chinese listed companies and asked whether, within a given sector, state-owned firms systematically have a higher savings rate. The first column of Table 4.5 reports an insignificant coefficient on the state-owned enterprise (SOE) dummy, which means that the answer is negative. Some state-owned firms might have a high savings rate because they pay insufficient dividends to shareholders, but non-state-owned firms might also have a high savings rate – probably because they are concerned with access to bank lending and other sources of external financing when they need to invest and expand.

In the second column of Table 4.5, we examine how the pattern evolves over time by including an interaction term between a time trend and the dummy for SOEs. The result indicates that, in the earlier part of the sample (2000–03), it was indeed the case that SOEs had a higher savings rate. In the latter part of the sample (2004–07), however, the reverse is true: non-SOEs tended to have a higher savings rate.

Even though non-SOEs do not have the same kind of corporate governance, their high savings rate can be understood through the lens of the difficulty they

Table 4.5 Chinese corporate gross savings (as a share of assets)

	China firm sample:		*Cross-country sample:*	
	Comparing SOEs with non-SOEs		*Comparing Chinese firms with world average*	
State-owned dummy	0.003	0.027*		
	[0.010]	[0.016]		
State-owned dummy*trend		–0.007*		
		[0.004]		
China dummy			0.0713	0.105**
			[0.0533]	[0.049]
China*time trend				–0.0092
				[0.0062]
Firm size	0.058**	0.059**	0.223**	0.22**
	[0.018]	[0.018]	[0.075]	[0.08]
Year dummies?	Yes	Yes	Yes	Yes
Sector dummies?	Yes	Yes	Yes	Yes
Observations	6,402	6,402	132,801	132,801
R-squared	0.086	0.087	0.265	0.265

Source: Bayoumi *et al.* (2010).

Note: Standard errors in parentheses. P-value levels: *** < 1 %; ** < 5 %; * < 10 %. Corporate gross savings rate is Winsorized at the 1 per cent level; standard errors are clustered at the country level (columns 3–4).

face in obtaining a bank loan. This problem is much more severe for newly established private firms, which are far from being eligible for listing on a stock exchange. This is where the sex ratio angle comes in.

A simple decomposition of China's manufacturing growth rate from 1995–2004 (using two censuses of all manufacturing firms in these two years) indicates that 70 per cent of the growth comes from domestic private firms. A further decomposition of private sector growth indicates that 70 per cent of that comes from extensive margin growth (that is, the formation and growth of new privately owned firms). In other words, the birth and growth of new private firms are a big part of China's growth story. Wei and Zhang (2011b) find that the desire to raise one's relative wealth – which is greatly exacerbated by a rising sex ratio imbalance – has inspired much more private business formation. In Figure 4.3, we plot the average growth rate in the number of domestic private firms (for all regions with a common sex ratio) against the local sex ratio. There is a clear and strong positive relationship between the two. This positive relationship continues to hold when we control for other determinants of private business formation, such as local income, education level, initial business

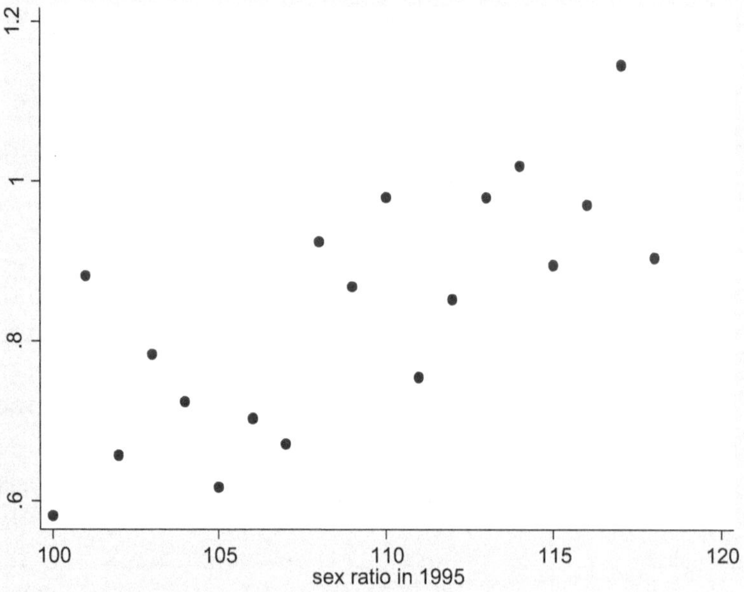

Figure 4.3 Initial sex ratios and growth rates of private firms, 1995–2004

Source: Wei and Zhang (2011b).

Note: On the horizontal axis is the sex ratio for the age cohort 5 to 19 in 1995 inferred from the 1990 Population Census. On the vertical axis is the growth rate in the number of private firms from 1995–2004, averaged over all counties that had the same value sex ratio (up to a basis point).

development and the age structure of the local population. Household-level data indicate that families with a son who live in regions with a high sex ratio are more likely to choose to be entrepreneurs (business owners or self-employed). Across regions, we estimate that variations in the sex ratio might account for half of the regional variations in the rate of private business formation. The relationship also holds after we do instrumental variable regressions and perform a placebo test. The instruments are regional variations in the financial penalties for violating birth quotas 15 years before and the fraction of local population that is exempted from birth quotas. We can reject the hypothesis that these are weak instruments. We also show that these instruments have a high correlation with the local sex ratio, and they are uncorrelated with the error term in the main regression. The two stage least square regressions suggest that the relationship is likely to be causal: a higher local sex ratio causes more new private firms to emerge.

Again, since new private firms have concerns about access to external financing, they have to keep most of their profits within the same for reinvestment. As a result, a combination of rising sex ratios and financial market frictions has produced a rise in corporate savings in the private sector.

3.3 How does a higher sex ratio raise the household savings rate?

The connection between the higher sex ratio and higher household savings is even more direct. Before we go to that evidence, it is useful to comment on some common misconceptions. Some researchers and opinion leaders contend that the Chinese household savings rate cannot be an important part of China's current account surplus story because: (a) Chinese household income as a share of national income has been falling in recent years; and (b) in any case, corporate savings (and also government savings) have shown a strong increase in recent years. I disagree with this contention. First, the household share in national income might well be underestimated due to under-reporting of income for tax-avoidance or evasion purposes. As the range of "gray income" rises over time, the scope for under-reporting of national income might also have increased. Second, even though the Chinese corporate savings rate appears high in an absolute sense, it is in fact part of an international pattern. Bayoumi *et al.* (2010) formally document this pattern. Columns 3 and 4 of Table 4.5 present the relevant statistical evidence on this issue. In comparison, Chinese household savings as a share of national savings has no peer in the world. This suggests that, to understand why China's national savings rate is so much higher than other countries, corporate savings is no more important than household savings after all.

Back to the connection between the sex ratio and the household savings rate: Xiaobo Zhang and I have documented relevant evidence (Wei and Zhang, 2011a). First, across regions in China, those with a higher sex ratio also tend to have a higher savings rate, holding constant the age structure of the local population, income level, social safety net and other factors.

Second, across households with a son, those residing in a region with a higher sex ratio save more (holding constant family income and other characteristics). In comparison, for households with a daughter, the savings rate is uncorrelated with the local sex ratio. The sex ratio effect is significant. While the Chinese household savings rate approximately doubled from 16 per cent (of disposable income) in 1990 to 31 per cent in 2007, we estimate that the rise in the sex ratio explains more than half the increase in the household savings rate.

3.4 Overall savings rate

I have argued so far that the rising sex ratio in China in recent years has been an important factor underlying both a rising corporate savings rate and a rising household savings rate. To the extent that government revenue tends to be plentiful when the economy is growing well, the higher sex ratio has likely contributed to a rise in the government savings rate as well (though we do not have rigorous proof of this last point).

In Figure 4.4, we import from Wei and Zhang (2011a) a time-series plot of China's national savings rate, together with a plot of China's sex ratio for those aged 20 years (or the sex ratio at birth lagged by 20 years, to be precise). The two lines have a striking coherence. Of course, formal regression analysis confirms that the two are highly related.

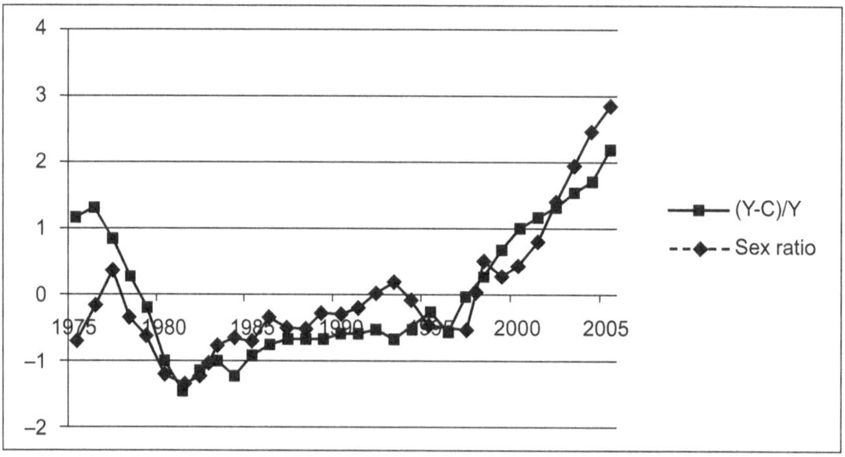

Figure 4.4 Sex ratios and saving rates

Source: Wei and Zhang (2011a).

Note: The sex ratio is defined as the ratio at birth 20 years earlier. The saving rate is defined as the ratio of GDP to private and government consumption to total GDP, which is available from the *China Statistical Yearbook 2007*. Both variables have been re-scaled by subtracting the mean and dividing by the standard deviation.

Qingyuan Du and I have also examined the connection between local sex ratios and local private sector savings rates (the sum of household and corporate savings rates) across countries in 2006 (Du and Wei, 2010). After controlling for per capita income, the share of the population enrolled in the social security system, the age structure of the population and continent dummies, we find that the national sex ratio is a statistically significant predictor of the national private sector savings rate. This relationship continues to hold if we exclude China from the sample.

As long as the sex ratio imbalance significantly raises the national savings rate, and the national investment rate does not have a correspondingly large change, a higher sex ratio would produce a higher current account surplus (without any policy actions on the nominal exchange rate front). Du and Wei (2010) have formalized this logic and provided some cross-country evidence that is consistent with this idea.

3.5 The sex ratio imbalance as a factor underlying the exchange rate

When the economy-wide savings rate rises, the real exchange rate (defined as the price of non-tradable goods relative to tradable goods) falls. To see this, we note that a rise in the savings rate implies a reduction in demand for both internationally traded goods and non-tradable goods. Since the price of internationally traded goods is approximately pinned down by the world market, this translates into a reduction in the relative price of non-tradable goods, and hence a decline in the value of the real exchange rate.

The high sex ratio imbalance also motivates people – especially parents with a son – to work harder and longer (in order to create more wealth and be more competitive in the marriage market). As the non-tradable sector is likely to be more labor intensive than the tradable sector, this leads to a faster expansion of the non-tradable sector relative to the tradable sector. This puts additional downward pressure on the value of the real exchange rate.

Putting the two channels together, a rise in the sex ratio generates a real exchange rate that appears too low relative to purchasing power parity (or relative to the standard approach used by the IMF). Of course, other factors have also contributed to an increase in the aggregate savings rate (for example, a rise in income volatility) or an increase in the effective labor supply (for example, gradual relaxation of restrictions on rural–urban migration). These factors would reinforce the Darwinian mechanism discussed here, causing the real exchange rate to fall further and the current account to rise even more.

While the sex ratio imbalance can induce a current account surplus without currency manipulation, the rises in the savings rate and current account are still socially inefficient. While households raise their savings rates to out compete other families in the marriage market, the number of men who cannot get married in the aggregate will not be affected by the savings behaviour. Therefore, the extra savings (and the associated current account surplus) is socially wasteful.

Without an effective mechanism for households to coordinate their actions, however, no individual household dares to unilaterally cut their savings rate or work effort.

4. The risks of a misdiagnosis

If the perspective in this chapter has some validity, then the ferocious fixation of international financial institutions and some G20 discussions might not be the most productive in terms of finding solutions to the global current account imbalances. But is the fixation simply "much ado about nothing", or does it pose risks to the world economy?

In a world with limited staff resources (that is, the world we live in), the fixation on fixed exchange rates becomes a costly distraction for the staff and management of international financial institutions. This happened in the years leading up to the GFC. There was very little effort going into uncovering other potentially systematically important risk factors, such as weak financial regulations, predatory lending practices and over-accumulation of risks in major financial institutions.

Just before the GFC became headline news, the staff of international financial institutions was accused of being "asleep at the wheel" for not acting vigorously enough to solve the exchange rate problem. In retrospect, the accusation was misplaced. If these institutions were asleep at the wheel – in the sense of overlooking the danger signs just under their noses – they were essentially overworked by being asked to drive a car on a road that led nowhere.

The fixation on the fixed exchange rate regime poses another risk, as governments in both surplus and deficit countries are mentally distracted from finding other ways to deal with the structural problems that led to the global imbalances. Of course, this is not to say that a change in the real exchange rate has no effect on current accounts. Rather, a move to a more flexible exchange rate does not reliably move the real exchange rate in the right direction.

If the higher sex ratio imbalance is a significant reason for the current account surplus, then policies that help to reduce the sex ratio imbalance can also help to narrow current account imbalances over time. Perhaps in future policy dialogue, instead of another push for more flexible exchange rates, it would be more productive to consider social policies – including family planning policies and women's social status in particular – in the context of national savings and current account imbalances. If they start now, they will not solve the global imbalances right away; however, if they do not, the world might still be talking about current account imbalances 10 years down the road.

Notes

1 This chapter was written at the invitation of Professor Jenny Corbett, and draws on various joint research projects with Xiaobo Zhang, Menzie Chinn, Qingyuan Du, Tamim Bayoumi and Hui Tong over the past few years. Part of the

underlying research has been supported by a US National Science Foundation grant and the general research fund of Columbia Business School, which I gratefully acknowledge. Any errors in the chapter are entirely mine, and not those of my collaborators, the funding agencies or any institutions with which I have an affiliation.

2 G20 Communiqué, Meeting of Finance Ministers and Central Bank Governors, 17–18 November 2007, Cape Town, South Africa.

3 We have also employed the *de jure* index based upon the IMF's *Annual Report on Exchange Arrangements and Exchange Restrictions,* instead of the de facto measures. The results indicate no systematic relationship.

4 We check for higher-order auto-regressive terms, and find that an AR(1) is sufficient for the annual data. The sole exception is for the category of non-industrial countries (and non-industrial ex-oil exporters) under a fixed exchange rate regime. In that case, the second lag is typically statistically significant. The pattern of persistence, however – as measured by the sum of the auto-regressive coefficients – is unchanged relative to the baseline specification.

References

Bayoumi, T., Tong, H. and Wei, S. (2010) 'The Chinese corporate savings puzzle: a firm-level cross-country perspective', *NBER Working Paper* 16432; and forthcoming in J. Fan and R. Morck (eds), *Capitalizing China*, Chicago: University of Chicago Press.

Chinn, M.D. and Wei, S. (forthcoming) 'A faith-based initiative meets the evidence: does a flexible exchange rate regime really facilitate current account adjustment?', *Review of Economics and Statistics.*

Du, Q. and Wei, S. (2010) 'A sexually unbalanced model of current account imbalances', *NBER Working Paper* 16000.

———. (2011) 'Sex ratios and exchange rates', *NBER Working Paper* 16788.

Levy-Yeyati, E. and Sturzenegger, F. (2005) 'Classifying exchange rate regimes: deeds vs. words', *European Economic Review*, 49: 1603–35.

Reinhart, C.M. and Rogoff, K. (2004) 'The modern history of exchange rate arrangements: a reinterpretation', *Quarterly Journal of Economics*, 119: 1–48.

Wei, S. and Zhang, X. (2011a) 'The competitive saving motive: evidence from rising sex ratios and savings rates in China', *Journal of Political Economy*, June.

———. (2011b) 'Sex ratios, entrepreneurship, and economic growth in the People's Republic of China', *NBER Working Paper* 16800.

Appendix

Table 4.6 Ln(real exchange rate) and the sex ratio, using private credit to GDP ratio as the measure of financial development

	(1) All countries	*(2) All countries*	*(3) All countries*	*(4) Excluding major oil exporters*	*(5) Excluding majoroil exporters*	*(6) Excluding major oil exporters*	*(7) Excluding major oil exporters*
Sex ratio			4.290**	4.012**	3.193*	3.408**	3.500**
			(1.667)	(1.713)	(1.797)	(1.568)	(1.754)
Ln(GDP per capita)	0.318**	0.190**	0.236**	0.233**	0.360**	0.402**	0.359**
	(0.030)	(0.038)	(0.041)	(0.044)	(0.073)	(0.063)	(0.073)
Private credit (% of GDP)		0.004**	0.004**	0.004**	0.003**	0.002**	0.002**
		(0.001)	(0.001)	(0.001)	(0.001)	(0.001)	(0.001)
Fiscal deficit					0.007	0.002	0.005
					(0.009)	(0.008)	(0.009)
Terms of trade					0.0002	0.001	0.0003
					(0.001)	(0.001)	(0.001)
Capital account openness					0.060**	0.029	0.058**
					(0.027)	(0.024)	(0.027)
Dependency ratio					0.009**	0.010**	0.008*
					(0.004)	(0.004)	(0.004)

	(1) All countries	*(2) All countries*	*(3) All countries*	*(4) Excluding major oil exporters*	*(5) Excluding majoroil exporters*	*(6) Excluding major oil exporters*	*(7) Excluding major oil exporters*
Crawling peg (RR)						0.397**	
						(0.075)	
Managed floating (RR)						0.036	
						(0.077)	
Free floating (RR)						0.081	
						(0.119)	
Intermediate (LYS)							0.078
							(0.092)
Float (LYS)							0.145*
							(0.085)
Observations	142	132	132	123	92	89	92
R-squared	0.444	0.542	0.564	0.579	0.706	0.801	0.716

Source: Du and Wei (2011).

Note: Dependent variable = ln(RER). Standard errors in parentheses; ** $p < 0.05$; * $p < 0.1$.

Table 4.7 Ln(real exchange rate) and the sex ratio, using financial system sophistication as the measure of financial development

	(1) *All countries*	(2) *All countries*	(3) *All countries*	(4) *Excluding major oil exporters*	(5) *Excluding major oil exporters*	(6) *Excluding major oil exporters*	(7) *Excluding major oil exporters*
Sex ratio			– 6.192**	– 6.255**	– 5.051*	– 4.664*	– 4.430
			(1.964)	(1.995)	(2.500)	(2.802)	(2.908)
Ln(GDP per capita)	0.318**	0.480**	0.443**	0.447**	0.529**	0.526**	0.531**
	(0.030)	(0.082)	(0.077)	(0.088)	(0.123)	(0.119)	(0.127)
Financial system sophistication		0.170*	0.252**	0.245**	0.099	0.034	0.086
		(0.089)	(0.086)	(0.099)	(0.110)	(0.121)	(0.116)
Fiscal deficit					– 0.022	– 0.014	– 0.025
					(0.015)	(0.015)	(0.017)
Terms of trade					– 0.004	– 0.006**	– 0.005
					(0.003)	(0.003)	(0.003)
Capital account openness					0.063	0.058	0.073
					(0.042)	(0.047)	(0.047)
Dependency ratio					0.014**	0.017**	0.017*
					(0.007)	(0.007)	(0.008)
Crawling peg (RR)						– 0.285*	
						(0.147)	

	(1) *All countries*	(2) *All countries*	(3) *All countries*	(4) *Excluding major oil exporters*	(5) *Excluding major oil exporters*	(6) *Excluding major oil exporters*	(7) *Excluding major oil exporters*
Managed floating (RR)						0.045	
						(0.102)	
Free floating (RR)						0.053	
						(0.173)	
Intermediate (LYS)							0.052
							(0.137)
Float (LYS)							0.044
							(0.125)
Observations	142	54	54	49	43	42	43
R-squared	0.444	0.748	0.791	0.797	0.844	0.866	0.845

Source: Du and Wei (2011).

Note: Dependent variable = log(RER). Standard errors in parentheses; ** $p < 0.05$; * $p < 0.1$.

Table 4.8 Real exchange rate undervaluation and excess current account: the case of China

	% of RER undervaluation					*Excess (non-governmental) current account*				
	(1) Only BS	*(2) FD + BS*	*(3) Add GD + TT + KA*	*(4) Add DR*	*(5) Add SR*	*(1) Only BS*	*(2) FD + BS*	*(3) Add GD + TT + KA*	*(4) Add DR*	*(5) Add SR*
Financial development index										
Private credit (% of GDP)	55.26	43.45	35.44	17.91	7.86	13.52	12.06	11.39	8.97	2.01
Financial system sophistication	55.26	46.38	31.31	16.78	2.24	13.52	10.26	10.11	7.97	0.37

Source: Du and Wei (2001), *NBER Working Paper* 16000.

Note: Excess RER undervaluation = model prediction – actual log RER (a positive number describes percentage undervaluation); excess current account = private sector current account (that is, current account net of government savings) – model prediction; the five columns include progressively more regressors: (1) the only regressor (other than the intercept) is log income – a proxy for the Balassa–Samuelson (BS) effect; (2) add financial development (FD) to the list of regressors; (3) add government fiscal deficit (GD), terms of trade (TT), and capital account openness (KA); (4) add the dependence ratio (DR); (5) add the sex ratio (SR). The last two rows correspond to estimates when two different proxies for financial development are used. The first row uses the ratio of credit to the private sector to GDP, and the second row uses an index of local financial system sophistication from the *Global Competitiveness Report*.

5 Do Asian countries fear appreciation against the renminbi?

Victor Pontines and Reza Siregar

1. Introduction

It has been argued that one of the biggest inconsistencies in the global economy today is the fact that emerging Asian economies have rebounded faster than any other region, with a widening gap between their average growth rate and that of developed economies, yet most of their currencies have fallen since 2008 in real trade-weighted terms (The Economist, 2009). Moreover, there are ongoing concerns about the global consequences of exceptionally loose monetary policy in the United States and other developed markets as capital flows to emerging markets around the globe, especially in Asia, have been picking up and fears of appreciating local currencies remain a key policy concern.

Against this backdrop, the objectives of our chapter are as follows. The first is to investigate and assess the exchange market interventions carried out by selected central banks in the East and Southeast Asian region – namely, Bank Indonesia, Bank of Korea, Bangko Sentral Ng Pilipinas, Bank of Thailand and the Monetary Authority of Singapore. For this purpose, and noting that these five Asian countries do not release their respective foreign exchange positions to the public, we will imperfectly resort to exploiting the underlying concept of an exchange market pressure (EMP) and construct the EMP index for these five major Asian currencies. In doing so, we hope that, based on the sign and magnitudes of the EMP index, we are able to initially ascertain the de facto exchange rate policy stance of these five Asian countries. This is understandably important as four of the five countries we examine have officially adopted inflation-targeting regimes and as such, we intrinsically expect that being official inflation targeters should lead to greater flexibility in their exchange rates. In conformity with the voluminous literature on the fear of floating, however, there is a general reluctance on the part of emerging market countries, including the five economies examined here, to float their currencies freely.[1]

Nonetheless, a current nuance of the apparent move towards allowing some greater flexibility in exchange rates is that, for various reasons, it is possible that the degree of flexibility is significantly higher on one side of the market.[2] In other words, the monetary authorities in these Asian economies can asymmetrically manage their exchange rates wherein they can allow for some currency depreciation while substantially limiting the extent of currency appreciation. For lack of better alternatives, this exchange rate intervention behaviour has been called by Levy-Yeyati and Sturzenegger (2007) "fear of floating in reverse" or "fear of appreciation". Accordingly, the next important objective of this chapter is to verify evidence of asymmetrical exchange rate behaviour – that is, the presence, if any, of fear of appreciation on the part of the five monetary authorities mentioned. Lastly, we also investigate whether this fear, if it exists, extends not just to the exchange rates of the five Asian currencies with respect to the US dollar but also vis-à-vis the Chinese renminbi.

There have been a few recent works that examine such central bank aversion to exchange rate appreciations in East Asia.[3] None of these earlier studies, however, goes further to examine possible factors contributing to this asymmetrical exchange rate behaviour in Asia. In particular, none has considered the plausible influence of the Chinese renminbi on asymmetrical exchange rate management of these Asian currencies, especially after the 2005 exchange rate policy reform in China.[4] It is quite surprising that, in spite of the rapidly emerging role of the Chinese economy in Asia in particular and in the world in general, to our knowledge, the literature has been silent on the possible influence of the renminbi with regard to the issue of asymmetrical exchange rate behaviour in Asia.

In view of the potential ramifications of this fear of appreciation in Asia for the issue of global rebalancing, let alone that it touches on sensitive regional "competitiveness" issues (we will expound upon the second point later in our analysis), it is a logical and interesting research issue that is worth pursuing. Our findings confirm those of earlier works, that is, the existence of a general fear of appreciation with respect to the US dollar. In addition to this finding, however, we have found that there is an even greater dimension to this story: the greater fear of appreciation against the renminbi than against the US dollar, especially prior to the Global Financial Crisis (GFC).

The chapter is structured as follows: discussion on exchange rate intervention and its underlying motivation is presented next. Section 3 discusses model specifications and the econometric testing employed to assess the degree of asymmetrical exchange rate behaviour. The key empirical findings are analyzed and highlighted in Section 4. In the following section, we present and examine bilateral trade patterns of the five Asian economies. The main objective of the section is to further substantiate the analysis presented in Section 4. A brief concluding section ends the paper.

2. Exchange rate intervention and exchange market pressure

As is illustrated and documented in early seminal works, countries often intervene to limit sudden or large currency depreciation (Calvo and Reinhart, 2002) or strongly fear a sudden or large currency appreciation (Levy-Yeyati and Sturzenegger, 2007). In other words, even under an observed shift to flexible exchange rate regimes, the pursuit of an active exchange rate policy as part of a "leaning-against-the-wind exchange rate policy" might still be the norm.[5] To initially investigate the possibility of what can be labelled an "asymmetrical exchange rate regime", we resort to the useful and commonly applied concept of an EMP index in the spirit of Kaminsky and Reinhart (1998) and Kaminsky and Reinhart (1999), which can be formally expressed as follows

$$EMP_{i,t} = \frac{\Delta e_{i,t}}{e_{i,t}} - \frac{\sigma_e}{\sigma_r}\frac{\Delta r_{i,t}}{r_{i,t}} + \frac{\sigma_e}{\sigma_{\text{int}}}\Delta \text{int}_{i,t} \tag{1}$$

where ($EMP_{i,t}$) is the exchange market pressure index for country (i) in period (t); $e_{i,t}$ is the unit of country *i's* currency per US dollar in period t; (σ_e) is the standard deviation of the rate of change in the exchange rate $\left(\frac{\Delta e_{i,t}}{e_{i,t}}\right)$; ($r_{i,t}$) is the gross foreign reserves of country (i) in period t; and (σ_r) is the standard deviation of the rate of change in reserves $\left(\frac{\Delta r_{i,t}}{r_{i,t}}\right)$; ($\text{int}_{i,t}$) is the nominal interest rate for country (i) in period; and (σ_{int}) is the standard deviation of the change in the nominal interest rate ($\Delta\text{int}_{i,t}$).

In short, an EMP index is a weighted average of the changes in the nominal exchange rate in foreign exchange reserves, and in nominal interest rates. In particular, the weights of the interest rate and reserve fluctuations depend on the relative size of their standard deviations – (σ_r) and (σ_{int}), respectively – against that of the exchange rate (σ_e).[6] Hence, a positive (negative) EMP index suggests the presence of selling/depreciation (buying/appreciation) pressures against the local currency.

Given the lack of either official disclosure on the foreign exchange intervention or the currency composition and denominations of foreign exchange reserves of the five economies included in our study, we follow the standard approach of calculating the EMP based on the US dollar exchange rate and the foreign exchange reserves expressed in US dollars. For the basic purpose of tracing the presence of active foreign exchange market intervention, it is sufficient for the EMP construction to be derived as above.

In general, we found all currencies included in our study experienced buying pressure (negative EMP) before the GFC of 2000–07 and for most of 2008–10, with the exception of the last quarter of 2008 and the first quarter of 2009, when the currencies of most emerging markets were under selling pressure following the closure of Lehman Brothers (Figure 5.1). We also found, during most parts of 2000–10, a steady accumulation of foreign exchange reserves. Combining this evidence of buying/appreciation pressures and reserve accumulation, one cannot dismiss the possibility of a "leaning-against-the-wind" policy stance adopted by the central banks of these countries during the period of observation. The trends and individual components of the EMP provide indications of policy interventions to manage the volatility of the local currencies.[7] More importantly, the initial evidence also shows that the efforts tend to be biased towards mitigating appreciation pressures rather than depreciation pressures. Hence, there seems to be evidence of asymmetrical exchange rate

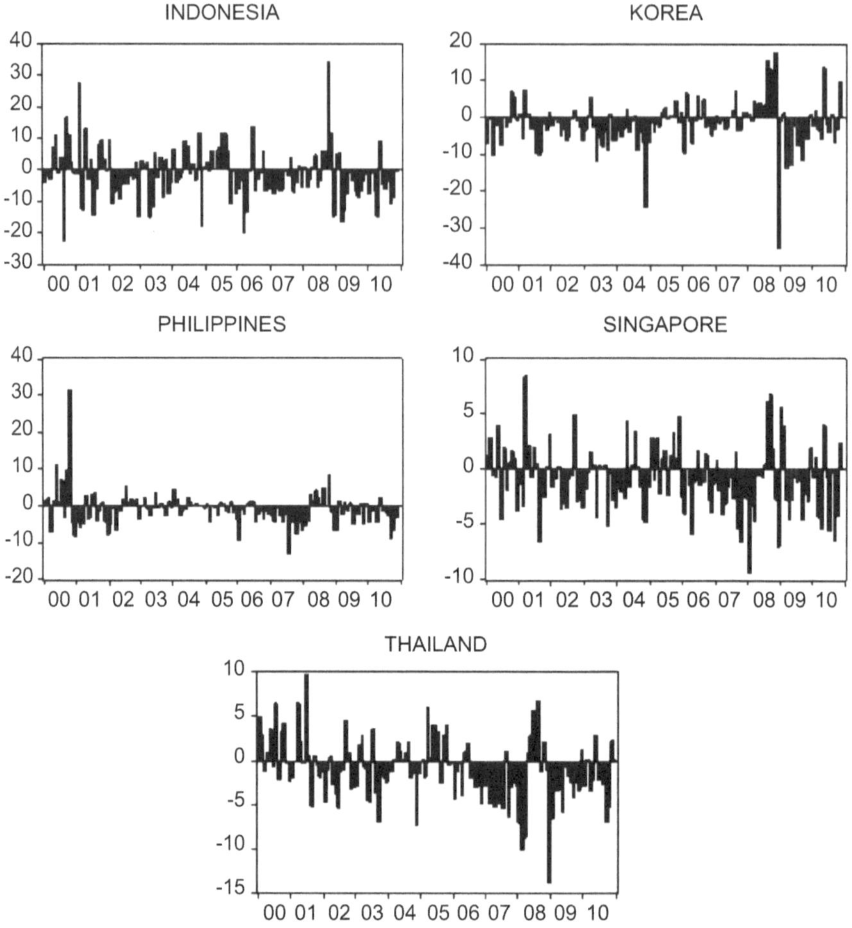

Figure 5.1 Exchange market pressure index

intervention behaviour. To verify this conjecture, a set of empirical testing will be carried out to formally confirm the presence of fear of appreciation and to trace the possible role of the Chinese renminbi in this asymmetrical exchange rate intervention behaviour.

3. Empirical approach

The aim of this section and the one that follows is to investigate and assess the existence of such forms of asymmetric exchange rate behaviour. In order to achieve this objective, we employ a class of a regime-switching model known as the smooth transition auto-regressive (STAR) model and in particular a certain type of regime-switching model known as the LSTR2 model. This is nothing but a logical method to capture this form of exchange rate behaviour, as the use of this model allows one to explicitly measure the thresholds on both sides of the market, that is, appreciation and depreciation thresholds. A brief technical discussion of the underlying mechanics of the LSTR2 model and how these appreciation and depreciation thresholds are derived from this LSTR2 model is provided in Appendix A.[8] In a nutshell, the LSTR2 model involves the estimation of two threshold parameters c_L (the lower or appreciation threshold) and c_H (the upper or depreciation threshold). The comparison of the magnitudes of these lower (c_L) and upper (c_H) threshold parameters reflects the relative tolerance of monetary authorities to exchange rate variations. To be specific, if the upper threshold, c_H is larger than the (absolute value of the) lower threshold, c_L, this suggests an aversion of monetary authorities to currency appreciations. This interpretation is possible since the exchange rate data used in the estimation are defined in terms of the local currency with respect to the US dollar or the Chinese renminbi, thus the limit or tolerance of monetary authorities to an appreciation of the local currency corresponds to the "lower" threshold (c_L), whereas the tolerance of monetary authorities to local currency depreciation corresponds to the "upper" threshold (c_H).

4. Empirical results

Our estimation is based on weekly data for the five Asian countries: Indonesia, Korea, the Philippines, Singapore and Thailand. We divided the estimation into three distinct periods: pre-GFC (January 2000–December 2006), GFC (January–July 2009), and post-GFC (August 2009–March 2011).[9] All nominal exchange rate (domestic currency per US dollar and Chinese renminbi, respectively) data for these countries are obtained from the Pacific Exchange Rate Service (http://fx.sauder.ubc.ca). The rationale for the choice of the three distinct periods is based on the view that the bulk of reserve accumulation occurred during the pre-GFC period, as evidenced from official reserves data and numerous academic studies; the period of the GFC captures the massive volatilities experienced by the countries examined and, consequently, led to the drawdown or de-accumulation of reserves by these same countries; while the post-GFC period corresponds with the several months after the collapse of Lehman Brothers, and is in agreement with official announcements and publications by international multilateral institutions that a global economic recovery is under way.

In general, the construction of STAR models follows the same steps as the ARIMA-Box-Jenkins modelling approach,[10] wherein the modelling cycle consists of model specification, parameter estimation and diagnostic evaluation. While the linearity tests conducted easily reject in favour of STAR-type models in all cases, in view of the stated objective of this chapter, it is only sensible that we automatically resort to fitting a LSTR2 model to the data and leave until the diagnostic stage the question of whether this choice is appropriately supported by the data.[11] Appendix Tables 5.B1a–c present the estimation results of our LSTR2 models for the pre-GFC (Table 5.B1a), GFC (Table 5.B1b), and post-GFC periods (Table 5.B1c), in that order, using the first-difference of the log of the nominal exchange rate defined as the domestic currency per US dollar. The Appendix Tables 5.B2a–c present the estimation results of our LSTR2 models using the first-difference of the log of the nominal exchange rate defined as the domestic currency per Chinese renminbi for the same respective periods of the pre-GFC (Table 5.B2a), GFC (Table 5.B2b), and post-GFC periods (Table 5.B2c), also in that order.

In every table, the first two rows of results present the auto-regressive order p chosen (first row) and the optimal delay lag length d (second row).[12] From these reported p and d values in each table, Appendix Tables 5.B1a–c and 5. B2a–c also report the corresponding estimation results of fitting LSTR2 models for the five East Asian currencies. The majority of the estimated coefficients in each table are statistically different from zero. More importantly, as reported in the last row of Appendix Tables 5.B1a–c and 5.B2a–c, the residuals from the fitted LSTR2 models are all random and white noise, which suggests the suitability of fitting an LSTR2 model in the nominal exchange rate data of the five East Asian currencies.

We now turn to our main focus: the lower or appreciation threshold (c_L) and upper or depreciation thresholds (c_H) from the fitted LSTR2 models, which are presented in Table 5.1. This table is divided into three panels: the upper panel contains the estimated lower and upper thresholds for the pre-GFC period, the middle panel reports the lower and upper thresholds for the GFC period, and the lower panel contains the lower and upper thresholds for the post-GFC period. Each period then reports the lower and upper thresholds for the two nominal exchange rate definitions of the domestic currency with respect to the US dollar and the Chinese renminbi, respectively. Turning first to the estimated lower and upper thresholds for the pre-GFC period (domestic currency with respect to the US dollar), these are at 1.34 and 3.83 per cent, respectively, for the Indonesian rupiah; 1.49 and 2.12 per cent for the Korean won; –1.8 and 3.88 per cent for the Philippine peso; –0.39 and 0.71 per cent for the Singapore dollar; and –0.07 and 1.9 per cent for the Thai baht. This shows that in all five of the East Asian currencies considered, the upper threshold, c_H, is larger than the (absolute value of the) lower threshold, c_L, which indicates a lower threshold tolerance or aversion from the concerned monetary authorities in these countries to currency appreciations against the US dollar. This is likewise the outcome we obtain when we examine the case of the nominal exchange rate defined in terms of the domestic currency per Chinese renminbi: 0.84 and 7.02 per cent, respectively, for the Indonesian rupiah; 1.2 and 2.49 per cent for the Korean won; 0.26 and 0.24 per cent for the Philippine peso; 0.57 and 1.93 per cent for the Singapore dollar; and 0.95 and 1.96 per cent for the Thai baht.

In other words, our results firmly support the case that during the pre-GFC period the monetary authorities in these five countries exhibited a lower threshold tolerance of, or aversion to, currency appreciations regardless of whether one looks at the nominal exchange rate defined as the domestic currency against the US dollar or the Chinese renminbi. More interestingly, it is clear from the

Table 5.1 Threshold values (per cent)

	Pre-GFC period, January 2000–December 2006			
	per US$		*per Chinese renminbi*	
	Lower threshold	*Upper threshold*	*Lower threshold*	*Upper threshold*
	(cL)	*(cH)*	*(cL)*	*(cH)*
Indonesian rupiah	1.34 (0.01)***	3.83 (0.28)***	0.84 (0.07)***	7.02 (0.06)***
Korean won	1.49 (0.04)***	2.12 (0.08)***	1.20 (0.18)***	2.49 (1.09)**
Philippine peso	–1.80 (0.18)***	3.88 (0.03)***	0.26 (0.02)***	0.24 (0.06)***
Singapore dollar	–0.39 (0.11)***	0.71 (0.13)***	0.57 (0.02)***	1.93 (0.02)***
Thai baht	–0.07 (0.01)***	1.90 (0.08)***	0.95 (0.05)***	1.96 (0.05)***
	GFC period, January 2007–July 2009			
	per US$ per Chinese renminbi			
	Lower threshold	*Upper threshold*	*Lower threshold*	*Upper threshold*
	(cL)	*(cH)*	*(cL)*	*(cH)*
Indonesian rupiah	–0.78 (0.02)***	0.88 (6.9)	–1.46 (0.07)***	–0.24 (0.04)***
Korean won	–0.37 (0.02)***	1.61 (1.20)	–3.17 (0.19)***	10.0 (27.4)
Philippine peso	–2.57 (0.06)***	–1.58 (0.05)***	–1.76 (0.34)***	–0.80 (0.10)***
Singapore dollar	–2.07 (0.17)***	–1.11 (4.15)	–2.40 (0.05)***	–0.22 (0.04)***
Thai baht	–3.02 (0.23)***	–1.25 (0.16)***	–1.43 (0.02)***	0.58 (0.47)

(*Continued*)

Table 5.1 (Continued)

	Post-GFC period, August 2009–March 2011			
	per US$		*per Chinese renminbi*	
	Lower threshold	*Upper threshold*	*Lower threshold*	*Upper threshold*
	(cL)	*(cH)*	*(cL)*	*(cH)*
Indonesian rupiah	0.44 (0.06)***	1.31 (0.23)***	0.59 (0.04)***	1.35 (0.32)***
Korean won	–1.60 (0.09)***	3.09 (0.07)***	–1.64 (0.18)***	3.08 (0.15)***
Philippine peso	0.22 (0.05)**	2.12 (0.13)***	0.84 (0.06)***	1.77 (0.08)***
Singapore dollar	0.10 (0.01)***	0.24 (0.01)***	0.09 (0.05)	0.63 (0.10)***
Thai baht	–0.69 (0.10)***	0.87 (0.02)***	0.10 (0.07)	0.22 (0.08)***

Note: Numbers in parentheses are standard errors. Significance levels: * 10%; ** 5%; *** 1%.

absolute differences between c_H and c_L that, with the lesser exception of the Philippine peso, the remainder of the East Asian currencies considered exhibit a much greater aversion to appreciations when the Chinese renminbi is used as the comparator base currency. Furthermore, apart from the clear absence of a relative tolerance or allowance for sizeable appreciations against the Chinese renminbi, we also observe a greater relative tolerance (based on c_H) for currency depreciations against the Chinese renminbi than against the US dollar.

According to our findings, however, this phenomenon of fear of appreciation all but disappeared during the height of our chosen period of the GFC. Understandably, the preference of the monetary authorities in these countries is to avoid a free fall in the value of their currencies, so they adopt the typical strategy during financial turmoil of resisting or leaning against the significant selling pressures that are brought to bear on these currencies by international financial markets. In light of the proposed testing strategy laid out in this chapter, this is interpreted as either significantly negative lower and upper thresholds or a significantly negative lower threshold but with an insignificant upper threshold.[13] As reported in the middle panel of Table 5.1, the former applies to the cases of the Philippine peso, Singapore dollar and Thai baht vis-à-vis the US dollar, as well as the cases of the Indonesian rupiah, Philippine peso and Singapore dollar vis-à-vis the Chinese renminbi. The latter applies to the cases of the Indonesian rupiah and Korean won vis-à-vis the US dollar, as well as to the cases of the Korean won and Thai baht, this time vis-à-vis the Chinese renminbi.

Once this tumultuous period of the GFC subsided, can we find the reappearance of behaviour akin to the pre-GFC period of fear of, or aversion to, currency appreciation? And, more so, similar to what we find in the pre-GFC period, is this fear of or aversion to appreciations exemplified to a greater extent in the case of the Chinese renminbi than with the US dollar in the aftermath of the GFC?

As to the first question, based on the most recent data available at the time of writing, there are indications that the GFC only briefly and temporarily interrupted this behaviour, and as such, this phenomenon might have reasserted itself on the part of the monetary authorities in these countries. To varying degrees, all five countries show a revealed preference for limiting the extent of strengthening their currencies against the US dollar (0.44 and 1.31 per cent, respectively, for the Indonesian rupiah; –1.60 and 3.09 per cent for the Korean won; 0.22 and 2.12 per cent for the Philippine peso; 0.10 and 0.24 per cent for the Singapore dollar; and –0.7 per cent and 0.87 per cent for the Thai baht).

In other words, it is understandable that after coming out of a tumultuous period punctuated by sharp and volatile movements in their exchange rates, it is necessary for these countries to slow the pace of the depreciation of their currencies with respect to the US dollar, while at the same time retaining their preference to restrain the strengthening of their currencies against the US dollar. For instance, when compared with their respective pre-GFC behaviour, we observed that this analysis applies in the cases of the Indonesian rupiah, Singapore dollar and Thai baht. In the case of the Korean won, however, which can be depicted as the most affected amongst the five Asian currencies in the group during the GFC, we observe some loosening in the resistance to the appreciation of this currency against the US dollar after the GFC, which is in marked contrast with the outcome found during the pre-GFC period. Furthermore, to some extent, this alleged reappearance, akin to the pre- GFC period, of fear of or aversion to currency appreciations can also be argued to apply in the case of the Chinese renminbi as the base comparator currency (0.59 and 1.35 per cent, respectively, for the Indonesian rupiah; –1.64 and 3.08 per cent for the Korean won; 0.84 and 1.77 per cent for the Philippine peso; 0.09 and 0.63 per cent for the Singapore dollar; and 0.1 and 0.22 per cent for the Thai baht).

With regard to the second question posed earlier, as to whether the pre-GFC finding of a greater fear of appreciation against the Chinese renminbi than the US dollar also applies in the aftermath of the GFC – as depicted in the lower panel of Table 5.1, the relative values of the lower and upper thresholds seem to indicate that the greater fear of appreciation of these currencies pre-GFC with respect to the Chinese renminbi than against the US dollar is not yet strongly supported in the data. Only the further passage of time can validate this important exchange rate policy question for this set of economies.

5. Bilateral trade patterns and beyond: the dominant role of mainland China

How can we possibly explain the renminbi having such an influence on the Asian currencies? One of the frequently advanced factors behind the increasing influence of the Chinese renminbi is the rise of China as a major trading partner of countries around the globe, including the five Asian economies in our study. In fact, China has become both a major exporter and a major importer of tradable goods in Asia. China, the second-largest economy in the world, ultimately accounted for about 50 per cent of all trade flows in imported inputs in Asia in 2009 – more than double its share in 1995 (International Monetary Fund [IMF], 2011). At the same time, China's share of direct and indirect intermediate goods exports within Asia doubled to nearly 30 per cent in 2009 – from 15 per cent a decade earlier.

A simple calculation of trade ratios for all five Asian economies in terms of their bilateral trade patterns with China, the United States and Japan consistently reveals the rapidly emerging dominant role of China as a major trading partner (Figures 5.C1–C9 in Appendix C).[14] The steep increase in total trade with China started to be noticeable in the early 2000s – only a few years after the 1997 East Asian crisis in all five of the Asian economies examined here. The monthly total trade of Indonesia with China, for instance, was averaging only about 52 per cent and 31 per cent of the country's trade with the United States and Japan, respectively, in 2000. In 2006, just before the outbreak of the sub-prime crisis, the average monthly trade with China rose to less than 10 per cent of the trade with the US economy. By 2010, Indonesia's average monthly trade with China was about 70 per cent higher than with the United States, and about 1.1 times the monthly trade with Japan. The story of rising Chinese influence and trade importance for these major East and Southeast Asian economies can be very much repeated for all five economies included in our study. In particular, the rapid rise of China's bilateral trade with its regional neighbours is most evident in the case of Korea. By the end of 2010, Korea's monthly trade with China was averaging about 2.4 times the country's trade with the traditional markets: the United States and Japan.

More importantly for policymakers in these East and Southeast Asian regions, maintaining trade surpluses with China is critical to achieving an overall strong current account position. With the exception of Indonesia and Singapore, and to a lesser extent the Philippines, the other major Asian countries had successfully maintained trade surplus positions during the past decade with China. Korea and Thailand, in particular, saw a growing trade surplus with China during the latter half of the past decade. Indonesia, on the other hand, saw its monthly marginal trade surplus of about US$70 million during the first half of the 2000s (until 2006) turn into a deficit of about US$150 million following the sub-prime crisis. As an export-processing economy, Singapore has been the processing hub of imported goods from all three major trading partners (China, Japan and the United States).

To understand further the influence of Chinese trade on these five Asian economies, it is imperative to look further into the structures of trade in what is the world's second-largest economy. It is estimated that processing trade accounted for more than 40 per cent of China's total trade by the mid-2000s, and these processing trades explained most of China's trade balances with its trading partners globally (Xing, 2011).[15] Four of the East and Southeast Asian economies examined here – namely, Korea, the Philippines, Thailand and Singapore – have been competing in this processing trade. In 2008, these four economies were in fact listed as among the top 10 sources of China's processing imports (Xing, 2011). Korea, for example, exported about US$60 billion worth of China's processing imports, while the processing exports of Thailand, the Philippines and Singapore were worth about US$12.5 billion, US$10 billion and US$8.8 billion, respectively.

China has also been the largest exporter of labour-intensive goods to the rest of the world and a major competitor for a number of labour-abundant East and Southeast Asian economies examined here – namely, Indonesia, the Philippines and Thailand. Studies such as Thorbecke (2011) and Thorbecke and Zhang (2009) found labour-intensive exports from China and Association of South-East Asian Nations (ASEAN) countries to be very sensitive to exchange rates in both the exporting country and other countries exporting labour-intensive products to third markets. Based on panel data analysis looking at about 30 countries over the 1987–2006 period, Thorbecke and Zhang (2009) reported that for China, a 10 per cent appreciation of the renminbi would reduce labour-intensive exports by about 17 per cent, and a 10 per cent depreciation among competing countries would decrease exports by about 9 per cent. Similarly, analysing an annual panel data set including exports to 25 countries over the

1983–2007 period, Thorbecke (2010) found that for ASEAN countries, a 10 per cent appreciation in the exporting country would reduce that country's labour-intensive exports by about 20 per cent, and a 10 per cent depreciation among competing countries would decrease ASEAN countries' exports by about 12 per cent. These results support the claim that profit margins for these goods are thin, and that exchange rates play a critical role in the overall competitiveness of the labour-intensive export products of these economies.

Going forward, the influence of the Chinese renminbi and the exchange rate policy of China are likely to gain further momentum with the internationalization of its currency. As a result of the use of the renminbi for conducting trade and investment, coupled with the gradual movement of the renminbi towards greater exchange rate flexibility, there will be a pressing need to strengthen regional cooperation in the broad arena of trade and finance. For example, in order to ensure stability in trade and investment activities between and during the peak of the recent sub-prime GFC, the monetary authorities of Hong Kong, Indonesia, Malaysia, Korea and Singapore signed swap agreements, denominated in renminbi, with the Central Bank of China (Table 5.2). In fact, this swap arrangement has been widely extended by the Chinese central bank to other trading partners outside the region.[16]

Table 5.2 People's Bank of China's swap agreements with Asian central banks

Counterparty central bank	*Date of announcement*	*Terms of agreements*	*Amount (RMB billion)*	*Stated purpose*
Bank of Korea	12 December 2008	3	180.0	Address short-term liquidity in financial system and improve bilateral trade
Hong Kong Monetary Authority	20 January 2009	3	200.0	Extend short-term liquidity support to mainland operations of Hong Kong banks
Bank Negara Malaysia	8 February 2009	3	80.0	Bilateral trade and investment
Bank Indonesia	23 March 2009	3	100.0	Bilateral trade and investment
Monetary Authority of Singapore	23 July 2010	3	150.0	Bilateral trade and investment

Source: Web site of the People's Bank of China (http://www.pbc.gov.cn/publish/english/963/index.html).Visited December 2010.

6. Conclusion

Our finding that there is a greater fear of appreciation against the renminbi than against the US dollar, especially prior to the GFC, supports the claim that links the exchange rate policy of China to the overall fear of appreciation in Asia. Bergsten (2004), for instance, asserts that China continued to "strengthen its competitiveness" by "riding the dollar down", which in turn "severely truncated the adjustment process" because other Asian countries fear losing competitiveness against China and thus block their appreciation against the US dollar. This will preserve appreciation expectations among other Asian currencies and fuel further demand for emerging market currencies that foster a further need to intervene to prevent currency appreciation. This will likely derail the supposed global rebalancing process (Kiguel and Levy-Yeyati, 2009). This in turn implies that only if China allows the renminbi to rise, will other Asian countries be likely to follow suit.

A joint or regional action in which economies in the region, including China, can collectively appreciate is a logical and effective mechanism that can not only promote currency stability in the region but can also do so without running the risk of altering price competitiveness. If this is to occur, only then will Asia play its full part in the issue of global rebalancing. Indeed, a recent review of the empirical evidence suggests that concerted appreciations in East Asia would help to rebalance processing trade in the region (Thorbecke, 2012).

Notes

1 The typical reasoning advanced is that in the presence of large stocks of unhedged foreign currency-denominated debt and high pass-through, allowing currencies to float freely means tolerating the substantial exchange rate volatility that ensues, which can be harmful to the economy.
2 See, for instance, Stigler *et al.* (2009) for this set of plausible reasons.
3 See, for instance, Ramachandran and Srinivasan (2007), Srinivasan *et al.* (2009) and Pontines and Rajan (2010).
4 In July 2005, the People's Bank of China (PBC) announced its policy intention to set the value of the renminbi with reference to a basket of foreign currencies, and to allow the currency to move more flexibly. The outcome was arguably a more measured and deliberate approach akin to a managed crawl, whereby the currency was allowed to appreciate by about 20 per cent against the US dollar from 2005 to late 2008.
5 The earlier study of Almekinders and Eijffinger (1996) finds that during the post-Louvre period, US and German central banks tried to counteract appreciations of their currency more strongly than depreciations.
6 The weights are also designed to ensure that no single variable's fluctuation could potentially dominate the overall movements of the EMP index. The standard deviation of exchange rate is adopted as the "numerator", as exchange rate volatility (standard deviation) tends to be significantly higher than the rates for the other two variables. See, Eichengreen *et al.* (1995, 1996).
7 Data on the breakdowns of the EMP index can be made available upon request.
8 In general, the construction of STAR models follows the same steps as in the ARIMA-Box-Jenkins modelling approach, wherein the modelling cycle consists of model specification, parameter estimation and diagnostic evaluation.

9 The growth rates of these economies rebounded at the end of the third quarter 2009 from three quarters of economic slowdowns following the collapse of Lehman Brothers in the final quarter of 2008.
10 See Box and Jenkins (1970).
11 For more discussion of this procedure, see Terasvirta (1998).
12 The reported auto-regressive order *p* was chosen according to the partial autocorrelation function (PACF) and selection criterion such as the Akaike information criterion; whereas the reported optimal delay lag length *d* was chosen according to the smallest *p*-value of the linearity tests. These results are not reported here for the sake of brevity, but are available from the authors upon request.
13 Both of these cases are the results we expect and this is reasonably logical since in any crisis situation, the preference of a monetary authority is to mitigate or alleviate the pressure of its currency depreciating or sliding in a free fall such that both threshold parameters (cL and cH) must either be significantly negative (indicating its preference for its currency to strengthen) or, to a lesser extent, a significantly negative lower threshold but with an insignificant upper threshold (again to indicate that it is willing to accept a much stronger currency in a crisis situation, while averting the possibility of a free fall in the value of its own currency).
14 The calculation of the trade ratio proceeds as follows. We take the ratio of total trade (exports plus imports) with China and total trade with the United States and Japan, respectively. So, for the case of Indonesia, for instance, the ratio of total bilateral exports and imports of Indonesia with China against the total bilateral exports and imports of Indonesia with the United States is calculated. We also do this for the ratio of total bilateral exports and imports of Indonesia with China against the total bilateral exports and imports of Indonesia with Japan. An increasing ratio, therefore, suggests the relative increasing role of China in the bilateral trade patterns of the five Asian economies, and a diminishing one for both the United States and Japan.
15 A typical example of processing trade is iPhone trade between the People's Republic of China (PRC) and the United States. This advanced mobile phone is assembled exclusively in China. All the components, however, are produced in Germany, Japan, Republic of Korea, Taipei, China and the United States. Components are shipped to, and the final products are fully assembled in, the PRC before being exported to the rest of the world (Xing, 2011).
16 Since the onset of the GFC, China has also signed swap arrangements with Belarus, Argentina, Iceland, New Zealand and Uzbekistan.
17 The other possible choice of the transition function is given by the exponential transition function $F(\gamma,c;\, y_{t-d}) = 1 - \exp(-\gamma(y_{t-d} - c)^2)$. One limiting behaviour of the ESTAR model is that for large values of γ, this model becomes practically indistinguishable from a linear model.

References

Almekinders, G.J. and Eijffinger, S.C.W. (1996) 'A friction model of daily Bundesbank and Federal Reserve Bank intervention', *Journal of Banking and Finance*, 20: 1365–80.

Bergsten, F. (2004) 'Bush needs to make a decisive change of course', *Financial Times* (14 December): 13.

Box, G. and Jenkins, G. (1970) *Time Series Analysis: Forecasting and Control*, San Francisco: Holden Day.

Calvo, G.A. and Reinhart, C. (2002) 'Fear of floating', *The Quarterly Journal of Economics*, CXVII: 379–408.

Economist (2009) 'Emerging Asian economies: on the rebound' *The Economist* (13 August). Online. Available HTTP: http://www.economist.com/node/14209825.

Eichengreen, B., Rose, A. and Wyplosz, C. (1995) 'Exchange market mayhem: the antecedents and aftermaths of speculative attacks', *Economic Policy*, 21: 249–312.

———. (1996) 'Contagious currency crises: first tests', *Scandinavian Journal of Economics*, 98: 463–84.

International Monetary Fund (IMF) (2011) *Asia Pacific Regional Economic Outlook*, April, Washington, DC: IMF.

Kaminsky, G. and Reinhart, C. (1998) 'Leading indicators of currency crisis', *IMF Staff Papers* 45.

———. (1999) 'The twin crises: the causes of banking and balance of payments problems', *American Economic Review*, 89: 537– 60.

Kiguel, A. and Levy-Yeyati, E. (2009) 'Back to 2007: fear of appreciation in emerging economies', *VOX*. Online. Available HTTP: http://www.voxeu.org.

Levy-Yeyati, E. and Sturzenegger, F. (2007) 'Fear of floating in reverse: exchange rate policy in the 2000s', mimeo.

Pontines, V. and Rajan, R. (2010) 'Foreign exchange market intervention and reserve accumulation in East Asia: is there evidence of "fear of appreciation"?', *Economics Letters* (forthcoming).

Ramachandran, M. and Srinivasan, N. (2007) 'Asymmetric exchange rate intervention and international reserve accumulation in India', *Economics Letters*, 94: 259–65.

Srinivasan, N., Mahambare, V. and Ramachandran, M. (2009) 'Preference asymmetry and international reserve accretion in India', *Applied Economics Letters*, 16: 1543–46.

Stigler, M., Patnaik, I. and Shah, A. (2009) 'Asymmetries in central bank intervention', mimeo.

Terasvirta, T. (1998) 'Modelling economic relationships with smooth transition regressions', in A. Ullah and D.E.A. Giles (eds) (1998) *Handbook of Applied Economic Statistics*, New York: Marcel Dekker.

Thorbecke, W. (2010) 'An empirical analysis of ASEAN's labor-intensive exports', *Journal of Asian Economics*, 21: 505–13.

———. (2011) 'The effect of exchange rate changes on trade in East Asia', *Asian Development Bank Institute Working Paper Series* 263 (January).

———. (2012) 'East Asian supply chains and relative prices: a survey of the evidence', *RIETI Discussion Paper Series* 12-P-006.

Thorbecke, W. and Zhang, H. (2009) 'The effect of exchange rate changes on China's labor-intensive manufacturing exports', *Pacific Economic Review*, 14: 389–409.

Xing, Y. (2011) 'Processing trade, exchange rates, and the People's Republic of China bilateral trade balances', *ADBI Working Paper Series* 270 (March).

Appendix A

Smooth Transition Auto-Regressive (STAR) model

The STAR model is a nonlinear time-series model that allows the variable under investigation – in the present case denoted as $\Delta\ln exr$, the first difference of the log of the nominal exchange rate (local currency per US dollar or the Chinese renminbi) – to adjust smoothly every moment within different regimes. This model may be written as

$$\Delta \ln exr = \alpha_0 + \sum_{i=1}^{p} \alpha_i(\Delta \ln exr_{t-i}) + \left[\beta_0^* + \sum_{i=1}^{p} \beta_i^*(\Delta \ln exr_{t-i})\right] F(\Delta \ln exr_{t-d}) + \varepsilon_t \qquad (1a),$$

where α_0 is the linear intercept term; α_i $(i = 1, \ldots, p)$ stand for the linear auto-regressive parameters; β_0^* is the nonlinear intercept term; $\beta_1^*(i = 1, \ldots, p)$ stand for the nonlinear auto-regressive parameters; $F(\Delta\ln exr_{t-d})$ is the transition function that characterized the smooth transition between two regimes that depend on the lagged term of the first difference of the log of the nominal exchange rate; $\Delta\ln exr_{t-d}$, where d is the delay lag length, and ε_t is a white noise with zero mean and constant variance.

Depending on the specification of the transition function, the natural starting point in describing the STAR model is the two-regime LSTR1 model with the following general logistic transition function, which takes values in the interval between zero and one

$$F(\gamma, c; y_{t-d}) = \frac{1}{1 + \exp(-\gamma(y_{t-d} - c))}, \qquad \gamma > 0 \qquad (2a),$$

where γ is the slope parameter (the magnitude of which measures the speed of transition between the two regimes); c is the threshold parameter (the value of which indicates the location of the transition); and y_{t-d} is the transition variable with the associated delay parameter d.

It turns out that a variant of the LSTR1 model is well suited to testing whether East Asian currencies exhibit aversion to appreciations. In particular, one can resort to the LSTR2 model suggested in Terasvirta (1998).[17] The transition function of the LSTR2 model is the second-order logistic function

$$F(\gamma, c_L, c_H; y_{t\text{-}d}) = \frac{1}{1 + \exp(-\gamma(y_{t\text{-}d} - c_L)(y_{t\text{-}d} - c_H))}, \quad \gamma > 0 \qquad (3a).$$

Notice that the LSTR2 transition function resembles the transition function of the LSTR1 model but the LSTR2 transition function involves two threshold parameters: c_L (the lower or appreciation threshold) and c_H (the upper or depreciation threshold). These lower (c_L) and upper (c_H) threshold parameters measure the relative tolerance of monetary authorities to exchange rate variations. To be more specific, if the upper threshold, c_H, is larger than the (absolute value of the) lower threshold, c_L, this suggests monetary authorities' aversion to currency appreciations.

Appendix B

Estimation results

Table 5.B1a Estimation results of LSTR2 models for East Asian currencies vis-à-vis the US dollar (pre-GFC sample period, weekly data, January 2000–December 2006)

	Indonesian rupiah	*Korean won*	*Philippine peso*	*Singapore dollar*	*Thai baht*
P	5	1	3	8	1
d	2	3	1	5	9
Linear part					
Intercept	0.037	0.004	0.001	–0.000	–0.000
	(0.01)***	(0.00)	(0.00)	(0.00)	(0.00)
$\Delta\ln exr_{t\text{-}1}$	–0.478	–0.708	0.369	0.365	0.471
	(0.15)***	(0.26)**	(0.06)***	(0.08)***	(0.07)***
$\Delta\ln exr_{t\text{-}2}$	–0.889		0.170	–0.005	
	(0.38)**		(0.04)***	(0.10)	
$\Delta\ln exr_{t\text{-}3}$	–0.579		0.062	0.038	
	(0.16)***		(0.05)	(0.09)	
$\Delta\ln exr_{t\text{-}4}$	0.123			–0.182	
	(0.12)			(0.10)*	
$\Delta\ln exr_{t\text{-}5}$	–0.271			0.248	
	(0.10)***			(0.15)*	
$\Delta\ln exr_{t\text{-}6}$				–0.027	
				(0.10)	
$\Delta\ln exr_{t\text{-}7}$				–0.091	
				(0.14)	
$\Delta\ln exr_{t\text{-}8}$				–0.222	
				(0.13)*	
Nonlinear part					
Intercept	–0.037	–0.005	–0.096	–0.000	0.001
	(0.01)***	(0.00)	(0.01)***	(0.00)	(0.00)
$\Delta\ln exr_{t\text{-}1}$	0.893	1.023	–2.311	–0.056	–0.319
	(0.15)***	(0.27)***	(0.23)***	(0.18)	(0.10)***

	Indonesian rupiah	*Korean won*	*Philippine peso*	*Singapore dollar*	*Thai baht*
$\Delta\ln exr_{t-2}$	0.823 (0.39)**		–1.791 (0.29)***	–0.181 (0.17)	
$\Delta\ln exr_{t-3}$	0.827 (0.17)***		3.870 (0.76)***	–0.101 (0.16)	
$\Delta\ln exr_{t-4}$	–0.189 (0.13)			0.229 (0.19)	
$\Delta\ln exr_{t-5}$	0.187 (0.12)			–0.197 (0.19)	
$\Delta\ln exr_{t-6}$				–0.229 (0.17)	
$\Delta\ln exr_{t-7}$				0.425 (0.19)**	
$\Delta\ln exr_{t-8}$				0.412 (0.22)*	
LB-*Q* test	0.20	0.72	0.67	0.74	0.33

Note: *p* is the number of lags of the linear auto-regressive model; *d* is the optimal delay parameter; numbers in parentheses are standard errors, whereas numbers in the LB-Q test are *p*-values. Significance levels: * 10%; ** 5%; *** 1%.

Table 5.B1b Estimation results of LSTR2 models for East Asian currencies vis-à-vis the US dollar (GFC sample period, weekly data, January 2007–July 2009)

	Indonesian rupiah	*Korean won*	*Philippine peso*	*Singapore dollar*	*Thai baht*
p	2	1	2	1	1
d	4	12	1	2	5
Linear part					
Intercept	0.000 (0.01)	0.002 (0.00)	–0.142 (0.08)*	–0.010 (0.00)**	0.007 (0.00)
$\Delta\ln exr_{t-1}$	0.206 (0.13)	–0.216 (0.12)*	–6.567 (3.74)*	–0.974 (0.50)**	1.704 (0.91)*
$\Delta\ln exr_{t-2}$	0.242 (0.13)**		–1.971 (0.86)**		
Nonlinear part					
Intercept	0.001 (0.00)	–0.002 (0.00)	0.143 (0.075)*	0.010 (0.00)**	–0.007 (0.00)
$\Delta\ln exr_{t-1}$	–0.358 (0.29)	0.911 (0.18)***	6.735 (3.73)*	1.310 (0.50)***	–1.679 (0.92)*
$\Delta\ln exr_{t-2}$	–0.839 (0.36)**		2.047 (0.87)**		
LB-*Q* test	0.57	0.58	0.62	0.13	0.16

Note: *p* is the number of lags of the linear auto-regressive model; *d* is the optimal delay parameter; numbers in parentheses are standard errors, whereas numbers in the LB-Q test are *p*-values. Significance levels: * 10%; ** 5%; ***1%.

Table 5.B1c Estimation results of LSTR2 models for East Asian currencies vis-à-vis the US dollar (post-GFC sample period, weekly data, August 2009–March 2011)

	Indonesian rupiah	*Korean won*	*Philippine peso*	*Singapore dollar*	*Thai baht*
p	1	1	1	1	1
d	2	2	1	7	11
Linear part					
Intercept	–0.002	–0.001	–0.010	–0.014	–0.001
	(0.00)	(0.00)	(0.00)***	(0.01)**	(0.00)
$\Delta \ln exr_{t-1}$	–0.840	0.607	1.237	–1.259	0.577
	(0.35)**	(0.13)***	(0.37)***	(0.86)	(0.12)***
Nonlinear part					
Intercept	0.001	0.006	0.009	0.013	0.003
	(0.00)	(0.00)	(0.004)**	(0.00)***	(0.00)*
$\Delta \ln exr_{t-1}$	1.077	–1.364	–1.242	1.398	–0.837
	(0.37)***	(0.26)***	(0.42)***	(0.88)	(0.28)***
LB-Q test	0.75	0.97	0.16	0.98	0.40

Note: p is the number of lags of the linear auto-regressive model; d is the optimal delay parameter; numbers in parentheses are standard errors, whereas numbers in the LB-Q test are p-values. Significance levels: * 10%; ** 5%; *** 1%.

Table 5.B2a Estimation results of LSTR2 models for East Asian currencies vis-à-vis the Chinese renminbi (pre-GFC sample period, weekly data, January 2000–December 2006)

	Indonesian rupiah	*Korean won*	*Philippine peso*	*Singapore dollar*	*Thai baht*
P	3	1	1	1	1
D	2	4	5	1	11
Linear part					
Intercept	0.003	0.004	0.017	0.005	0.004
	(0.00)	(0.00)	(0.00)***	(0.00)**	(0.00)***
$\Delta \ln exr_{t-1}$	–0.528	1.316	–2.248	–0.236	–0.180
	(0.13)***	(0.23)***	(0.16)***	(0.29)	(0.16)
$\Delta \ln exr_{t-2}$	0.166	0.297			
	(0.20)	(0.19)			
$\Delta \ln exr_{t-3}$	0.072				
	(0.11)				

	Indonesian rupiah	*Korean won*	*Philippine peso*	*Singapore dollar*	*Thai baht*
Nonlinear part					
Intercept	–0.003 (0.00)	–0.005 (0.00)	–0.016 (0.00)***	–0.006 (0.00)***	–0.004 (0.00)***
$\Delta\ln exr_{t-1}$	0.976 (0.14)***	–1.099 (0.24)***	2.349 (0.17)***	0.496 (0.30)*	0.516 (0.17)***
$\Delta\ln exr_{t-2}$	–0.267 (0.21)	–0.316 (0.194)			
$\Delta\ln exr_{t-3}$	0.114 (0.12)				
LB-*Q* test	0.19	0.76	0.18	0.13	0.60

Note: *p* is the number of lags of the linear auto-regressive model; *d* is the optimal delay parameter; numbers in parentheses are standard errors, whereas numbers in the LB-Q test are *p*-values. Significance levels: * 10%; ** 5%; *** 1%.

Table 5.B2b Estimation results of LSTR2 models for East Asian currencies vis-à-vis the Chinese renminbi (GFC sample period, weekly data, January 2007–July 2009)

	Indonesian rupiah	*Korean won*	*Philippine peso*	*Singapore dollar*	*Thai baht*
P	2	5	1	1	3
D	6	2	9	1	8
Linear part					
Intercept	0.003 (0.00)	0.004 (0.00)**	–0.004 (0.00)	0.007 (0.00)**	0.002 (0.00)
$\Delta\ln exr_{t-1}$	0.255 (0.33)	0.253 (0.10)***	–0.350 (0.43)	1.299 (0.33)***	0.257 (0.12)**
$\Delta\ln exr_{t-2}$	0.819 (0.42)**	–0.229 (0.12)**			–0.171 (0.13)
$\Delta\ln exr_{t-3}$		–0.010 (0.09)			–0.157 (0.13)
$\Delta\ln exr_{t-4}$		–0.411 (0.085)***			
$\Delta\ln exr_{t-5}$		0.337 (0.09)***			
Nonlinear part					
Intercept	–0.002 (0.00)	0.006 (0.01)	0.006 (0.003)**	–0.006 (0.00)**	–0.001 (0.00)
$\Delta\ln exr_{t-1}$	–0.041 (0.38)	0.119 (0.47)	0.678 (0.44)	–1.054 (0.35)***	0.005 (0.19)
$\Delta\ln exr_{t-2}$	–0.921 (0.46)**	0.983 (0.24)***			0.530 (0.20)**

(*Continued*)

Table 5.B2b (Continued)

	Indonesian rupiah	*Korean won*	*Philippine peso*	*Singapore dollar*	*Thai baht*
$\Delta \ln exr_{t-3}$		−0.546 (0.34)			0.523 (0.18)**
$\Delta \ln exr_{t-4}$		1.508 (0.40)***			
$\Delta \ln exr_{t-5}$		−0.392 (0.66)			
LB-*Q* test	0.55	0.14	0.73	0.17	0.47

Note: *p* is the number of lags of the linear auto-regressive model; *d* is the optimal delay parameter; numbers in parentheses are standard errors, whereas numbers in the LB-Q test are *p*-values. Significance levels: * 10%; ** 5%; *** 1%.

Table 5.B2c Estimation results of LSTR2 models for East Asian currencies vis-à-vis the Chinese renminbi (post-GFC sample period, weekly data, August 2009–March 2011)

	Indonesian rupiah	*Korean won*	*Philippine peso*	*Singapore dollar*	*Thai baht*
p	1	3	3	1	1
d	4	2	3	7	11
Linear part					
Intercept	−0.002 (0.00)	−0.004 (0.00)	−0.087 (0.06)	−0.003 (0.00)	−0.004 (0.00)
$\Delta \ln exr_{t-1}$	−0.982 (0.35)***	0.617 (0.15)***	−0.328 (0.73)	0.589 (0.32)*	1.526 (1.605)
$\Delta \ln exr_{t-2}$		−0.282 (0.14)***	0.189 (0.85)		
$\Delta \ln exr_{t-3}$		0.106 (0.137)	7.938 (5.00)		
Nonlinear part					
Intercept	0.002 (0.00)	0.008 (0.01)	0.086 (0.06)	0.002 (0.00)	0.003 (0.00)
$\Delta \ln exr_{t-1}$	1.180 (0.37)***	−1.628 (0.58)***	0.411 (0.74)	−0.549 (0.35)	−1.119 (1.62)
$\Delta \ln exr_{t-2}$		0.343 (0.24)	−0.384 (0.86)		
$\Delta \ln exr_{t-3}$		−0.162 (0.263)	−8.060 (5.01)		
LB-*Q* test	0.68	0.98	0.70	0.43	0.55

Note: *p* is the number of lags of the linear auto-regressive model; *d* is the optimal delay parameter; numbers in parentheses are standard errors, whereas numbers in the LB-Q test are *p*-values. Significance levels: * 10%; ** 5%; *** 1%.

Appendix C

Trade ratios for the five Asian economies in terms of their bilateral trade patterns with China, the United States and Japan

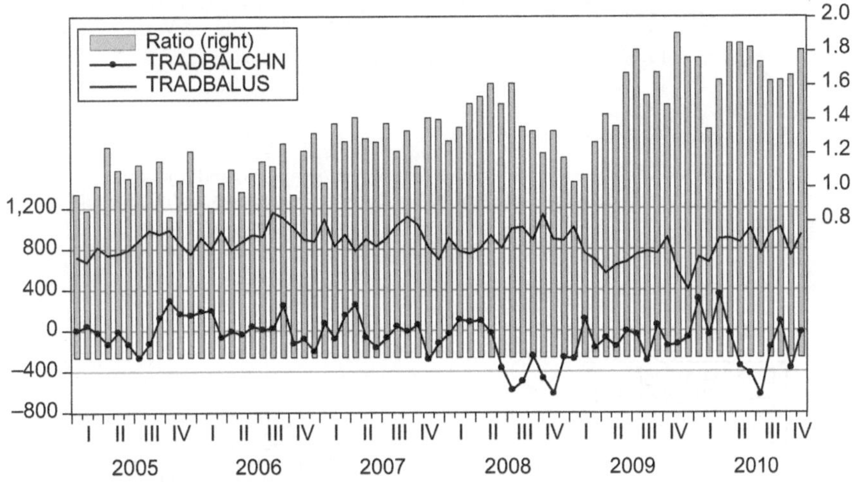

Figure 5.C1 Indonesia trade

Note: Ratio is the ratio of total trade with China (exports and imports) and total trade with the United States. TRADBALCHN and TRADBALUS are trade balances with China and the United States, respectively. Trade balance is calculated as export minus import.

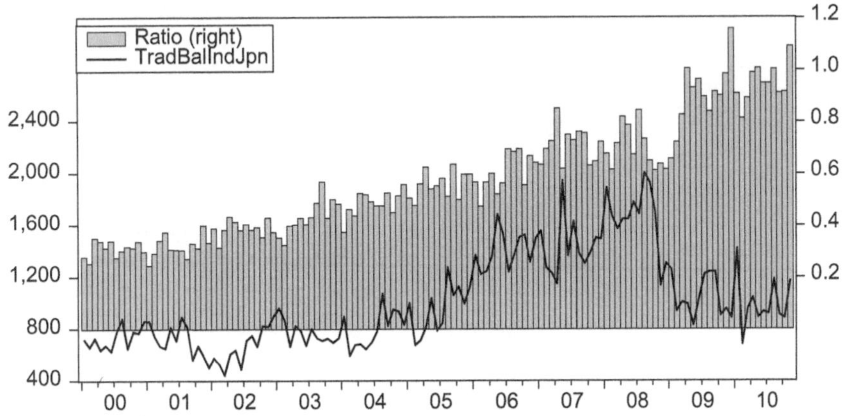

Figure 5.C2 Indonesia–Japan–China trade

Note: Ratio is the ratio of total trade with China (exports and imports) and total trade with Japan. TRADBALJPN is trade balance with Japan. Trade balance is calculated as export minus import.

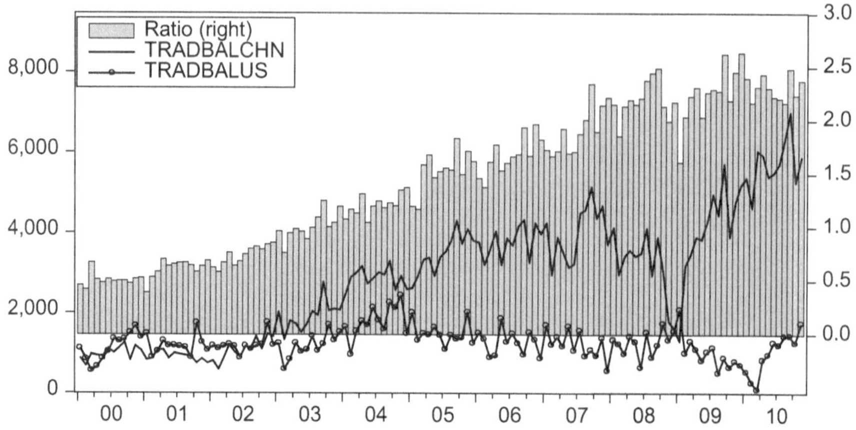

Figure 5.C3 Korea–China–US trade

Note: Ratio is the ratio of total trade with China (exports and imports) and total trade with the United States. TRADBALCHN and TRADBALUS are trade balances with China and the United States, respectively. Trade balance is calculated as export minus import.

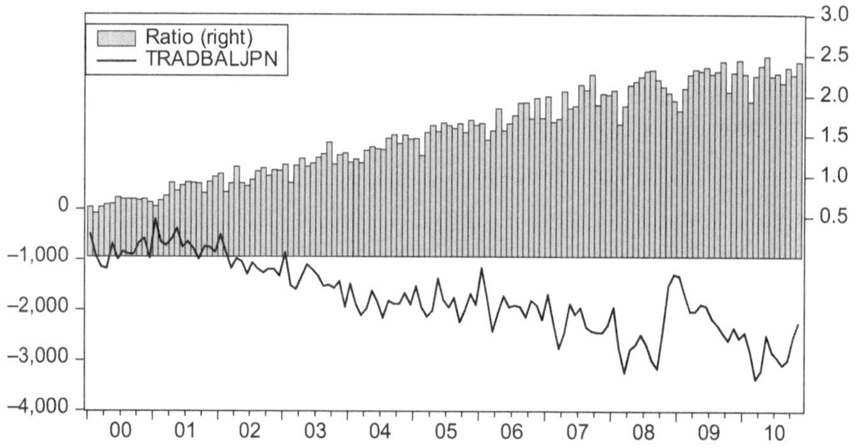

Figure 5.C4 Korea–China–Japan trade

Note: Ratio is the ratio of total trade with China (exports and imports) and total trade with Japan. TRADBALJPN is trade balance with Japan. Trade balance is calculated as export minus import.

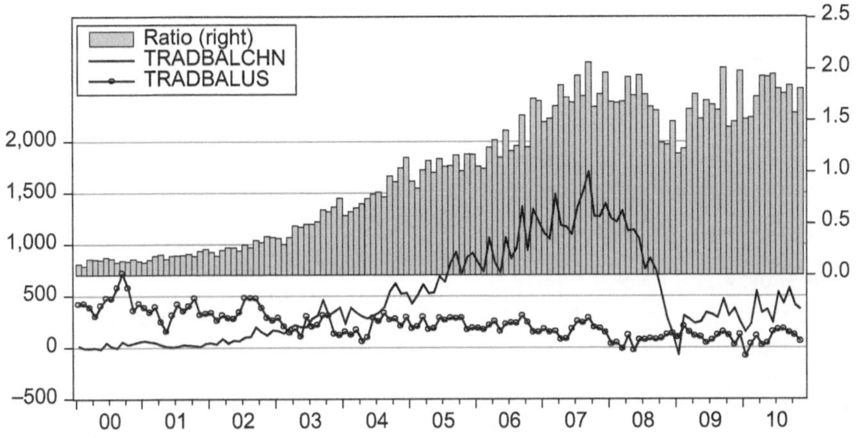

Figure 5.C5 The Philippines–China–US trade

Note: Ratio is the ratio of total trade with China (exports and imports) and total trade with the United States. TRADBALCHN and TRADBALUS are trade balances with China and the United States, respectively. Trade balance is calculated as export minus import.

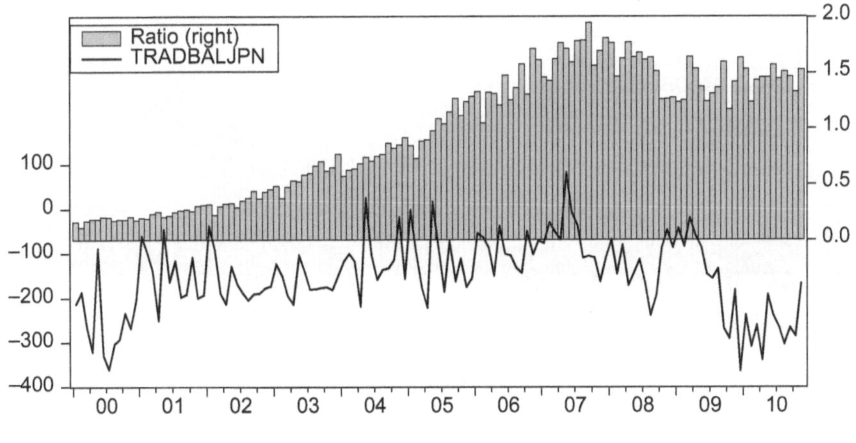

Figure 5.C6 The Philippines–China–Japan trade

Note: Ratio is the ratio of total trade with China (exports and imports) and total trade with Japan. TRADBALJPN is trade balance with Japan. Trade balance is calculated as export minus import.

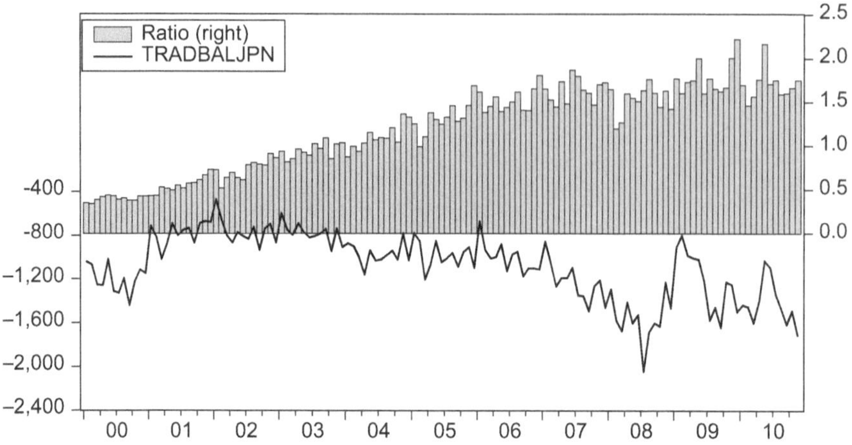

Figure 5.C7 Thailand–China–US trade

Note: Ratio is the ratio of total trade with China (exports and imports) and total trade with the United States. TRADBALCHN and TRADBALUS are trade balances with China and the United States, respectively. Trade balance is calculated as export minus import.

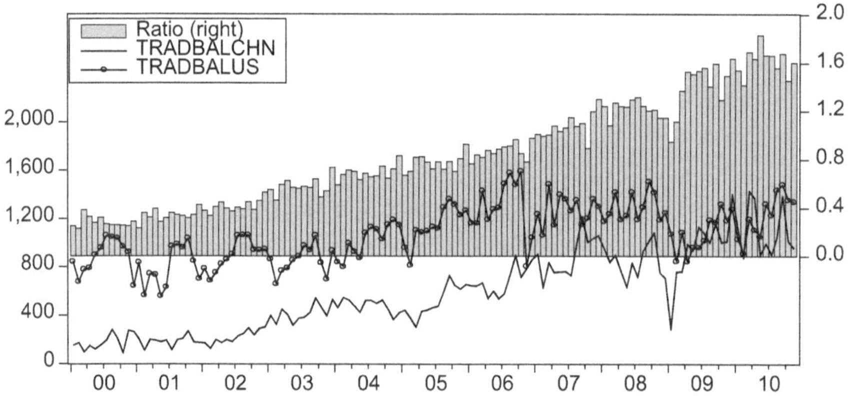

Figure 5.C8 Thailand–China–Japan trade

Note: Ratio is the ratio of total trade with China (exports and imports) and total trade with Japan. TRADBALJPN is trade balance with Japan. Trade balance is calculated as export minus import.

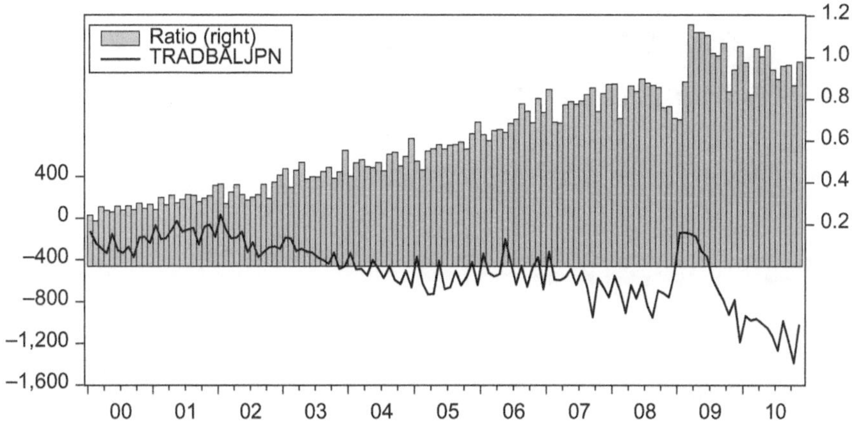

Figure 5.C9 Singapore–China–US trade

Note: Ratio is the ratio of total trade with China (exports and imports) and total trade with the United States. TRADBALCHN and TRADBALUS are trade balances with China and the United States, respectively. Trade balance is calculated as export minus import.

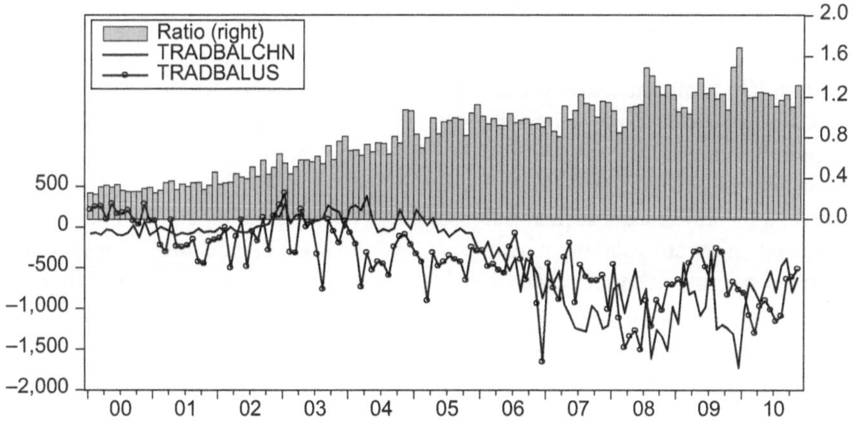

Figure 5.C10 Singapore–China–Japan trade

Note: Ratio is the ratio of total trade with China (exports and imports) and total trade with Japan. TRADBALJPN is trade balance with Japan. Trade balance is calculated as export minus import.

6 What drives some countries to hoard foreign reserves?

Dyna Heng and Jenny Corbett

1. Introduction

> The lack of a clear benchmark for the appropriate level of precautionary reserves, and for the appropriate use of reserves, is a problem, both at the country level and at the global level.
>
> —Olivier Jeanne[1]

Over the past two decades, East Asian economies have accumulated a large amount of foreign reserves. The reserves in the region were merely US$0.7 trillion before the Asian crisis in 1997, but rose ninefold to about US$6 trillion in 2010. This amount is more than half of the total global foreign reserves.

Four major motivations behind this rapid reserve build-up, as is often suggested, are precautionary self-insurance against crisis (Aizenman and Lee, 2008), mercantilism to stimulate growth (Dooley *et al.*, 2004), supporting the overall banking system and insuring against financial instability (Obstfeld *et al.*, 2010), and managing exchange rate volatility (Levy-Yeyati and Sturzenegger, 2006). These four rationales become even stronger amid increasing global capital flows, which are often volatile and potentially destabilizing. Capital flows, for instance, increase output volatility (Mendoza and Terrones, 2008), cause real exchange rate appreciation and thus loss of competitiveness (Corden, 1993), and drive asset bubbles (Grenville, 2008).

Reserve build-up, however, involves some types of domestic risks and costs (Pineau *et al.*, 2006). The most significant include inflationary pressure, asset bubbles, misallocation of domestic bank lending, complications in the management of monetary policies, sterilization costs, and potentially sizeable capital losses on central banks' balance sheets. Conflict between reserve accumulation (that is, as a result of intervention in foreign exchange markets) and inappropriate increases in money supply, for instance, could cause inflation and asset price bubbles. Sterilization costs – as another example – can be a considerable drain on a country's budget when the reserves are excessive (Rodrik, 2006).[2]

To dampen the macroeconomic effects associated with reserve accumulation and capital inflows, countries have applied various policies such as modest capital controls, sterilized foreign exchange intervention and fiscal tightening. As these policies have generally not proved effective in many cases, a satisfactory way of managing capital flows and reserve build-up is yet to be discovered.

In this chapter, we hypothesize that the development of a deep and active financial sector attenuates the impact of capital flows on the demand for reserves. Capital inflows influence reserve demand via their volatility, potential destabilizing effects, and the risks of sudden stop and reversal (Frankel, 2010; Jeanne, 2010; Kaminsky *et al.*, 2004). Financial development, meanwhile, reduces the impacts of capital flows on real exchange rate appreciation (Saborowski, 2009), and lowers output and macroeconomic volatility (Raddatz, 2006). The main reason is that a well-functioning financial market enables efficient utilization of capital inflows, mobilizes resources, facilitates risk diversification and provides access to global liquidity during shocks (Beck and Levine, 2004; Beck *et al.*, 1999; King and Levine, 1993).

We present a model in which the state holds reserves in order to supply foreign exchange liquidity in underdeveloped financial markets. Our theoretical argument is that with the low capacity of the private sector to meet liquidity demand when financial markets are underdeveloped, the state plays a role in supplying additional liquidity. Thus, in our model, the development of the financial system reduces the monetary authority's motivation to hoard reserves for liquidity provision.

Using annual data for 12 East Asian economies between 1980 and 2009, we empirically examine the motives for foreign reserve accumulation and analyze the effects of capital flows and financial development on reserve demand. Fixed effects and alternative measures of financial development are also introduced to check the robustness of the estimations. We confirm the precautionary motives and financial stability motives for reserve demand in Asia. Our results also consistently suggest that financial sector development reduces the impacts of capital flows on the demand for reserves.

This chapter contains three innovations. First, our analysis concentrates on East Asian economies that attract a large share of global capital flows. Second, we formally take into account the level of financial development in discussing foreign reserve demand and capital flows. Third, we introduce a "rationalized" monetary policy reaction and the concept of private and public liquidity provision – first analyzed by Holmström and Tirole (1998) – into the framework set-up by Obstfeld *et al.* (2010).

The chapter is structured as follows: the next section describes the recent trends in foreign reserve accumulation among Asian emerging-market economies. Section 3 provides a short review of the current state of understanding on foreign reserve accumulation and its nexus with capital flows and financial development. Section 4 introduces the theoretical underpinnings of the analysis. The formal model is presented in Appendix A. Section 5 presents the empirical investigation. Section 6 discusses the results. Section 7 concludes and sheds some light on policy implications in reserve accumulation. An appendix presents a model explaining the motives for reserve accumulation and the role of the private sector in liquidity provision.

2. Recent trends in foreign reserve accumulation among Asian economies

As can be seen in Figure 6.1, there are three features of the trend of reserve accumulation over the past two decades. First, reserves grew rapidly in 2002–07, at a pace three times more than that of 1999–2001. Second, central banks in East Asia, particularly China, accounted for the bulk of the build-up. Among the reserve accumulators, Asian economies are among the 10 largest reserve holders: China, Japan, Taiwan, Korea, India, Hong Kong, Singapore and Malaysia. The share of foreign reserves held by Asian economies increased from 45 per cent in 1995 to 66 per cent in 2010. Third, few monetary authorities held an increasingly larger share of the reserve holding. China and Japan accounted for more than half the total world reserve accumulation.

As shown in Figure 6.2, Hong Kong accumulates the highest percentage of reserves-to-GDP (121 per cent), followed by Singapore (106 per cent), Taiwan (94 per cent), Malaysia (50 per cent), and China (49 per cent).

As shown in Figures 6.3, 6.4 and 6.5, ratios of reserves to imports for many Asian economies are far above the traditional rule of thumb, which is three to four months' coverage. Taiwan, for example, would be able to finance its imports for about two years with its reserves. Similarly, as can be seen in Figure 6.6, China's ratio of reserves to short-term external debt reaches a value of about 10, which is much higher than 1, suggested by the Greenspan–Guidotti rule. In addition, as shown in Figures 6.7 and 6.8, the reserves to broad money ratios in many Asian economies have increased significantly above the threshold

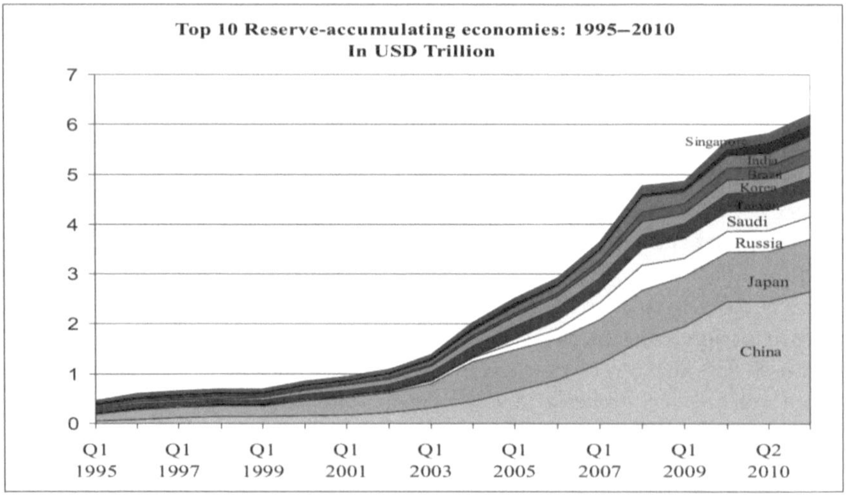

Figure 6.1 Top 10 reserve-accumulating economies: 1995–2010 (in USD trillion)

Source: Foreign exchange (series code: 1D.DZF), International Financial Statistics, IMF, (accessed 19 December 2010); Central Bank of the Republic of China (Taiwan).

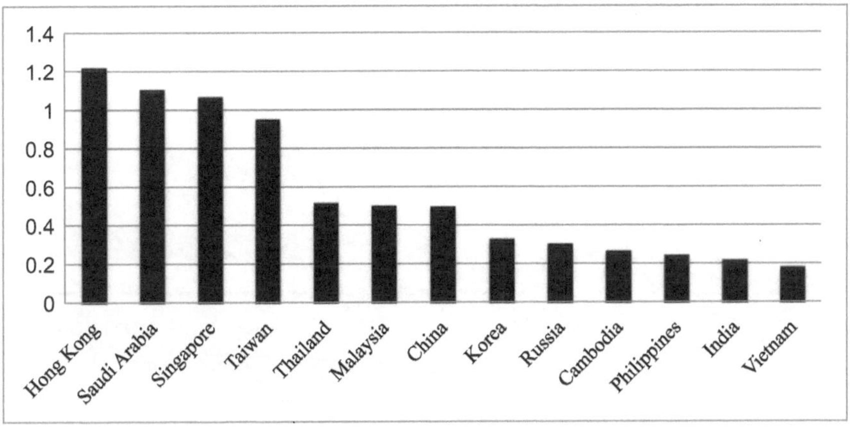

Figure 6.2 Reserves/GDP in 2010

Source: International Financial Statistics, IMF. GDP from World Economic Outlook, IMF, (accessed 23 December 2010); Central Bank of the Republic of China (Taiwan).

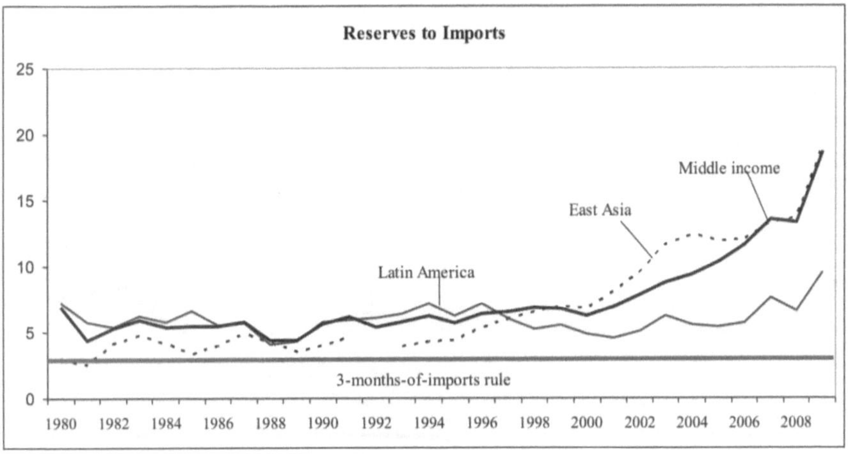

Figure 6.3 Reserves to imports

Source: World Development Indicators, World Bank (accessed 28 December 2010); Central Bank of the Republic of China (Taiwan).

values, which are suggested to be between 5 and 20 per cent. In Singapore, for example, the ratio is about 90 per cent.

Traditional indicators (see Box 6.1) for reserve adequacy suggest that in emerging Asian economies, the stock of foreign reserves might be substantially in excess. The unprecedented accumulation in several key Asian economies indicates that factors other than purely precautionary motives might be driving

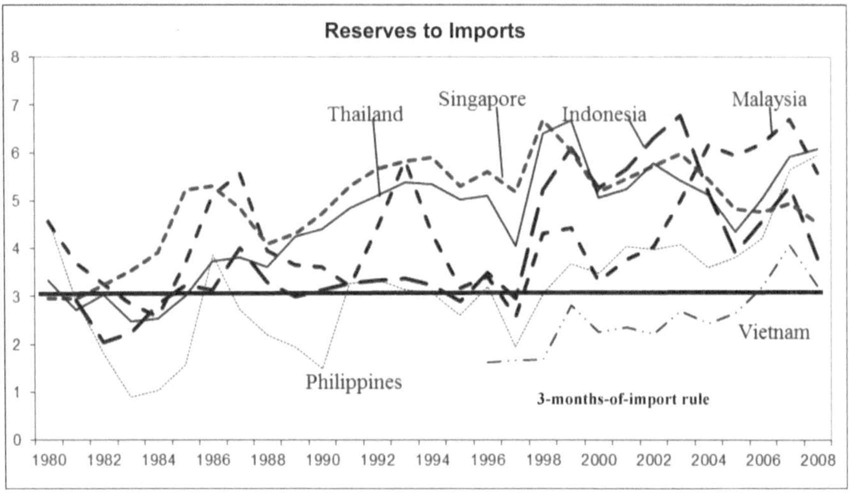

Figure 6.4 Reserves to imports

Source: World Development Indicators, World Bank (accessed 28 December 2010); Central Bank of the Republic of China (Taiwan).

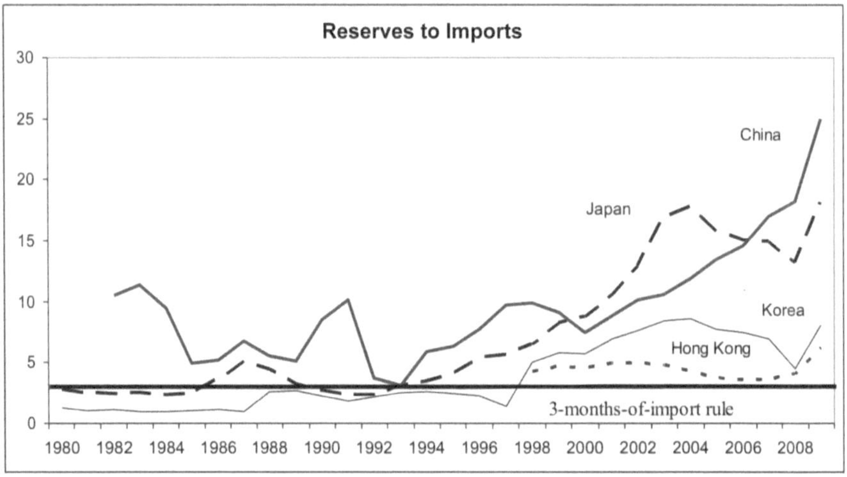

Figure 6.5 Reserves to imports

Source: World Development Indicators, World Bank (accessed 28 December 2010); Central Bank of the Republic of China (Taiwan).

the rapid build-up of international reserves (Aizenman and Lee, 2008). The evidence also suggests that limiting vulnerability has probably not been the primary motive for recent reserve build-ups in most economies. Nonetheless, determining the optimal level of foreign reserves is not straightforward as it is

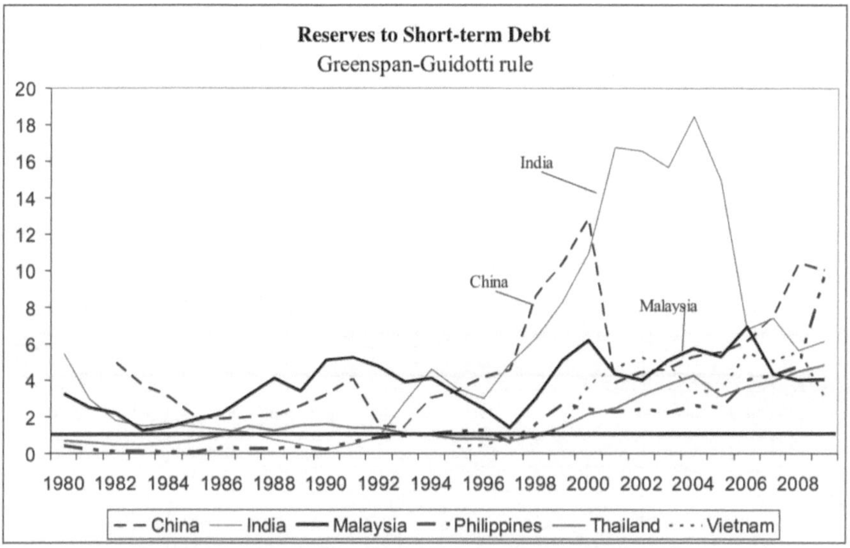

Figure 6.6 Reserves to short-term debt (Greenspan–Guidotti rule)

Source: Authors' calculation; World Development Indicators, World Bank (accessed 28 December 2010); Central Bank of the Republic of China (Taiwan).

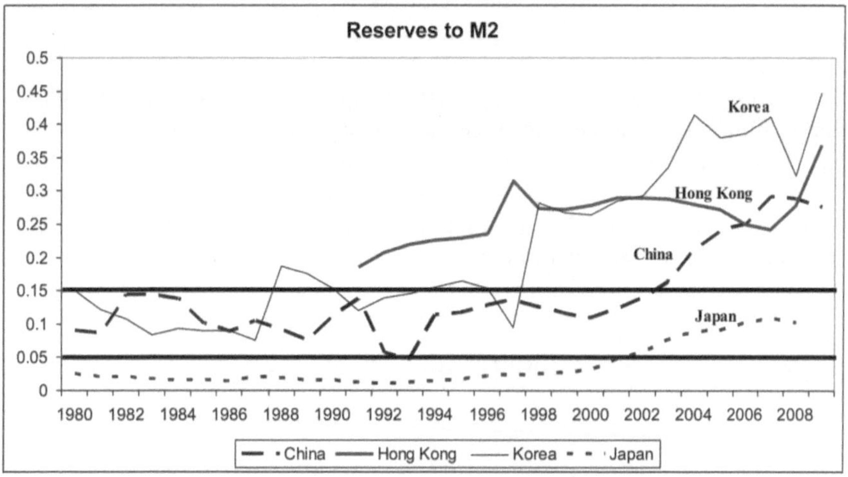

Figure 6.7 Reserves to M2

Source: Authors' calculation; World Development Indicators, World Bank (accessed 28 December 2010); Central Bank of the Republic of China (Taiwan).

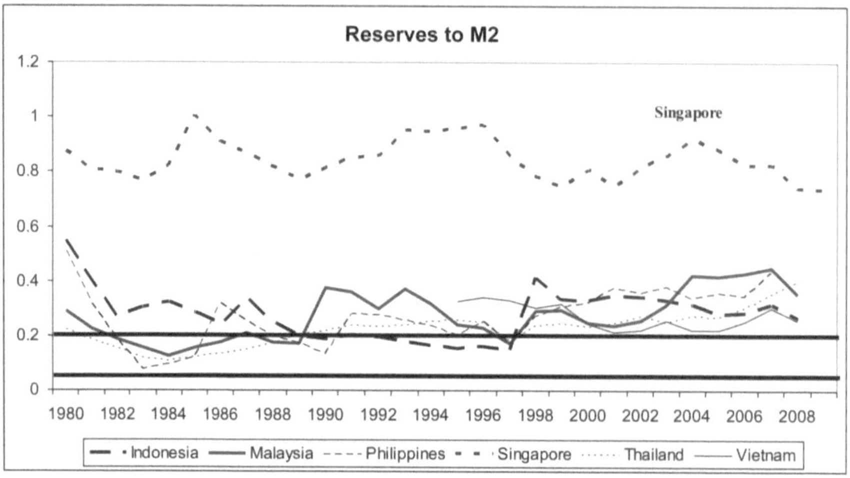

Figure 6.8 Reserves to M8

Source: Authors' calculation; World Development Indicators, World Bank (accessed 28 December 2010); Central Bank of the Republic of China (Taiwan).

subject to uncertainty and institutional factors such as the degree of capital mobility, financial liberalization, or the weakness of the domestic banking system. Under financial globalization, the high volatility of capital flows complicates the conduct of monetary policy and exchange rate policy, and has impacts on an economy's ability – particularly those with underdeveloped financial markets – to deal with sudden capital inflows and outflows. This environment indeed influences the desired stock of foreign reserves (see Box 6.2 for the case of South Korea during the 2008 crisis).

de Beaufort Wijnholds and Kapteyn (2001) argue that the old rule of thumb – reserves should be equivalent to three months of imports – is obsolete and that a new benchmark that takes into account capital flows is needed. They argue that the new benchmark should consist of the sum of short-term debt (external drain) and an allowance for possible capital flight by domestic residents (internal drain), taking into account differences in country risk and the exchange rate regime.

Box 6.1 Traditional indicators for reserve adequacy

Ratio	*Value*	*Notes*
Reserves to imports	3 to 4	This ratio represents the number of months for which an economy could support its current level of imports if all other revenues were to stop. As a rule of thumb, countries should hold foreign reserves in order to cover their imports for three to four months.

Reserves to short-term external debt	1	This ratio, known as the Greenspan–Guidotti rule, reflects an economy's ability to service its existing short-term external debt (debt maturing within a year) in the case of a sharp deterioration in the external financing conditions. Typically, the country is prudent if the ratio is equal to 1 (Garcia and Soto, 2006; Rodrik and Velasco, 1999).
Reserves to broad money (M2)	0.05 to 0.2	This ratio reflects the potential for resident-based capital flight from the domestic currency because broad money indicates a country's exposure to the withdrawal of assets. If the ratio is close to zero, broad money largely exceeds foreign reserves. In the case of an exchange rate peg regime, the lower the ratio, the higher the potential for capital flight in the event of negative money demand shocks. This ratio has indeed increased in most Asian economies since the 1997 Asian crisis (see de Beaufort Wijnholds and Kapteyn, 2001).

3. Literature review

3.1 Reserve demand

Three major theoretical explanations stand out in the literature on reserve demand: precautionary motives, mercantilist motives and financial stability motives. In the precautionary view, countries accumulate foreign reserves as self-insurance to avoid costly liquidation of long-term projects (Aizenman and Lee, 2008), and to smooth domestic absorption as a cushion against sudden stops in capital inflows (Jeanne and Rancière, 2006) when the economy is susceptible to sudden stops. In addition, countries can use international reserves to smooth the impact of capital-flow volatility, to manage an adjustable-peg or managed-floating exchange rate regime (Frankel and Jovanovic, 1981), and to stabilize output (Aizenman and Marion, 2004; Garcia and Soto, 2006; Jeanne and Rancière, 2006). Similarly, foreign reserves can be used to stabilize fiscal expenditure in countries with limited taxation capacity and sovereign risk, and limited access to the global capital market (Aizenman and Marion, 2004).

In the mercantile view, reserve accumulation is the result of a growth strategy by keeping exchange rates undervalued to stimulate export growth and competitiveness (Dooley *et al.*, 2004). Moreover, foreign reserves can serve as "collateral" for encouraging foreign direct investment (FDI). Similarly, foreign reserve accumulation can occur in the aftermath of a growth strategy that combines export promotion and credit subsidization – known as "financial mercantilism" (Aizenman and Lee, 2008). The development experience of East Asia suggests the prevalence of export promotion by preferential financing, which effectively subsidizes investment in targeted sectors (Aizenman and Lee, 2008). The promotion was achieved in several ways, including through direct subsidies funded by state banks; by means of financial repression where favoured sectors enjoyed preferential access to cheaper external debt; or through "moral suasion" where private banks were encouraged to provide favourable financing.

In the financial stability view, a major motivation for central banks to hold foreign reserves is to support the overall banking system and to insure against financial instability (Obstfeld *et al.*, 2010). In this view, financial shock is not simply a "sudden stop", in which case countries would need to hold reserves only in proportion to their short-term external debt (Greenspan–Guidotti rule). Given such motivation and the desire for exchange rate stability and vulnerability to portfolio shifts by domestic residents, the monetary authority needs to hold reserves proportional to the size of its banking system.

3.2 Capital flows, reserve accumulation and financial development

In this section, we connect the link between capital flows, reserve accumulation and financial development. Despite the benefits of capital flows on investment and growth (Bosworth *et al.*, 1999; Mileva, 2008; Mody and Murshid, 2005), capital flows can have a direct impact on macroeconomic stability and then affect reserve demand through at least three channels, as can be seen in Box 6.2.

First, capital flows affect reserve demand through increased output volatility as they are more often pro-cyclical than countercyclical (Kaminsky *et al.*, 2004; Mendoza and Terrones, 2008; Reinhart and Reinhart, 2008). Sudden changes in the direction of capital flows, for instance, tend to induce or exacerbate boom–bust cycles in economies that lack a deep and well-functioning financial sector (Aghion *et al.*, 2005). This relation implies that increases in capital flows tend to increase output volatility, which motivates more precautionary demand for foreign reserves.

Second, capital inflows influence reserve demand through their appreciation impacts on the real exchange rate and thus have negative effects on the external competiveness of recipient economies (Athukorala and Rajapatirana, 2003; Corden, 1993). As Asian economies are fearful of appreciation (Pontines and Yongqiang, 2010), central banks are induced to intervene in foreign exchange markets by buying reserves to "lean against the wind" when there is upward pressure on exchange rates. The reasons for such intervention could be that a fixed or relatively rigid exchange rate can provide benefits in terms of macroeconomic stability, particularly to developing countries where financial

Box 6.2 List of explanatory variables for reserve build-up

Variables	*Sign*	*Notes*
GDP per capita	+/–	GDP per capita can reflect the stage of economic development. It is expected to be positively/negatively linked to reserve accumulation according to the stage of the economy.
Capital flows (Hot money)	+	A potential indicator of hot money flows to a country is the sum of the current account and net FDI inflows scaled by GDP. A negative value indicates the level of short-term flows needed to finance a current account deficit. A positive value might reflect a current account surplus and positive net FDI inflows. This indicator could be construed as a possible inducement for appreciation pressure on the currency, in which there would be a positive link to reserve accumulation.
Broad money	+	Broad money often indicates a country's exposure to the withdrawal of assets or resident-based capital flight from the domestic currency. Thus, it is used as a proxy for potential liquidity demand. Broad money is expected to be positively linked to reserve accumulation.
Trade	+	Trade openness might require foreign reserve demand for transaction. Also, a conventional rule of thumb suggests that a country should hold reserves enough to finance three or four months of imports without income flows. For this reason, as a precautionary demand, a country can hold more for self-insurance. Thus, imports/GDP is expected to be positively linked to reserve accumulation (*Source*: WDI, the World Bank).
Financial development	–	A high level of financial sector development could mobilize resources more efficiently and would be less vulnerable to crises. Thus, it is expected to reduce demand for a reserve build-up. A country's total equity and debt liability is used as an indicator of capital market development and as a proxy for the country's access to the international financial market.
Interaction term (Capital flows and financial development)	–	The interaction term captures the marginal effect of capital flows on reserve demand. It is expected to take a negative sign given the hypothesis that increases in financial development could help attenuate the impact of capital flows on reserve demand.
Financial openness (Chinn–Ito)	+	We adopt the Chinn–Ito Index. Higher financial openness suggests vulnerability to external financial shocks and is expected to increase precautionary demand for reserves.

Exchange rate fluctuation	+/–	On the one hand, exchange rate fluctuation within a certain range would result in less government intervention in the foreign exchange market, thus less reserve build-up. On the other hand, greater real exchange rate volatility is empirically linked to lower growth and financial instability – notably, in financially underdeveloped countries. Also, a higher level of reserves is empirically linked to reduced exchange rate volatility (Hviding *et al.*, 2004). This variable is expected to be positively linked to reserve holding.

development is limited and the capital market is closed (Aghion *et al.*, 2009). On the contrary, real exchange rate volatility reduces growth in countries with relatively weak financial development (Aghion *et al.*, 2009). In such cases, reserve accumulation is a result of intervening in foreign exchange markets or stabilizing the real exchange rate in the presence of volatile terms-of-trade shocks and potentially destabilizing capital flows.

Third, capital inflows motivate reserve demand when they drive up equity and asset prices (Grenville, 2008; Schadler, 2008), reduce the quality of assets, and adversely affect the maturity and currency composition of the balance sheets of the private sector. This contributes to greater financial fragility, which increases the odds of a currency crisis (Kaminsky and Reinhart, 1999). Real estate booms and asset price bubbles can amplify financial fragility and crisis risks, thus making the economy particularly vulnerable to financial shocks and crises (Reinhart and Rogoff, 2008). In such cases, a reserve build-up can also be associated with the growing fragility of a country's banking system. This is because concerns about financial stability lead countries to hoard foreign reserves for liquidity provision to mitigate the possible transmission of a banking crisis to a currency crisis during shocks.

Analysis of the three transmission types implies that the development of the financial sector can attenuate the reserve demand by weakening the impacts of capital flows on output volatility, the real exchange rate and financial fragility. First, a more developed financial system is associated with lower output volatility across countries (Beck *et al.*, 1999). Second, a deep and active financial sector can provide broad investment opportunities, direct capital inflows towards their most productive use, mitigate investment demand constraints (Ötker-Robe *et al.*, 2007), and thus reduce real exchange rate appreciation (Saborowski, 2009). Third, financial development has a large causal effect in the reduction of macroeconomic volatility as a result of liquidity provision by the financial sector (Raddatz, 2006), which then requires less liquidity provision by the government.

Different strands of the literature discussed above underline: (i) the motivation to accumulate reserves; (ii) the potentially adverse impacts of capital inflows on the recipient economies and thus on the reserve build-up; and (iii) the importance of the financial market in mobilizing and allocating resources efficiently to attenuate the impacts. These findings shape our hypothesis that the impacts of capital flows on reserve demand could be attenuated by the development of deep financial markets and institutions.

4. Theoretical motivation based on liquidity view

The theoretical framework underpinning our analysis rests on three important strands of the literature: foreign reserve accumulation, liquidity provision and financial development. We take into account the concept of liquidity in the model as it plays an essential role in the literature of financial crisis. Higher liquidity can significantly decrease countries' vulnerability to external shock in the face of weak domestic fundamentals (Mulder and Bussière, 1999). Similarly, in the model of the amplification mechanism of financial shock, liquidity provision by the central bank can alleviate the crisis (Krishnamurthy, 2010).

Drawing on the work of Holmström and Tirole (1998), we introduce the concept of private versus public supply of liquidity (domestic versus international liquidity) into the framework in Obstfeld *et al.* (2010). In the case of liquidity demand shock, domestic residents or firms can meet liquidity by issuing claims on their productive assets or by using a credit line (Holmström and Tirole, 1998). When financial markets are not developed well enough to provide these options, however, the government might need to step in to supply additional liquidity. The underdeveloped financial markets could be caused by collateral constraints (Caballero and Panageas, 2005). In these circumstances, the build-up of foreign reserves is motivated by the government's role in supplying additional liquidity to domestic economic agents during a liquidity shock – that is, a sudden stop or capital outflows, with the presence of an underdeveloped capital market that fails to fully meet liquidity demand. This relation implies that the development of a deep and active financial market could bring about two benefits. First, it could promote resource mobilization for more private liquidity provision. Second, it can reduce the impacts of capital flows on macroeconomic and exchange rate volatility, and vulnerability to financial crisis. These two benefits, therefore, can attenuate the state's motivation to hoard reserves.

The theoretical reasoning outlined above motivates our simple modelling of the relationship between the demand for liquidity, the level of financial sector development and an economy's international reserve accumulation. In the model outlined in the Appendix, we follow Obstfeld *et al.* (2010) in deriving the liquidity demand in a domestic economy. Unlike the framework set out in Obstfeld *et al.* (2010), however, in which the central bank sells foreign reserves passively, we introduce a monetary reaction function based on optimizing behaviour to motivate its intervention. Furthermore, as noted earlier, our model also introduces concepts of private versus public liquidity provision and the level of capital market development.

5. Empirical approach

We turn to an empirical investigation on the liquidity demand, financial development and reserve accumulation. Based on the theoretical motivation outlined in the previous section and Appendix A, the reduced form for our empirical study can be simplified as

$$reserves = \alpha_1 + \alpha_2 Capflows_{it} + \alpha_3 Findev_{it} + \alpha_4 CapFin_{it} + \alpha_5 X_{it} + \eta_{it} + \varepsilon_{it}, \qquad (1)$$

where *Reserves* is the amount of foreign reserves, *Capflows* is capital inflows, *Findev* is financial development, and *Capfin* is the interaction terms between capital flows and financial development. X_{it} is a vector of control variables including GDP per capita, broad money, trade, exchange rate stability and financial openness, which are often included in the literature. η is the fixed effect and ε is the error term. We also include a dummy for the post-Asian crisis period, POST, in order to capture potential differences in reserve accumulation patterns across countries between the pre- and post-Asian crisis periods.

The parameters of main interest are α_3 and α_4, which capture the effects of financial development and the interaction of capital flows and financial development on reserve accumulation, respectively. If financial development can attenuate the impact of capital flows on reserve accumulation, then α_4 should be negative and statistically significant. Meanwhile, we expect the coefficient of capital flows, α_2, to be positive and that of financial development, α_3, to be negative.

For potential liquidity demand, we use broad money over GDP. Using broad money as a proxy for possible liquidity demand is motivated by (de Beaufort Wijnholds and Kapteyn, 2001), the Early Warning System literature, and the financial stability model presented by Obstfeld *et al.* (2010). Short-term external debt can also be a good proxy for liquidity demand. Given data availability, however, broad money (M2) is preferred in this analysis.

Financial development is a broad economic concept, within which there is a large literature on the measurement of financial development (see, for example, Beck *et al.*, 1999). Among all measures, the sum of total external equity liability and debt liability is used as an indicator of a country's level of financial development in terms of access to external financial resources. The measure of financial market development as the extent of external liabilities is based on the assumption that countries with less developed domestic financial markets also have fewer external liabilities. Thus, this measure will be used for our main regressions and analysis. Besides, the total stock value traded, measures financial market liquidity while, stock market capitalization, reflects the size and depth of the market. These alternative measures will be used for a robustness check in the next section.

For financial openness, the Chinn–Ito Index (2008) is used. This index is based on the binary dummy variables that codify the restriction on cross-border financial transactions reported in the International Monetary Fund's *Annual*

Report on Exchange Arrangements and Exchange Restriction (*AREAER*). A higher value signals a higher degree of openness to financial transaction.

For capital flows, we follow Mendoza (2010) by using the sum of the current account and net FDI inflows scaled by GDP. This measure captures more of the short-term component of capital flows (hot money) – considered to be volatile and potentially destabilizing in the literature. A negative value indicates the level of short-term flows needed to finance a current account deficit. A positive value might reflect a current account surplus and positive net FDI inflows. This indicator could be construed as a possible inducement for appreciation pressure on the currency, in which there would be a positive link to reserve accumulation.

Our annual data sample covers 30 years from 1980 to 2009 and includes 12 Asian economies.[3] (See Box 6.2 for an explanation of each variable and the Appendix for data sources.)

6. Regression results and analysis

Table 6.1 reports the results of regressions with a log of reserve accumulation over GDP as the dependent variable. Column 1 shows the result of regression with a country fixed effect while column 2 includes country and year fixed effect. In columns 3 and 4, we add capital flows, financial development, and the interaction terms with country fixed effect and country and year fixed effect, respectively.

We observe that broad money and trade are positive and significant in all regressions while the post-crisis period is positive and significant in columns 1 and 3 (country fixed effect). These results confirm the precautionary motives and financial stability motives for reserve accumulation among Asian economies. Based on the results, a 10 per cent increase in broad money over GDP leads to about a 5 per cent increase in reserves over GDP. Similarly, when trade over GDP increases by 10 per cent the reserves over GDP ratio would increase by about 7 per cent.

In columns 3 and 4, we find that the coefficient of capital flows is positive and significant. This finding implies that a 10 percentage point increase in the capital flows ratio would lead to about a 26 per cent increase in the reserves-to-GDP ratio.[4] This effect is fairly high, but is evidenced by some Asian economies' behaviour. In our sample, an average capital inflow is 4 per cent while the average increase in reserves-to-GDP ratio is 14 percentage points.

We also find that the interaction terms between capital flows and financial development have the expected sign and are significant. The results confirm our hypothesis that financial development attenuates the impacts of capital flows on reserve accumulation. The implication here is that although capital inflows could motivate reserve accumulation, a well-functioning financial system could help reduce the impacts of capital flows on reserve hoarding. In other words, the magnitude of the impacts of capital flows on reserve demand decreases with a higher level of financial development due to the efficient absorption of capital inflows.

Table 6.1 Regression result with log (foreign reserves/GDP) as dependent variable

	(1)	*(2)*	*(3)*	*(4)*
lnGDPPC	0.153	–0.099	0.175	–0.1
	(0.12)	(0.053)*	(0.10)	(0.042)**
lnM2	0.542	0.485	0.528	0.427
	(0.242)**	(0.162)**	(0.210)**	(0.126)***
lnTrade	0.73	0.758	0.683	0.774
	(0.239)**	(0.110)***	(0.217)***	(0.128)***
Evol	–1.604	–3.631	–1.446	–3.979
	(1.03)	(2.21)	(1.14)	(2.29)
Kaopen	0.137	0.022	0.19	0.04
	(0.08)	(0.06)	(0.081)**	(0.05)
Post-crisis	0.469		0.471	
	(0.237)*		(0.217)*	
Capital inflows			2.057	2.721
			(1.091)*	(1.009)**
Financial development			–0.009	–0.08
			(0.06)	(0.06)
Cap*Fin			–1.094	–1.044
			(0.361)**	(0.298)***
Observations	326	327	322	322
Country fixed effect	Yes	Yes	Yes	Yes
Year fixed effect	No	Yes	No	Yes
R-squared	0.9	0.85	0.91	0.87

Note: Robust standard errors in parentheses. Significance levels: * 10%; ** 5%; *** 1%.
Financial Development 1 (Fin.Dev1) is the sum of total external equity liability and debt liability.

More interestingly, if financial development increases by 10 percentage points, the impact of capital flows on reserve demand will be reduced by 11 per cent. Based on the results of our empirical analysis, we can also determine the threshold level of financial development around which the effects of capital flows on reserve accumulation are neutralized. To do this, we differentiate the model in equation 10 (in column 4) with respect to capital flows.

$$\frac{\Delta Reserves}{\Delta CapFlows} = 2.72 - 1.044 * FinDev$$

The threshold level of financial development is about 2.6, which is equivalent to 260 per cent of GDP in terms of access to international financial resources. This is indeed a high level of financial development. In our data, only Hong Kong and Singapore have such financial size and depth. Nonetheless, the threshold itself is not important. Rather, an essential implication is that the high level of financial sector development attenuates the impacts of capital flows on reserve accumulation.

6.1 Robustness check

To conduct a robustness check, we use domestic credit and market capitalization over GDP (DCMCAP) and domestic market liquidity (total stock value traded over GDP, SVT) as alternative proxies of financial development and resource mobilization for liquidity provision by the private sector. The results are presented in Table 6.2. We observe that the results are not quantitatively much different from our earlier findings. The coefficients of broad money, trade and the post-Asian crisis period dummy remain positive and significant. The interaction terms between capital flows and financial development are all negative and remain statistically significant. The results confirm our hypothesis that financial development attenuates the impact of capital flows on reserve accumulation. Based on the results, a 10 per cent increase in financial development reduces the impacts of capital flows on reserve accumulation by between 6 and 10 per cent.

7. Conclusion

This chapter has examined the motives for foreign reserve accumulation and analyzed the effects of capital flows and financial development on reserve demand in the Asian region. We have presented a model in which a state holds reserves to supply foreign exchange liquidity in underdeveloped financial markets. Our theoretical argument is that with the low capacity of the private sector to meet liquidity demand due to underdeveloped financial markets, the state plays a role in supplying additional liquidity. Thus, in our model, the development of the financial system weakens the monetary authority's motivation to hoard reserves for liquidity provision.

Using annual data for 12 East Asian economies between 1980 and 2009, our results confirm the presence of a precautionary motive and a financial stability motive in hoarding reserves. By using various measures of financial development, we also consistently found that financial sector development reduces the impacts of capital flows on reserve demand.

It is widely believed that a deep financial sector helps allocate resources efficiently. In extending this concept to precautionary reserve holdings to provide liquidity provision against shock, an important implication is that financial

Table 6.2 Robustness check with access to international market (external access)

	(1)	*(2)*
lnGDPPC	–0.114	–0.126
	(0.036)***	(0.048)**
lnM2	0.633	0.505
	(0.238)**	(0.172)**
lnTrade	0.683	0.636
	(0.084)***	(0.091)***
Evol	–4.506	–4.089
	(2.328)*	(2.34)
Kaopen	0.00	–0.02
	(0.04)	(0.05)
Capital inflows	2.523	1.79
	(0.692)***	(0.668)**
DCMCAP	–0.051	
	(0.09)	
Cap*DCMCAP	–0.59	
	(0.214)**	
SVT		0.186
		(0.100)*
Cap*SVT		–0.989
		(0.331)**
Observations	242	247
Country fixed effect	Yes	Yes
Year fixed effect	Yes	Yes
R-squared	0.88	0.87

Note: Robust standard errors in parentheses. Significance levels: * 10%; ** 5%; *** 1%.
DCMCAP is domestic credit and market capitalization over GDP while SVT is total stock value trade over GDP.

development could help reduce reserve demand due to capital flows and their macroeconomic consequences.

Our finding in this chapter suggests that an important part of a long-term policy in dealing with capital flows is the development of a deep and active financial sector. Also, as capital flows can be volatile and potentially have destabilizing effects on macroeconomic management, the policy recommendation in favour of financial sector development becomes even stronger.

Notes

1 Jeanne (2010).
2 Sterilization cost is the spread between interest paid on external borrowing and the returns from investment of reserves. For such costs, Rodrik (2006) provides an estimate of 1 per cent of GDP when the reserve level is 30 per cent of GDP.
3 China, Hong Kong, India, Indonesia, Japan, Korea, Malaysia, the Philippines, Singapore, Taiwan, Thailand and Vietnam.
4 1 unit increase in capital flows (a 100 percentage *point* increase) would lead to a 260 per cent increase in the reserves-to-GDP ratio. (See page 43, Chapter 2, of Wooldridge, *Introductory Econometrics: A Modern Approach*, second edition). In other words, 0.1 unit increase (a 10 percentage *point* increase) would lead to 26 per cent increase in reserves ratio.

References

Aghion, P., Angeletos, G.M., Banerjee, A. and Manova, K. (2005) 'Volatility and growth: credit constraints and productivity-enhancing investment', *NBER Working Paper* 11349.

Aghion, P., Bacchetta, P., Rancière, R. and Rogoff, K. (2009) 'Exchange rate volatility and productivity growth: the role of financial development', *Journal of Monetary Economics*, 56: 494–513.

Aizenman, J. and Lee, J. (2008) 'Financial versus monetary mercantilism: long-run view of large international reserves hoarding', *World Economy*, 31: 593–611.

Aizenman, J. and Marion, N. (2004) 'International reserve holdings with sovereign risk and costly tax collection', *The Economic Journal*, 114: 569–91.

Athukorala, P. and Rajapatirana, S. (2003) 'Capital inflows and the real exchange rate: a comparative study of Asia and Latin America', *The World Economy*, 26: 613–37.

de Beaufort Wijnholds, J.O. and Kapteyn, A. (2001) 'Reserve adequacy in emerging market economies', *IMF Working Paper* 01/43.

Beck, T. and Levine, R. (2004) 'Stock markets, banks, and growth: panel evidence', *Journal of Banking and Finance*, 28: 423–42.

Beck, T., Levine, R. and Loayza, N. (1999) 'Finance and the sources of growth', *Policy Research Working Paper Series* 2057, World Bank.

Bosworth, B.P., Collins, S.M. and Reinhart, C.M. (1999) 'Capital flows to developing economies: implications for saving and investment', *Brookings Papers on Economic Activity*: 143–80.

Caballero, R. and Panageas, S. (2005) 'Insurance and reserves management in a model of sudden stops', mimeo, MIT.

Calvo G.A. and Reinhart, C.M. (2002) 'Fear of floating', *The Quarterly Journal of Economics*, 117: 379–408.

Chinn, M. and Ito, H. (2008) 'A new measure of financial openness', *Journal of Comparative Policy Analysis: Research and Practice*, 10: 309–22.

Corden, W.M. (1993) *Economic Policy, Exchange Rates, and the International System*. Oxford: Oxford University Press.

Dooley, M., Folkerts-Landau, D. and Garber, P. (2004) 'The revived Bretton Woods system: the effects of periphery intervention and reserve management on interest rates and exchange rates in center countries', *NBER Working Paper* 10332.

Frankel, J. (2010) *Monetary Policy in Emerging Markets*. Amsterdam: Elsevier.

Frankel, J. and Jovanovic, B. (1981) 'Optimal international reserves: a stochastic framework', *The Economic Journal*, 91: 507–14.
Garcia, P. and Soto, C. (2006) 'Large hoarding of international reserves: are they worth it?' in R. Caballero, C. Calderon and L.F. Cespedes (eds) , *External Vulnerability and Preventive Policies*, Santiago: Central Bank of Chile.
Grenville, S. (2008) 'Central banks and capital flows', *Asian Development Bank Institute Discussion Paper* 87.
Holmström, B. and Tirole, J. (1998) 'Private and public supply of liquidity', *Journal of Political Economy*, 106: 1–40.
Hviding, K., Nowak, M. and Ricci, A. (2004) 'Can higher reserves help reduce exchange rate volatility?', *IMF Working Paper* 04/189.
Jeanne, O. (2010) 'Dealing with volatile capital flows', *Peterson Institute for International Economics Policy Brief* (July).
Jeanne, O. and Rancière, R. (2006) 'The optimal level of international reserves for emerging market countries: formulas and applications', *IMF Working Paper* 06/229.
Kaminsky, G. and Reinhart, C. (1999) 'The twin crises: the causes of banking and balance-of-payments problems', *American Economic Review*, 89: 473–500.
Kaminsky, G., Reinhart, C. and Végh, C. (2004) 'When it rains, it pours: procyclical capital flows and macroeconomic policies', *NBER Macroeconomics Annual*, 19: 11–53.
King, R.G. and Levine, R. (1993) 'Finance and growth: Schumpeter might be right', *The Quarterly Journal of Economics*, 108: 717–37.
Krishnamurthy, A. (2010) 'Amplification mechanisms in liquidity crises', *American Economic Journal: Macroeconomics*, 2: 1–30.
Lane, P.R. and Milesi-Ferretti, G.M. (2007) 'The external wealth of nations mark ii: revised and extended estimates of foreign assets and liabilities, 1970–2004', *Journal of International Economics*, 73: 223–50.
Levy-Yeyati, E. and Sturzenegger, F. (2006) 'Fear of floating in reverse: exchange rate policy in the 2000s', mimeo, Kennedy School of Government, Harvard University.
Mendoza, R.U. (2010) 'Was the Asian crisis a wake-up call?: Foreign reserves as self-protection', *Journal of Asian Economics*, 21: 1–19.
Mendoza, E.G. and Terrones, M. (2008) *An Anatomy of Credit Booms: Evidence from Macro Aggregates and Micro Data*, Cambridge, Mass.: National Bureau of Economic Research.
Mileva, E. (2008) *The Impact of Capital Flows on Domestic Investment in Transition Economies*, Frankfurt am Main: European Central Bank.
Mody, A. and Murshid, A.P. (2005) 'Growing up with capital flows', *Journal of International Economics*, 65: 249–66.
Mulder, C.B. and Bussière, M. (1999) 'External vulnerability in emerging market economies – how high liquidity can offset weak fundamentals and the effects of contagion', *IMF Working Paper* 99/88.
Obstfeld, M., Shambaugh, J. and Taylor, A. (2010) 'Financial stability, the trilemma, and international reserves', *American Economic Journal: Macroeconomics*, 2: 57–94.
Ötker-Robe, I., Polaski, Z., Topf, B. and Vávra, D. (2007) 'Coping with capital inflows: experiences of selected European countries', Washington, DC: International Monetary Fund.

Pineau, G., Dorrucci, E., Comelli, F. and Lagerblom, A. (2006) 'The accumulation of foreign reserves', *Occasional Paper Series*, 43, European Central Bank.

Pontines, V. and Rajan, R.S. (2011) 'Foreign exchange market intervention and reserve accumulation in emerging Asia: is there evidence of fear of appreciation?', *Economics Letters*, 111: 252–5.

Pontines, V. and Yongqiang, L. (2010) 'Regime dependence, Mrs. Machlup's wardrobe and the accumulation of international reserves in Asia', *Economics Letters*, 110: 231–4.

Raddatz, C. (2006) 'Liquidity needs and vulnerability to financial underdevelopment', *Journal of Financial Economics*, 80: 677–722.

Reinhart, C.M. and Rogoff, K. (2008) 'This time is different: a panoramic view of eight centuries of financial crises', *NBER Working Paper* 13882

Reinhart, C.M. and Reinhart, V. (2008) *Capital Flow Bonanzas: An Encompassing View of the Past and Present*, Cambridge, Mass.: National Bureau of Economic Research.

Rodrik, D. (2006) 'The social cost of foreign exchange reserves', *International Economic Journal*, 20: 253–66.

Rodrik, D. and Velasco, A. (1999) 'Short-term capital flows', *NBER Working Paper* 7364.

Saborowski, C. (2009) *Capital Inflows and the Real Exchange Rate: Can Financial Development Cure the Dutch Disease?*, Washington, DC: International Monetary Fund.

Schadler, S. (2008) 'Managing large capital inflows: taking stock of international experiences', *Asian Development Bank Institute Discussion Paper* 97.

Srinivasan, N., Mahambare, V. and Ramachandran, M. (2009) 'Preference asymmetry and international reserve accretion in India', *Applied Economics Letters*, 16: 1543–6.

Surico, P. (2008) 'Measuring the time inconsistency of US monetary policy', *Economica*, 75: 22–38.

Appendix A
The analytical model of reserve demand

A.1 The private sector

The economy in the model consists of two typical periods: t and t + 1. The exchange rate on date t + 1 is expressed as follows

$$e_{t+1} = e(\theta) = \alpha\theta \,, \tag{1}$$

where e is the foreign currency price of the domestic currency, and θ reflects the future state of the economy. Higher values of θ indicate more favourable states of the economy. Economic agents in the domestic economy have divergent views of the fundamental that will materialize in period t + 1. For a given θ, agents i expect that the fundamental will be $\theta + \varepsilon$, where the noise, ε_i, is uniformly distributed over the interval $[-\bar{\varepsilon}, \bar{\varepsilon}]$ and $\theta - \varepsilon_i > 0$. $i \in [0, 1]$ indexes domestic agents who are all risk neutral.

Assume that there is a liquidity shock – in other words, a sudden stop or capital flow reversal – which increases the demand for foreign currency and, for simplicity, that foreigners are not willing to hold the home currency at any price. In this case, the exchange rate will be determined by the exchange market involving only domestic residents, domestic financial institutions and the home monetary authority. We also assume that the monetary authority can prevent domestic interest rates from fully offsetting expected exchange rate changes, or that the increase in interest rate per se is so damaging to financial stability that home residents discount it. Transaction costs and interest gains that could potentially be earned from the currency position are ignored for simplicity here. In such circumstances, people fundamentally care about the exchange rate in period t + 1, compared with the exchange rate in period t. If θ is very low and the economic consequence from a liquidity shock is expected to continue when the financial market cannot function to fully offset the liquidity demand, then the average market forecast is for continuing home currency weakness. Domestic agents, however, hold divergent views on how weak the currency will be.

Assume that domestic agents hold a domestic liquid asset (that is, a bank deposit), the size of which is proportional to total liquid asset l_t at period t claimed by all domestic agents, and which can be sold for foreign exchange.

Banks' assets, however, are illiquid. Thus, if domestic agents liquidate their liquid asset, financial institutions can repay domestic residents only if they can mobilize resources domestically or internationally to fully meet liquidity demands or the domestic monetary authority intervenes to supply additional liquidity.

Given the assumptions, domestic agent i would trade the home currency for foreign exchange if the home currency is expected to fall from its current level, or

$$E_t\{e_{t+1} / (\theta + \varepsilon_i)\} = \alpha(\theta + \varepsilon_i) \le e_t . \tag{2}$$

For a given date, t, and exchange rate, e_t, the measure of agents such that

$$\alpha(\theta + \varepsilon_i) \le e_t, \text{ or } \varepsilon_i \le (e_t / \alpha) - \theta, \text{ is } \frac{1}{2\bar{\varepsilon}} \int_{-\bar{\varepsilon}}^{(\frac{e_t}{\alpha}) - \theta} dx = \frac{1}{2\bar{\varepsilon}} (\bar{\varepsilon} + \frac{e_t}{\alpha} - \theta). \tag{3}$$

Therefore, at date t, the demand for foreign exchange in terms of the home currency as a result of liquidity demand shock is

$$l_t^d = \frac{l_t}{2\bar{\varepsilon}} (\bar{\varepsilon} + \frac{e_t}{\alpha} - \theta), \tag{4}$$

where l_t^d is the total demand for foreign exchange liquidity.

A.2 Private liquidity supply

From here, we depart from Obstfeld's framework by introducing private liquidity supply. The financial institutions will coordinate to supply liquidity, the amount of which depends on the capacity of the financial sector to mobilize resources domestically or internationally to meet the liquidity demand. In this regard, the net liquidity demand is

$$l_t^d - l_t^s, \tag{5}$$

where l_t^s is the liquidity supply coordinated by all private financial institutions. If λ_t, for which $0 < \lambda < 1$ captures the level of the financial sector's ability to coordinate liquidity supply, $l_t^s = \lambda_t l_t^d$. Equation 5 can be rewritten as

$$(1 - \lambda_t) \frac{l_t}{2\bar{\varepsilon}} (\bar{\varepsilon} + \frac{e_t}{\alpha} - \theta). \tag{6}$$

Equation 6 implies that the level of financial development partly determines the net liquidity demand. Higher capacity to coordinate resources for liquidity supply would help offset the liquidity demand.

A.3 Public liquidity provision and central banks' reaction function

The central bank is assumed to intervene in the foreign exchange market to minimize the following intertemporal criterion

$$\min_{R_{t+1}} E_t\left\{L_t + \delta L_{t+1}\right\},$$

where δ is the discount factor and L_t is the loss function at period t. In specifying the function, we follow Surico (2008) and specifically Srinivasan *et al.* (2009) whose function captures the asymmetric preference on exchange rate stability. This is supported by the argument that emerging economies "fear floating" (see, for example, Calvo and Reinhart, 2002). Levy-Yeyati and Sturzenegger (2006) conjectured that exchange rate policy has evolved towards an apparent "fear of floating in reverse" or "fear of appreciation" whereby interventions have been aimed at limiting appreciation rather than depreciations. Pontines and Rajan (2011) confirm the existence of the asymmetry in central bank foreign exchange intervention responses to currency appreciation versus depreciation in India, Korea, the Philippines, Singapore, Thailand and Indonesia. In this regard, the monetary reaction function is

$$L_{t+1} = \frac{1}{2}\left(R_{t+1} - R^*\right)^2 + \frac{\beta}{2}\left\{\left(e_{t+1} - e^*\right)^2 + \frac{\gamma}{3}\left(e_{t+1} - e^*\right)^3\right\} \tag{7}$$

where $\beta > 0$ is the relative weight and γ is the asymmetric preference parameter on exchange rate stability. Here, R^* and e^* are the optimal level of foreign reserves and the target exchange rate, respectively. We express the reaction function in period t + 1 because we will later assume that the exchange rate at period t is the central bank's target rate. The loss function departs from the standard quadratic form in that policymakers are allowed to treat differently the rate of appreciating and depreciating pressure. It should be noticed that if $\gamma = 0$, the loss function becomes symmetric. If $\gamma > 0$, equation 13 implies that the rate of appreciation is weighted more heavily than the rate of depreciation.

In other words, if $\dfrac{\partial L_{t+1}}{\partial e_{t+1}} = \beta\left[e_{t+1} - e^* + \dfrac{\gamma}{2}\left(e_{t+1} - e^*\right)^2\right] > 0$

the exchange rate appreciation would increase the policymaker's loss.

Furthermore, since we take into account the central bank's motives for foreign exchange market intervention, it is assumed that the exchange rate depreciation/appreciation can be reduced by the central bank's intervention. That is,

$$e_{t+1} - e^* = a_0 + a_1 R_{t+1} + \epsilon_{t+1}, \tag{8}$$

where $a_1 > 0$ and ϵ_{t+1} are the error terms with zero mean and variance σ_ϵ^2. Minimizing equation 7 subject to equation 8 leads to the following intervention reaction function of the central bank

$$0 = R_{t+1} - R^* + \frac{\beta}{2} E_t\left[2a_1(e_{t+1} - e^*) + \gamma a_1\left(e_{t+1} - e^*\right)^2\right]. \tag{9}$$

Suppose that a central bank's optimal level of reserves is equal to the net liquidity demand in period t as expressed in equation 6. In other words, given the economic fundamentals, and with the underdeveloped financial market, the central bank would hold the necessary precautionary reserves to supply additional liquidity by selling R in foreign reserves, which is measured in foreign currency. Indeed, for emerging economies with a thin domestic bond market and shallow financial system, there might be no practical short-run means of managing the exchange rate other than reserve sales. The optimal level of reserves for the economy's central bank in period t is then given by

$$\frac{R^*}{e_t} = (1-\lambda_t)\frac{L}{2\bar{\varepsilon}}(\bar{\varepsilon} + \frac{e_t}{\alpha} - \theta). \tag{10}$$

Also, we assume that the exchange rate at period t is the target exchange rate aimed for by the central bank – that is, $e_t = e^*$. Thus, equation 15 can be transformed as

$$R_{t+1} = (1-\lambda_t)\frac{L_t}{2\bar{\varepsilon}}e_t\left(\bar{\varepsilon} + \frac{e_t}{\alpha} - \theta\right) + \frac{\beta}{2}E_t\left\{2a_1(\Delta e_t) + \gamma a_1(\Delta e_t)^2\right\}. \tag{11}$$

Equation 11 indicates that the reserve accumulation is influenced by the expected liquidity demand, the fundamentals of the economy, the central bank's target exchange rate, its preference on exchange rate fluctuation and the level of financial development. If the capacity of the financial market is high (high value of λ) then pressure on the currency would be smaller (small net liquidity demand), which requires less intervention by the government. Equation 11 could also partly explain why reserve levels in countries with a preference on exchange rate stability can be rather high.

Suppose there is a bad realization of θ, which causes a liquidity shock, and therefore pressure on the home currency as people liquidate their assets to speculate in foreign exchange. With the underdeveloped financial market, which cannot fully coordinate to meet the full liquidity demand, the monetary authority will then exercise its "lender-of last-resort" role by using its reserves to moderate the exchange rate fall. This is motivated by the central bank's desire to limit exchange rate volatility and to avoid a currency crisis. Nevertheless, with a huge liquidity demand shock, the pressure on the exchange rate will be greater and will require a bigger intervention if the economy's financial development is low.

Similarly, suppose there is upward pressure on the exchange rate as a result of capital inflows. The monetary authority with a preference on exchange rate stability would intervene by buying foreign currency and end up with reserve accumulation. If the financial sector is developed enough to efficiently allocate resources to productive investment rather than consumption, or to efficiently intermediate capital outflows to offset inflows, the intervention in the foreign exchange market by the central bank is less necessary. Less intervention should partly reduce the central bank's motivation to hoard reserves.

The model provides implications not only for the central bank's liquidity provision, but also for the active management of liquidity by the central bank that values macroeconomic and financial stability. Put simply, the role of states in easing illiquidity and providing liquidity increases when financial markets are underdeveloped and cannot fully guarantee liquidity during shocks. In other words, an open economy with less developed financial markets is expected to accumulate more reserves to ensure liquidity while limiting exchange rate and macroeconomic volatility. This implies that the motivation to hoard reserves could be mitigated partly by developing a deep financial sector. This theoretical framework provides the basis for the following empirical investigation.

Appendix B

B.1 List of economies in the sample

China, Hong Kong, India, Indonesia, Japan, Korea, Malaysia, Singapore, the Philippines, Taiwan, Thailand, Vietnam.

Table 6.B1 List of variables, definition and data source

Variables	*Definition*	*Source*
lnGDPPC	GDP per capita	World Development Indicators
lnM2	M2 over GDP	World Development Indicators
lnTrade	Export plus import over GDP	World Development Indicators
Exchange rate volatility	Annual standard deviation of monthly change in exchange rate	Authors' calculation based on exchange rates from IFS, IMF
Capital inflows (Hot money)	The sum of current account and net FDI inflows over GDP	Calculation based on data from IFS, IMF
Financial development	Total equity liability plus total debt liability over GDP	(Lane and Milesi-Ferretti, 2007). Updated until 2009
DCMCAP	Domestic credit and market capitalization over GDP	World Development Indicators
SVT	Total stock value traded over GDP	World Development Indicators
Financial openness	Chinn–Ito index (2008)	http://web.pdx.edu/~ito/Chinn-Ito_website.htm

Table 6.B2 Summary statistics

Variable	*Obs*	*Mean*	*Std Dev.*	*Min.*	*Max.*
ln(Reserves/GDP)	334	2.673	1.150	–0.724	4.799
lnGDPPC	359	7.914	1.574	4.576	10.645
lnM2	339	4.302	0.670	2.065	5.490
lnTrade	353	4.336	0.882	2.514	6.082
FX volatility	359	0.025	0.070	0.000	0.835
Financial openness	355	0.691	1.605	–1.844	2.478
Capital inflows	358	0.051	0.095	–0.086	0.469
Financial development	340	0.775	0.975	0.000	5.299
DCMCAP	242	2.099	1.346	0.289	7.416
SVT	252	0.623	0.868	0.000	7.558

7 Defining openness and economic interconnection in East and Southeast Asia

Tony Cavoli[1]

1. Introduction

The extent and magnitude of economic interconnections between countries – particularly in Asia – is an area of immense scholarly and policy debate. One of the most notable strands of this debate relates to the implications of economic interconnections for the creation of furthering economic ties between nations, either through trade and investment accords, regional integration initiatives (such as the Chiang Mai initiative) or indeed through the creation of closer monetary ties (see Rajan, 2008).

However, for such discussions to effectively bear fruit, there needs to be some consensus regarding the related questions of how to measure the extent of interconnection and what factors drive it. It is well known that there are a vast number of ways to measure the degree of integration, alternatively known as openness, or economic "interconnectedness", and that these measures individually only really highlight one or two salient characteristics of what one might regard as the total integration landscape for a country or a region. Some of the characteristics are financial, some real, some relate to labour movements, others to the convergence of institutions.

This chapter takes a multivariate view of measuring integration and presents an exploration of the extent of openness and interconnectedness in Asia by employing some of the better known measures of integration. Our focus will be to highlight bilateral and regional integration, but we will also examine some stylised facts regarding countries' openness by presenting some country aggregates. By using many measures, one should be able to investigate the extent to which an individual measure contributes to the overall level of integration. While each measure may not be perfect (after all, this is why there is such a large literature on each individual measure of real or financial integration), and while the list of measures adopted here may not be exhaustive, there is much value in gaining information about the level of integration in the region. This has significant policy implications about how, for instance, to orient policies of liberalization of both trade and finance and for the possibility of a future Asian monetary union. The countries that we will focus on here are the ASEAN+3 countries for the period 2000–09.

The measures presented in this chapter are summaries relating to two categories of integration – real and financial – in the spirit of using multiple measures. Perhaps surprisingly, there appears to be very little work of this type in this area – scholarly research preferring, it would appear, to pursue the option of refining individual measures rather than examining the interaction of individual measures in an attempt to ascertain a broader perspective of integration in the Asian region. This chapter does not deal with the measures of integration that take on political dimensions – such as the removal of trade barriers or capital controls, or the imposition of trade or investment agreements – which are in many respects the traditional way of assessing economic integration, as captured by the first three of Balassa's five stages of integration (Balassa, 1961). The issue of separating the political, or policy dimensions, and the economic characteristics has an analogy in the literature on regional economic integration. The term "regionalism" refers to integration efforts that are derived from policy, such as those stated above. "Regionalization", on the other hand, refers to integration that is measured by and reflected in economic data such as trade shares, investment flows and arbitrage conditions (see Pomfret, 2011). This chapter takes the latter approach and attempts to uncover whether countries are integrated though the behaviour of economic variables, and to provide some motivation about what might be possible if one takes a multivariate view of assessing economic interconnections.

This chapter is structured as follows: the next section provides a brief overview of the ways of measuring economic closeness and integration – focusing generally on the measures used in later sections of the paper. Some measures using country aggregates are also shown here for the purposes of illustrating the extent of openness for individual countries in Asia. Section 3 presents the data and methodology relating to the measures of bilateral and regional integration. Section 4 discusses the results and shows what it is possible to uncover when utilizing a multivariate approach to assessing economic interconnections. Section 5 presents some concluding remarks.

2. A note on measuring openness and integration

The measurement of the degree of economic integration takes on many dimensions; real versus financial, price based versus quantity based, regional versus global, and the list goes on. Below is a very brief summary of the main themes that emerge in the literature devoted to measuring openness and economic integration. The first is trade openness, defined in basic terms as possessing real and quantity dimensions. This particular measure picks up the real dimension of economic integration and examines the importance of the flow of goods and services in and out of a particular country.[2] There are many ways of calculating this measure, but generally speaking, we can measure it either in bilateral or regional terms (the next section will present one such measure), or indeed as a country aggregate. As such, and by way of establishing some stylised facts, Figure 7.1 presents the country level trade openness, measured as (imports +

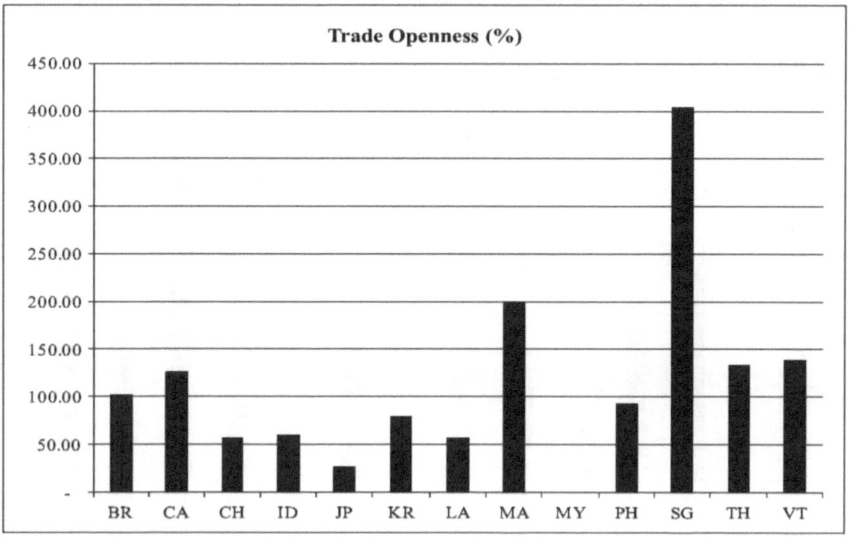

Figure 7.1 Trade openness

Source: World Development Indicators

exports)/GDP for the ASEAN+3 countries. The countries exhibiting a high level of openness are self-evident, with Singapore and Malaysia the highest and the larger economies of Japan, China and Korea among the lowest. It is typical (with particular regard to this measure) that countries with high GDPs will return lower ratios, and this is found to be the case here.

There are many different ways of measuring financial integration. The first is price-based measures such as covered, uncovered and real interest parity. While the literature on these measures is vast, it is worth noting that real interest parity is essentially made up of uncovered interest parity (UIP), purchasing power parity (PPP) and the Fisher effect (see Cavoli and Rajan, 2009), thus potentially capturing both real (PPP) and financial (UIP) elements of integration. The second measure relates to quantity-based measures and includes such measures as capital flows and capital openness. Figure 7.2 presents the capital flows/GDP ratio for each of the ASEAN+3 nations. In many respects, we are witnessing a repeat of the story from Figure 7.1, with Singapore and Malaysia (but also Vietnam and Thailand) showing higher values and both the larger and poorer economies revealing lower ratios.

Other quantity-based measures also include savings/investment correlations (Feldstein and Horioka, 1980). The intuition here is that in a closed economy, by definition, savings must equal investment (i.e. the correlation between savings and investment should be very high). At the other extreme, in highly integrated capital markets with a single world interest rate, domestic investment should be largely independent of domestic savings since the former can be financed via

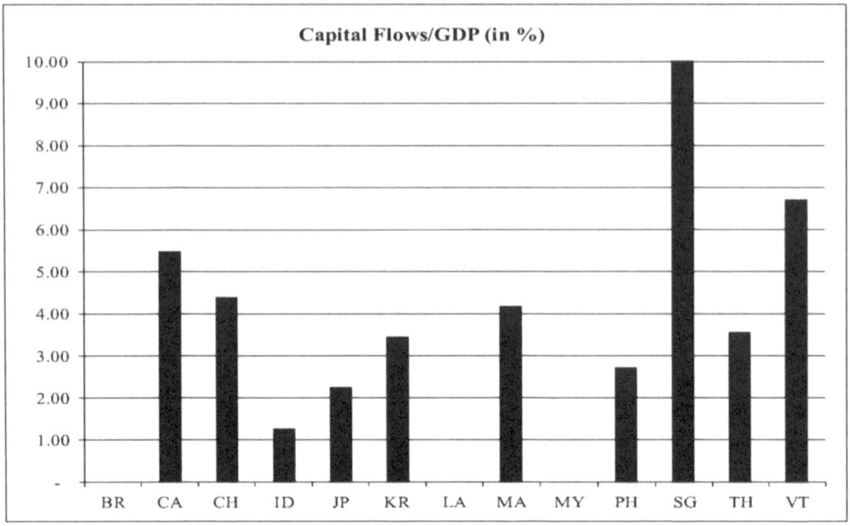

Figure 7.2 Capital flows/GDP

Source: World Development Indicators

foreign savings. Another relates to consumption correlations (Obstfeld, 1989). A high level of correlation of consumption between two economies is an indication that each country is accessing the same capital market to choose a time path for consumption that is outside of the path implied by available domestic resources. This implies that there is access or openness to international capital flows.[3]

A third way of measuring financial integration might be categorized as regulatory and/or institutional and might include regulatory measures designed to curb international capital flows (or indeed the liberalization of capital flows through the removal of capital controls) and stock market co-movements. Figure 7.3 presents, for each ASEAN+3 country, the well-known Chinn–Ito index of capital liberalization. While the quantity-based measures shown in Figures 7.1 and 7.2 tend to disadvantage countries with big incomes and or small trade/financial flows, the Chinn–Ito index does not. As such, Singapore remains highly open under this measure but Japan, China, Laos, Myanmar and Vietnam are said to be less integrated.

As mentioned in the previous section, this chapter presents an examination of economic interconnection that attempts to use multiple measures. It is worth noting at this point that attempts have been made to find a multivariate measure of integration. Takagi and Hirose (2001) and de Browuer (1999) have employed techniques that combine various measures of financial integration and reduce them to one measure. Chinn and Ito (2008) have also created a very well-known index of capital mobility/financial openness. The advantage of these techniques is that they capture the breadth of available measures of integration – information

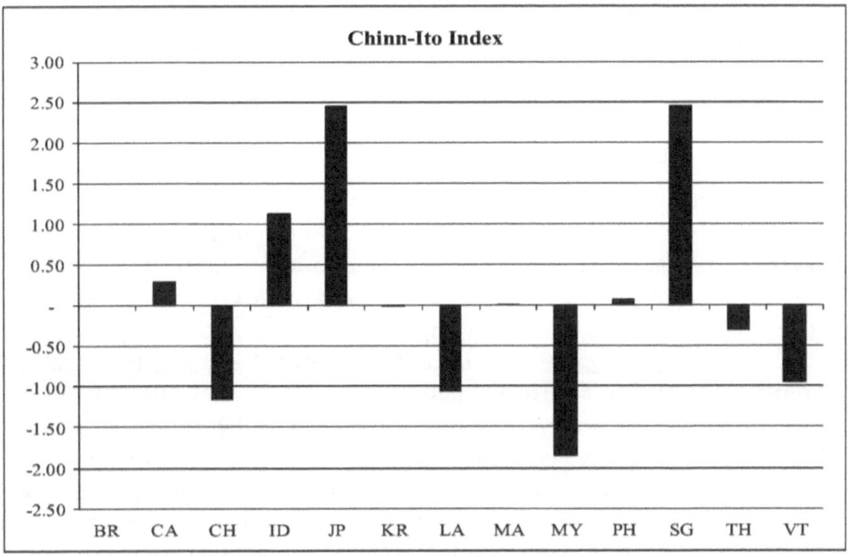

Figure 7.3 Chinn–Ito index

Source: World Development Indicators

is not simply lost by virtue of the non-employment of a measure. As such, the next section presents the measures that will be employed to calculate economic integration on a bilateral and regional basis. The measures have their roots in the above discussion and represent real and financial as well as price and quantity dimensions.

3. Data and measures

Having set the scene with a discussion of the broad measures of openness and interconnection, and established some stylized facts, we can now turn to measuring bilateral integration. We employ four measures in this study. Two measures are essentially quantity based – business cycle correlations (BCS) and trade openness. The other two measures are price based, namely deviations from relative PPP and deviations from UIP. A brief description of each of the measures proposed is given by the following. The first is a measure of the synchronicity of business cycles as captured by GDP correlations between country i and country/region j[4]

$$BCS(ij) = \rho_{GDPi,GDPj}, \qquad (1)$$

where *GDPi* is the annual growth rate of GDP for country *i*. The correlation coefficient is calculated from 12 monthly observations. A higher value implies greater integration, as it would suggest that the pair of countries for which the correlation is taken can be subject to, and react in the same way to, common shocks. We know from optimal currency area (OCA) literature of the importance of BCS in providing a signal for the plausibility of a regional zone of fixed exchange rates.

The second measure is given by the deviations from relative PPP (RPPD) between country *i* and country/region *j*. This is given by

$$\text{RPPD(ij)} = \text{ABS}(\Delta e_t^{d/f} + \pi_t^{f} - \pi_t^{d}) \tag{2}$$

where e_t is the nominal exchange rate at time *t* and π_t^f (π_t^d) refers to the foreign (domestic) inflation rate at time *t*. Here, a smaller value implies greater integration as the law of one price, with respect to goods prices, is more likely to hold. The absolute value is taken since, from the point of view of providing some assessment of integration, sign is less important than the distance from zero – one can have a large negative or a large positive RPPD and still be more or less equally connected to a partner country. Empirically, studies using PPP have enjoyed mixed success as a measure of integration. For the most part, recent testing of PPP has employed estimators favouring long run equilibrium relationships, (see Cavoli and Rajan, 2009). From the point of view of capturing the salient characteristics of integration, PPP assumes a degree of importance in extracting aspects of price convergence not picked up by other measures.

The third measure is trade openness or intensity (TI) between country *i* and country/region *j* as given by

$$\text{TI(ij)} = T_{ij}/T_{ALL} \tag{3}$$

where T_{ij} is the trade (exports plus imports) between country *i* and *j* and T_{ALL} is all trade recorded for each country pair within the sample examined (not double counted). As with its country aggregate counterpart, we scale the trade flows, here with T_{ALL} rather than GDP. A higher value means greater integration as it implies that trade between the country/region pair examined occupies a greater share of total trade in the region. Many other versions of trade intensity measures exist (see for example Imbs, 2006), where the measures effectively control for size effects (either in trade terms or GDP). The TI measure benefits from being simple to calculate and also has the virtue of providing a very clear and visible interpretation – the number presented reveals simply what proportion of total regional trade occurs between *i* and *j*. The cost of this simplicity is that larger country TI's more than likely exhibit an upward bias in their measure. This issue is partly addressed by normalizing the data – a procedure discussed below. The final measure here is given by deviations from UIP[5] between country *i* and country/region *j*. This is measured by

$$\text{UIP(ij)} = \text{ABS}(i_t^{d} - i_t^{f} - \Delta e_{t+1}^{d/f}), \tag{4}$$

where i_t^d *and* i_t^f refer to domestic and foreign interest rates respectively and $\Delta e_{t+1}^{d/f}$ refers to the expected rate of depreciation. A lower value implies greater integration between two countries or regions as the law of one price, with respect to financial assets, is more likely to apply. Like RPPD, absolute values are taken, and like RPPD, the literature on whether UIP holds is mixed (see de Brouwer, 1999; Chinn, 2006; Cavoli and Rajan, 2009). Like PPP, UIP is quite sensitive to econometric specification, time horizons used and the method by which expectations are captured in the estimates. However, UIP is underpinned by sound economic reasoning about the equalization of asset returns that provide information about the potential openness of economies, and can capture aspects of economic interconnections that other measures do not.

The objective is to use data that are readily and publically available so as to provide an easily estimated overall measure. Given the countries examined, these measures lend themselves appropriately as ways to ascertain the degree of integration between countries and regions because they are simple and easy to comprehend, data are readily available and, in the case of the parity conditions, they are underpinned by economic intuition about agent behaviour.

The main data source is the international integration statistics database of the ADB's Asia Recovery Integration Center[6], except for the data used to calculate the UIP and RPPP measures, which are from the International Monetary Fund's *International Financial Statistics*. The sample selected in this instance are data from 2000–09.

We employ the measures in the following way. For example, we can measure the extent of Indonesia's integration with, say, Malaysia by observing each measure *individually* between the two countries. We also measure Indonesia's integration with the other countries in the sample and therefore create a measure of a country's regional integration (i.e. the result of its bilateral integration with all other countries). We do this by calculating each measure with the other 12 countries bilaterally and then taking the average of these bilateral measures. Obviously, to derive the level of integration between a particular country and the region of which it is a member, the country is left out of the members group.

Once we have analyzed the individual measures of integration, we can create a measure of "overall" integration by imposing a cumulative normal distribution on all of the measures, such that they all map on to the same distribution. The normalized individual measures are then summed to create an overall measure. Each measure of integration against the defined regional groupings (as defined above) have been normalized to return a value between 0 and 1, where 0 represents the least integrated and 1 represents the most integrated. Prior to making these transformations, the UIP and RPPD are inverted such that a larger value now implies more integrated. Each value is then simply summed to present an overall measure of integration for each country against the regional groupings. Undertaking this process is important for two main reasons. First, it was possible to compare the raw measures across countries as normalization facilitates comparison across measures. For example, the comparison of, say, a raw UIP with a raw TI for a particular currency pair is difficult, but if the normalized UIP and TI values are 0.8 and 0.9 (80th and 90th percentile), it tells the reader immediately that each measure occupies roughly the same region in the distribution for this particular currency pair – indicating a high level of integration for both measures. The second reason for normalizing is to reduce the scale effects inherent in each measure. For instance, for UIP or RPPD, the figure returned could be anything above 0 (obviously depending on the extent of the deviation in each parity condition). Even once UIP and RPPD are inverted to return a larger value for higher integration, the range of values is infinite. Thus, normalizing essentially flattens the possible effects of scale of each measure by returning a figure between 0 and 1.[7]

4. Results

Table 7.1 presents the extent of bilateral integration for each measure – the highlighted numbers show some potentially interesting results. From Table 7.1a we can see that the level of BCS is high for Malaysia and the Philippines, Singapore and Thailand. The BCS for Japan–Philippines and Japan–Thailand is also high. The RPPD results in Table 7.1b also reveal a high level of integration (low RPPD) for pairings involving Malaysia and the Philippines. The same is found for the UIP measures in Table 7.1c and, albeit to a lesser extent, the trade intensity in Table 7.1d.

When one observes the quantity-based measure, TI intensity, the higher levels of integration occur in the larger economies of Japan, China and Korea. This possibly emphasizes the importance of size on trade flows as exposed by the particular measure employed in this chapter. We can see this effect most emphatically in the case of TI in Table 7.1c for the Japan–China, Japan–Korea and China–Korea pairings. The results for FI and PI also show that these pairs are significant but, additionally, reveal Singapore as an important source of openness when paired with the larger economies – notably Japan.

Table 7.2 presents the measure of the extent of integration of each country to the whole sample. It does this for each individual measure. To calculate this, we take the average of each country's bilateral integration for each measure. For the business cycle correlations, we see that that the ASEAN5 countries, especially Singapore, Malaysia and the Philippines, as well as Japan, are highly connected to the sample group. It is typically the ASEAN5 group that returns the lowest RPPP and UIP scores (indicating higher connections). For the trade intensity scores, it is the larger economies that, unsurprisingly, are better connected through trade flows.

We can also reveal, for each country, the Top 5 interconnections by measure. These are given in Table 7.3. A couple of observations stand out. The first is that the ASEAN5 group, especially Malaysia and Singapore, appear in individual countries' Top 5 more often than others. The second is that, outside the ASEAN5 group, Japan appears most often and across all of the measures utilized. This is a solid indicator of the role of Japan, and the major centre of Singapore, as a conduit for integration in the region. It is very clear from this table that the ASEAN5 group are the most connected through RPPD and UIP, which are manifestations of the law of one price. The large economies – Japan, China and Korea – are not as well connected generally. The areas where there is some evidence of integration are in the

Table 7.1a Business cycle synchronisation

	BR	*CA*	*CH*	*ID*	*JP*	*KR*	*LA*	*MA*	*MY*	*PH*	*SG*	*TH*	*VT*
BR	–												
CA	–8.44%	–											
PRC	–16.33%	61.57%	–										
ID	–59.60%	40.96%	78.27%	–									
JP	23.43%	66.44%	38.12%	32.90%	–								
KR	51.13%	–5.83%	0.79%	6.56%	71.33%	–							
LAO	–10.79%	38.46%	78.91%	76.90%	20.78%	–3.67%	–						
MA	–14.43%	40.08%	56.91%	59.60%	85.04%	63.82%	77.84%	–					
MY	–10.63%	42.34%	–3.09%	32.81%	66.07%	–1.03%	17.38%	62.59%	–				
PH	–10.16%	48.11%	58.69%	65.29%	85.69%	60.86%	59.76%	93.93%	48.98%	–			
SG	5.62%	64.11%	55.29%	61.15%	84.40%	63.36%	58.19%	87.67%	62.59%	94.82%	–		
TH	32.89%	32.52%	31.98%	24.68%	88.65%	57.88%	31.58%	90.77%	68.39%	81.87%	74.90%	–	
VT	5.27%	88.79%	74.24%	47.01%	82.61%	39.97%	55.52%	78.01%	13.30%	75.77%	75.84%	74.36%	–

Source: Cavoli 2012

Table 7.1b Relative PPP deviations

	BR	*CA*	*CH*	*ID*	*JP*	*KR*	*LA*	*MA*	*MY*	*PH*	*SG*	*TH*	*VT*
BR	–												
CA	0.09	–											
CH	0.13	0.42	–										
ID	0.33	0.01	0.80	–									
JP	0.24	0.32	0.25	0.31	–								
KR	0.37	0.02	0.56	0.21	0.11	–							
LA	0.29	0.18	0.46	0.14	0.68	0.26	–						
MA	0.12	0.11	0.30	0.11	0.21	0.07	0.27	–					
MY	1.69	1.38	0.28	1.50	1.68	1.70	1.28	1.51	–				
PH	0.01	0.09	0.49	0.08	0.23	0.12	0.29	0.02	1.52	–			
SG	0.04	0.13	0.26	0.12	0.19	0.08	0.31	0.02	1.52	0.04	–		
TH	0.03	0.06	0.27	0.05	0.26	0.12	0.22	0.05	1.51	0.03	0.07	–	
VT	0.13	0.07	0.51	0.13	0.32	0.35	0.20	0.17	1.35	0.14	0.18	0.12	–

Source: Cavoli 2012

Table 7.1c UIP deviations

	BR	*CA*	*CH*	*ID*	*JP*	*KR*	*LA*	*MA*	*MY*	*PH*	*SG*	*TH*	*VT*
BR	–												
CA	0.15	–											
CH	0.30	0.28	–										
ID	0.11	0.23	0.05	–									
JP	0.07	0.09	0.35	0.33	–								
KR	0.11	0.04	0.18	0.19	0.17	–							
LA	1.33	1.55	1.25	1.16	1.70	1.24	–						
MA	0.08	0.15	0.14	0.06	0.16	0.11	1.30	–					
MY	0.70	0.77	0.48	0.60	0.85	0.80	0.68	0.65	–				
PH	0.60	0.32	0.04	0.09	0.41	0.28	1.15	0.19	0.45	–			
SG	0.09	0.09	0.16	0.14	0.19	0.02	1.33	0.04	0.69	0.23	–		
TH	0.20	0.14	0.16	0.14	0.18	0.02	1.39	0.04	0.68	0.22	0.00	–	
VT	0.13	0.01	0.12	0.01	0.20	0.22	1.40	0.02	0.59	0.16	0.08	0.09	–

Source: Cavoli 2012

Table 7.1d Trade openness

	BR	*CA*	*PRC*	*ID*	*JP*	*KR*	*LAO*	*MA*	*MY*	*PH*	*SG*	*TH*	*VT*
BR	–												
CA	0.02%	–											
PRC	0.04%	0.04%	–										
ID	0.12%	0.01%	1.88%	–									
JP	0.32%	0.01%	23.08%	3.74%	–								
KR	0.11%	0.01%	12.76%	1.42%	9.07%	–							
LAO	0.00%	0.02%	0.02%	0.00%	0.00%	0.01%	–						
MA	0.05%	0.01%	3.34%	0.96%	4.12%	1.43%	0.00%	–					
MY	0.00%	0.00%	0.19%	0.02%	0.05%	0.04%	0.00%	0.05%	–				
PH	0.00%	0.00%	1.45%	0.20%	2.15%	0.70%	0.00%	0.58%	0.00%	–			
SG	0.08%	0.07%	3.26%	1.51%	4.30%	1.31%	0.08%	3.16%	0.22%	0.71%	–		
TH	0.05%	0.07%	2.65%	0.75%	4.91%	0.83%	0.15%	1.62%	0.31%	0.46%	0.83%	–	
VT	0.00%	0.05%	1.18%	0.18%	1.09%	0.61%	0.03%	0.31%	0.01%	0.13%	0.64%	0.40%	–

Source: Cavoli 2012

Table 7.2 Average regional integration by measure

	BR	*CA*	*CH*	*ID*	*JP*	*KR*	*LA*	*MA*	*MY*	*PH*	*SG*	*TH*	*VT*
BCS	–1%	42%	43%	39%	62%	34%	42%	65%	33%	64%	66%	58%	59%
RPPD	0.27	0.22	0.36	0.29	0.37	0.30	0.35	0.23	1.30	0.23	0.23	0.22	0.28
UIP	0.30	0.29	0.27	0.24	0.36	0.26	1.19	0.23	0.61	0.32	0.23	0.25	0.23
Trade	0.07%	0.03%	4.16%	0.90%	4.40%	2.36%	0.03%	1.30%	0.07%	0.53%	1.35%	1.09%	0.39%

Source: Author's calculations

quantity-based measures, BCS and trade intensity – especially trade intensity where they are quite strongly integrated with each other and where each large country routinely appears in the Top 5 of many of the other countries.[8]

The next set of results attempts to use all of the available measures to return an overall measure of integration that captures both real and financial dimensions. This facilitates the investigation of which individual measure might possibly drive the overall level of integration and, in doing so, addresses the question of what the possible sources of integration between countries in the region might be.

Table 7.4 presents the results of the normalized integration measure bilaterally. Unsurprisingly, the most integrated pair is Singapore–Malaysia, with 3.11. As with the previous results, we see that Singapore and Malaysia are solidly interconnected with most of the ASEAN5 and the larger economies. Of the big three economies, Japan remains the most integrated. The newer ASEAN members, for the most part, are not as well connected – Vietnam is an exception in some cases.

Figure 7.4 shows the overall normalized value for each country. As with the individual measures, we can take the average bilateral measures for the entire sample to present a picture of overall regional integration. Japan and the ASEAN5 are the most connected here, with Myanmar, Laos and Brunei the least.

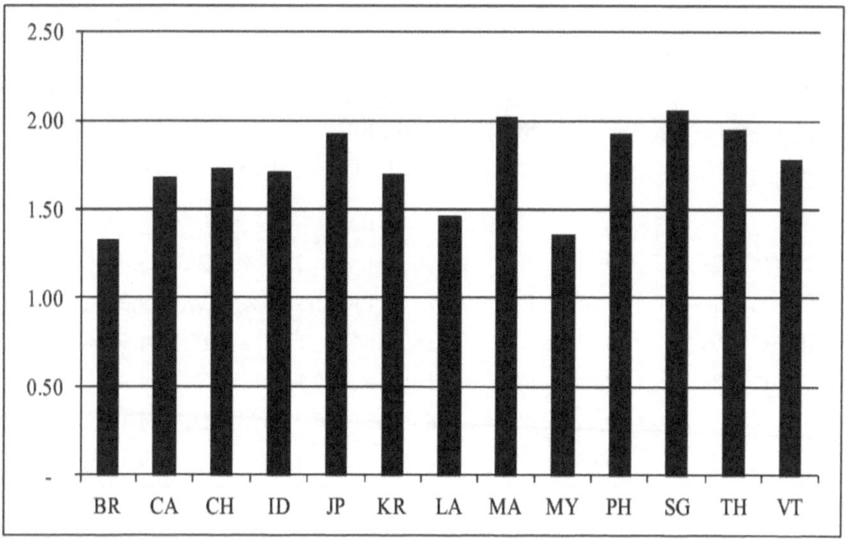

Figure 7.4 Total regional overall integration

Source: Author's calculations

Table 7.3 Top 5 interconnections by measure

BCS	*BR*		*CA*		*CH*		*ID*		*JP*		*KR*	
	KR	51%	VT	89%	LAO	79%	PRC	78%	TH	89%	JP	71%
	TH	33%	JP	66%	ID	78%	LAO	77%	PH	86%	MA	64%
	JP	23%	SG	64%	VT	74%	PH	65%	MA	85%	SG	63%
	SG	6%	PRC	62%	CA	62%	SG	61%	SG	84%	PH	61%
	VT	5%	PH	48%	PH	59%	MA	60%	VT	83%	TH	58%
	Ave	**24%**		**66%**		**70%**		**68%**		**85%**		**63%**
RPPD	**BR**		**CA**		**CH**		**ID**		**JP**		**KR**	
	PH	0.014	ID	0.007	BR	0.132	CA	0.007	KR	0.105	CA	0.0215
	TH	0.029	KR	0.0215	JP	0.251	TH	0.054	SG	0.189	MA	0.069
	SG	0.035	TH	0.062	SG	0.255	PH	0.084	MA	0.205	SG	0.084
	CA	0.092	VT	0.074	TH	0.272	MA	0.107	PH	0.229	JP	0.105
	MA	0.124	PH	0.091	MY	0.275	SG	0.123	BR	0.236	TH	0.118
	Ave	**0.06**		**0.05**		**0.24**		**0.08**		**0.19**		**0.08**
UIP	**BR**		**CA**		**CH**		**ID**		**JP**		**KR**	
	CA	0.15	VT	0.01	PH	0.04	VT	0.01	BR	0.07	SG	0.02
	CH	0.30	KR	0.04	ID	0.05	CH	0.05	CA	0.09	TH	0.02
	ID	0.11	JP	0.09	VT	0.12	MA	0.06	MA	0.16	CA	0.04
	JP	0.07	SG	0.09	MA	0.14	PH	0.09	KR	0.17	BR	0.11
	KR	0.11	TH	0.14	SG	0.16	BR	0.11	TH	0.18	MA	0.11
	Ave	**0.15**		**0.08**		**0.10**		**0.06**		**0.13**		**0.06**
TRADE	**BR**		**CA**		**CH**		**ID**		**JP**		**KR**	
	JP	0.32%	TH	0.07%	JP	23.08%	JP	3.74%	PRC	23.08%	PRC	12.76%
	ID	0.12%	SG	0.07%	KR	12.76%	PRC	1.88%	KR	9.07%	JP	9.07%
	KR	0.11%	VT	0.05%	MA	3.34%	SG	1.51%	TH	4.91%	MA	1.43%
	SG	0.08%	PRC	0.04%	SG	3.26%	KR	1.42%	SG	4.30%	ID	1.42%
	MA	0.05%	LAO	0.02%	TH	2.65%	MA	0.96%	MA	4.12%	SG	1.31%
	Ave	**0.14%**		**0.05%**		**9.02%**		**1.90%**		**9.10%**		**5.20%**

Source: Author's calculations

LA		*MA*		*MY*		*PH*		*SG*		*TH*		*VT*	
PRC	79%	PH	94%	TH	68%	SG	95%	PH	95%	MA	91%	CA	89%
MA	78%	TH	91%	JP	66%	MA	94%	MA	88%	JP	89%	JP	83%
ID	77%	SG	88%	MA	63%	JP	86%	JP	84%	PH	82%	MA	78%
PH	60%	JP	85%	SG	63%	TH	82%	VT	76%	SG	75%	SG	76%
SG	58%	VT	78%	PH	49%	VT	76%	TH	75%	VT	74%	PH	76%
	70%		**87%**		**62%**		**86%**		**84%**		**82%**		**80%**
LA		**MA**		**MY**		**PH**		**SG**		**TH**		**VT**	
ID	0.139	SG	0.015	CH	0.275	BR	0.014	MA	0.015	BR	0.029	CA	0.074
CA	0.179	PH	0.023	LA	1.278	MA	0.023	BR	0.035	PH	0.029	TH	0.122
VT	0.198	TH	0.049	VT	1.345	TH	0.029	PH	0.039	MA	0.049	ID	0.126
TH	0.223	KR	0.069	CA	1.382	SG	0.039	TH	0.069	ID	0.054	BR	0.131
KR	0.263	ID	0.107	ID	1.504	ID	0.084	KR	0.084	CA	0.062	PH	0.135
	0.20		**0.05**		**1.16**		**0.04**		**0.05**		**0.04**		**0.12**
LA		**MA**		**MY**		**PH**		**SG**		**TH**		**VT**	
MY	0.68	VT	0.02	PH	0.45	CH	0.04	TH	0.00	SG	0.00	CA	0.01
PH	1.15	TH	0.04	CH	0.48	ID	0.09	KR	0.02	KR	0.02	ID	0.01
ID	1.16	SG	0.04	VT	0.59	VT	0.16	MA	0.04	MA	0.04	MA	0.02
KR	1.24	ID	0.06	ID	0.60	MA	0.19	VT	0.08	VT	0.09	SG	0.08
CH	1.25	BR	0.08	MA	0.65	TH	0.22	BR	0.09	ID	0.14	TH	0.09
	1.09		**0.05**		**0.56**		**0.14**		**0.05**		**0.06**		**0.04**
LA		**MA**		**MY**		**PH**		**SG**		**TH**		**VT**	
TH	0.15%	JP	4.12%	TH	0.31%	JP	2.15%	JP	4.30%	JP	4.91%	PRC	1.18%
SG	0.08%	PRC	3.34%	SG	0.22%	PRC	1.45%	PRC	3.26%	PRC	2.65%	JP	1.09%
VT	0.03%	SG	3.16%	PRC	0.19%	SG	0.71%	MA	3.16%	MA	1.62%	SG	0.64%
PRC	0.02%	TH	1.62%	JP	0.05%	KR	0.70%	ID	1.51%	KR	0.83%	KR	0.61%
CA	0.02%	KR	1.43%	MA	0.05%	MA	0.58%	KR	1.31%	SG	0.83%	TH	0.40%
	0.06%		**2.74%**		**0.16%**		**1.12%**		**2.71%**		**2.17%**		**0.79%**

Table 7.4 Normalized overall integration using all four measures (min = 0, max = 4)

	BR	*CA*	*CH*	*ID*	*JP*	*KR*	*LA*	*MA*	*MY*	*PH*	*SG*	*TH*	*VT*
BR	–												
CA	1.33	–											
PRC	1.23	1.78	–										
ID	1.15	2.21	2.20	–									
JP	1.46	1.87	2.19	1.89	–								
KR	1.70	1.86	1.84	1.44	2.66	–							
LAO	1.16	1.56	1.92	2.00	1.30	1.19	–						
MA	1.28	1.67	2.15	2.05	2.50	2.22	1.94	–					
MY	1.11	1.52	1.21	1.41	1.79	1.15	1.26	1.75	–				
PH	1.81	1.78	1.99	2.05	2.28	1.96	1.77	2.71	1.60	–			
SG	1.73	1.93	2.13	2.08	2.52	2.32	1.75	3.11	1.77	2.55	–		
TH	2.00	1.73	1.79	1.77	2.56	2.13	1.48	2.64	1.84	2.56	2.81	–	
VT	1.33	2.64	2.05	2.03	2.11	1.61	1.75	2.25	1.23	2.03	2.08	2.08	–

Source: Author's calculations

As with the individual measures we can present the overall Top 5 integration – the results of which are given in Table 7.5. These tend to support the above results. Japan, Singapore and Malaysia are among the more connected countries and appear more frequently in the Top 5 than the others. In fact, if one was to examine the average Top 5, Singapore is the most connected with 2.66 (out of 4), Malaysia is second (2.64), Thailand third (2.54) and Japan fourth (2.50).

The newer ASEAN nations only really appear in the Top 5 of other newer ASEAN countries, or for mainland China. From the averages, the least connected is Brunei (1.74/4), with Myanmar (1.75) the second least integrated and Laos (1.88) the third least.

5. Conclusion

Three quite well-defined groups emerge from the above analysis. The first is the ASEAN5 group of countries: Singapore, Malaysia, the Philippines, Indonesia and Thailand. The second group represents the newer ASEAN nations: Brunei, Cambodia, Laos, Myanmar and Vietnam. The third are the region's large economies: China, Japan and Korea. In many respects, the extent of economic interconnection tends to organize around these groupings.

Clearly, the most integrated group is the ASEAN5. Not only is each country highly integrated with other members of the group, but Singapore and Malaysia – and to a slightly lesser extent Thailand – are particularly well connected to many

Table 7.5 Normalized overall integration Top 5

SG		*MA*		*TH*		*JP*		*PH*		*KR*		*VT*		*CH*		*ID*		*CA*		*LA*		*MY*		*BR*	
MA	3.11	SG	3.11	SG	2.81	KR	2.66	MA	2.71	JP	2.66	CA	2.64	ID	2.20	CA	2.21	VT	2.64	ID	2.00	TH	1.84	TH	2.00
TH	2.81	PH	2.71	MA	2.64	TH	2.56	TH	2.56	SG	2.32	MA	2.25	JP	2.19	PRC	2.20	ID	2.21	MA	1.94	JP	1.79	PH	1.81
PH	2.55	TH	2.64	JP	2.56	SG	2.52	SG	2.55	MA	2.22	JP	2.11	MA	2.15	SG	2.08	SG	1.93	PRC	1.92	SG	1.77	SG	1.73
JP	2.52	JP	2.50	PH	2.56	MA	2.50	JP	2.28	TH	2.13	TH	2.08	SG	2.13	PH	2.05	JP	1.87	PH	1.77	MA	1.75	KR	1.70
KR	2.32	VT	2.25	KR	2.13	PH	2.28	ID	2.05	PH	1.96	SG	2.08	VT	2.05	MA	2.05	KR	1.86	SG	1.75	PH	1.60	JP	1.46
Average	**2.66**		**2.64**		**2.54**		**2.50**		**2.43**		**2.26**		**2.23**		**2.14**		**2.12**		**2.10**		**1.88**		**1.75**		**1.74**

Source: Author's calculations; presented in descending order of average integration levels.

of the other countries in the whole sample. This occurs quite pervasively through the entire range of measures, regardless of the individual measure, and whether the measure was price or quantity based, or indeed possessed real or financial dimensions. However, it is the financial and price-based measures (UIP and RPPD) that more persuasively highlight the extent of integration of the ASEAN5 group. The larger "+3" countries exhibited higher levels of integration in the quantity measures, especially in trade intensity where they were highly connected to each other. This has a few possible implications. First, being mindful of the possible endogeneity issues – given the history of the creation of ASEAN and the resultant path dependence – the results suggest the possibility of ASEAN5 being influential as a bloc. Second, if one allows the data to drive the pursuit of an ongoing debate about the possibility of a monetary union in Asia, then it would appear that ASEAN is a grouping that is potentially open enough to be more able to entertain the notion of monetary integration than other groupings.

The newer ASEAN countries were the least integrated according to the measures presented in this chapter. Of these, Vietnam was the most connected to countries outside its cluster of economies. Myanmar and Laos were the least integrated generally. This is not a surprising result. Many of the countries in this cluster have emerging goods and financial markets and, up to this point, have escaped the radar in terms of the development of linkages with other countries in the region.

The larger economies showed a high degree of integration with each other only in the quantity-based measure of trade intensity. This is due to the sheer volume of trade between the three large economies. Of the large countries, Japan was clearly the most integrated with a number of other clusters, most notably the ASEAN5 group. This perhaps reveals the role this country has played over a long period in developing real and financial linkages in the region generally. However, it must be said that if monetary integration involving the three larger economies remains a possible policy objective in the region, then the above analysis does not really support it at this stage.

The quality of the results is dependent on the quality of the measures used. What can be observed from the above is that there is some consistency offered among the measures; we observe high levels of interconnection for many (not all) of the same countries across a range of measures. This should perhaps be a beginning point for further work in the area. Further work should involve a refinement of the measures used, and a more thorough statistical investigation of the information content in each of the measures, so as to avoid a possible overlap of information. Another obvious extension would be in the area of dynamics; to investigate how each measure might drive the level of integration over time. This is important first in ascertaining which countries are getting closer (or not!), and second, in revealing any breaks or regime shifts that might act as shocks to the pace of integration between countries over time. A third suggestion for further work would be to ascertain a benchmark for each measure, to show whether countries are ahead or behind when presented in comparison to the benchmark. Such improvements to the multivariate view would vastly improve the policy messages emanating from the integration measures going forward.

Notes

1 Many thanks to Jenny Corbett and Ying Xu for their valuable comments and suggestions on a previous version of this chapter. The usual caveat applies.
2 A country that is open to trade might also be open to capital flows; as such, there is some possible overlap with respect to this measure between the real and financial dimensions of integration.
3 We do not formally examine this particular measure of integration in this instance owing to a lack of ease in obtaining consumption data for all countries sampled in the later section. That said, it is generally well known that consumption is a significant proportion of national income and, as such, the business cycle correlations presented below offer an (imperfect) degree of substitutability for consumption correlations.
4 "S" for synchronicity. Like trade openness, this measure could quite possibly pick up real as well as financial dimensions. The financial characteristic may come from the same intuition as that which defines consumption correlations – given that in most cases consumption is a significant proportion of income.
5 Covered interest parity could be employed here. Typically, however, data on forward FX contracts are harder to procure for lesser developed economies.
6 Available at: "http://aric.adb.org/"
7 One can take averages rather than sums, but for the purpose of creating a comparison between measures, the effect is much the same.
8 As mentioned, the level of TI for the larger countries is almost certainly exaggerated due to the way that TI is constructed.

References

Balassa, B. (1961) *The Theory of Economic Integration*, Illinois: Irwin Homewood.

Cavoli, T. and Rajan, R.S. (2009) *Exchange Rate Regimes and Macroeconomic Management in Asia*, Hong Kong: Hong Kong University Press.

———. (2011) 'The real/financial dimensions to measuring regional economic integration in ASEAN and East Asia', in J. Corbett and Y. Xu (2011) (eds) *Achieving Sustainable Growth in East Asia*, ERIA Research Project Report 2010–28, Jakarta: ERIA, pp. 201–22.

———. (2012) 'Exploring dimensions of regional economic integration in Asia: more than the sum of its parts?' *Journal of Asian Economics*, 23: 643–53.

Chinn, M.D. (2006) 'The (partial) rehabilitation of interest rate parity in the floating rate era: longer horizons, alternative expectations, and emerging markets', *Journal of International Money and Finance*, 25: 7–21.

Chinn M.D. and Ito, H. (2008) 'A new measure of financial openness', *Journal of Comparative Policy Analysis*, 10: 309–22.

de Browuer, G. (1999) *Financial Integration in East Asia*, Cambridge: Cambridge University Press.

Feldstein, M. and Horioka, C. (1980) 'Domestic saving and international capital flows', *The Economic Journal*, 90: 314–29.

Imbs, J. (2006) 'The real effects of financial integration', *Journal of International Economics*, 68: 296–324.

Obstfeld, M. (1989) 'How integrated are world capital markets? Some new tests', in G. Calvo (2012) (ed) *Debt, Stabilization and Development*, Oxford: Basil Blackwell.

Pomfret, R. (2011) *Regionalism in East Asia: why has it flourished since 2000 and how far will it go?*, Singapore: World Scientific.

Rajan, R.S. (2008) 'Monetary and financial cooperation in Asia', in N. Kumar, K. Kesavapany and Y. Chaocheng (eds) (2008) *Asia's New Regionalism and Global Role: Agenda for the East Asia Summit*, Institute for South East Asian Studies (ISEAS): Singapore/Research and Information Systems for Developing Economies (RIS): New Delhi.

Takagi, S. and Hirose, K. (2001) *A Multivariate Approach to Financially Integrated Economies*, mimeo.

8 Choosing the best partners for risk-sharing integration

Achmad Maulana, Wei Feng and Jenny Corbett

1. Introduction

Initiatives towards regional integration have traditionally been based on political definitions of national and regional boundaries. Even if the move to integration is primarily trade driven, as it is in East Asia, rather than politically motivated, as it has arguably been in Europe, the definition of the region and the identity of the nation-states within the region are the result of political history. The choice of partners within an integrating region can therefore be somewhat arbitrary. When there are conditions on entry – for example, the Maastricht conditions in Europe – existing members of a region have some control over who joins. But it is rare that these conditions are set on the basis of which countries will contribute most to the economic welfare of the integrated group. Nor do individual countries usually pick their partners on the basis of welfare-maximizing conditions. Outcomes might be better if they did. The economic conditions for optimal currency unions are now well documented in the literature, and it is clear that currency unions that are very far from those conditions can face convulsions and disintegration.

In this chapter, we apply recently developed methods to show which groups of countries in the East Asian region would benefit most from closer financial integration. The benefits come both from improved stability of income and consumption streams and from the estimated welfare gains that these deliver. Section 2 of the chapter sets out the research questions in more detail in the context of the relevant literature. Section 3 describes the research methodology. Section 4 describes the results and Section 5 presents our conclusions.

2. Research questions

What is the benefit to countries from being able to reduce the volatility of their consumption when they have adverse economic events at home? If it were possible to perfectly smooth consumption streams (which would in theory maximize welfare), a given country would always consume a fixed fraction of aggregate world income regardless of the state of its economy. Known in the literature as "full diversification of risk", this would imply that if a country experienced an unusually positive outcome in its economy, it would pay some fraction of its increased income to countries with negative outcomes and vice versa. That ideal situation can be achieved only when countries have access to perfect and complete financial markets that would allow them to lend to and borrow from each other without friction, and give them a perfect ability to monitor and enforce contractual arrangements across borders. The absence of these conditions in the real world raises an important research and policy question: what second-best outcomes can be achieved by integrating financially with well-chosen partners?

Using this insight into the advantages of financial integration, we examine two questions in this chapter. First, which pool of countries gives the greatest benefit for regional risk-sharing opportunities in East Asia? Second, how large is the welfare gain from the optimal regional risk-sharing pool for countries in East Asia?

3. Literature review

3.1 Optimal risk

There is an abundant literature on the benefits of international risk-sharing, but it is clear that no countries in the world have yet achieved the condition of complete international sharing of risk.

The discussion of the measurement of countries' risk-sharing began when Lucas (1987) estimated the welfare cost of consumption uncertainty in the US economy. By proposing a method that compared countries' levels of utility under financial autarky with the levels of utility when countries can trade on international financial markets, Lucas argued that the gain from eliminating consumption variability was relatively small – that is, less than 1 per cent of lifetime consumption. The implication is that the cost of business cycles for the United States is insignificant. In the same spirit as Lucas, Obstfeld (1994) carefully distinguished the effects of risk-aversion and inter-temporal substitution on the gain from reducing consumption volatility. Though producing a higher figure for the gain of eliminating consumption variability than Lucas, Obstfeld's estimate was still low.

More recent work (Callen *et al.*, 2009) produces much larger welfare gains by examining the optimal country groupings for risk-sharing arrangements. The novelty of this approach relies on the fact that the reduction in volatility can be maximized by choosing partners who provide the best offsetting pattern of output variance. This suggests using the variance–covariance matrix to run a systematic search of the ideal pool from a group of countries worldwide. Callen *et al.* (2011) calculate the output volatility across a group of 74 countries and compare it with the volatility of output of each country individually. If the volatility of the combined output of the group is lower than individual country volatility, they conclude that there are potential welfare gains from international risk-sharing. Their estimates showed that the largest gains from risk-sharing were obtained in a group that consisted of less than 10 countries and that these gains could be quite large. These gains remain theoretical in the absence of some mechanism or institution to implement the risk-sharing and, clearly, weak institutions in any of the potential partners or a history of default on international obligations might undermine the feasibility of these first best risk-sharing pools.

3.2 Welfare implications

Many studies have tried to estimate the welfare effects of business cycles and international risk-sharing. Among these, Cole and Obstfeld (1991), Lucas (1987) and Tesar (1995) find low welfare gains (less than 0.5 per cent), while studies by Kim and Sheen (2007), Kim *et al.* (2006), Obstfeld (1994) and van Wincoop (1994, 1999) give larger numbers.

Cole and Obstfeld (1991) evaluate the gains from international risk-sharing using a simple general equilibrium model that incorporates output uncertainty. In a model that mimics selected moments of US and Japanese data to approximate the gain from international risk-sharing, the magnitude is about a 0.2 per cent increase in annual output. This gain, however, disappears once assumptions on preferences and technologies are altered. Tesar (1995) introduces different sources of uncertainty – market structure, country size, technology and preferences – and finds that the size of gains from risk-sharing range from 0 to 2 per cent of lifetime consumption. Such low results for the potential benefit of risk-sharing might explain why countries appear to have a strong bias towards domestic assets, low international consumption correlations and high correlations between domestic saving and investment (that is, a low level of international risk-sharing).

Van Wincoop (1999), estimating Organization for Economic Cooperation and Development (OECD) countries' potential welfare gain from risk-sharing, points out that the gains are sensitive to the parameterization of representative agents' preferences and to the assumption about the stochastic process and measurement of endowment. The first is important since it relates to the implicit risk-free interest rate, the rate of relative risk-aversion, and the elasticity of substitution between tradable and non-tradable goods. Using almost full information on the factors that determine the benefits of risk-sharing, van Wincoop (1999) estimates the welfare gain from risk-sharing in the range of a 1.1 per cent to a 7.4 per cent permanent increase in consumption over 50 and 100 year horizons.

Using the same framework as van Wincoop (1994, 1999), Kim *et al.* (2006) calculate the potential welfare gain for 10 Asian countries when they perfectly diversify idiosyncratic country-income shocks. For all these countries, they find that risk-sharing gains are an increase of between 1.4 per cent and 7 per cent in consumption. The gains are higher if the United States is included in the set of countries that is available as risk-sharing partners, and range from 2 per cent to almost 10 per cent. For the ASEAN5 sub-group, Kim *et al.* (2006) estimate an increase in annual consumption of about 2 per cent to 9.5 per cent for 10 and 50 year horizons. The gain for this group is higher than for the groups of Northeast Asia, developed countries and greater China.

4. Research methodology

The standard theory of risk-sharing between countries asserts that, with complete markets, each country within the group will consume a fixed amount of aggregate output, but it does not give any information on the appropriate measure of the welfare gain associated with risk-sharing. Our main objective – as with the literature reviewed above – is to estimate the scale of welfare gains from risk-sharing. We go beyond the standard results, however, by not only asking what the gains from risk-sharing versus no risk-sharing are, but also quantifying the effect of risk-sharing arrangements between different countries in East Asia.

The initial step is to calculate the variance of output growth rates for each country under autarky and within different risk-sharing pools and to then evaluate the welfare implications of the different pools.

We define a "pool" as any group of countries that engage in complete risk-sharing with each other (Callen *et al.*, 2011). While Callen *et al.* use a large group of countries, we choose to narrow our search for the optimal pool and consider 10 countries in the Asia Pacific region plus the United Kingdom. These countries are Australia, China, Indonesia, Japan, the Philippines, Malaysia, Singapore, South Korea, Thailand, the United States and the United Kingdom. Our data are real gross domestic product (GDP) in purchasing power parity (PPP) US dollars over the period 1980–2011, taken from the World Bank's *World Development Indicators* (World Bank, various years).[1]

4.1 GDP growth and variability

Figures 8.1 and 8.2 show the dynamics of GDP growth rates in the sample of countries between 1981 and 2011. The ASEAN5 countries had relatively more volatile income than their peers. All countries in the ASEAN5 experienced major downturns in their economic performance in 1998 and again in 2001 and 2009. While the impact of the Asian Financial Crisis (AFC) of 1998 was restricted to East Asian countries (excluding China), the more recent wave of crisis was experienced not only in East Asia but also in developed countries such as the United Kingdom and the United States. The coefficients of variation in Table 8.1 support the evidence of the graphs. This makes it clear that not only did levels of income fall, but growth rates also became significantly more volatile about the time of the AFC. The ability to smooth consumption in such circumstances could be very valuable to improving welfare. Tesar (1995) explains that models of international risk-sharing imply that, with high levels of risk-sharing, countries' consumption streams should be highly correlated with each other. Since idiosyncratic shocks would be removed, the only remaining shocks would be system-wide ones and all countries' consumption would move together. She shows, however, that consumption in most countries had low correlation with global consumption while output had higher correlation with global output. This is inconsistent with any significant risk-sharing. In Table 8.2, we report

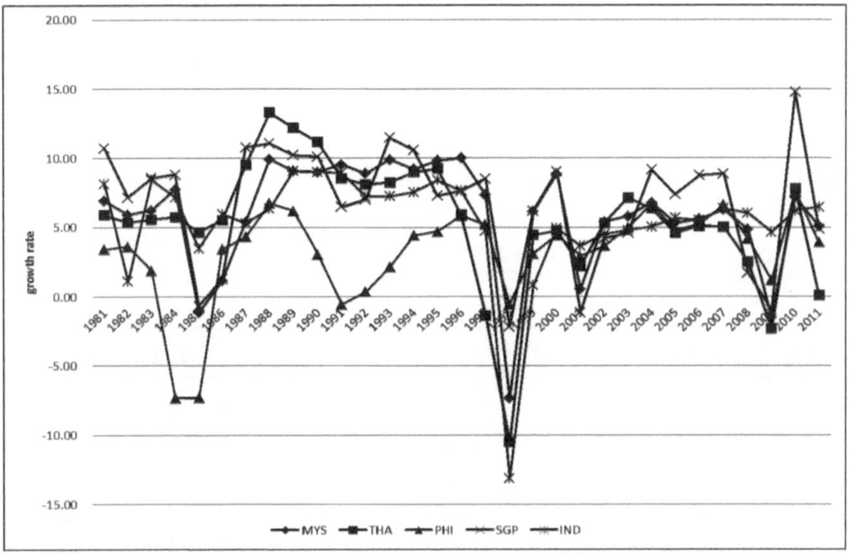

Figure 8.1 GDP growth across ASEAN5 countries, 1981–2011

Source: Data for all tables and charts are from World Bank's *World Development Indicators.*

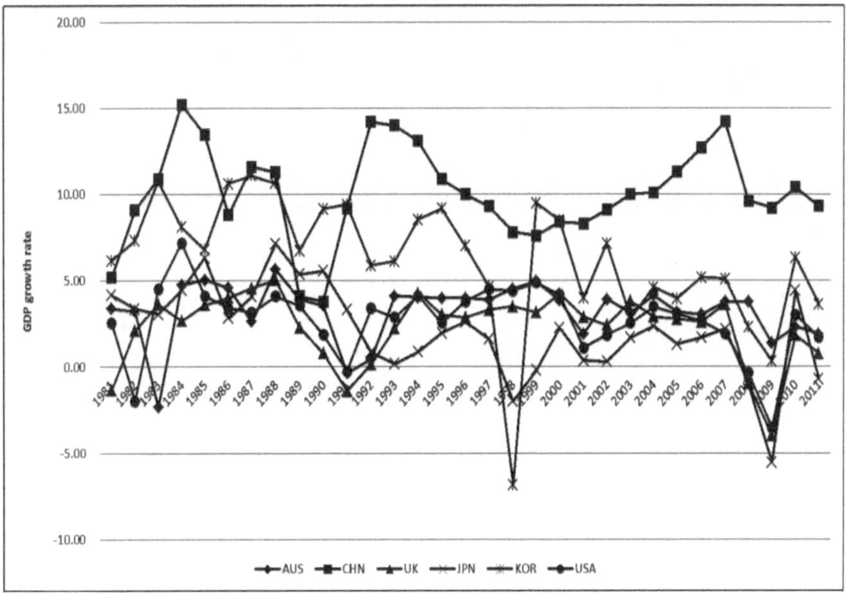

Figure 8.2 GDP growth across non-ASEAN5 countries, 1981–2011

Source: As for Table 8.1

correlations between global and country output and consumption for selected East Asian countries for the period 1981–2011. The results confirm Tesar's findings and reiterate the findings in several previous studies (Corbett and Maulana, 2010; Kim *et al.*, 2006) that risk-sharing activities are far from optimal for countries in the region. Correlations of consumption with global consumption are low in the region and are lower than for the developed-country benchmarks of the United States and the United Kingdom. Our data show – contrary

Table 8.1 Coefficients of variation of GDP growth rates

Country	*1980–85*	*1986–90*	*1991–95*	*1996–2000*	*2001–05*	*2006–11*
AUS	105.56	27.82	90.32	11.31	26.93	36.99
CHN	36.20	47.79	17.61	11.79	11.58	19.03
IDN	57.00	24.88	9.65	838.03	15.87	11.76
JPN	29.91	32.48	86.93	226.31	73.86	1964.60
KOR	22.87	18.48	21.61	145.64	35.98	57.93
MYS	69.42	53.01	4.49	141.41	51.30	67.77
PHL	–496.68	35.00	107.47	70.93	31.50	47.73
SGP	63.79	47.84	26.65	78.86	81.13	89.43
THA	9.05	29.24	5.63	1063.71	37.36	122.53
USA	103.22	25.96	65.94	9.24	39.87	274.07
UK	95.55	53.00	137.05	14.93	17.30	430.01

Source: Authors' calculations

Table 8.2 Correlations with global consumption and output

Country	*Corr(c(i),c(w))*	*Corr(y(i),y(w))*
AUS	0.27	0.37
CHN	–0.28	–0.16
IDN	0.06	0.21
JPN	0.51	0.55
KOR	0.32	0.25
MYS	0.17	0.30
PHL	0.18	0.24
SGP	0.36	0.40
THA	0.45	0.40
USA	0.45	0.56
UK	0.46	0.48

Source: Authors' calculations

In the absence of risk-sharing arrangements, any single country's change in consumption equals the change in its individual output (income). That is, $C_t^j = Y_t^j$. The corresponding Epstein-Zin utility function at initial period $t = 0$ for an individual country, j, is

$$U_0^j = U\left(C_0^j, \mu_j, \sigma_j^2\right) = C_0^j\left(1 - \beta exp\left[(1-\theta)\left(\mu_j - \frac{1}{2}\gamma\sigma_j^2\right)\right]\right)^{-(1/(1-\theta))} \tag{5}$$

If a risk-sharing arrangement were in place, the Epstein-Zin utility would be given by

$$U_t = U\left(\underline{C}_t, \underline{\mu}, \underline{\sigma}\right) = \underline{C}_t\left(1 - \beta exp\left[(1-\theta)\left(\underline{\mu} - \frac{1}{2}\gamma\underline{\sigma}^2\right)\right]\right)^{-(1/(1-\theta))} \tag{6}$$

The parameter θ is the inverse of the inter-temporal elasticity of substitution in consumption, γ is the parameter of relative risk-aversion, β is the discount rate and $\sigma^2{}_j, \underline{\sigma}^2$ are individual and pool-wide variance, respectively.

There are two points to be noted from (5) and (6). First, since $(\mu - \frac{1}{2}\gamma\sigma^2)$ positively affects the level of period t utility, it follows that the smaller the variance of pool-wide GDP, the bigger is the increase in the "certainty equivalent" utility. The scale of the effect is given by the size of the parameter for risk-aversion, γ: a higher risk-aversion coefficient will lead to greater welfare gains from a given reduction in variance. Second, as the term for the inverse of inter-temporal substitutionθ, increases, the welfare gain coming from a decrease in variance is reduced.

With the measures for country welfare specified in (5) and (6), we can now assess the scale of the welfare gain associated with moving from the autarky position to the risk-sharing arrangement. Full risk-sharing within the pool ensures individual country j's consumption grows with pool-wide output at rate $\underline{\mu}$ and fluctuates with pool-wide output variance, $\underline{\sigma}^2$. Substituting, we can calculate the welfare gain as

$$\delta = \frac{C_0^j\left(1 - \beta exp\left[(1-\theta)\left(\mu_j - \frac{1}{2}\gamma\sigma j^{2}\right)\right]\right)^{-(1/(1-\theta))}}{\underline{C}_j\left(1 - \beta exp\left[(1-\theta)\left(\underline{\mu} - \frac{1}{2}\gamma\underline{\sigma}^2\right)\right]\right)^{-(1/(1-\theta))}}. \tag{7}$$

The welfare function (7) has three constituent parts: (i) the difference between individual and pool-wide volatilities; (ii) the expected difference between growth in country j in autarky and the growth of the pool; and (iii) the ratio between the initial consumption of the individual country with no risk-sharing and the initial average consumption of the countries in the pool. In order to isolate the effects due directly to the diversification gain that country j will receive under risk-sharing, we set $\mu_j = \underline{\mu}$ and $C_0^j = \underline{C}_0$, thus assuming that growth and consumption levels are equal in country j and the pool.[3] This approach also abstracts

In the absence of risk-sharing arrangements, any single country's change in consumption equals the change in its individual output (income). That is, $C_t^j = \Upsilon_t^j$. The corresponding Epstein-Zin utility function at initial period $t = 0$ for an individual country, j, is

$$U_0^j = U\left(C_0^j, \mu_j, \sigma_j^2\right) = C_0^j\left(1 - \beta exp\left[(1-\theta)\left(\mu_j - \frac{1}{2}\gamma\sigma_j^2\right)\right]\right)^{-(1/(1-\theta))} \tag{5}$$

If a risk-sharing arrangement were in place, the Epstein-Zin utility would be given by

$$U_t = U\left(\underline{C}_t, \underline{\mu}, \underline{\sigma}\right) = \underline{C}_t\left(1 - \beta exp\left[(1-\theta)\left(\underline{\mu} - \frac{1}{2}\gamma\underline{\sigma}^2\right)\right]\right)^{-(1/(1-\theta))} \tag{6}$$

The parameter θ is the inverse of the inter-temporal elasticity of substitution in consumption, γ is the parameter of relative risk-aversion, β is the discount rate and $\sigma^2{}_j, \underline{\sigma}^2$ are individual and pool-wide variance, respectively.

There are two points to be noted from (5) and (6). First, since $(\mu - \frac{1}{2}\gamma\sigma^2)$ positively affects the level of period t utility, it follows that the smaller the variance of pool-wide GDP, the bigger is the increase in the "certainty equivalent" utility. The scale of the effect is given by the size of the parameter for risk-aversion, γ: a higher risk-aversion coefficient will lead to greater welfare gains from a given reduction in variance. Second, as the term for the inverse of inter-temporal substitutionθ, increases, the welfare gain coming from a decrease in variance is reduced.

With the measures for country welfare specified in (5) and (6), we can now assess the scale of the welfare gain associated with moving from the autarky position to the risk-sharing arrangement. Full risk-sharing within the pool ensures individual country j's consumption grows with pool-wide output at rate $\underline{\mu}$ and fluctuates with pool-wide output variance, $\underline{\sigma}^2$. Substituting, we can calculate the welfare gain as

$$\delta = \frac{C_0^j\left(1 - \beta exp\left[(1-\theta)\left(\mu_j - \frac{1}{2}\gamma\sigma j^2\right)\right]\right)^{-(1/(1-\theta))}}{\underline{C}_j\left(1 - \beta exp\left[(1-\theta)\left(\underline{\mu} - \frac{1}{2}\gamma\underline{\sigma}^2\right)\right]\right)^{-(1/(1-\theta))}}. \tag{7}$$

The welfare function (7) has three constituent parts: (i) the difference between individual and pool-wide volatilities; (ii) the expected difference between growth in country j in autarky and the growth of the pool; and (iii) the ratio between the initial consumption of the individual country with no risk-sharing and the initial average consumption of the countries in the pool. In order to isolate the effects due directly to the diversification gain that country j will receive under risk-sharing, we set $\mu_j = \underline{\mu}$ and $C_0^j = \underline{C}_0$, thus assuming that growth and consumption levels are equal in country j and the pool.[3] This approach also abstracts

In the absence of risk-sharing arrangements, any single country's change in consumption equals the change in its individual output (income). That is, $C_t^j = Y_t^j$. The corresponding Epstein-Zin utility function at initial period $t = 0$ for an individual country, j, is

$$U_0^j = U\left(C_0^j, \mu_j, \sigma_j^2\right) = C_0^j\left(1 - \beta exp\left[(1-\theta)\left(\mu_j - \frac{1}{2}\gamma\sigma_j^2\right)\right]\right)^{-(1/(1-\theta))} \tag{5}$$

If a risk-sharing arrangement were in place, the Epstein-Zin utility would be given by

$$U_t = U\left(\underline{C}_t, \underline{\mu}, \underline{\sigma}\right) = \underline{C}_t\left(1 - \beta exp\left[(1-\theta)\left(\underline{\mu} - \frac{1}{2}\gamma\underline{\sigma}^2\right)\right]\right)^{-(1/(1-\theta))} \tag{6}$$

The parameter θ is the inverse of the inter-temporal elasticity of substitution in consumption, γ is the parameter of relative risk-aversion, β is the discount rate and $\sigma^2{}_j, \underline{\sigma}^2$ are individual and pool-wide variance, respectively.

There are two points to be noted from (5) and (6). First, since $(\mu - \frac{1}{2}\gamma\sigma^2)$ positively affects the level of period t utility, it follows that the smaller the variance of pool-wide GDP, the bigger is the increase in the "certainty equivalent" utility. The scale of the effect is given by the size of the parameter for risk-aversion, γ: a higher risk-aversion coefficient will lead to greater welfare gains from a given reduction in variance. Second, as the term for the inverse of inter-temporal substitutionθ, increases, the welfare gain coming from a decrease in variance is reduced.

With the measures for country welfare specified in (5) and (6), we can now assess the scale of the welfare gain associated with moving from the autarky position to the risk-sharing arrangement. Full risk-sharing within the pool ensures individual country j's consumption grows with pool-wide output at rate $\underline{\mu}$ and fluctuates with pool-wide output variance, $\underline{\sigma}^2$. Substituting, we can calculate the welfare gain as

$$\delta = \frac{C_0^j\left(1 - \beta exp\left[(1-\theta)\left(\mu_j - \frac{1}{2}\gamma\sigma j^2\right)\right]\right)^{-(1/(1-\theta))}}{\underline{C}_j\left(1 - \beta exp\left[(1-\theta)\left(\underline{\mu} - \frac{1}{2}\gamma\underline{\sigma}^2\right)\right]\right)^{-(1/(1-\theta))}}. \tag{7}$$

The welfare function (7) has three constituent parts: (i) the difference between individual and pool-wide volatilities; (ii) the expected difference between growth in country j in autarky and the growth of the pool; and (iii) the ratio between the initial consumption of the individual country with no risk-sharing and the initial average consumption of the countries in the pool. In order to isolate the effects due directly to the diversification gain that country j will receive under risk-sharing, we set $\mu_j = \mu$ and $C_0^j = \underline{C}_0$, thus assuming that growth and consumption levels are equal in country j and the pool.[3] This approach also abstracts from the possibility of transfers on entry between countries in the pool. We therefore focus entirely on the welfare implications of the fall in volatility associated with international risk-sharing and preserve the emphasis in Obstfeld (1994).

From (7), it is clear that the gain from international risk-sharing will be smaller for a country that has similar volatility measures in both the pooled and autarky situations. If volatility is related to size, then countries' relative sizes matter in explaining the gain. Further, we assume that shocks to consumption follow a random walk (Callen *et al.* [2011] explain what happens if the random-walk assumption is relaxed), so we do not consider situations where certain countries are systematically subject to consumption shocks.

Following the strategy of Callen *et al.* (2011), we use a (weighted) variance of the growth rate of output as a metric for output uncertainty. To estimate the covariance matrix, Callen *et al.* assume that the change in growth rates of GDP is identically distributed over windows of observations. This assumption allows them to decompose the resulting variance of country pools into the sum of each country's growth rate plus covariances between countries within the pool.[4]

We adapt Callen *et al.*'s (2011) criterion to select the "preferred" pool of countries by selecting the combination of countries that gives the minimum variance of the growth rate of GDP for the pool. Theoretically, if there is full integration and complete markets for a pool of countries then each country in the pool will consume a constant fraction of pool output. This implies that the percentage change in consumption for all countries in the pool will be equal to the percentage change in pool-wide output and will change only along with pool uninsurable risks. For this reason, we focus on the comparison of the volatility (variance) of pool-wide GDP with the volatility (variance) of each country's GDP (rather than using consumption variances).

Identifying the countries that give the minimum variance of the growth rate of pool-wide GDP is not a trivial task, given the large number of possible combinations. To cover all combinations would take 2,047 calculations. Following Callen *et al.* (2011) we use recursive searches to implement an exhaustive search method to analyze all possible combinations. The method compares all pools of a given size p and chooses the best pool for each group of size p (the group size ranges from two to 10, so we assess the welfare gains of each best pool of a different size).

We implement our best-pool-finding algorithms using *Matlab*. This program starts the search for the best pool for one country and loops through sequential searches. At each iteration of the loop, we use a subsequent procedure to find the optimal pool by calculating the welfare gain for groups of a particular size for each country. This subsequent procedure – the core component of our algorithm – consists of the following three steps.

Step 1

We find the maximum welfare gain for the current country among all C_N^k possible candidates, where N denotes the number of countries and k is the current pool size. Generating all possible country combinations is the primary task, and it is important to make sure that the current country is in any pool. In each iteration, we calculate the welfare gain of the current pool with the formula

$$\delta^j = \frac{C_0}{C_0^j} \frac{\left\{1 - \beta \exp\left[(1-\theta)\left(\underline{\mu} - \frac{1}{2}\gamma \underline{\sigma}^2\right)\right]\right\}^{-(1/1-\theta)}}{\left\{1 - \beta \exp\left[(1-\theta)\left(\mu_j - \frac{1}{2}\gamma \sigma_j^2\right)\right]\right\}^{-(1/1-\theta)}} - 1$$

This is compared with the largest welfare gain that has been found so far, and used to update the maximum welfare gain if necessary. At the end of the loop, we thus identify the maximum welfare gain that can be achieved.

Step 2

We calculate the group variance using the formula

$$Var(g_p) = Var\left(\sum_{i=1}^{p} w_i g_i\right) = \sum_{i}^{p} w_i^2 Var(g_i) + \sum_{i=1}^{p}\sum_{j=i}^{p} w_i w_j Cov(g_i, g_j) \text{ for } i \neq j$$

This step paves the way for the calculation of welfare gain in Step 1 and will identify the current pool size, the name of the optimal pool, the group variance of the pool and the welfare gain.

Step 3

If the current pool size has not reached the threshold of the previous highest welfare gain, another recursion with a new pool size that is one larger than the current size would take place. Finally, each country's optimal pool, with varying pool sizes, can be identified.

5. Results[5]

We are now in a position to present the variance and welfare calculations for each of the nine East Asian countries when paired with combinations of our group of 11 countries and to derive the optimal groupings between them.

We focus on the variances and welfare gains of the best pool for each country, rather than the variance and welfare calculations for all possible pools. As noted above, under the assumptions that the initial consumption levels are equal under autarky and in the best pool, and that all share an equal growth rate of 3 per cent, the gains to pooling come only from reduced variance and not from joining pools of a higher growth rate.

We present two countries here as examples, Indonesia from the ASEAN5 and Australia from the non-ASEAN5. The detailed results for all countries are presented in Appendix A and the graphs for all countries, excluding Indonesia and

Australia, are presented in Appendix B. We use the same parameter values as Cole and Obstfeld (1991), Obstfeld (1994), Tesar (1995) and Callen *et al.* (2011), which are regarded as global "norms". These are the discount rate $\beta = 0.95$, the coefficient of risk-aversion $\gamma = 5$, the inverse of the inter-temporal substitution rate $\theta = 2$, and an expected growth rate of 3 per cent. In the figures, the left axis shows the variance, while the right axis represents the welfare gain.

Figure 8.3 shows that for Indonesia, the United Kingdom – rather than any ASEAN5 country – is the best single partner and that different integration pools would yield welfare gains in the range from 4.09 per cent to 4.36 per cent of consumption. The U shape of the figure shows that, as variance reduces, welfare increases but at a diminishing rate, that is reduced variance has a decreasing impact on the welfare gain. The best pool for Indonesia is a combination of Australia, China, the Philippines and the United Kingdom, which will achieve a welfare gain of 4.36 per cent of consumption. This pool has the lowest variance at 0.000192. The best pool size is achieved with four partners: beyond four, the welfare gain begins to decrease. The U-shaped pattern is replicated in other studies and some authors argue this is may be caused by larger enforcement costs (Imbs and Mauro 2007; Callen *et al.* 2011). Enforcement costs are not explicitly considered in our welfare calculation, so the more mundane explanation must lie with increases in covariance between partners as the numbers go beyond the optimum. Significantly, the optimal pool for Indonesia is not the current ASEAN

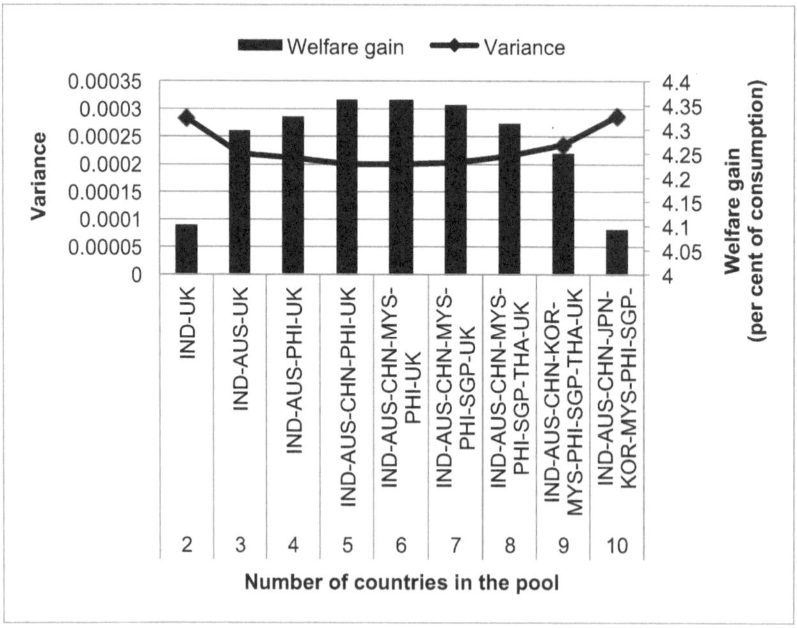

Figure 8.3 Dynamics of Indonesia's optimal pool

Source: Authors' calculations

group, but a mix of regional partners such as China and Australia, with the non-regional United Kingdom contributing to welfare gains. The results highlight the limits that may be imposed by a purely regional focus for integration for Indonesia. Callen *et al.* also note that geographical constraints can affect the ability to diversify risks in emerging markets if countries can only pool with certain countries. Welfare gains may be lower than integrating without geographical constraints. Another important finding is that the AUS-IND-CHN-PHI-UK pool is the most common optimal group – it appears more frequently than any other combination in the best pool for each of the 11 countries. We return to this point later.

Australia's results are presented as an example of a non-ASEAN5 country. From Figure 8.4, Australia's best pool size is four and marginal gains will decrease for larger sizes. This is similar to Indonesia: as variance reduces welfare improves but reductions in variance have a decreasing impact on the welfare gain. In Australia's case the maximum welfare gain reaches 0.24 per cent of consumption, while the minimum variance is 0.0001992. Compared with Indonesia, the welfare gain achieved by Australia, even with its optimal partners, is smaller. A striking difference for Australia compared with the other countries is that combined welfare gains become negative in pools of nine countries and above. Combinations of ten countries will worsen welfare in Australia. Although the best single pair for Australia is with Malaysia, the best pool is AUS-CHN-IND-PHI-UK, which does not contain Malaysia at all. Using our search algorithm, the optimal pool may not always include the initial best pair of countries, in contrast with the results in Corbett and Maulana (2011).

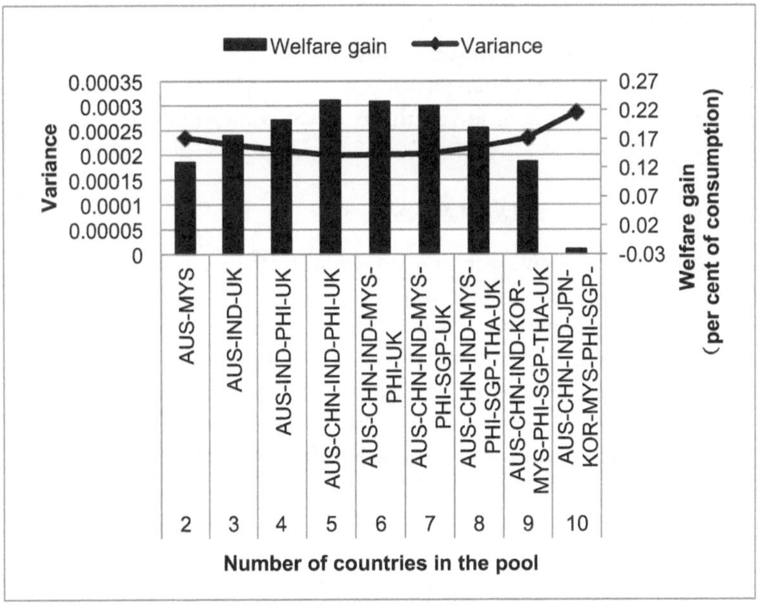

Figure 8.4 Dynamics of Australia's optimal pool

Source: Authors' calculations

5.1 Optimal pools for ASEAN5 countries

Examining the optimal combinations for the ASEAN5 countries with the group of 11 and calculating the scale of the welfare gain from the reduction in volatility, reveals some interesting results. Table 8.A1 in Appendix A presents the variances for all countries, the pool variances and the welfare gains. It emerges that as a single partner, Australia is the ideal partner for four countries (Indonesia is an exception), while the United Kingdom is the ideal partner for Indonesia. All five countries in the ASEAN group reach their maximum benefits in combinations with five or fewer partners, and in these combinations, the pool variance decreases significantly. This means that these countries gain considerably from the reduction in the volatility of combined growth. The largest variance reduction comes from being integrated with the first partner, and the proportional decrease in the variance is smaller as more partners are added into the pool. The percentage increase in welfare gain is correspondingly bigger in the initial pool compared with the subsequent additions to the pool.

Amongst the ASEAN5 countries, Thailand seems to achieve the biggest welfare gain at greater than 5 per cent of annual consumption (Thailand's maximum welfare gain is about 5.978 per cent of consumption with its optimal pool of six: THA-AUS-CHN-IND-PHI-UK). Singapore follows Thailand, gaining nearly 5 per cent of consumption in all pools. Indonesia and Malaysia gain more than 4 per cent from pooling, while the Philippines achieves less but still gains more than 3 per cent. The other four ASEAN5 countries have very similar situations.

Australia is in the best pool for four of the countries of the region and is the best initial partner; bringing the bulk of the benefits to any pool. If the ASEAN countries want to establish risk-sharing arrangements, Australia is a critical partner to achieve maximum potential benefits. A pooling of AUS-CHN-IND-PHI-UK is optimal or close to optimal for all the ASEAN countries.

5.2 Optimal pools for the non-ASEAN5 countries

Table 8.A2 in Appendix A shows the best pool and welfare gains for the non-ASEAN5 countries (Australia, United Kingdom, China, Japan and Korea). As for the ASEAN5 countries, the percentage welfare gain is larger from the initial combination with the best partner, increasing at a diminishing rate as more countries are added to the pool. The scale of welfare gains achieved by non-ASEAN countries is smaller than for the ASEAN5 countries. The maximum gains for the other three countries, excluding South Korea, are less than 2 per cent. The optimal pool size for non-ASEAN5 countries is typically six or fewer. In Japan, the optimal pool size is five. Japan's largest welfare gain is about 1.2 per cent of consumption.

It is noteworthy that when considering the best single partner for the non-ASEAN countries (not necessarily the optimal pool) none of them is best paired with an ASEAN country, except Australia where the best single pair is with Malaysia. For China, the United Kingdom is the ideal partner, while the best partner for Japan is the United States and for South Korea the best partner is Australia. It appears that limiting integration to regional groups would not be in the best interests of most of these countries, although one grouping stands out as presenting near optimal gains for all. The best grouping for China is UK-AUS-PHI-IND. The best group for Japan is AUS-CHI-IND-PHI-UK (though the welfare gain is only marginally better than a single partnering with the United States), and the best group for South Korea is AUS-CHI-IND-PHI-UK. Along with the results from the ASEAN countries, it appears that a core group of Australia, China, Indonesia, Philippines and the United Kingdom would provide the bulk of gains for most partners. As more partners join, there are slight reductions in the welfare benefits for some partners, which presents challenges to calculating the best pooling for all countries in the region simultaneously.

5.3 Who gains most?

Figure 8.5 shows the significant variation in the welfare gain across all 11 countries. Thailand, Singapore and Indonesia benefit more than any other country,

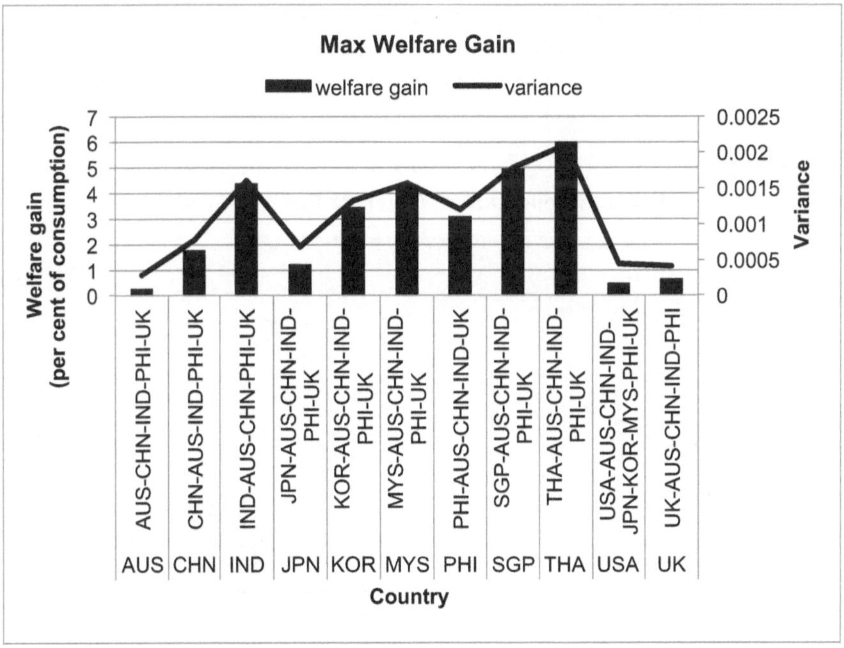

Figure 8.5 Maximum welfare gain of each country

Source: Authors' calculations

Notes: The left axis shows the percentage welfare gain for each country in its optimal of pool (varying sizes for each country); the right axis shows the variance of individual country's income.

while Australia, the United Kingdom and the United States benefit relatively less. The outcome is the result of the link between reduced volatility of GDP and the benefits from smoothing consumption. Because of the assumption that each country's consumption and expected growth rate will be the same as the average of the whole pool both before and after integration, countries with more volatility in the GDP growth rate achieve greater reduction in volatility (and therefore assumed smoothing of consumption and welfare gain) compared with countries with less volatility initially. The more volatile the income of the country, the more benefit it will derive from pooling. Another contributing factor is the nature of the individual and global business cycle. From Table 8.2, both the United States and United Kingdom have higher correlations with world growth. As Lewis (2000) points out, the higher initial correlation with the world explains why the US' benefits from pooling are lower than other countries; in effect the United States is already integrated with the whole world.

Figure 8.6 shows the welfare implications of different pool sizes, and reinforces the results in Figure 8.5: no matter what the pool size, countries with larger volatility of output gain more from pooling. Strikingly, the results show the largest welfare gain among Asian countries is as much as 5.5 per cent of annual consumption. While Kim *et al.* (2006) found a range from 1.4 per cent to 7 per cent welfare gain from integration in 10 Asian countries (using different methods from ours), many estimates for other country groups have been lower, as noted in the literature review above.

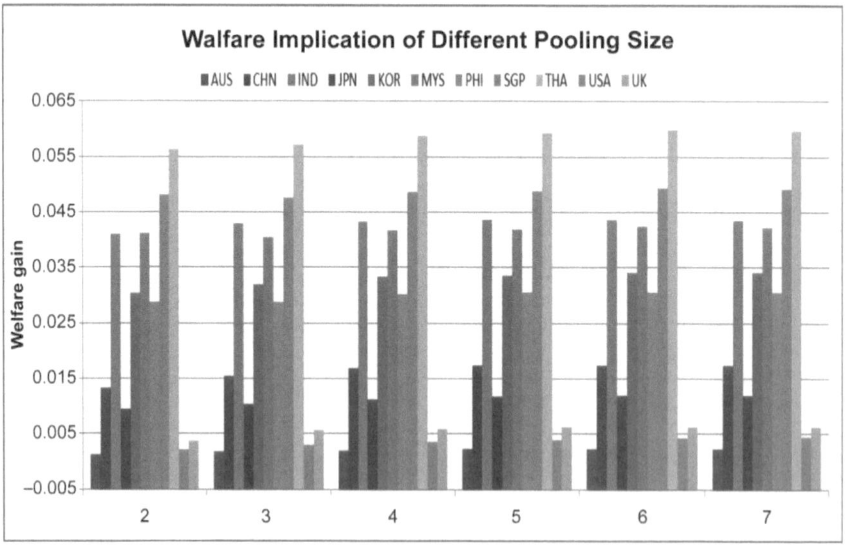

Figure 8.6 Welfare implication of different pooling size

Source: Author's calculations

Table 8.3 Optimal pool for each country

Country	*Optimal pool*
AUS	AUS-CHN-IND-PHI-UK
CHN	CHN-AUS-IND-PHI-UK
IND	IND-AUS-CHN-PHI-UK
JPN	JPN-AUS-CHN-IND-PHI-UK
KOR	KOR-AUS-CHN-IND-PHI-UK
MYS	MYS-AUS-CHN-IND-PHI-UK
PHI	PHI-AUS-CHN-IND-UK
SGP	SGP-AUS-CHN-IND-PHI-UK
THA	THA-AUS-CHN-IND-PHI-UK
USA	USA-AUS-CHN-IND-JPN-KOR-MYS-PHI-UK
UK	UK-AUS-CHN-IND-PHI

Source: Authors' calculations

5.4 Ideal partners and most common combinations

From Table 8.A1 and Table 8.A2 in Appendix A, it is clear that Australia is the ideal partner for many countries among the 11 considered here. Furthermore, the most common best combination is AUS-CHN-PHI-IND-UK. This group is contained in every best pool for all these countries, as shown in Table 8.3. This combination is clearly not the same as any current Asian political grouping. Somewhat surprisingly, the United Kingdom, a European country, brings benefits as an integration partner to the Asian countries, while the United States, despite its low volatility and status as the most developed country in the world, does not enter into any best combination at all. This may be due, as noted above, to the close connection between the US business cycle and the cycles of the other countries (i.e. despite low variance, the covariance is high so it does not provide additional risk-sharing). This mirrors the finding of Imbs and Mauro (2007) that France was not contained in any optimal pool because its growth cycle tends to be closely related to the growth of the other 74 countries in their study. Thus France's high covariance with the other countries in the sample removed it from the best pools.

5.5 Impact from different parameter assumptions

So far we have assumed constant global norms for the key parameters $\beta = 0.95$, $\theta = 2$, $\gamma = 5$. But it is likely that the risk-aversion parameters and the intertemporal substitution rate are not constant, and indeed they may be very sensitive to the scale of welfare gains. Here, following Obstfeld (1994) and Lewis (2000), we introduce different values of risk-aversion and the inverse of intertemporal substitution to gauge the effect on the welfare gains and the composition of the best pools.

Table 8.4 Impacts on welfare gain for China with different risk-aversion

Optimal pool	*gamma = 3*	*gamma = 5*	*gamma = 7*
CHN-UK	0.7918	1.3329	1.8848
CHN-AUS-PHI	0.9216	1.5513	2.1935
CHN-AUS-IND-UK	1.0008	1.6846	2.382
CHN-AUS-IND-PHI-UK	1.0371	1.7455	2.4681
CHN-AUS-IND-MYS-PHI-UK	1.0357	1.7433	2.4649
CHN-AUS-IND-MYS-PHI-SGP-UK	1.031	1.7353	2.4537

Source: Authors' calculations

Table 8.5 Impacts on welfare gain with different theta for China

Optimal pool	*theta = 2*	*theta = 4*	*theta = 10*
CHN-UK	0.7918	0.7522	0.3049
CHN-AUS-PHI	0.9216	0.8743	0.3539
CHN-AUS-IND-UK	1.0008	0.9486	0.3837
CHN-AUS-IND-PHI-UK	1.0371	0.9825	0.3973
CHN-AUS-IND-MYS-PHI-UK	1.0357	0.9813	0.3968
CHN-AUS-IND-MYS-PHI-SGP-UK	1.031	0.9768	0.395

Source: Authors' calculations

Tables 8.4 and 8.5 show the welfare impact from different risk-aversion values using China as an example (further examples for the non-ASEAN countries are shown in Appendix C). With $\gamma = 3$, $\gamma = 5$, $\gamma = 7$, it is clear that with smaller coefficients of risk-aversion, the welfare gains become smaller. This is true for all countries and is to be expected since the welfare value of reduced volatility of GDP will be lower for more risk-loving countries. Clearly this also has implications for the scale of welfare gains estimated earlier. If lower-income countries in the region have high risk-aversion, then the scale of welfare gain from pooling will be even larger than calculated earlier.

Table 8.5 presents similar results with different values for θ, the inverse of the inter-temporal rate of substitution. Lower values result in countries benefitting more from the pool. A decrease in θ means the elasticity of inter-temporal substitution increases, so consumers value future gains in consumption certainty more highly and the welfare gains from consumption smoothing increase (Lewis, 2000). The welfare impacts in other countries are similar to those in China.

6. Conclusions

To assess the gains from financial integration this chapter investigated the welfare gain from reducing the volatility of GDP, since financial integration opens the possibility to smooth consumption in the face of output uncertainty. With complete risk-sharing, changes in consumption will be equal to changes in the combined output of the integrated group, and the consumption level of an individual country will be identical to the average consumption in the pool. On entering a risk-sharing arrangement the individual country's welfare gain derives from the benefits of the fall in volatility of consumption.

In this chapter, we have focussed exclusively on the implication for welfare gains from this potential reduction in volatility. We sought the best groupings of partner countries for each country in a group of nine Asian and two external partners and quantified the largest welfare gain attainable. Building on the method in Corbett and Maulana (2011), originally derived from Imbs (2006), a recursive and a systematic search method is adopted to calculate all possible country groupings using a *Matlab* programming computational algorithm to do the exhaustive search. Calculating first the variance of the individual country, then the variance of different pools and finally calculating the welfare gains, we compared each possible group. The initial estimates were done using two assumptions: that the initial consumption level under autarky was equal to the average for the pool, and that all countries had the same growth rate. The result is that reducing volatility increases welfare at a diminishing rate. We presented the best pool and the biggest welfare gains available for each country and showed that the potential welfare gains for the ASEAN5 countries are larger than in the non-ASEAN5 countries. In particular, Thailand, Singapore and Indonesia potentially gain more than other countries, while the developed countries of Australia, the United Kingdom and the United States will gain relatively little. The largest welfare gain (Thailand) exceeds 5 per cent of consumption, making our estimates relatively large by comparison with other literature (though not out of line with estimates for developing countries). When considering integration with a single partner alone, Australia is the ideal partner for most of the countries considered here, and the most commonly occurring optimal pool is AUS-CHN-PHI-IND-UK.

Changing the assumptions of constant coefficients of risk-aversion and the inverse of the inter-temporal substitution rate affects the welfare gain, with higher risk-aversion and higher inter-temporal substitution rates (i.e. greater value on future certainty) increasing the potential gains.

There remain many limitations with this method of assessing the welfare effects of financial integration. It does not consider factors affecting the implementation and enforcement of financial integration arrangements, such as enforcement costs and institutional quality. It also does not take account of other elements of integration arrangements, such as trade integration. We consider only 11 countries, so the possible pools are restricted, and we may be missing the benefits of wider global diversification. In addition, by imposing the two assumptions discussed above, the analysis focusses only on the pure diversification gain from reducing volatility. It would be useful (though difficult) to consider the effect of relaxing these two assumptions in the future so that the potential gains from joining groups with higher levels of consumption and faster growth could also be considered.

What does emerge clearly, however, is that there are considerable potential welfare gains for countries in Asia from smoothing consumption and output uncertainty through financial integration. The best welfare gains can be achieved by choosing the most appropriate partners, and the chief virtue to be sought in a partner is the ability to offset the home country's volatility. Australia is found to be the ideal partner to five countries, and pools that include Australia, China, Philippines, Indonesia and the United Kingdom regularly emerge as the best for many countries in the region. Each country has a different maximum size for its best group, but a group with these five would capture the bulk of welfare gains for many participants. As group size gets bigger there are varying declines in welfare gains for some partners, so there are challenges in finding a strictly optimal group for all. From a welfare point of view, however, it is clear that current political and geographical groupings are not the best combinations for financial integration, and limiting integration arrangements on the basis of geography will limit their value.

Notes

1 Callen *et al.* (2011) note that the overall result of their analysis is similar when they use the *Penn World Tables* (PWT) data set.

2 Limpert *et al.* (2001) point out that when a variable has low mean values, large variance and is non-negative then it is innocuous to assume the variable has a log normal distribution.

3 Callen *et al.* (2011) extend the welfare calculation by allowing differential growth rates between countries and the pool and differentials in initial consumption levels. In the Appendix, we show the effects of assuming different growth rates for all countries, but do not examine different growth rates for individual countries.

4 Callen *et al.* (2011) also test a different stochastic process for the growth rates of GDP and find that the main result of the analysis is largely unaffected.

5 Our results depend heavily on the estimation of the variance–covariance matrices of GDP growth rates, and these will be appropriate only if those series are statistically stable over time. Using the Augmented Dickey Fuller (ADF) test, unit roots are rejected in all countries' GDP growth rates, excluding Japan, so we conclude that our estimator for the variance–covariance matrices is justifiable. The results of the ADF test for the unit root component for each country's growth of GDP are available upon request.

References

Callen, M., Imbs, J. and Mauro, P. (2011) 'Pooling risk among countries', mimeo, revised version of CEPR DP 6461. Online. Available HTTP: <http://www.jeanimbs.com/papers2_files/Pooling_22July2011.pdf>.

Cole, H.L. and Obstfeld, M. (1991) 'Commodity trade and international risk-sharing: how much do financial markets matter?', *NBER Working Paper* 3027.

Corbett, J. and Maulana, A. (2010) 'Consumption risk-sharing and its implications for financial integration: the case of nine East Asian countries' in C. Findlay, F. Parulian and J. Corbett (eds), *Linkages between Real and Financial Aspects of Economic Integration in East Asia,* ERIA Research Project Report 2009-1, Jakarta: ERIA pp. 43–64.

Corbett, J. and A. Maulana (2011), 'Choosing Partners for Integration: maximising Benefits from Risk Sharing' in Corbett, J. and Y. Xu (eds.), *Achieving Sustainable Growth in East Asia,* ERIA Research Project Report 2010-28, Jakarta: ERIA, pp. 223–256.

Epstein, L.G. and Zin, S.E. (1989) 'Substitution, risk-aversion, and the temporal behavior of consumption and asset returns: a theoretical framework', *Econometrica,* 54: 937–69.

Imbs, J. (2006) 'The real effects of financial integration', *Journal of International Economics,* 68: 296–324.

Imbs, J. and Mauro, P. (2007) 'Pooling Risk Among Countries', *IMF Working Paper* 07/132 and CEPR Discussion Paper 6461.

Kim, D. and Sheen, J. (2007) 'Consumption risk-sharing within Australia and with New Zealand', *The Economic Record,* 83: 46–59.

Kim, S., Kim, S.H. and Wang, Y. (2006) 'Financial integration and consumption risk-sharing in East Asia', *Japan and the World Economy,* 18: 143–57.

Lewis, K. (2000) 'Why do stocks and consumption imply such different gains from international risk-sharing?', *Journal of International Economics,* 52: 1–35.

Limpert, E., Stahel, W.A. and Abby, M. (2001) 'Log-normal distributions across the sciences: keys and clues', *Bioscience,* 51: 341–52.

Lucas, R.E. Jr. (1987) *Model of Business Cycles,* Oxford: Blackwell.

Obstfeld, M. (1994) 'Evaluating risky consumption paths: the role of intertemporal substitutability', *European Economic Review,* 38: 1471–86.

Tesar, L. (1995) 'Evaluating the gains from international risk-sharing', *Carnegie-Rochester Conference Series on Public Policy* 42(June): 95–143.

van Wincoop, E. (1994) 'Welfare gains from international risk-sharing?', *Journal of Monetary Economics,* 34: 175–200.

van Wincoop, E. (1999) 'How big are potential welfare gains from international risk-sharing?', *Journal of International Economics,* 47: 109–35.

World Bank (various years) *World Development Indicators,* Washington, DC: World Bank.

Appendix A

Ideal risk-sharing partners

Table 8.A1 Ideal risk-sharing partners for ASEAN5 countries

Country	*2*	*3*	*4*	*5*	*6*	*7*
Indonesia Variance (0.001603) Welfare gain	IND-UK 0.0002829 [4.1022]	IND-UK-AUS 0.0002196 [4.2983]	IND-UK-AUS-PHI 0.0002106 [4.3264]	IND-UK-AUS-CHN-PHI 0.0001992 [4.3618]	IND-AUS-CHN-MYS-PHI-UK 0.0001999 [4.3594]	IND-AUS-CHN-MYS-PHI-SGP-UK 0.0002026 [4.3513]
Philippines Variance (0.001198) Welfare gain	PHI-AUS 0.0002608 [2.8720]	PHI-AUS-MYS 0.0002589 [2.8778]	PHI-AUS-IND-UK 0.0002106 [3.0257]	PHI-AUS-CHN-IND-UK 0.0001992 [3.0606]	PHI-AUS-CHN-IND-MYS-UK 0.0001999 [3.0583]	PHI-AUS-CHN-IND-MYS-SGP-UK 0.0002026 [3.0503]
Singapore Variance (0.001779) Welfare gain	SGP-AUS 0.0002423 [4.8019]	SGP-AUS-MYS 0.0002592 [4.7492]	SGP-AUS-IND-UK 0.0002214 [4.8670]	SGP-AUS-IND-PHI-UK 0.0002141 [4.8899]	SGP-AUS-CHN-IND-PHI-UK 0.0002006 [4.9318]	SGP-AUS-CHN-IND-MYS-PHI-UK 0.0002026 [4.9258]
Malaysia Variance (0.001566) Welfare gain	MYS-AUS 0.0002352 [4.1273]	MYS-AUS-PHI 0.0002589 [4.0540]	MYS-AUS-IND-UK 0.0002204 [4.1732]	MYS-AUS-IND-PHI-UK 0.0002138 [4.1936]	MYS-AUS-CHN-IND-PHI-UK 0.0001999 [4.2367]	MYS-AUS-CHN-IND-PHI-SGP-UK 0.0002026 [4.2285]
Thailand Variance (0.002102) Welfare gain	THA-AUS 0.0003179 [5.6325]	THA-AUS-UK 0.0002912 [5.7167]	THA-AUS-IND-UK 0.000239 [5.8812]	THA-AUS-CHN-IND-UK 0.0002264 [5.9207]	THA-AUS-CHN-IND-PHI-UK 0.0002082 [5.9780]	THA-AUS-CHN-IND-PHI-SGP-UK 0.000211 [5.9693]

Source: Authors' calculations

Notes: In calculating the welfare gains, we use the following parameters $\beta = 0.95$, $\theta = 2$, $\gamma = 5$, $\mu = \mu_i = 3$ per cent.

Table 8.A2 Ideal risk-sharing partners for non-ASEAN5 countries

Country	*2*	*3*	*4*	*5*	*6*	*7*
Australia	AUS-MYS	AUS-IND-UK	AUS-IND-PHI-	AUS-CHN-IND-	AUS-CHN-IND-	AUS-CHN-IND-
Variance(0.000279)	0.0002352	0.0002196	UK 0.0002106	PHI-UK 0.0001992	MYS-PHI-UK	MYS-PHI-SGP-UK
Welfare gain	[0.1289]	[0.1754]	[0.2023]	[0.2363]	0.0001999 [0.2341]	0.0002026 [0.2262]
Korea	KOR-AUS	KOR-AUS-PHI	KOR-AUS-CHN-	KOR-AUS-CHN-	KOR-AUS-CHN-	KOR-AUS-CHN-
Variance(0.001320)	0.0003353	0.0002792	PHI 0.0002365	PHI-UK 0.0002278	IND-PHI-UK	IND-PHI-SGP-UK
Welfare gain	[3.0306]	[3.2029]	[3.3343]	[3.3610]	0.0002105 [3.4144]	0.0002131 [3.4061]
Japan	JPN-USA	JPN-CHN-USA	JPN-AUS-CHN-	JPN-AUS-CHN-	JPN-AUS-CHN-IND-	JPN-AUS-CHN-
Variance(0.000676)	0.0003670	0.0003340	UK 0.0003077	PHI-UK 0.0002884	PHI-UK 0.0002811	IND-MYS-PHI-UK
Welfare gain	[0.9334]	[1.0328]	[1.1123]	[1.1702]	[1.1924]	0.0002824 [1.1885]
China	CHN-UK	CHN-AUS-	CHN-AUS-IND-	CHN-AUS-IND-	CHN-AUS-IND-	CHN-AUS-IND-
Variance(0.000776)	0.0003357	PHI 0.0002634	UK 0.0002193	PHI-UK 0.0001992	MYS-PHI-UK	MYS-PHI-SGP-UK
Welfare gain	[1.3329]	[1.5513]	[1.6846]	[1.7455]	0.0001999 [1.7433]	0.0002026 [1.7353]

Source: Authors' calculations

Notes: In calculating the welfare gains, we use the following parameters $\beta = 0.95$, $\theta = 2$, $\gamma = 5$, $\mu = \mu_j = 3$ per cent.

Appendix B

Best pool and welfare gain for all countries

The following figures show the change in variance and welfare for each principal country with different numbers of countries in the pool, and the optimal pool in each case. The parameter values for calculating welfare are as described in the text.

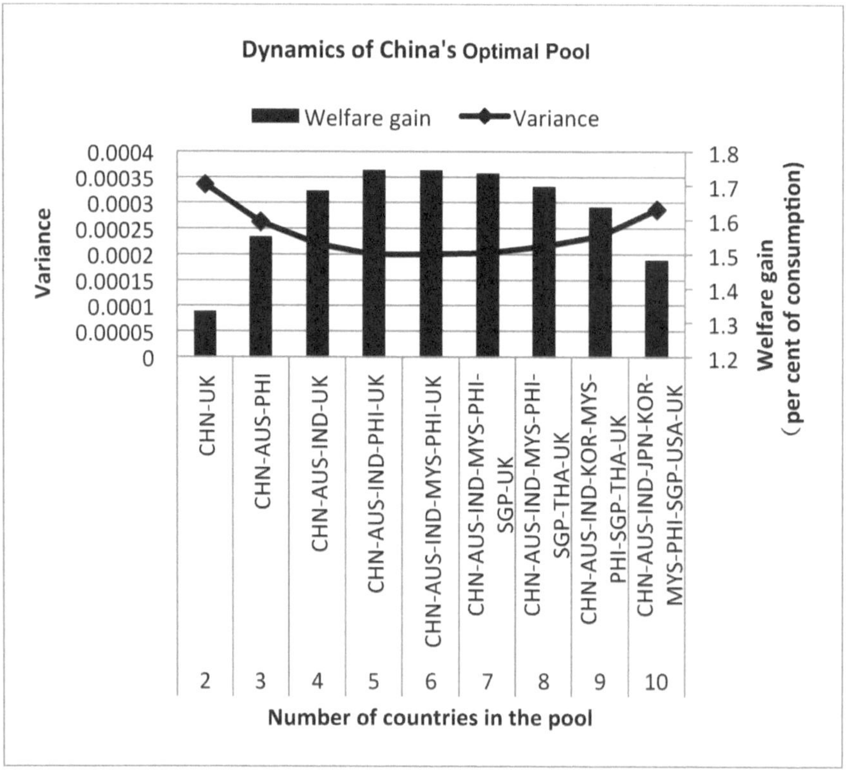

Figure 8.B1 Dynamics of China's optimal pool

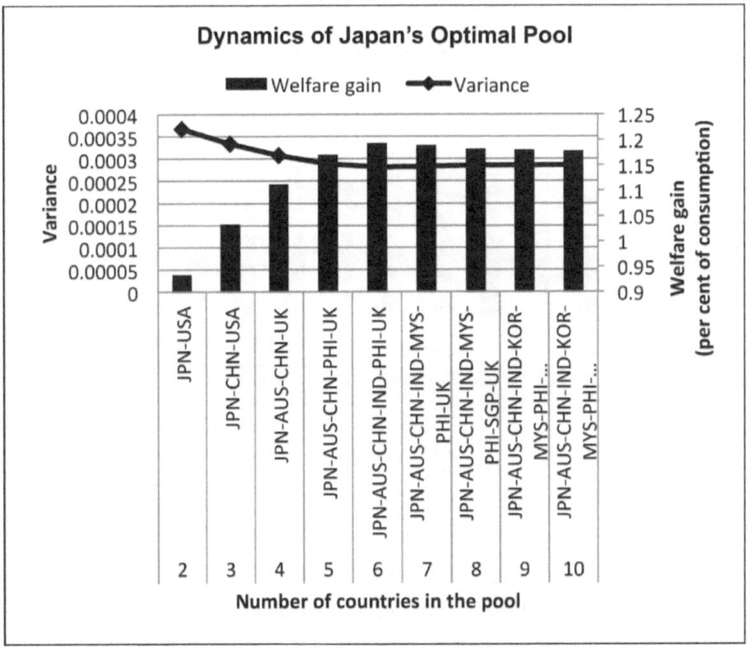

Figure 8.B2 Dynamics of Japan's optimal pool

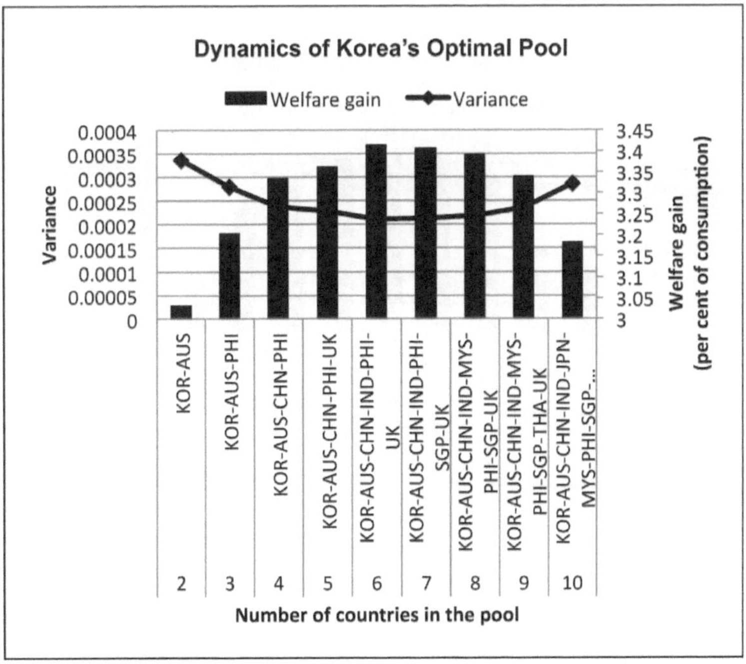

Figure 8.B3 Dynamics of Korea's optimal pool

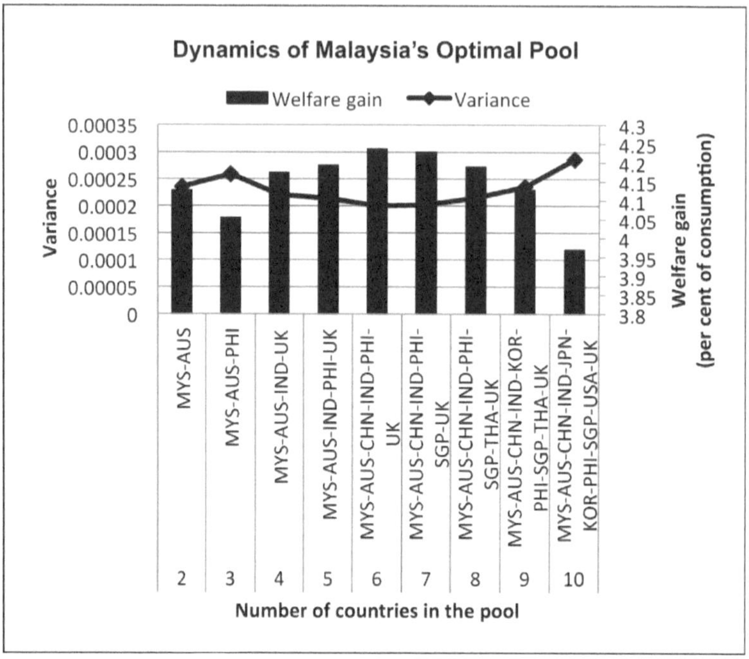

Figure 8.B4 Dynamics of Malaysia's optimal pool

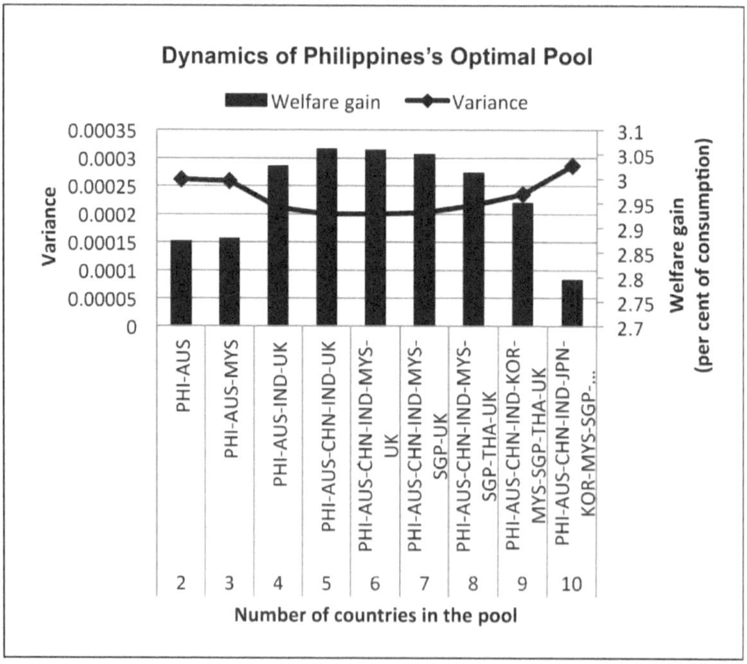

Figure 8.B5 Dynamics of the Philippines's optimal pool

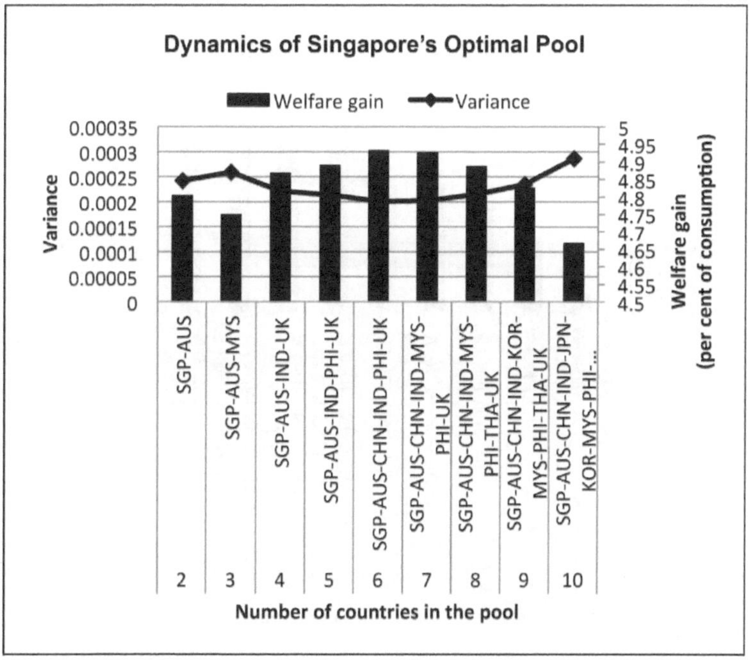

Figure 8.B6 Dynamics of Singapore's optimal pool

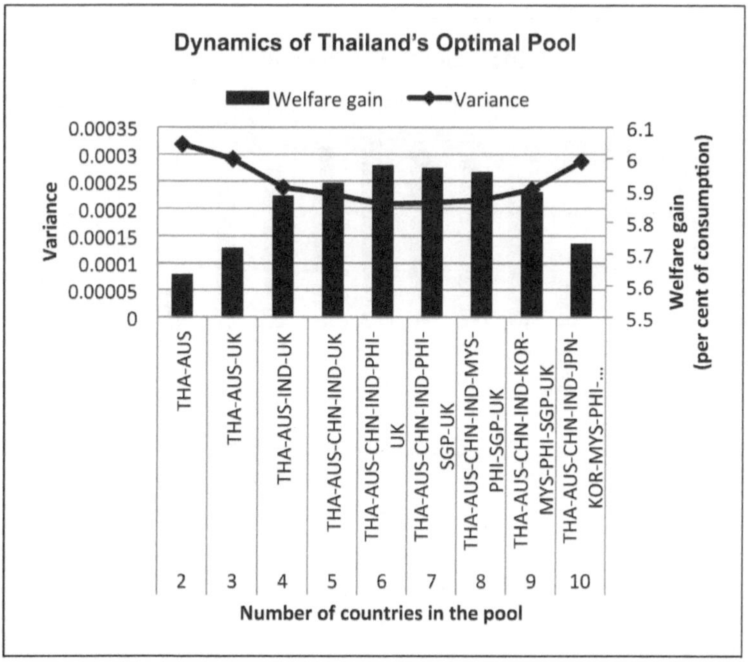

Figure 8.B7 Dynamics of Thailand's optimal pool

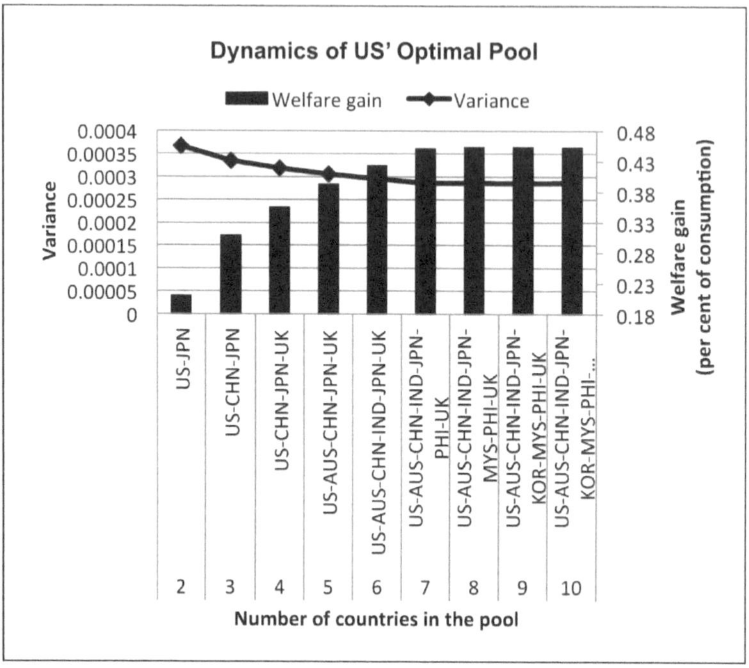

Figure 8.B8 Dynamics of the United States' optimal pool

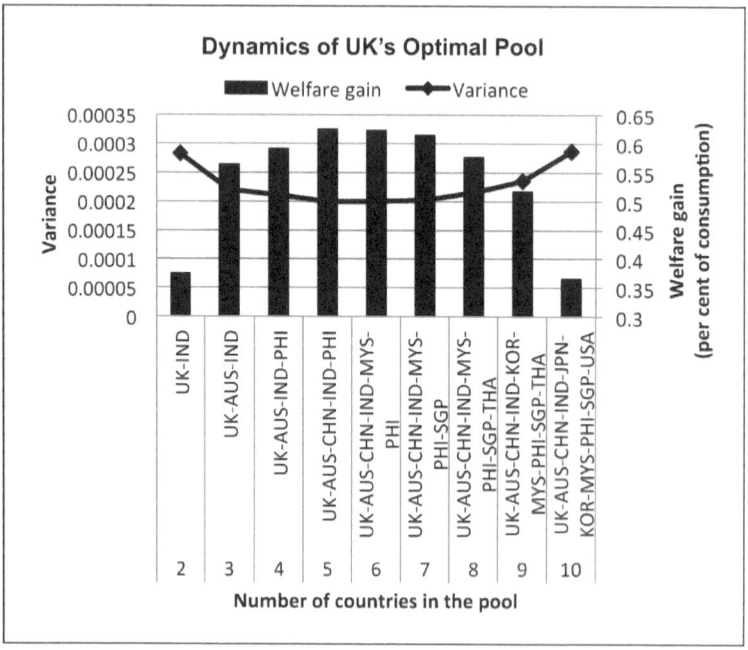

Figure 8.B9 Dynamics of the United Kingdom's optimal pool

Appendix C

Effect of different values for the coefficients of risk-aversion and inverse of the elasticity of inter-temporal substitution in consumption

We illustrate the impact on welfare of different values for the coefficients of risk-aversion (gamma) and of the elasticity of inter-temporal substitution in consumption (theta) for the non-ASEAN countries. Tables 8.C1 and 8.C2 show the effect of setting gamma equal to 3 and 7. Tables 8.C3 and 8.C4 show the effect of setting theta equal to 4 and 10. As noted in the text, with larger risk-aversion, the welfare gains become larger. With larger elasticity of inter-temporal substitution the gains become smaller.

Table 8.C1 Ideal risk-sharing partners for non-ASEAN5 countries (gamma = 3)

Country	*2*	*3*	*4*	*5*	*6*	*7*
Australia Variance(0.000279) Welfare gain	AUS-MYS 0.0002352 [0.0771]	AUS-IND-UK 0.0002196 [0.1049]	AUS-IND-PHI-UK 0.0002106 [0.1210]	AUS-CHN-IND-PHI-UK 0.0001992 [0.1413]	AUS-CHN-IND-MYS-PHI-UK 0.0001999 [0.1400]	AUS-CHN-IND-MYS-PHI-SGP-UK 0.0002026 [0.1353]
Korea Variance(0.001320) Welfare gain	KOR-AUS 0.0003353 [1.7878]	KOR-AUS-PHI 0.0002792 [1.8895]	KOR-AUS-CHN-PHI 0.0002365 [1.9670]	KOR-AUS-CHN-PHI-UK 0.0002278 [1.9828]	KOR-AUS-CHN-IND-PHI-UK 0.0002105 [2.0143]	KOR-AUS-CHN-IND-PHI-SGP-UK 0.0002131 [2.0094]
Japan Variance(0.000676) Welfare gain	JPN-USA 0.0003670 [0.5552]	JPN-CHN-USA 0.0003340 [0.6143]	JPN-AUS-CHN-UK 0.0003077 [0.6616]	JPN-AUS-CHN-PHI-UK 0.0002884 [0.6961]	JPN-AUS-CHN-IND-PHI-UK 0.0002811 [0.7093]	JPN-AUS-CHN-IND-MYS-PHI-UK 0.0002824 [0.7070]
China Variance(0.000776) Welfare gain	CHN-UK 0.0003357 [0.7918]	CHN-AUS-PHI 0.0002634 [0.9216]	CHN-AUS-IND-UK 0.0002193 [1.0008]	CHN-AUS-IND-PHI-UK 0.0001992 [1.0371]	CHN-AUS-IND-MYS-PHI-UK 0.0001999 [1.0357]	CHN-AUS-IND-MYS-PHI-SGP-UK 0.0002026 [1.0310]

Source: Authors' calculations

Table 8.C2 Ideal risk-sharing partners for non-ASEAN5 countries (gamma = 7)

Country	*2*	*3*	*4*	*5*	*6*	*7*
Australia Variance(0.000279) Welfare gain	AUS-MYS 0.0002352 [0.1811]	AUS-IND-UK 0.0002196 [0.2464]	AUS-IND-PHI-UK 0.0002106 [0.2843]	AUS-CHN-IND-PHI-UK 0.0001992 [0.3320]	AUS-CHN-IND-MYS-PHI-UK 0.0001999 [0.3289]	AUS-CHN-IND-MYS-PHI-SGP-UK 0.0002026 [0.3179]
Korea Variance(0.001320) Welfare gain	KOR-AUS 0.0003353 [4.3166]	KOR-AUS-PHI 0.0002792 [4.5620]	KOR-AUS-CHN-PHI 0.0002365 [4.7490]	KOR-AUS-CHN-PHI-UK 0.0002278 [4.7870]	KOR-AUS-CHN-IND-PHI-UK 0.0002105 [4.8629]	KOR-AUS-CHN-IND-PHI-SGP-UK 0.0002131 [4.8512]
Japan Variance(0.000676) Welfare gain	JPN-USA 0.0003670 [1.3183]	JPN-CHN-USA 0.0003340 [1.4585]	JPN-AUS-CHN-UK 0.0003077 [1.5708]	JPN-AUS-CHN-PHI-UK 0.0002884 [1.6526]	JPN-AUS-CHN-IND-PHI-UK 0.0002811 [1.6839]	JPN-AUS-CHN-IND-MYS-PHI-UK 0.0002824 [1.6784]
China Variance(0.000776) Welfare gain	CHN-UK 0.0003357 [1.8848]	CHN-AUS-PHI 0.0002634 [2.1935]	CHN-AUS-IND-UK 0.0002193 [2.3820]	CHN-AUS-IND-PHI-UK 0.0001992 [2.4681]	CHN-AUS-IND-MYS-PHI-UK 0.0001999 [2.4649]	CHN-AUS-IND-MYS-PHI-SGP-UK 0.0002026 [2.4537]

Source: Authors' calculations

Notes: gamma = 7

Table 8.C3 Ideal risk-sharing partners for non-ASEAN5 countries (theta = 4)

Country	*2*	*3*	*4*	*5*	*6*	*7*
Australia	AUS-MYS	AUS-IND-UK	AUS-IND-PHI-UK	AUS-CHN-IND-PHI-UK	AUS-CHN-IND-MYS-PHI-UK	AUS-CHN-IND-MYS-PHI-SGP-UK
Variance(0.000279)	0.0002352	0.0002196	0.0002106	0.0001992	0.0001999	0.0002026
Welfare gain	[0.0724]	[0.0984]	[0.1136]	[0.1326]	[0.1313]	[0.1269]
Korea	KOR-AUS	KOR-AUS-PHI	KOR-AUS-CHN-PHI	KOR-AUS-CHN-PHI-UK	KOR-AUS-CHN-IND-PHI-UK	KOR-AUS-CHN-IND-PHI-SGP-UK
Variance(0.001320)	0.0003353	0.0002792	0.0002365	0.0002278	0.0002105	0.0002131
Welfare gain	[1.7168]	[1.8124]	[1.8852]	[1.9000]	[1.9295]	[1.9249]
Japan	JPN-USA	JPN-CHN-USA	JPN-AUS-CHN-UK	JPN-AUS-CHN-PHI-UK	JPN-AUS-CHN-IND-PHI-UK	JPN-AUS-CHN-IND-MYS-PHI-UK
Variance(0.000676)	0.0003670	0.0003340	0.0003077	0.0002884	0.0002811	0.0002824
Welfare gain	[0.5268]	[0.5825]	[0.6270]	[0.6594]	[0.6718]	[0.6696]
China	CHN-UK	CHN-AUS-PHI	CHN-AUS-IND-UK	CHN-AUS-IND-PHI-UK	CHN-AUS-IND-MYS-PHI-UK	CHN-AUS-IND-MYS-PHI-SGP-UK
Variance(0.000776)	0.0003357	0.0002634	0.0002193	0.0001992	0.0001999	0.0002026
Welfare gain	[0.7522]	[0.8743]	[0.9486]	[0.9825]	[0.9813]	[0.9768]

Source: Authors' calculations

Notes: theta = 4

Table 8.C4 Ideal risk-sharing partners for non-ASEAN5 countries (theta = 10)

Country	2	3	4	5	6	7
Australia	AUS-MYS	AUS-IND-UK	AUS-IND-PHI-UK	AUS-CHN-IND-PHI-UK	AUS-CHN-IND-MYS-PHI-UK	AUS-CHN-IND-MYS-PHI-SGP-UK
Variance(0.000279)	0.0002352	0.0002196	0.0002106	0.0001992	0.0001999	0.0002026
Welfare gain	[0.0292]	[0.0397]	[0.0458]	[0.0534]	[0.0529]	[0.0511]
Korea	KOR-AUS	KOR-AUS-PHI	KOR-AUS-CHN-PHI	KOR-AUS-CHN-PHI-UK	KOR-AUS-CHN-IND-PHI-UK	KOR-AUS-CHN-IND-PHI-SGP-UK
Variance(0.001320)	0.0003353	0.0002792	0.0002365	0.0002278	0.0002105	0.0002131
Welfare gain	[0.6991]	[0.7373]	[0.7664]	[0.7722]	[0.7840]	[0.7822]
Japan	JPN-USA	JPN-CHN-USA	JPN-AUS-CHN-UK	JPN-AUS-CHN-PHI-UK	JPN-AUS-CHN-IND-PHI-UK	JPN-AUS-CHN-IND-MYS-PHI-UK
Variance(0.000676)	0.0003670	0.0003340	0.0003077	0.0002884	0.0002811	0.0002824
Welfare gain	[0.2135]	[0.2359]	[0.2538]	[0.2669]	[0.2718]	[0.2710]
China	CHN-UK	CHN-AUS-PHI	CHN-AUS-IND-UK	CHN-AUS-IND-PHI-UK	CHN-AUS-IND-MYS-PHI-UK	CHN-AUS-IND-MYS-PHI-SGP-UK
Variance(0.000776)	0.0003357	0.0002634	0.0002193	0.0001992	0.0001999	0.0002026
Welfare gain	[0.3049]	[0.3539]	[0.3837]	[0.3973]	[0.3968]	[0.3950]

Source: Authors' calculations

Notes: theta = 10

9 The influences of international and domestic shocks on East Asia

Mardi Dungey and M. Tugrul Vehbi

1. Introduction

Economic modelling for open economies in an empirically coherent and theoretically acceptable manner is a pressing problem. The increasing global financial integration of Asian economies over the past few decades and the effects of two significant financial crises in 1997–98 and 2007–08 encompass the effects of international conditions in models of Asia and make this an important research imperative.

Developments in the modelling frameworks used by many central banks internationally have favoured the use of Dynamic Stochastic General Equilibrium (DSGE) models. These have a coherent theoretical structure based on fundamental microeconomic relationships and can be reduced to a tractable empirical specification. They also, however, present a number of problems. First, the parameter estimates produced across a range of countries do not seem to reflect the diversity observed in the data (see, for example, Beltran and Draper, 2008; Canova and Sala, 2007). Second, these models have not yet produced credible open-economy results – for example, in Justiniano and Preston (2010), the DSGE does not come close to replicating the basic observed correlation between Canadian and American GDP growth.

An alternative approach is provided by Structural Vector Auto Regression (SVAR) models, which combine empirical coherence with restrictions imposed by a broad theoretical framework chosen by the researcher. A number of contributions have illustrated the increasing importance of using SVARs for identifying structural shocks in small, open economies, such as the work of Buckle *et al.* (2007), Cushman and Zha (1997), Dungey and Pagan (2009), Dungey and Vehbi (2010), Kim and Roubini (2000) and Mountford (2005). In addition to the different data sets used, a distinctive characteristic of these studies is the way in which they identify the structural shocks from the system.

This chapter takes the open-economy SVAR approach developed in Dungey and Pagan (2009) and Dungey and Vehbi (2010) – previously applied to Australia and the United Kingdom respectively – and applies it to the Association of South-East Asian Nations (ASEAN) region. The purpose of the chapter is to investigate the historical evolution of domestic responses to domestic and external output shocks originating in the United States and China during the period 1986–2009. Despite their structural differences, the majority of the industrialized countries in the East Asian region can be considered small, open economies that are heavily dependent on the economic performance of the United States. The most dramatic instance of this is the recent US-originated sub-prime crisis, which adversely affected most of the East Asian economies, with countries such as Taiwan and Singapore experiencing the greatest impact, further reflecting their strong dependence on external markets. Policy responses to the crisis also varied across the Asian economies depending on individual economic stances prior to the onset of the crisis, varying from significant tightening of monetary policy in Korea and Taiwan to using fiscal stimulus in China and Japan.

The countries analyzed in this chapter are Singapore, Thailand, the Philippines, Malaysia and Indonesia. A key advantage of the model framework in comparison with the methods used in previous studies is that it specifically accounts for the mixed nature of the data and cointegration between some variables, therefore taking into account, and indeed taking advantage of, the known empirical and theoretical relationships linking open economies to the international environment. The novel identification scheme of the structural shocks on the other hand ensures that the model has similar theoretical underpinnings to a standard New Keynesian DSGE model.

This chapter contributes to a mounting literature on small, open-economy modelling, including, for example, Beenstock and Longbottom (1981), Dennis *et al.* (2007), Leitemo (2006) and Ravn (1992), and to the emerging literature on combining methods of identification in VAR models in Dungey and Fry (2009). In this model, exclusion restrictions and cointegration are combined to identify the model, while maintaining the empirical coherence in the spirit of Akram and Nymoen (2009), who demonstrate the policy-related importance of models providing sound representations of the underlying data. The combination of identification methods harnesses the empirical properties of the data, employing a mix of I(1) and I(0) variables while identifying and recovering the effects of permanent and temporary shocks.

This chapter is structured as follows: the next section reviews the related literature, followed by a presentation of the theoretical framework in Section 3. Section 4 introduces econometric specification and identification. Section 5 presents empirical results. Section 6 compares responses to the United States' and China's output shocks across countries, and the final section concludes and draws policy implications.

2. Related literature

Several papers have examined the effects of structural shocks on East Asian economies using open-economy SVARs. A commonly raised issue in the majority of these studies is whether to explore the possibility of forming a monetary union in the East Asian region, similar to the European Monetary Union

(EMU), which was launched in Europe in 1999. Using a three-variable VAR model comprising global, regional and local outputs of seven East Asian economies and EMU countries, Chow and Yoonbai (2003) compare the degree of homogeneity among the East Asian countries with that of EMU countries. Their main finding is that each country in the region is sufficiently unique, implying that it would be costly to adopt a common currency peg. Zhang *et al.* (2004) also use a three-variable SVAR model to identify the respective demand, supply and monetary policy shocks in 10 East Asian countries in order to explore the feasibility of a monetary union in the region. Overall, they do not find strong evidence in favour of integration. In a similar study, Huang and Feng (2006) use a four-variable SVAR model to analyze various types of shocks in East Asian economies. Although their results are in line with the findings of Zhang *et al.* (2004), they also point out that several countries in the region have symmetric responses to shocks with equal magnitudes, suggesting the possibility of a feasible monetary union in the future. Finally, using the methodology proposed by Chow and Yoonbai (2003), Hsu (2010) finds that most East Asian economies have become relatively symmetric in terms of economic shocks and adjustments, implying that a common currency area might become viable through deepening regional integration. A recent working paper by Zhang *et al.* (2010) is closest to our study from a methodological perspective, using a SVAR model with block exogeneity to investigate whether external shocks originating in the United States played a dominant role in influencing the macroeconomic fluctuations in East Asia during the period 1978–2007. The authors find that the influence of US shocks on real output fluctuations in the East Asian region are very strong.

Our methodology, outlined in the following section, contributes to and extends the existing literature in two main areas. First, by incorporating long-run cointegration restrictions, the model specifically accounts for stationary versus non-stationary data properties and explicitly identifies the permanent and temporary shocks. Second, the model framework strongly emphasizes the role of exchange rates in the transmission of foreign shocks to the domestic economy by allowing the real exchange rate to react to all variables contemporaneously. This in turn is a reflection of the forward-looking nature of this variable. This chapter also uses extended sample sizes compared with the ones used in these studies to include the recent sub-prime-related financial crisis.

3. Theoretical framework

The standard macroeconomic framework for small, open economies with inflation-targeting monetary policy represented in contemporary research revolves around a three-equation model. Closed-economy representations include those in the standard graduate textbook of Woodford (2003), while extensions to the open-economy can be found in Gali and Monacelli (2005), Monacelli (2005) and the papers gathered in Gali (2008). The Gali and Monacelli (2005) framework underpins the theoretical specification of this chapter.

Building from standard New Keynesian assumptions of utility maximizing consumers in an economy with profit-maximizing producers who face Calvo pricing, and where consumers have preferences over both domestic and foreign-produced consumption goods, the model can be summarized with three standard equations representing an open-economy IS curve, a Phillips curve and an exchange rate equation. In the Monacelli (2005) extension to the Gali and Monacelli (2005) approach, imperfect pass-through of exchange rate shocks is assumed. In addition to these three equations, the system includes a monetary policy reaction function taking the form of a Taylor rule. The structure of the theoretical model takes the form

$$y_t = \mu E_t y_{t+1} + (1-\mu) y_{t-1} - \phi(r_{t-1} - E_{t-1}\pi_t) + \theta_1 \Delta q_t + \theta_2 y_t^* + \epsilon_{AD_t} \quad (1)$$
$$\mu_t = \delta E_t \pi_{t+1} + (1-\delta)\pi_{t-1} + \lambda y_t + \theta_3 \Delta q_t + \epsilon_{AS_t} \quad (2)$$
$$r_t = \rho r_{t-1} + (1-\rho)(\beta E_t \pi_{t+1} + \gamma y_t + \epsilon_{MP_t} \quad (3)$$
$$E_t \Delta q_{t+1} = (r_t - E_t \pi_{t+1}) - (r_t^* - E_t \pi_{t+1}^*) - \epsilon_{RER_t}, \quad (4)$$

where (y_t) and (y_t^*) represent domestic and foreign output gaps, (r_t) and (πt) are the interest rate and inflation, (q_t) is the real exchange rate and ϵ_{AD_t}, ϵ_{AS_t}, ϵ_{MP_t} and ϵ_{RER_t} represent the aggregate demand, aggregate supply, monetary policy and real exchange rate shocks respectively.

The theoretical specification should not be viewed as a constraining influence on the empirical coherence of the application. Rather the theory helps to motivate and justify empirical restrictions. Thus, we do not propose to follow the usual Bayesian approach of estimating the deep parameters of the particular theoretical specification. Rather, the empirical relationships in the data will be dominant, but identification will be aided by the use of a coherent theoretical framework. This will be achieved using the specification outlined in the next section.

4. Econometric specification and identification

Suppose that the economy is described by a VAR (p) model of the form

$$y_t = A_1 y_{t-1} + A_2 y_{t-2}, + \ldots + A_p y_{t-p} + u_t, \quad (5)$$

where the *A's* are ($n * n$) coefficient matrices, y_t is a ($n \times 1$) vector of observable variables and u_t is an ($n * 1$) vector of unobservable error terms with $u_t \sim (0, \Sigma_u)$.

Assuming that all the variables are at most difference stationary, the generic model can be written as a VECM of the form

$$B_0 \Delta y_t = \Pi^* y_{t-1} + \Gamma_1^* \Delta y_{t-1} + \ldots + \Gamma_{p-1} \Delta y_{t-p+1} + \varepsilon_t, \quad (6)$$

where the Γ^**'s* are ($n \times n$) matrix of short-run coefficients, Π^* is the structural matrix and ε_t is an ($n \times 1$) structural form error with zero mean and covariance matrix I_K B_0 is a ($n \times n$) matrix of contemporaneous relations among the variables in y_t.

Assuming that the B_0 matrix is invertible, equation (6) can be written as

$$\Delta y_t = \Pi y_{t-1} + \Gamma_1 \Delta y_{t-1} + \ldots + \Gamma_{p-1} \Delta y_{t-p+1} + \varepsilon_t , \tag{7}$$

where $\Pi_t = B_0^{-1}\Pi^*$, $\Gamma_j = B_0^{-1}\Gamma_j^*$ $(j = 1, \ldots, p-1)$ and $u_t = B_0^{-1}\varepsilon_t$, which relates the reduced form errors, u_t's, to the underlying structural errors ε_t's. When Π has a reduced rank of $r \leq n-1$ then Π can be written as $\Pi = \alpha\beta'$, where β is an $(n \times r)$ matrix that contains the long-run relationship and α is an $(n \times r)$ matrix of the "speed of adjustment" coefficients and the u_t is a white-noise error with zero mean and a covariance matrix Σ_u. Substituting Π into equation (7) produces the model in error correction form

$$\Delta y_t = \alpha\beta' y_{t-1} + \Gamma_1 \Delta y_{t-1} + \ldots + \Gamma_{p-1} \Delta y_{t-p+1} + u_t. \tag{8}$$

As the u_t's are the reduced form residuals, and are generally strongly correlated, the effects of a single shock on the whole system cannot be isolated without imposing restrictions on the system. Multiplying both sides by B_0 gives

$$\begin{aligned} B_0 u_t &= \varepsilon_t \\ \Sigma &= B_0^{-1}\Sigma_S (B_0)', \end{aligned} \tag{9}$$

where Σ, B_0 and Σ_S are all $(n \times n)$ matrices. Exact identification of Σ_S requires the imposition of $(n^2 - n)/2$ additional restrictions on B_0^{-1}. While traditional VAR models use a Cholesky-type recursive identification scheme to identify the structural errors, the structural approach differs by the ability to choose any restrictions on B_0 so as to achieve identification.

The existence of cointegration among the $I(1)$ variables could also provide extra identifying restrictions. According to Granger's Representation Theorem, equation (8) has the following Beveridge–Nelson Moving Average (MA) representation (see Lutkepohl and Kratzig, 2004, for details)

$$y_i = F\Sigma_{i=1}^{t} u_t + \Sigma_{j=0}^{\infty} u_{t-j} + y_0^*, \tag{10}$$

where the matrix $F = \beta_\perp \left(\alpha'_\perp \left(I_n - \Sigma_{i-1}^{p-1}\Gamma_i\right)\beta_\perp\right)^{-1} \alpha'_\perp$ and y_0^* contain the initial values. It is important to note that the rank of F is $n - r$, where r is the number of cointegrating vectors. Therefore there are $n - r$ independent common trends. The second term in the expression is an infinite order polynomial with coefficients F_j^* going to zero as $j \to \infty$. Hence it represents the transitory shocks to the system. The long-run effects of shocks are represented by the first term in equation (10), $F\Sigma_{i=1}^{t} u_{it}$, which captures the common stochastic trends. The common driving stochastic trends are the variables $\alpha'_\perp \Sigma_{i=1}^{t} u_i$, where their factor loadings are given by $\beta_\perp \left(\alpha'_\perp \left(I_n - \Sigma_{i=1}^{p-1}\Gamma_i\right)\beta_\perp\right)^{-1}$. By replacing u_t's with their structural counterparts, we obtain

$$y_t = F\sum_{i=1}^{t} B_0^{-1}\varepsilon_t + \sum_{j=0}^{\infty} F_j^* B_0^{-1}\varepsilon_{t-j} + y_0^*, \tag{11}$$

where the effects of both short and long-run structural shocks can be obtained. The long-run effects can be captured by FB_0^{-1}, which has a rank $n - r$ since $rk(F) = n - r$, and B_0 is not singular. Therefore, while r of the structural shocks have transitory effects, $n - r$ of them will have a permanent effect (linearly independent) and can be restricted to zero providing $r(n - r)$ independent restrictions. Given exact identification of the $\sum_\varepsilon$ requires $(n^2 - n)/2$ independent restrictions; $r(n - r)$ of them can be identified using the cointegration relationship alone.

Using the Wold decomposition theorem, Δy_t can be written as

$$\Delta y_t = C(L)u_t, \tag{12}$$

or as its structural counterpart as

$$\Delta y_t = C(L)B_0^{-1}\varepsilon_t, \tag{13}$$

where $C(L)$ is a polynomial of order q in the lag operator. Assuming that the first $(n - r)$ shocks are permanent (ε_{1t}), we can write Δy_t as

$$\Delta y_t = C(L)B_0^{-1}\binom{\varepsilon_{1t}}{\varepsilon_{2t}}. \tag{14}$$

For the remaining shocks, ε_{2t}, to be transitory requires

$$FB_0^{-1}\begin{pmatrix} 0_{(n-r)*r} \\ I_{r+k} \end{pmatrix} = G\alpha = 0, \tag{15}$$

which implies that $\alpha_1 = 0$, where α_1 is the $(n - r) * r$ matrix of adjustment coefficients of the $I(1)$ variables that give rise to the permanent shocks driving the cointegrating relationships (see Pagan and Pesaran, 2009, for details). An important implication of this result is that it precludes the use of error correction terms in equations that define the permanent shocks.

Using (15), the permanent component of Υ_t can be written as

$$\Delta y_t^p = FB_0^{-1}\varepsilon_t. \tag{16}$$

Given equation (16) and following Dungey and Pagan (2009), equation (8) can be written in "gap deviation" form, $\tilde{y}_t = y_t - y_t^p$, as the following

$$B^*(L)\Delta\tilde{y}_t = \alpha^*\beta' y_{t-1} - \sum_{j=1}^{p-1}\Delta y_{t-j}^p + B_0^{-1}\varepsilon_t, \tag{17}$$

where $\alpha^* = B_0^{-1}\alpha$. Since the gap variables are correlated with both the error correction terms and the changes in permanent components, exclusion of error correction terms will result in misspecification (see Dungey and Pagan, 2009, for more details). Therefore the conventional use of the output gap will be replaced with the differenced output together with the corresponding error correction term for this variable.

4.1 Handling exchange rate regime changes

A significant feature of recent history for many ASEAN economies is the change from fixed or managed exchange rate regimes to a floating environment, which mainly occurred about the time of the 1997–98 Asian Financial Crisis. This is particularly evident for Thailand, Malaysia, Indonesia and the Philippines – the sample countries considered here – where substantial currency devaluations were observed in the second half of 1997. This poses considerable challenges to the empirical identification of the model presented above. In particular, in a fixed exchange rate regime, a monetary policy reaction function of the form of equation (3) does not pertain, nor do the Phillips or IS curves react to exchange rate changes in the same way across fixed and floating regimes. Furthermore, the exchange rate equation given in equation (4) is not relevant. One way to address this problem within the New Keynesian framework described above is to augment the expression of equations (1) to (4) to incorporate the regime shift as follows

$$\begin{aligned} y_t &= \mu E_t y_{t+1} + (1-\mu) y_{t-1} - \varnothing (r_{t-1} - E_{t-1}\pi_t) + \theta_2 y_t^* \\ &\quad + I_t \left[\mu E_t y_{t+1} + (1-\mu) y_{t-1} - \varnothing (r_{t-1} - E_{t-1}\pi_t) + \theta_1 \Delta q_t + \theta_2 y_t^* \right] + \varepsilon_{AS_t} \end{aligned} \tag{18}$$

$$\pi_t = \delta_1 E_t \pi_{t+1} + (1-\delta_1)\pi_{t-1} + \lambda_1 y_t + I_t \begin{bmatrix} \delta_1 E_t \pi_{t+1} + (1-\delta_1)\pi_{t-1} \\ + \lambda_1 y_t + \theta_3 \Delta q_t \end{bmatrix} + \varepsilon_{AS_t} \tag{19}$$

$$r_t = I_t \left[\rho r_{t-1} + (1-\rho)(\beta E_t \pi_{t+1} + \gamma y_t) \right] + \varepsilon_{MP_t} \tag{20}$$

$$E_t \Delta q_{t+1} = I_t \left[(r_t - E_t \pi_{t+1}) - (r_t^* - E_t \pi_{t+1}^*) + \varepsilon_{RER_t} \right], \tag{21}$$

where I_t is an indicator variable taking the value 1 in the floating exchange rate regime period and 0 in the fixed rate period. This provides a straightforward means of accounting for the structural shift induced by the exchange rate regime. Its advantage is that it retains the use of longer-term relationships in the model, particularly the relationship across international output, while respecting that the relationships between different parts of the economy must change with such a dramatic policy change. This representation can be easily accommodated within the econometric framework laid out in the previous sub-section. Given the lack of sufficient data available in the sub-periods identified as fixed and floating regimes, this adaptation is not, however, practically feasible. Instead, we estimate the individual country models using the whole sample period of 1986Q1–2009Q4, while imposing a step dummy for the crisis period to avoid parameter instability.

5. Empirical results

The model presented in Section 4 suggests that data for output, inflation, interest rates and exchange rates are pertinent inputs to the model. Figures 9.A1–9.A5 in Appendix A map these data from 1986Q1–2009Q4 for each of Singapore, Thailand, the Philippines, Indonesia and Malaysia. Variable definitions and their sources are provided in Appendix B.

The most immediately notable feature of these figures is the financial crisis in Asia in 1997–98. The switch from a fixed to a floating exchange rate regime is immediately obvious for all countries with the exception of Singapore, which already had a floating exchange rate regime prior to the crisis. A serious recession eventuated in many cases, and International Monetary Fund (IMF) support programs were implemented shortly thereafter. Likewise, inflation shows a dramatic decrease and, as a general consequence of the adoption of an inflation targeting/floating exchange rate regime, interest rate volatility generally declines. Singapore and the Philippines weathered the crisis more easily than the other economies and did not experience prolonged periods of recession. For Singapore, this was due to the fact that it was already operating under a floating exchange rate regime prior to the crisis. A more evident feature in most of the countries' data is the relatively large rise in inflation in 2007–08 and the subsequent falls in 2009, which were associated with oil price volatility. Consequently, in the following, we augment the specification of the Phillips curve with exogenous oil price inflation; Kim and Roubini (2000) are among a number of authors who include oil prices in VAR models.

Table 9.1 presents Augmented Dickey Fuller (ADF) test results of the data for each of the countries' variables. In each case, the results show that the output and exchange rate series can be regarded as non-stationary. This in turn raises the possibility that these series are cointegrated. Theoretically, this

Table 9.1 Augmented Dickey Fuller unit root test

Levels	y^*	y	Π	r	q	*oil*
Singapore						
ADF statistic	–1.92	1.59	2.33	3.21*	–1.3	9.0*
Crit. val. (5 %)	–3.45	3.45	2.89	2.89	2.89	1.94
Philippines						
ADF statistic	–1.92	1.91	1.66	3.63*	1.47	9.01*
Crit. val. (5 %)	–3.45	3.45	2.89	2.89	2.89	1.94
Thailand						
ADF statistic	–1.92	2.18	2.11	2.48	1.73	9.01*
Crit. val. (5 %)	–3.45	3.45	2.89	2.89	2.89	1.94
Indonesia						
ADF statistic	–1.92	1.96	6.64*	3.50*	1.81	9.01*
Crit. val. (5 %)	–3.45	3.45	2.89	2.89	2.89	1.94
Malaysia						
ADF statistic	–1.92	1.70	2.44	3.50*	1.69	9.01*
Crit. val. (5 %)	–3.45	3.45	2.89	2.89	2.89	1.94

Note: * Denotes rejection of the null of a unit root at 5% confidence level.

supports an open-economy IS curve, or traditional models of the equilibrium exchange rate such as the Mundell–Fleming model, where the equilibrium exchange rate is a function of the current account balance, which is a function of domestic and foreign outputs. This cointegrating relationship – estimated for each country model separately – is an important part of our model design. Inflation rates are well known to fail to reject the null of a unit root. In general, this outcome represents a highly persistent price process, which is estimated with poor precision. In the case of the inflation rates for Singapore, the Philippines, Thailand and Malaysia, the AR (1) coefficients in ADF regressions are 0.49, 0.68, 0.34 and 0.29 respectively. Therefore, it is appropriate to treat the inflation rates as I(0) processes together with the inflation rate of Indonesia, which is shown to be stationary. Interest rates for all countries except Thailand are found to be stationary. All interest will also be treated as I(0) processes, given that they are the policy instruments of monetary authorities.

5.1 Results from the data-consistent SVECM

This section implements the SVECM models for each country, for the sample period of 1986Q1–2009Q4. Two additions to the generic specification are made. The first is the addition of a dummy for the Asian Financial Crisis period – defined as 1997Q3–1998Q4 in each equation. The second is the addition of oil price inflation as an exogenous variable entering the AS equation. As the interest rate and inflation rate are I(0) variables, this is respected by the addition of pseudo-ecm terms, consisting of the lagged level of the dependent variable to correct for the level effect that would be lost if using a standard VECM. The structural form specification of the system can be represented as follows, using the form of equation (6) and clearly showing the restrictions in the system.

$$\begin{bmatrix} 1 & 0 & 0 & 0 & 0 \\ b_{21}^{0} & 1 & 0 & 0 & 0 \\ 0 & b_{32}^{0} & 1 & 0 & 0 \\ 0 & b_{42}^{0} & b_{43}^{0} & 1 & 0 \\ b_{51}^{0} & b_{52}^{0} & b_{53}^{0} & b_{54}^{0} & 1 \end{bmatrix} \Delta \Upsilon_t = \begin{bmatrix} 0 & 0 & 0 \\ 0 & 0 & 0 \\ 0 & \alpha_{32} & 0 \\ 0 & \alpha_{42} & \alpha_{43} \\ \alpha_{51} & \alpha_{52} & \alpha_{53} \end{bmatrix} \begin{bmatrix} \beta_{11} & 1 & 0 & 0 & \beta_{51} \\ 0 & 0 & 1 & 0 & 0 \\ 0 & 0 & 1 & 1 & 0 \end{bmatrix} \Upsilon_{t-1}$$

$$+ \begin{bmatrix} b_{11}^{l} & 0 & 0 & 0 & 0 \\ b_{21}^{l} & b_{22}^{l} & b_{23}^{l} & b_{24}^{l} & b_{25}^{l} \\ 0 & b_{32}^{l} & b_{33}^{l} & 0 & b_{35}^{l} \\ 0 & b_{42}^{l} & b_{43}^{l} & b_{44}^{l} & 0 \\ b_{51}^{l} & b_{52}^{l} & b_{53}^{l} & b_{54}^{l} & 1 \end{bmatrix} \Delta \Upsilon_{t-1} \tag{22}$$

$$+ \begin{bmatrix} 0 \\ 0 \\ c \\ 0 \\ 0 \end{bmatrix} Oil + \begin{bmatrix} \varepsilon_t^{AD^*} \\ \varepsilon_t^{AD} \\ \varepsilon_t^{AS} \\ \varepsilon_t^{MP} \\ \varepsilon_t^{RER} \end{bmatrix}$$

The set of restrictions defined in equation (22) follows several considerations regarding the structure of the model. First, in line with the small, open economy assumption, the foreign economy does not respond to the current values of domestic variables. More importantly, the international linkages apply only through output with no direct linkages through inflation and interest rates, reflecting a New Keynesian IS curve. The monetary authority sets the interest rates with respect to current values of output and inflation. Finally, the real exchange rate equation reacts to all of the variables contemporaneously, reflecting the fact that exchange rates are forward-looking variables (Kim and Roubini, 2000).

5.1.1 Singapore

The impulse responses for the Singaporean economy to foreign and domestically sourced aggregate demand shocks are presented in Figures 9.1 and 9.2.

A shock to the foreign output equation results in permanently higher foreign output and permanently higher domestic output, which reflects the permanent nature of the shock captured by our model (see Figure 9.1). Initially, Singaporean output rises by about 0.8 of the rise in the foreign output; after three years, the multiplier of the foreign shock on domestic output is greater than 1,

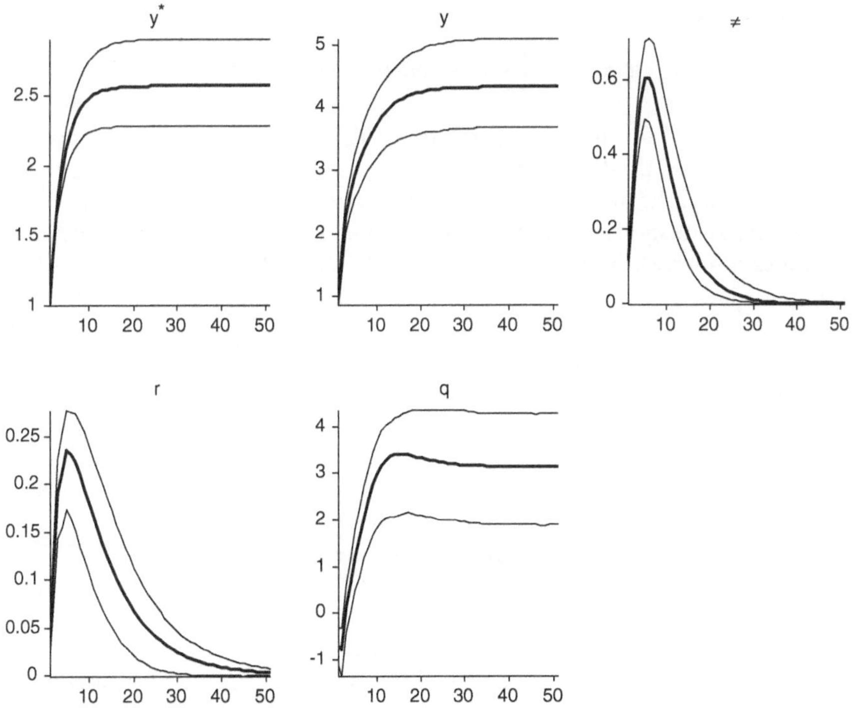

Figure 9.1 Impulse response functions (foreign output shock)

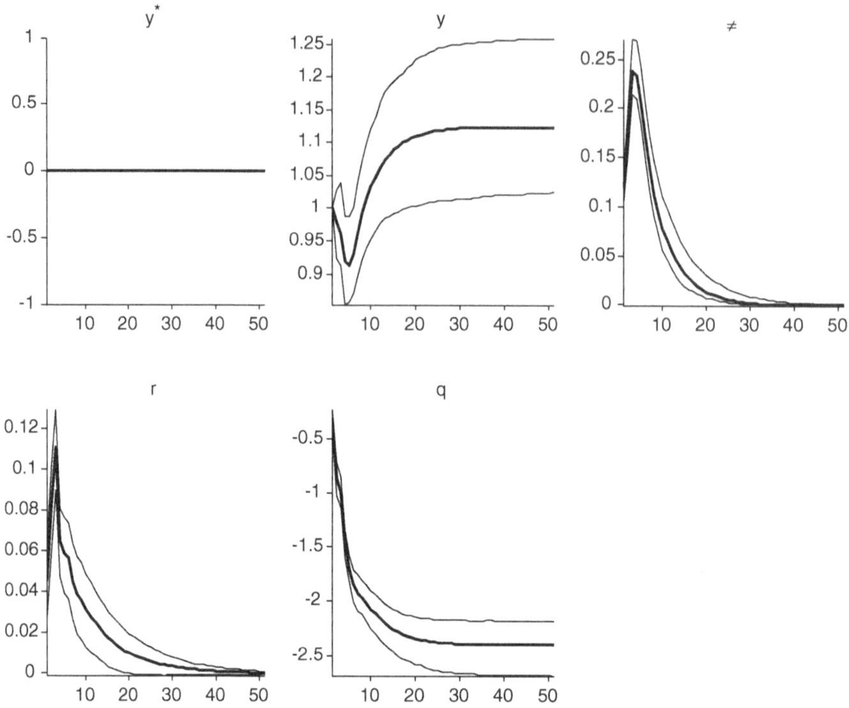

Figure 9.2 Impulse response functions (domestic output shock)

settling at about 1.06 in the longer term. This implies that the Singaporean economy will bear the full impact of foreign output shocks in the long-run, reflecting its high degree of openness. The output shock leads to an increase in Singaporean inflation resulting in a corresponding response from the monetary authorities to increase interest rates. As a result, this inflationary pressure eases after approximately four years. The initial appreciation of Singapore's domestic currency is followed by a permanent depreciation due to the decline in real interest rates and the permanent increase in domestic output.

Domestically sourced output shocks result in a permanently higher output in Singapore, although the long-run multiplier on the shock is not as high as for the foreign-sourced shocks (see Figure 9.2). The inflation increases as a result of the increased demand, which is followed by a higher interest rate response of the central bank to control inflation. The increased output results in a permanent currency appreciation despite the decline in real interest rates. We do not report the other impulses from the model, but rather note that the model does not display a price puzzle or exchange rate puzzle.

Figure 9.3 presents the contributions of shocks associated with each of foreign aggregate demand, domestic aggregate demand, aggregate supply, monetary policy and the real exchange rate to the variation in output over the entire sample period.

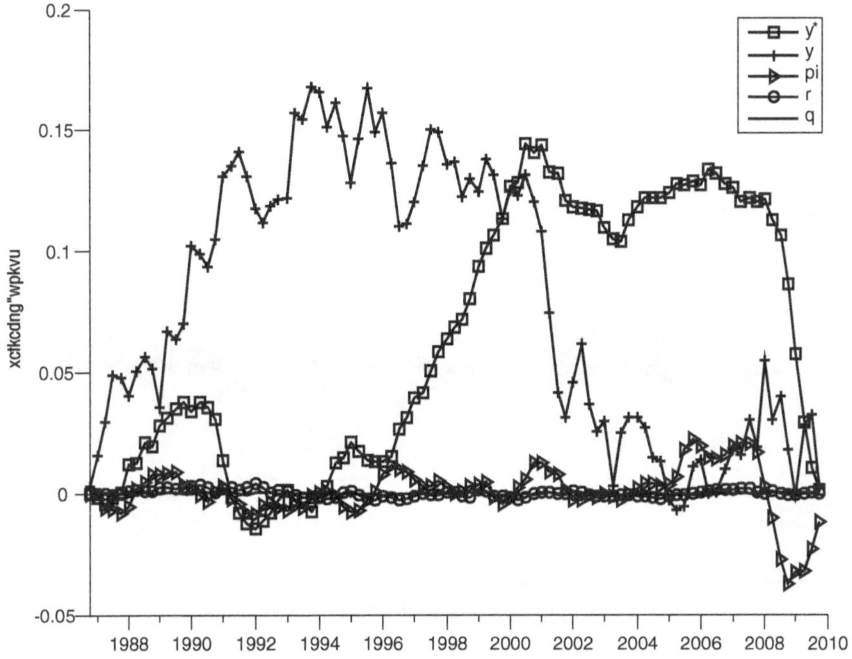

Figure 9.3 Historical decomposition of output

As initial conditions might be important, analysis is restricted to exclude the two years following the beginning of the sample. The most striking feature of the figure is the dramatic change in the relative importance of foreign and domestic aggregate demand shocks to variation in Singaporean output. Prior to 2001, domestically sourced shocks were the largest contributor, peaking from March 1994 until the middle of 1997, corresponding with the onset of the financial crisis. In June 2001, the foreign shocks exceeded the contribution of domestic shocks for the first time. After that time, the contribution of foreign-sourced aggregate demand shocks to Singaporean output can be seen to remain high and positive, while the contribution of domestic shocks shows a steep decline. This situation persisted until September 2007, after which the positive impact of foreign-sourced shocks is dramatically reduced. This is unsurprising given the onset of the Global Financial Crisis – and additionally, a relatively large negative component sourced from inflationary shocks. Singapore experienced strong inflation followed by deflation in this period, even after accounting for the effects of oil price movements at this time.

The effects of the inflationary pressures in Singapore late in the sample can also be observed in Figure 9.4, which depicts the historical decomposition of inflation variation over the sample.

The relatively large contribution of positive inflation shocks in the period from March 2008 to the end of the sample dwarfs all other sources during the

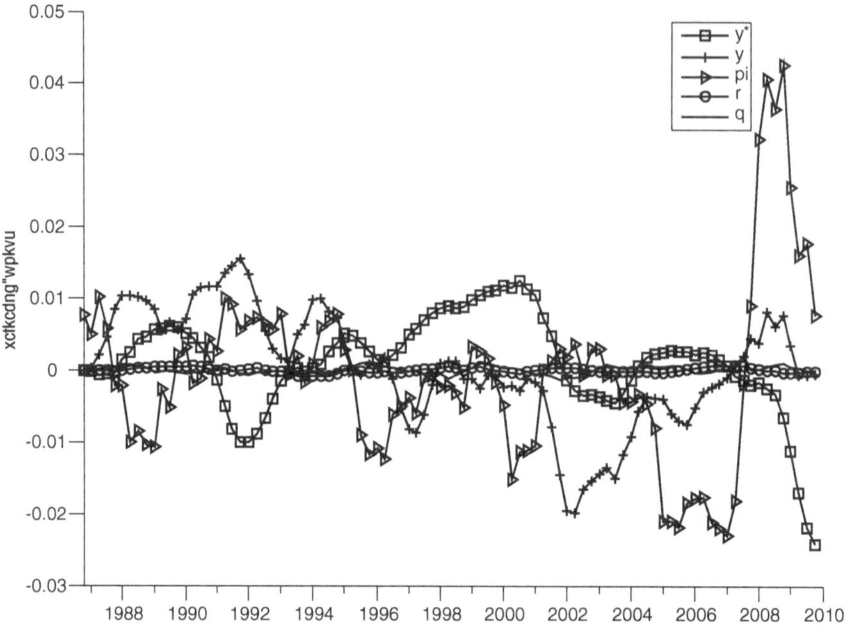

Figure 9.4 Historical decomposition of inflation

period. At the same time, it can be seen that there are substantial offsetting effects on inflation from foreign-sourced output shocks – again, presumably relating to the downturns experienced by many economies in response to the Global Financial Crisis. Domestic output shocks in the final two years of the sample initially contributed positively to inflation variation but more recently have been offsetting inflation pressures. About the time of the Asian Financial Crisis, the impact of lower domestic output shocks can be clearly seen as reducing pressure on inflation while at the same time foreign output shocks were providing some inflationary stimulus. In the period after the Asian Financial Crisis, foreign output shocks contributed more negatively than domestic output shocks, and, from 2004 to 2008, foreign inflation shocks were an important source of downward pressure on inflation volatility.

In summary, the Singaporean economy has had a dramatic change of focus regarding the sources of output variation over the sample, with foreign-based shocks becoming more significant than they were in the pre-Asian crisis period. Domestic conditions on the other hand have become less influential.

5.1.2 The Philippines

The empirical identification of the model for the Philippines is the same as that given in equation (22), including the crisis dummy variable and exogenous oil

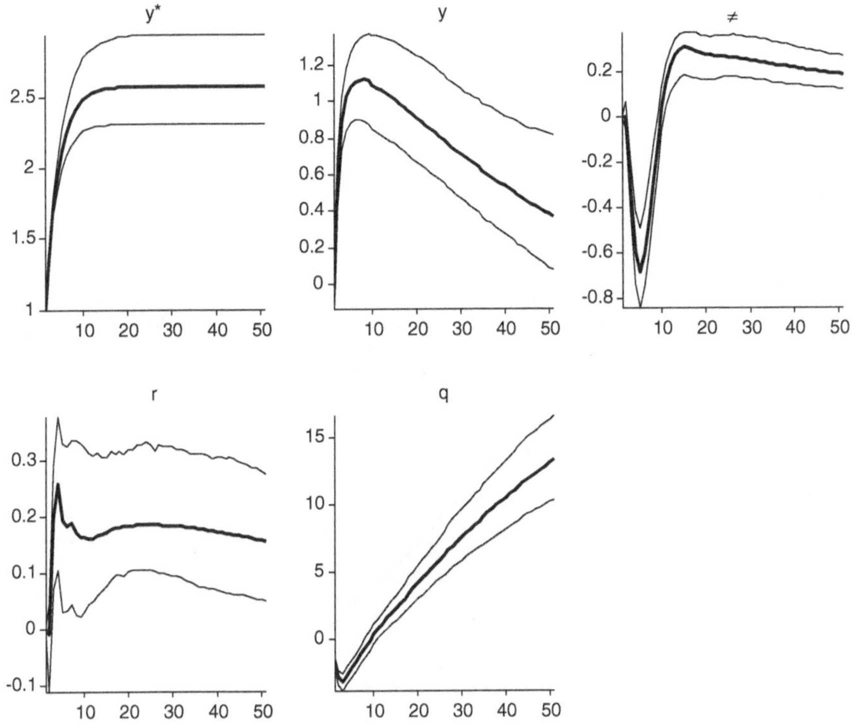

Figure 9.5 Impulse response functions (foreign output shock)

price inflation in the Phillips curve equation. We find that it is feasible to estimate this model for the entire sample period of 1986Q1–2009Q4, despite the change in exchange rate regime during this period.

The impulse responses of the Philippines economy to shocks sourced from foreign output are shown in Figure 9.5.

In this case, the long-run effect of the foreign output shock on domestic output is lower than in Singapore – presumably a reflection of its less open nature. The effect dissipates very slowly over the 10 year period shown. Although there is no initial significant positive inflationary response to the shock, inflation picks up as the higher growth rates continue. Inflation returns to equilibrium in the long-run in response to the higher interest rates. This might be a result of the mixed exchange rate regime data in the sample. The higher real interest rates are clearly associated with an initial appreciation of the Philippine peso.

A domestically sourced output shock shown in Figure 9.6 also results in higher real interest rates. Although the initial impact on inflation is significantly positive, it rapidly reverts to an insignificant effect, while nominal interest rates are significantly higher. In this case, the Philippine peso appreciates rapidly yet this is subsequently eroded over the 10 year horizon. The presence of the price

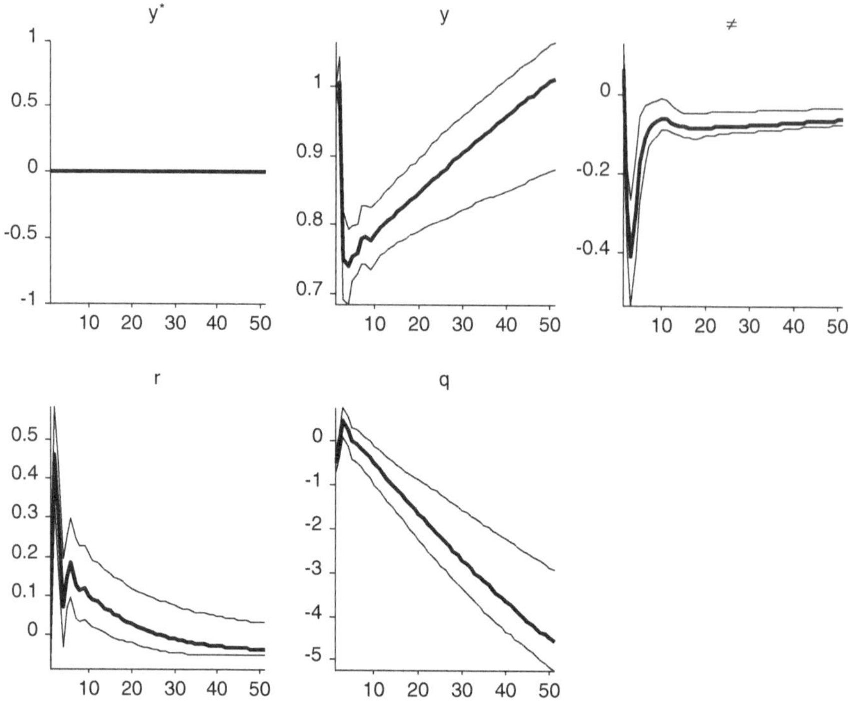

Figure 9.6 Impulse response functions (domestic output shock)

puzzle in this model also indicates that it is not yet a satisfactory representation of the Philippines economy.

The historical decomposition of output in the Philippines is shown in Figure 9.7. It shows the substantial impact of domestic economic output shocks throughout the period. These were particularly prominent during the decade 1993–2003, with the impact of the financial crisis in Asia causing a pronounced effect in 1997. This could be interpreted as the model failing to incorporate sufficient richness to model the Philippine economy. Other potential indicators of development, population growth, climatic conditions and the effects of the US military presence might need to be incorporated in the model. The figure also shows the increased effect of international output shocks to domestic output variation during the period from 1995. This effect builds until 2001, after which international effects have a less pronounced, but nevertheless positive, impact on domestic output variation. In the past two years, the impact of the Global Financial Crisis on reduced international demand is clearly evident in the negative contribution of international output shocks to domestic output variability.

Figure 9.8 shows the historical decomposition of inflation for the Philippines. The contributions of shocks other than domestic shocks to inflation variation

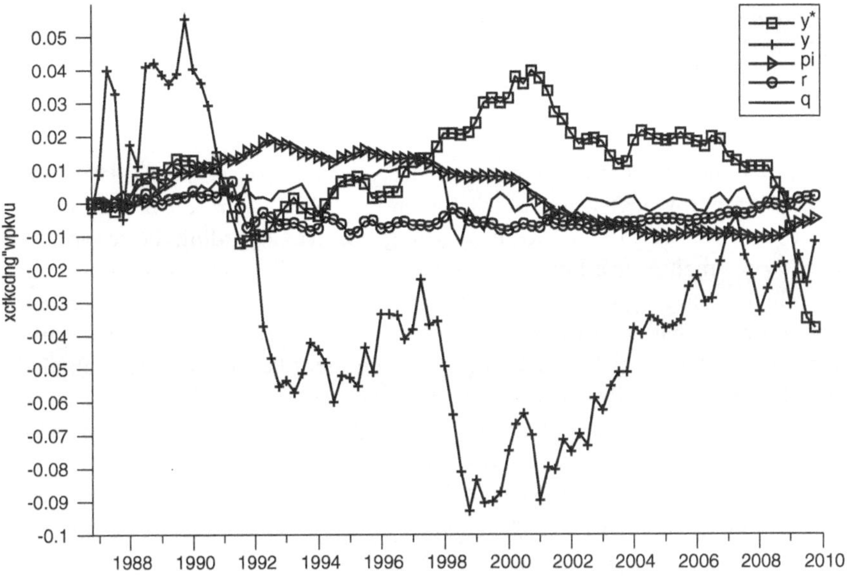

Figure 9.7 Historical decomposition of output

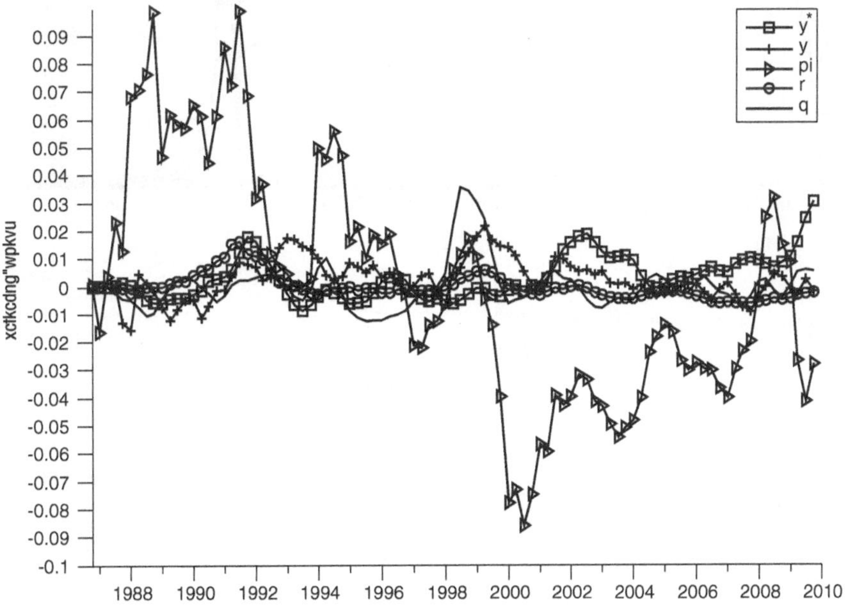

Figure 9.8 Historical decomposition of inflation

are minimal. This reflects the fact that the model is limited in providing an empirical specification of the inflationary process in the Philippines.

5.1.3 Thailand

After experiencing a period of export-led economic growth during 1986–95, the Thai economy began slowing by the end of 1995 as a result of weakening export performance. Heightened by growing concerns regarding the economy's ability to maintain a fixed exchange rate regime, capital inflows reversed substantially, exerting significant pressure on the exchange rate. The subsequent devaluation of Thailand's currency in July 1997 is largely responsible for igniting the Asian Financial Crisis. Using the same identification structure applied in the Singapore and Philippines models, we estimate the model for Thailand for the entire sample period of 1986Q1–2009Q4. Figure 9.9 shows the impulse response functions of Thailand's domestic variables to a US shock. The permanent US shock increases Thailand's output significantly, with an average multiplier of 1 within the first year following the shock. As a result, inflation

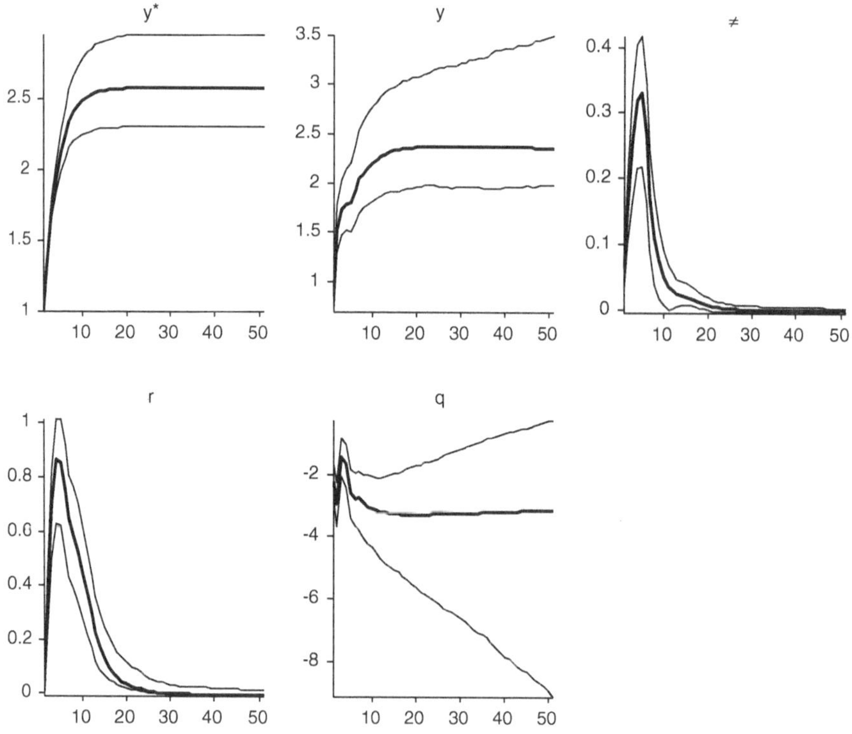

Figure 9.9 Impulse response functions (foreign output shock)

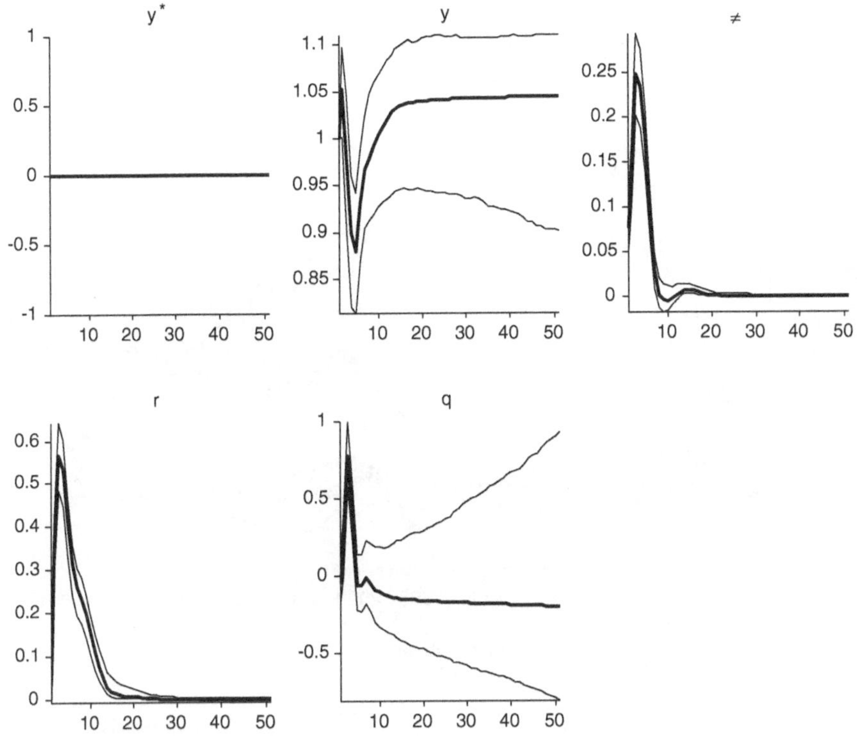

Figure 9.10 Impulse response functions (domestic output shock)

increases and the central bank responds by increasing interest rates above the level of inflation, thereby reducing the prevailing excess demand and increased inflation. Consequently, the currency appreciates as a result of higher real interest rates.

The impulse responses from a domestically sourced output shock are shown in Figure 9.10, showing an output, inflation and interest rate increase in response to the shock. The long-run response of output is similar in magnitude to the original shock, while the inflation response peaks in the second year following the shock and takes more than five years to fully dissipate. Interest rates follow a similar pattern, which mirrors the inflation outcome. This is not unexpected since Thailand follows an inflation-targeting monetary policy regime for the period post-1997.

Figure 9.11 shows the historical decomposition of Thailand's domestic output. It can be seen that the contribution of foreign shocks begins to increase following the financial crisis in Asia, reflecting the increasing openness of the economy due to the floating exchange rate regime, and matches the contribution of domestic shocks after 2006. Figure 9.12 shows the historical

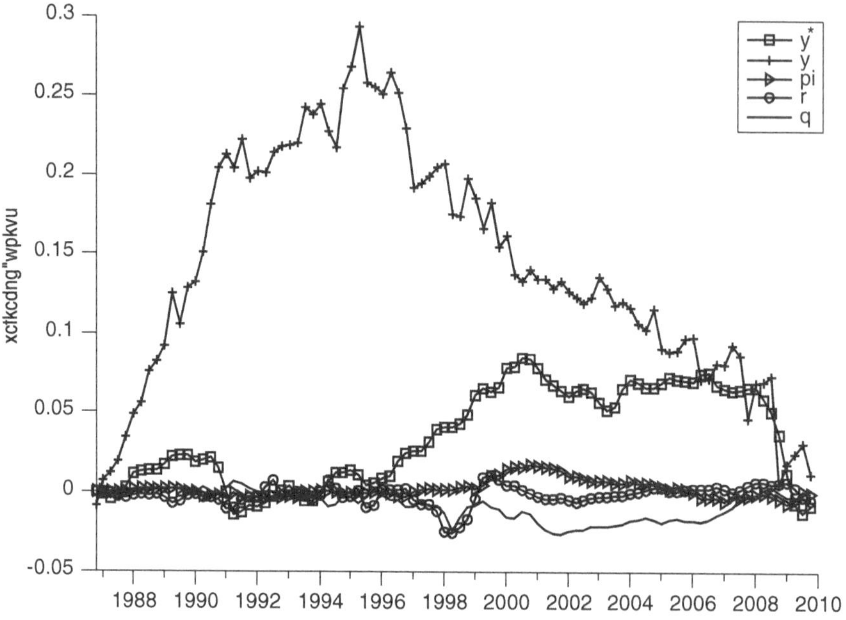

Figure 9.11 Historical decomposition of output

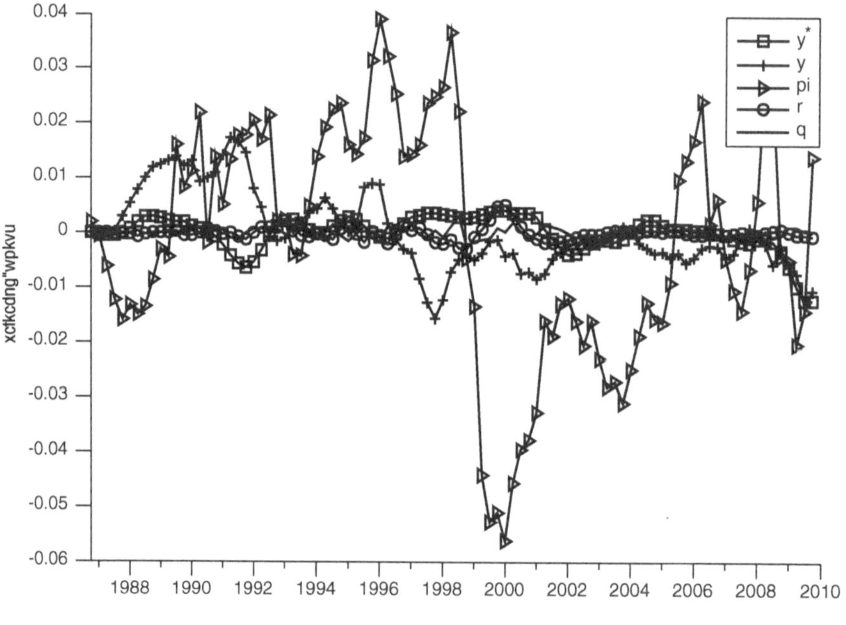

Figure 9.12 Historical decomposition of inflation

decomposition of Thailand's inflation and strongly suggests that the majority of the inflationary pressure in Thailand is driven by domestically sourced inflationary shocks (traditionally associated with supply shocks in many VAR models).

5.1.4 Malaysia

Figure 9.13 shows the impulse responses of real output growth to the US shock. It can be seen that domestic output increases at the same pace as both inflation and foreign output increase. The interest rate increase is only slightly higher than the increase in inflation, which results in an initial currency appreciation. The overall responses to a domestic output shock (Figure 9.14) follow a similar pattern to other countries examined.

The historical decomposition of Malaysian output is shown in Figure 9.15. Similar to the case of Singapore, here we observe an increase in the contribution of foreign-sourced shocks following the Asian crisis, and a corresponding

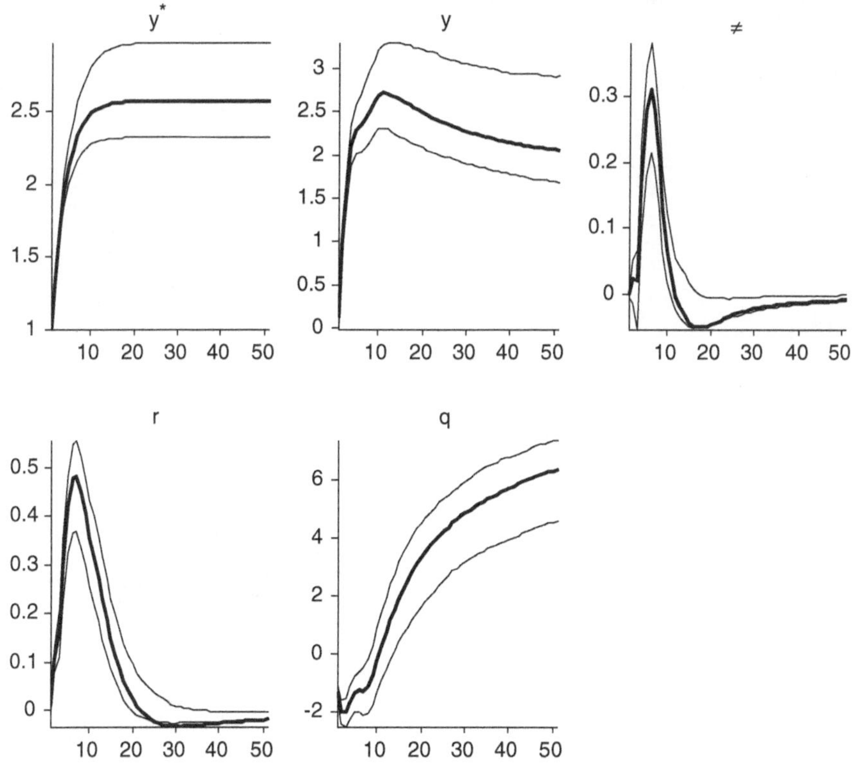

Figure 9.13 Impulse response functions (foreign output shock)

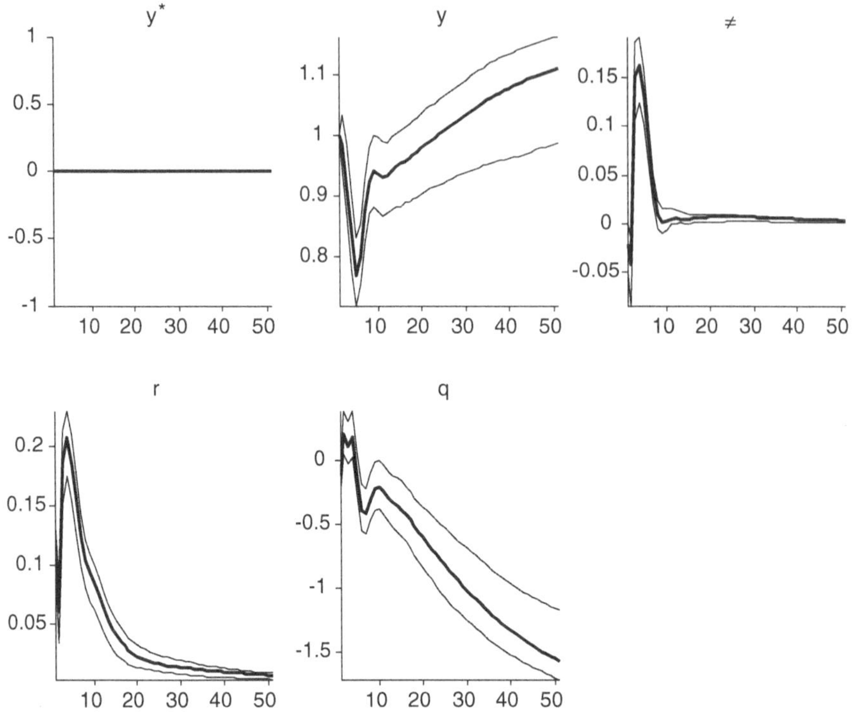

Figure 9.14 Impulse response functions (domestic output shock)

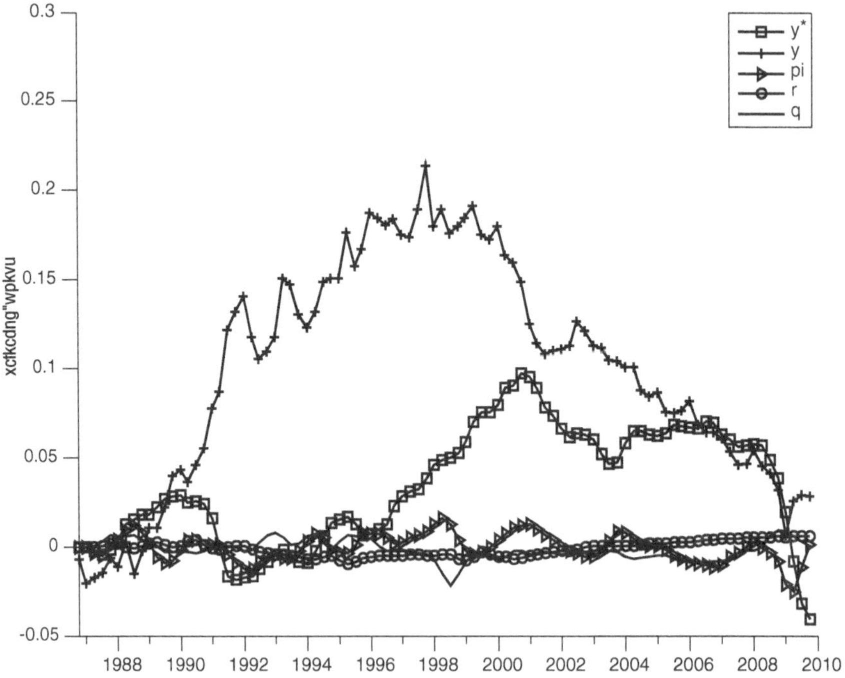

Figure 9.15 Historical decomposition of output

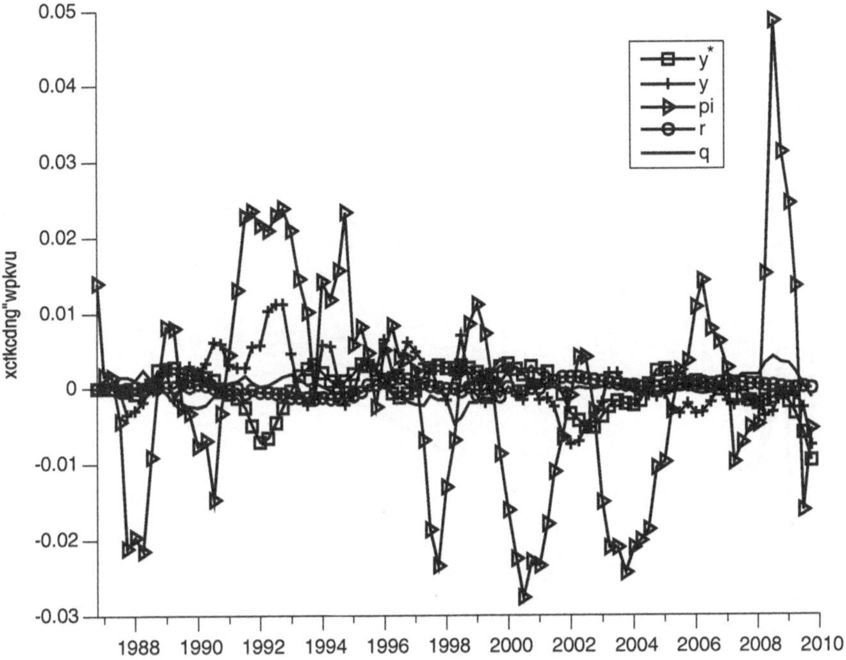

Figure 9.16 Historical decomposition of inflation

decline in the contribution of domestically sourced shocks. The historical decomposition of inflation on the other hand shows that inflation is rather persistent and is affected mainly by its past behaviour.

5.1.5 Indonesia

Indonesia's output response to a foreign output shock is relatively milder than in other economies and is not persistent. Inflation initially drops, followed by a subsequent decline in interest rates. Inflation picks up again after eight quarters and, in turn, interest rates increase. The initial increase in real interest rates causes currency appreciation, which quickly reverts as real interest rates decline. The overall responses of Indonesia's endogenous variables to both domestic and foreign shocks, on the other hand, show that further work is needed to enhance the model dynamics.

The historical decomposition of output shown in Figure 9.19 reflects the relatively closed structure of the Indonesian economy, where the domestically sourced shocks play a major role in output variations. The negative impact of foreign-sourced shocks is evident after 2008. The decomposition of inflation shown in Figure 9.20 on the other hand, does not point to any major contributor to the inflation variation where all the shocks have sizeable impacts.

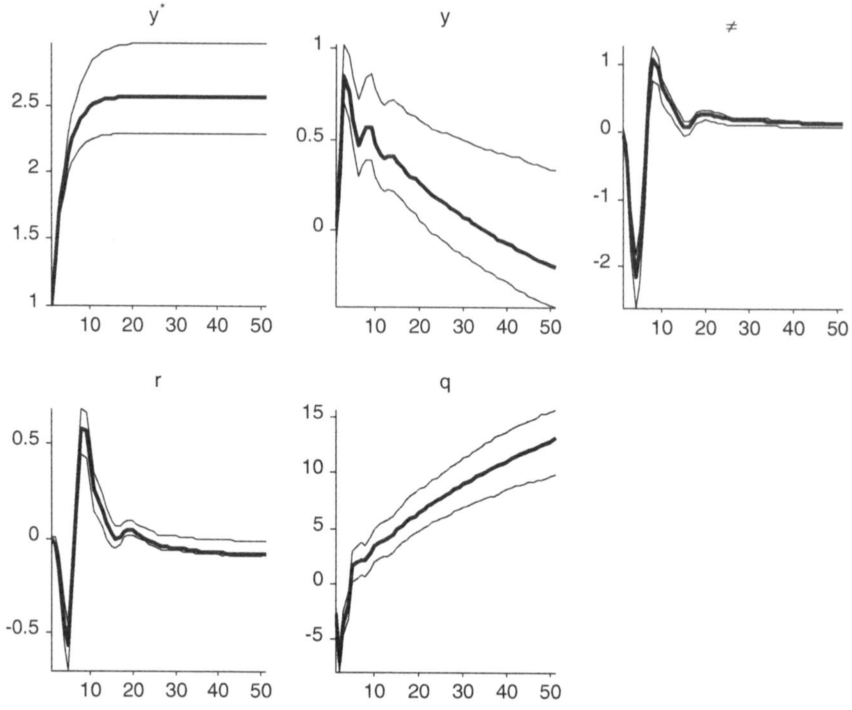

Figure 9.17 Impulse response functions (foreign output shock)

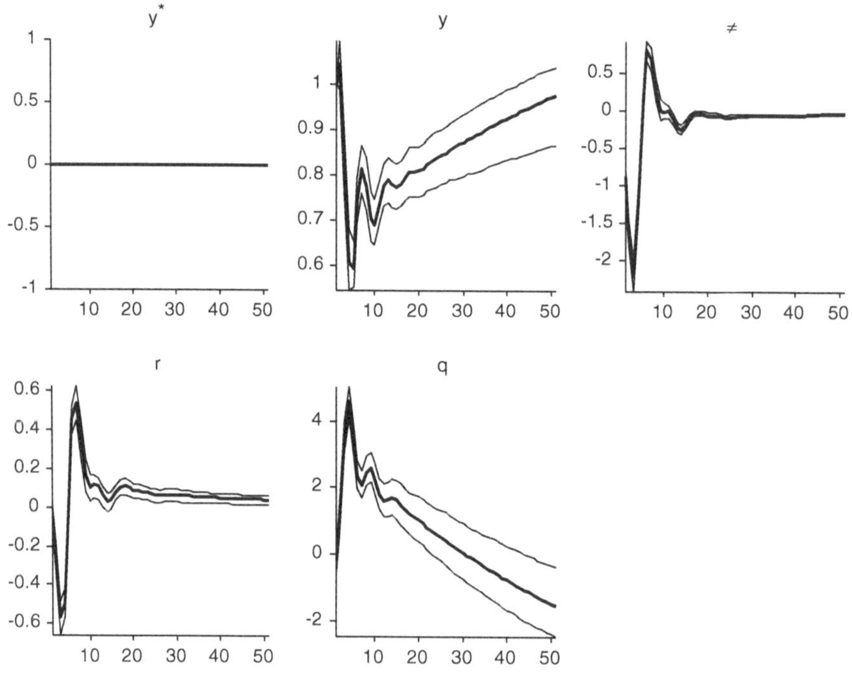

Figure 9.18 Impulse response functions (domestic output shock)

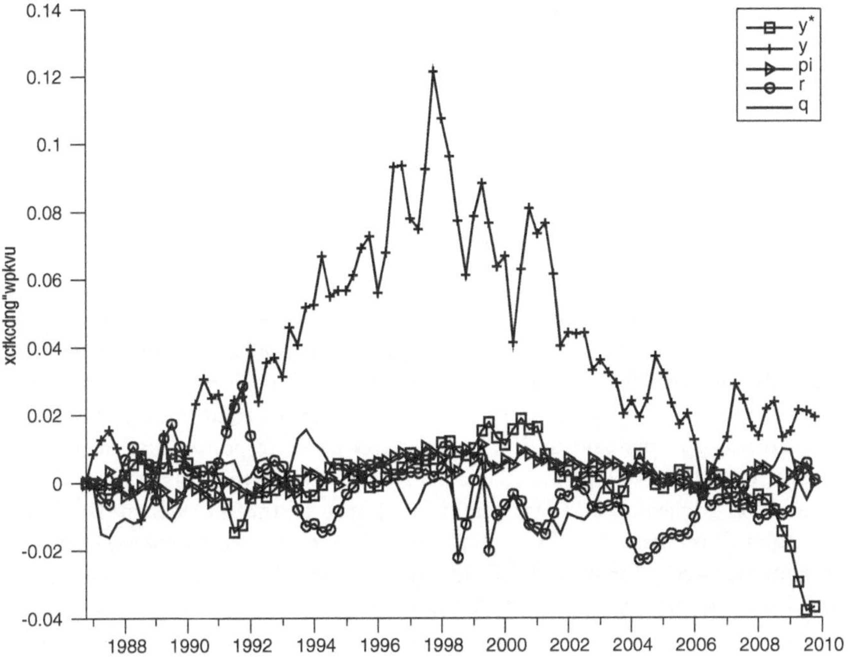

Figure 9.19 Historical decomposition of output

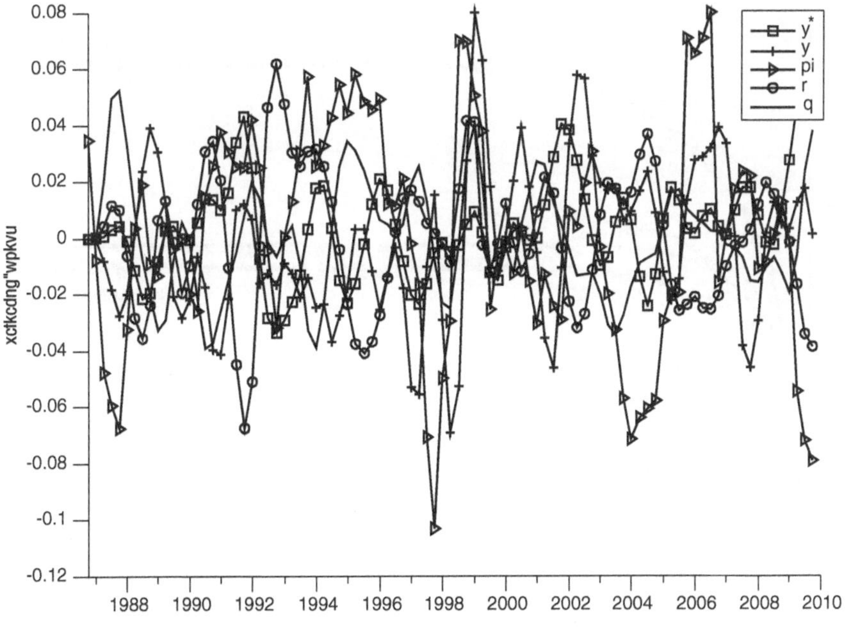

Figure 9.20 Historical decomposition of inflation

6. Comparison of responses to the United States' and China's output shocks across countries

This section compares the relative impact of foreign shocks on each of the individual countries' variables. Initially, the responses to a US output shock are reported. Furthermore, we re-estimate each country model using China as the foreign country and report the corresponding results.

6.1 US output shock

Figure 9.21 shows that output in Singapore is the most sensitive to a foreign shock, followed by Thailand and Malaysia; the Singaporean response is almost double that in Thailand. These results are unsurprising given the high degree of openness of these three countries, with the shares of total trade to GDP of 283, 146 and 108 per cent in 2009, respectively. The responses do not monotonically relate to trade openness; Thailand is more open than Malaysia in these measures yet Malaysia has a larger initial response to the shock than Thailand (although this is reversed in the longer term). This might also reflect the changes in regime occurring for both Thailand, which adopted a flexible exchange rate and inflation targeting during the Asian crisis, and Malaysia, which conversely reduced capital inflow and decreased exchange rate flexibility during the crisis. Alternatively, in the Philippines and Indonesia, the expansionary response of

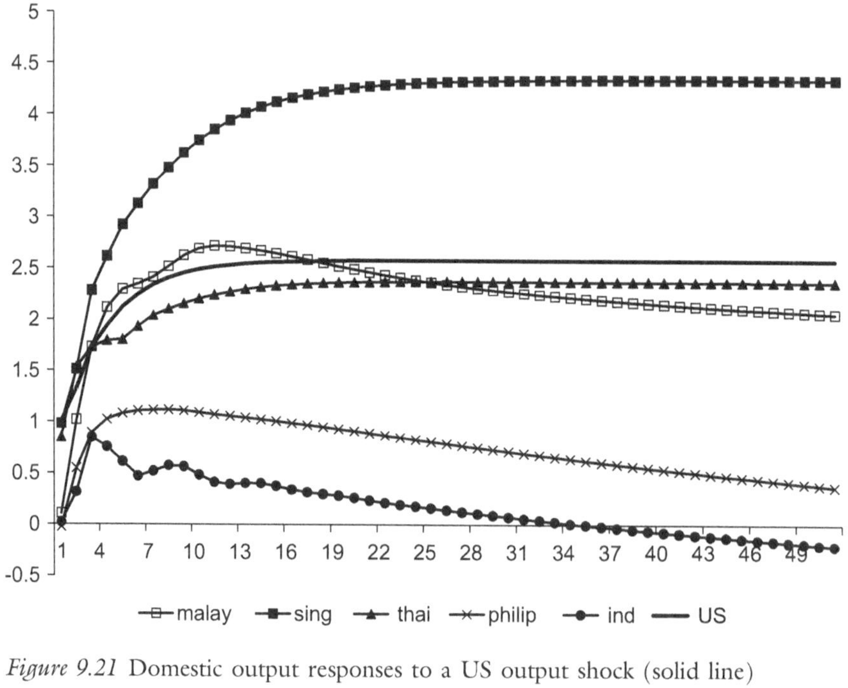

Figure 9.21 Domestic output responses to a US output shock (solid line)

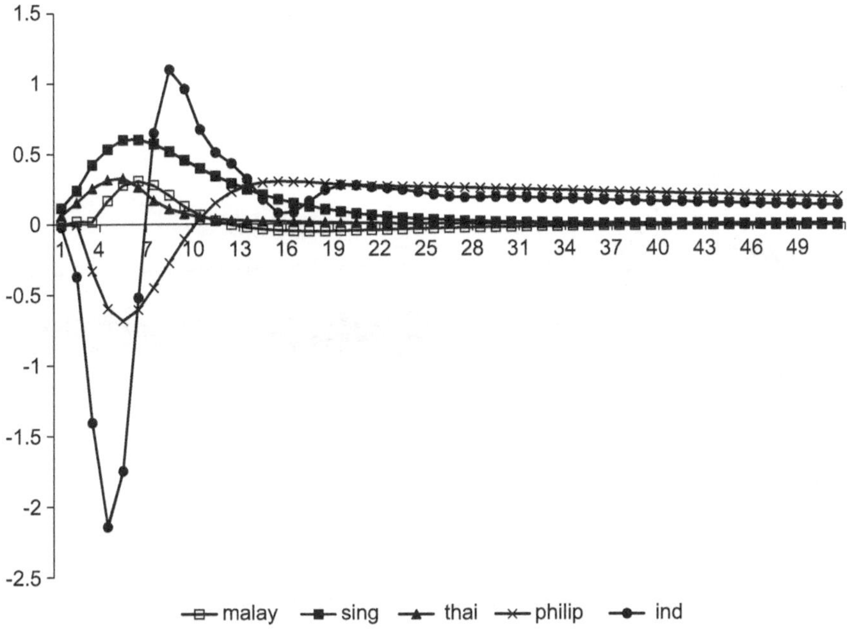

Figure 9.22 Inflation responses to a US output shock

output to a foreign output shock is less pronounced – consistent with the relatively more closed characteristics of these two economies (trade represents 51 and 39 per cent of GDP respectively in these economies).

Figure 9.22 presents the responses of inflation to the US output shock. It can be observed that the responses of Singapore, Thailand and Malaysia are highly synchronized where inflation picks up following the increased aggregate demand in the economy. The responses of the Philippines and Indonesia on the other hand are negative, with a more pronounced deflationary effect in the case of Indonesia. The impact of the recession on these results in Indonesia following the IMF programs there in 1997 needs to be further examined.

The interest rate responses to the US shock presented in Figure 9.23 show that the central banks react to the inflation increases by increasing interest rates, with the exception of Indonesia, where an initial reduction in interest rates is observed. This price puzzle for the Indonesian economy leads us to suspect that further analysis of the Indonesian situation is required. This is consistent with the inflationary outcomes observed previously.

Finally, Figure 9.24 presents the responses of each country's real exchange rate to the US output shock. The initial impact of the shock on the currencies of all countries is an appreciation, which is very short-lived in the case of Singapore. This is partly a reflection of the relatively mild interest rate response we observed in the case of Singapore. It is important to note, however, that it is notoriously difficult to explain the behaviour of real exchange rates.

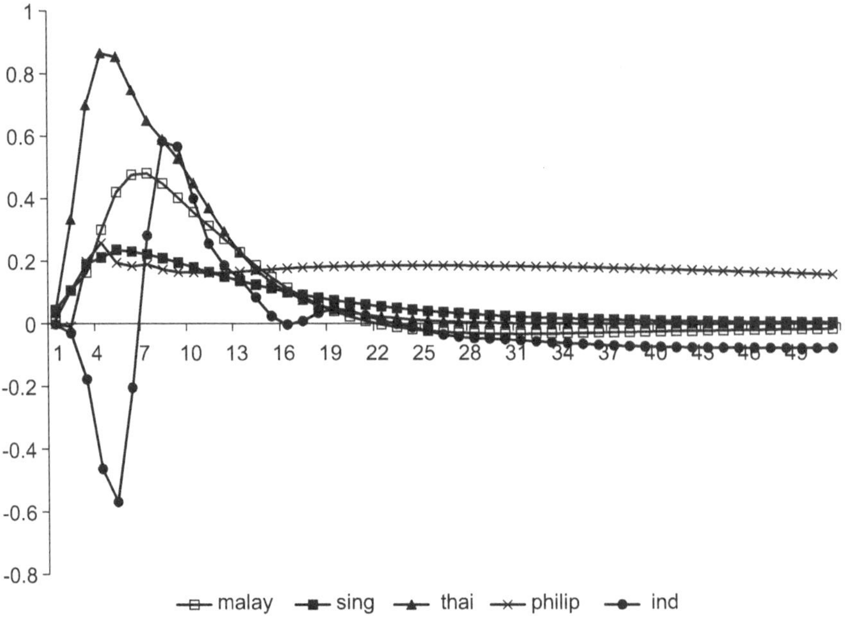

Figure 9.23 Interest rate responses to a US output shock

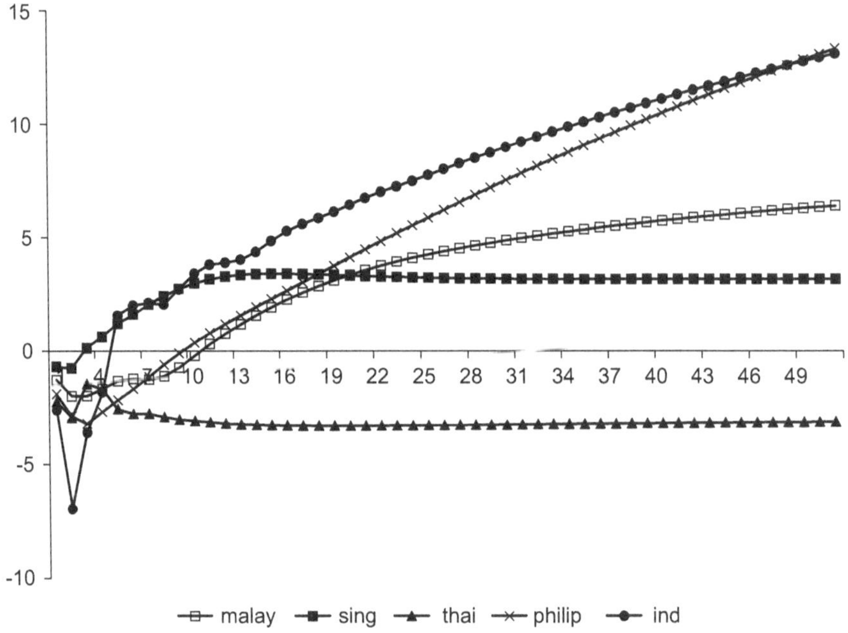

Figure 9.24 Real exchange rate responses to a US output shock

6.2 Chinese output shock

The impulse responses of each of the five East Asian countries to an external output shock originating in China are shown in Figure 9.25. Overall, the output responses are positive in the short- and medium-term, with the exception of the Philippines, where a small negative result is evident. On the other hand, the Chinese shocks are comparatively less important as a source of real output fluctuations in East Asia. This is consistent with the findings of Zhang *et al.* (2010). The inflation and interest rate responses are positive in the short run with the exception of the Philippines and Indonesia. All the countries experience currency depreciations with similar magnitudes in response to the output shock from China. The evidence from this section strongly suggests that when modeling East Asian economies, more explanatory power is gained by using the US economy as the proxy for global economic conditions than by using China. This is despite China's growing importance to these economies and to the world as a whole. Some of this might be due to the importance of the United States as the final source of much consumer demand for Asian production, as well as the fact that many international trade contracts continue to be priced in US dollars. Both of these factors lead to the view that the United States is a closer indicator of international economic conditions than fluctuations in Chinese conditions at this point. The exchange rate responses to the Chinese output shock shown in Figure 9.28, compared with the exchange rate responses to US

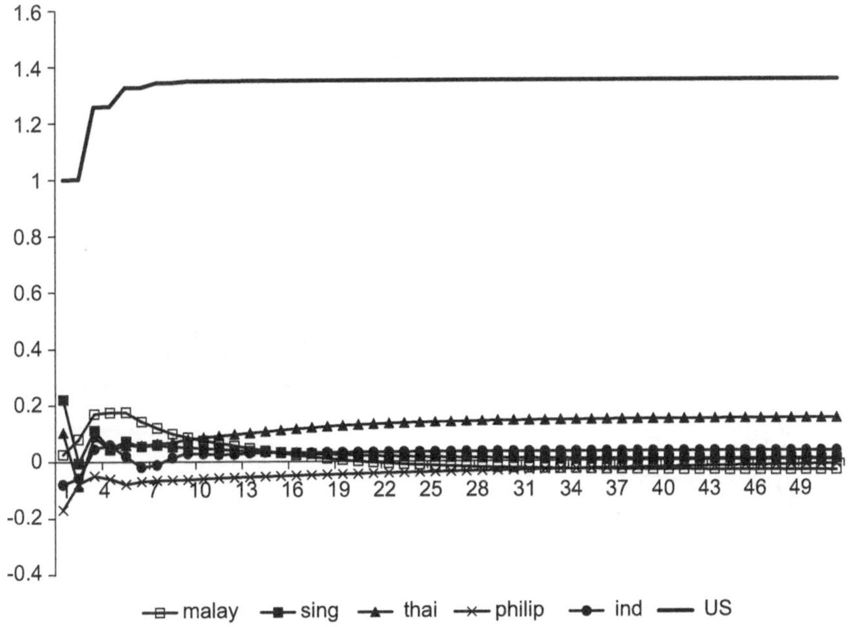

Figure 9.25 Domestic output responses to a Chinese output shock (solid line)

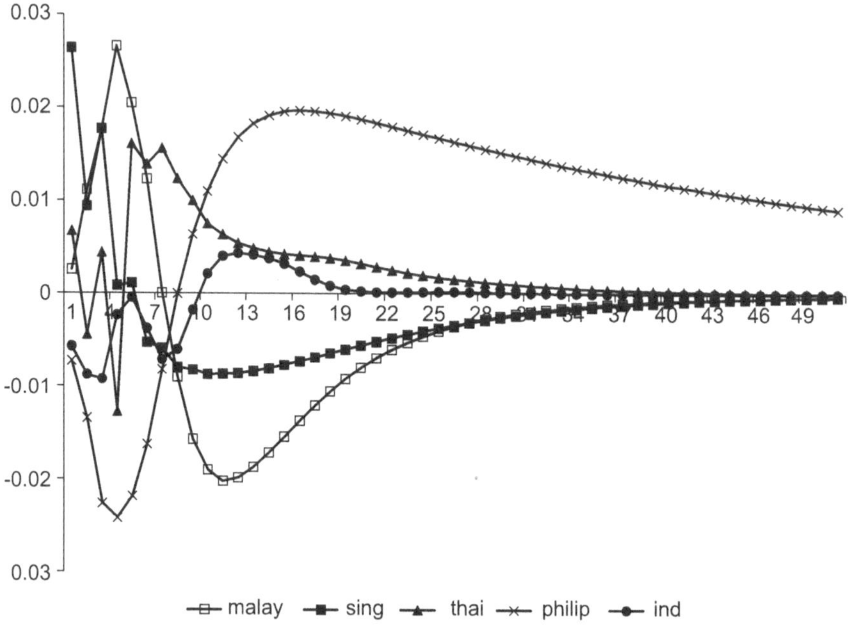

Figure 9.26 Inflation responses to a Chinese output shock

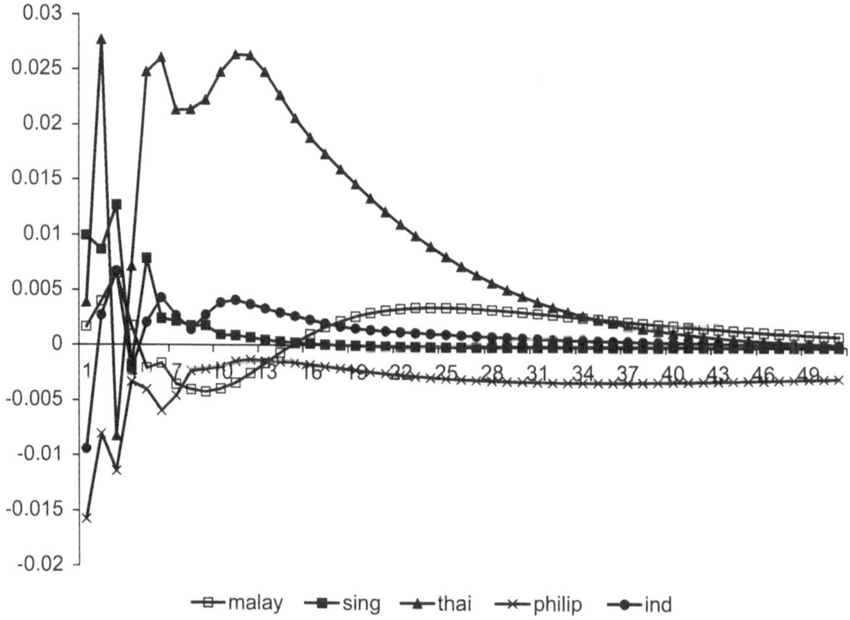

Figure 9.27 Interest rate responses to a Chinese output shock

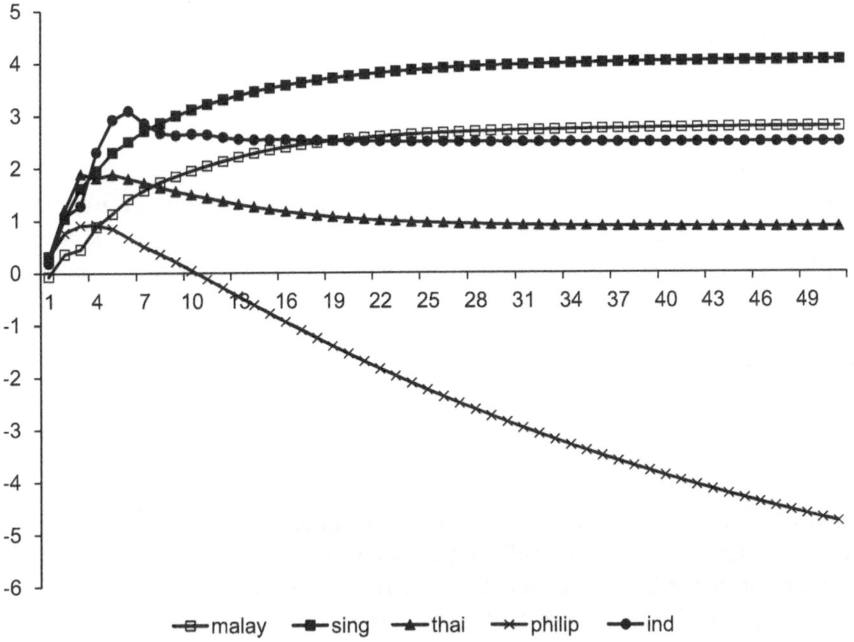

Figure 9.28 Real exchange rate responses to a Chinese output shock

output shocks in Figure 9.24, strongly support the importance of the US dollar in international transactions that impact on the Asian economies. Further work is required in this area, which specifically incorporates both the United States and China as external influences, allowing for the interaction between these economies in order to more effectively model the effect of international conditions on Asian economies.

7. Conclusion

Modelling the macroeconomic relationships in the small, open economies of Asia presents a number of challenges. The relatively short data samples and changing monetary policy and exchange rate regimes during the past 20 years have proven to be significant impediments to the implementation of many modelling frameworks. This chapter has, however, successfully applied a SVECM framework with underlying modern New Keynesian theoretical foundations, taking into account the nature of the underlying data. We harness the mixed I(0) and I(1) nature of the data to provide additional identification and specifically account for the presence of cointegrating relationships between variables where the empirical evidence is compelling. The framework is applied to each of the economies of Singapore, Malaysia, Thailand, the Philippines and Indonesia. In all but the case of Indonesia, we are able to find a specification that does not result in the macroeconomic price and exchange rate puzzles common in this modelling framework. This is a particularly rewarding outcome in a challenging empirical environment. We present the historical analysis of the evolution of shocks in each country, and are able to successfully tie these to the underlying economic events during the sample period.

The framework particularly allows us to investigate the response of the Asian economies to international shocks. In the first instance, we examine how the economies of Singapore, Malaysia, Thailand, the Philippines and Indonesia respond to shocks generated via the US economy. We show that the responses generally reflect the degree of openness of each of these economies – with Singapore (the most open) responding to a far greater degree to US-generated shocks than Indonesia (the least open economy).

The growth of the Chinese economy over the past two decades leads us to consider the alternative of shocks driven by Chinese output shocks in a separate implementation of the model. We find that the Chinese shocks do not have the same impact as US-generated shocks on any of the Asian economies, which we suggest reflects both the role of the United States as the source of much final consumer demand for Asian trade and the importance of the US dollar as the currency of denomination for much international trade and portfolio flows.

The implication for policymakers is that despite the rapid growth of China's importance to countries in this region, external influences are currently better represented by the United States. In the future, this might no longer be the case. To understand more fully the development of these effects, future research should examine a time-varying parameter specification to evaluate the changing nature of these relationships, and accommodate the inter-linkages between the United States and China in understanding the ultimate sources of shocks and their direct and indirect effects on the economic outcomes in East Asia.

References

Akram, Q.F. and Nymoen, R. (2009) 'Model selection for monetary policy analysis: how important is empirical validity?', *Oxford Bulletin of Economics and Statistics*, 75: 35–68.

Beenstock, M. and Longbottom, J.A. (1981) 'The term structure of interest rates in a small open economy', *Journal of Money, Credit and Banking*, 13: 44–59.

Beltran, D.O. and Draper, D. (2008) 'Estimating the parameters of a small open economy DSGE model: identifiability and inferential validity', *International Finance Discussion Papers*, 955, Board of Governors of the Federal Reserve System.

Buckle, R.A., Kim, K., Kirkham, H., McLellan, N. and Sharma, J. (2007) 'A structural VAR business cycle for a volatile small open economy', *Economic Modelling*, 24: 990–1017.

Canova, F. and Sala, L. (2007) 'Back to square one: identification issues in DSGE models', *Banco de España Working Papers*, 0715.

Chow, H.K. and Yoonbai, K. (2003) 'A common currency peg in East Asia? Perspectives from Western Europe', *Journal of Macroeconomics*, 25: 331–50.

Cushman, D. and Zha, T. (1997) 'Identifying monetary policy in a small open economy under flexible exchange rates', *Journal of Monetary Economics*, 39: 433–48.

Dennis, R., Leitemo, K. and Söderström, U. (2007) 'Monetary policy in a small open economy with a preference for robustness', *CEPR Discussion Papers*, 6067.

Dungey, M. and Fry, R. (2009) 'The identification of fiscal and monetary policy in a structural VAR', *Economic Modelling*, 26: 1147–60.

Dungey, M. and Pagan, A.R. (2009) 'Extending a SVAR model of the Australian economy', *Economic Record*, 85: 1–20.

Dungey, M. and Vehbi, M. (2010) 'The term premium and the UK economy 1980–2007', *Centre for Financial Analysis and Policy Working Paper Series*, 10, University of Cambridge.

Gali, J. (2008) *Monetary Policy, Inflation, and the Business Cycle: An Introduction to the New Keynesian Framework*, Princeton, NJ: Princeton University Press.

Gali, J. and Monacelli, T. (2005) 'Monetary policy and exchange rate volatility in a small open economy', *Review of Economic Studies*, 72: 707–34.

Hsu, H.F. (2010) 'Is a common currency area feasible for East Asia? A multivariate structural vector autoregression approach', *Asian Economic Journal*, 24: 391–411.

Huang, Y. and Feng, G. (2006) 'Is currency union a feasible option in East Asia?: A multivariate structural VAR approach', *Research in International Business and Finance*, 20: 77–94.

Justiniano, A. and Preston, B. (2010) 'Monetary policy and uncertainty in an empirical small open-economy model', *Journal of Applied Econometrics*, 45: 561–86.

Kim, S. and Roubini, N. (2000) 'Exchange rate anomalies in the industrial countries: a solution with a structural VAR approach', *Journal of Monetary Economics*, 45: 561–86.

Leitemo, K. (2006) 'Targeting inflation by forecast feedback rules in small open economies', *Journal of Economic Dynamics and Control*, 30: 393–413.

Lutkepohl, H. and Kratzig, M. (2004) *Applied Time Series Econometrics*, Cambridge: Cambridge University Press.

Monacelli, T. (2005) 'Monetary policy in a low pass-through environment', *Journal of Money, Credit, and Banking*, 37: 1047–66.

Mountford, A. (2005) 'Leaning into the wind: a structural VAR investigation of UK monetary policy', *Oxford Bulletin of Economics and Statistics*, 67: 597–621.

Pagan, A. and Pesaran, M. (2009) 'Econometric analysis of structural systems with permanent transitory shocks', *Journal of Economics, Dynamics and Control*, 32: 3376–95.

Ravn, M. (1992) 'Business cycles in the U.K.: a small open economy in the interdependent world', *Economics Working Papers*, 1992–12, School of Economics and Management, University of Aarhus.

Woodford, M. (2003) *Interest & Prices: Foundations of a Theory of Monetary Policy*, Princeton, NJ: Princeton University Press.

Zhang, Z., Sato, K. and McAleer, M. (2004) 'Asian monetary integration: a structural VAR approach', *Mathematics and Computers in Simulation*, 64: 447–58, MSSANZ/IMACS 14th Biennial Conference on Modelling and Simulation.

———. (2010) 'Identifying shocks in regionally integrated East Asian economies with structural VAR and block exogeneity', *Working Papers in Economics*, 10/23, University of Canterbury, Department of Economics and Finance.

Appendix A
Variable plots

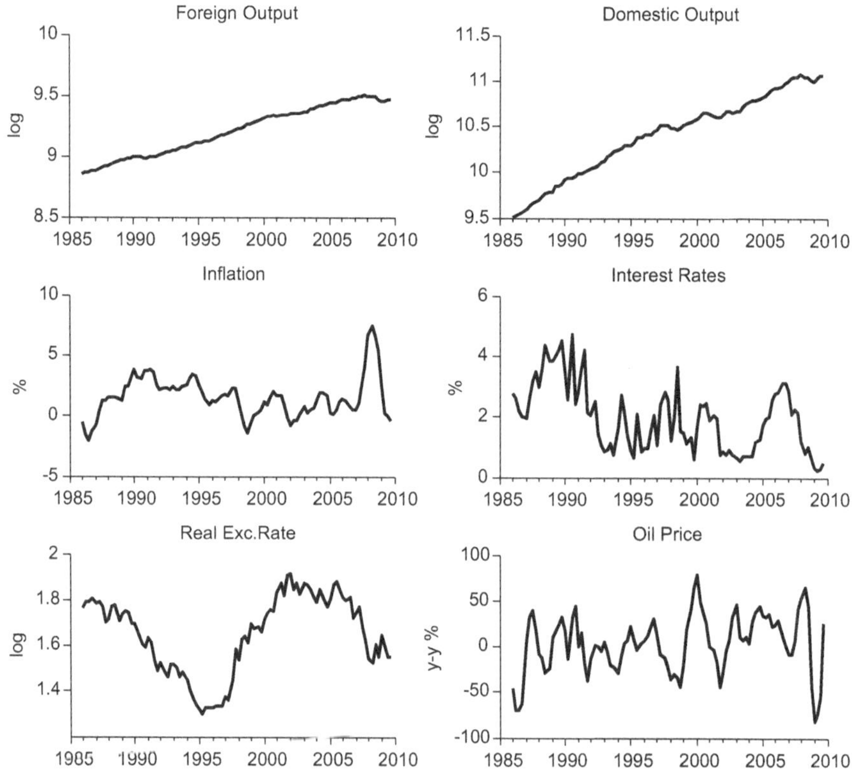

Figure 9.A1 Singapore's variable plots

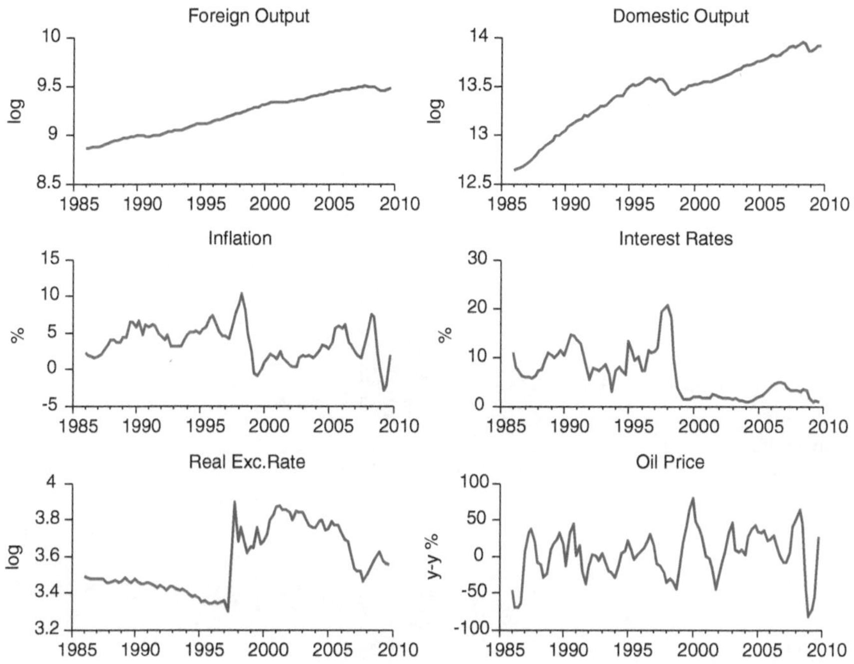

Figure 9.A2 Thailand's variable plots

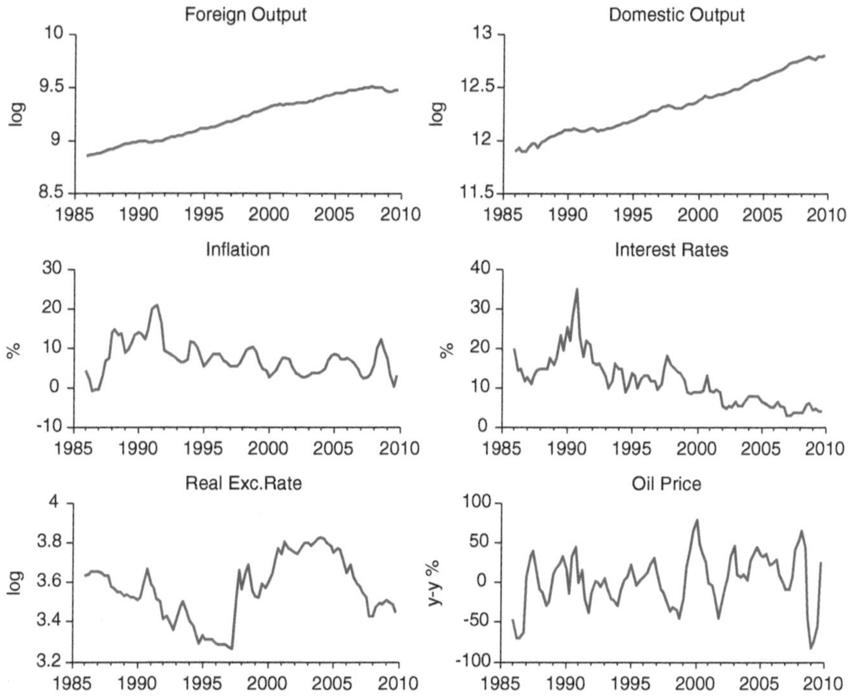

Figure 9.A3 The Philippines' variable plots

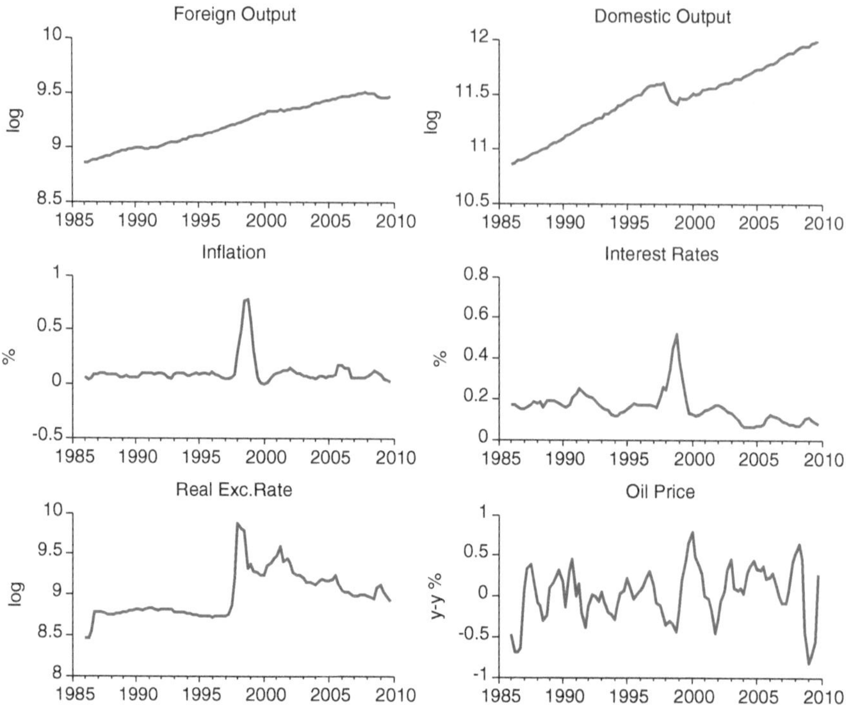

Figure 9.A4 Indonesia's variable plots

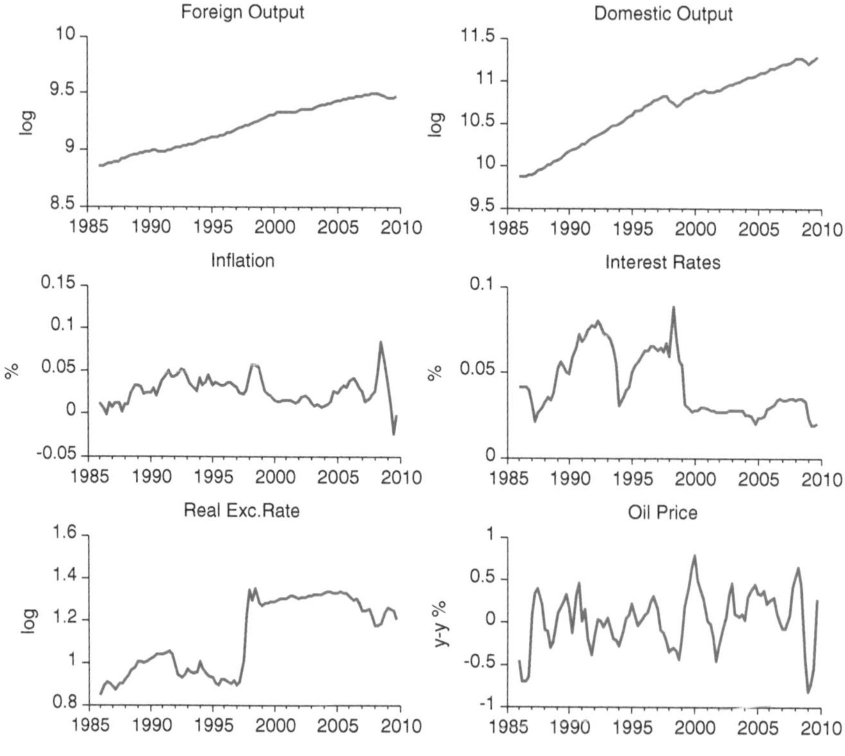

Figure 9.A5 Malaysia's variable plots

Appendix B

Variable descriptions

Data	*Description*	*Source*
y*	log US Real GDP, constant prices, national currency	IFS
y	log Real GDP, constant prices, national currency	IFS, Datastream, Tilak Abeysinge s homepage (http://courses.nus.edu.sg/course/ecstabey/Tilak.html)
π	CPI, % change per annum	IFS, Datastream
r	Treasury Bill rate, % per annum	IFS, Datastream
q	Real exchange rate, (nominal exchange rate as local currency per unit of foreign currency times the ratio of foreign and domestic CPIs)	IFS, Datastream
oil	Oil prices	Spot Oil Price, West Texas Intermediate, $ per barrel, FRED Database

10 International bank claims to East Asian economies

Stabilizers or destabilizers?

Victor Pontines and Reza Siregar[1]

1. Introduction

There is an intense, ongoing debate about the consequences of increased internationalization or globalization of banking. In the past, foreign banks often looked more attractive to host country authorities because they seemed to provide greater transfer of know-how and technology to emerging markets. At the outset of the recent global sub-prime financial crisis, the focus of host country authorities shifted more towards financial stability concerns. There is evidence to support the view that foreign bank entry into domestic banking systems is a stabilizing force for the host economy and results in more efficient allocation of scarce resources. Much of the analysis, however, has been in the context of shocks originating in emerging countries.

The claim that the globalization of banking has brought forth stable financial markets in host economies is in fact at odds with the view that such financial linkages have "fuelled the fire" of the transmission of financial stress from advanced economies to emerging countries, as was illustrated by the Global Financial Crisis (GFC) of 2007–09. During the recent sub-prime financial crisis, cross-border bank lending has also been found to be a key transmission channel through which stresses in the international financial markets were transmitted to emerging markets (Cetorelli and Goldberg, 2008, 2010).

Against this backdrop, understanding the determining factors behind the flows of lending of these international banks is therefore critical, especially for domestic policy makers. Our study examines push and pull factors that drive movements in the cross border loans of banks from three of the Organization for Economic Cooperation and Development (OECD) countries (the United Kingdom, the United States and Japan) to five major Southeast Asian economies (Indonesia, Malaysia, the Philippines, Thailand and Singapore) and Korea.

We extend limited works on the cross-border lending to East Asian economies, such as Siregar and Choy (2010), by focussing on the periods before and after the sub-prime financial crisis. At the peak of the sub-prime crisis – the second half of 2008 to the first half of 2009 – international banks' consolidated lending contracted sharply, driven predominantly by the sudden reversal of cross-border lending (Takats, 2010). Furthermore, the recent trend indicates that cross-border loans of these international banks to emerging markets in Asia dropped more significantly than the local claims of their subsidiaries or branches. This is in sharp contrast with the experience of the Latin American emerging economies. As will be elaborated further, banks from the three OECD economies have predominantly been responsible for the volatilities and significant fall in international bank claims to these major Asian economies during the last global financial meltdown.

While there is a general decline in international bank lending affecting all the emerging Asian economies in our study, some of these countries experienced a much worse, sudden stop of bank flows than others during the GFC (Figure 10.1). It is therefore worthwhile to compare and contrast these cross-country experiences and draw lessons from their diversity. The contagion effect is also interesting and important to examine here. For example, van Rijckeghem and Weder (2003) have shown that fluctuations in foreign bank claims in one country might spill over to other countries that hold claims from the same foreign banks.

In short, this study seeks to address a number of rising policy concerns from the aftermath of the recent sub-prime crisis: Did foreign bank lending decline sharply and transmit financial shocks from the advanced economies to the emerging markets in East and Southeast Asia? Was the decline driven by the drying up of supply of foreign bank loans or more by the sharp decline in the demand for this funding? Does the greater exposure of foreign banks to a host country lower the sensitivity of its claims to shocks? Are other countries affected by movements in international banks' claims on another country when they owe from the same international banks? At the outset, we want to assess the stability of these foreign bank loans. If there is a lesson to be learned from the GFC, it is that central banks around the globe have come to appreciate that monetary stability – particularly price stability during the great moderation in the early to mid-2000s – does not necessarily lead to financial stability. Hence, it is timely to revisit the role of foreign banks and ask: has the cross-border bank lending of foreign banks had a stabilizing or destabilizing effect?

The chapter is structured as follows: the next section presents a number of stylized facts on the relevant cross-border lending. The data description, working model and empirical testing are presented in Section 3. Discussion of the empirical findings and, more importantly, policy implications, are given in Section 4. The chapter ends with a concluding remark.

2. Stylized facts and motivation

Foreign banks' operations in emerging markets across the global banking system, including those of the Asian economies, increased dramatically from the second half of the 1990s. The emerging markets, in general, do not rely on foreign deposits for funding, but they usually turn to international banks for credit lines for exports (Mihaljek, 2010). For most East and Southeast Asian economies, the rise of the international banks' presence started with the first phase of reform and deregulation of the banking sector in the late 1980s and early 1990s. For

Indonesia

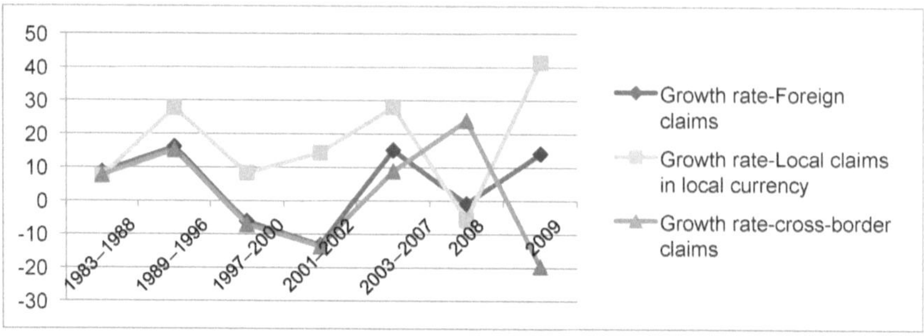

Korea

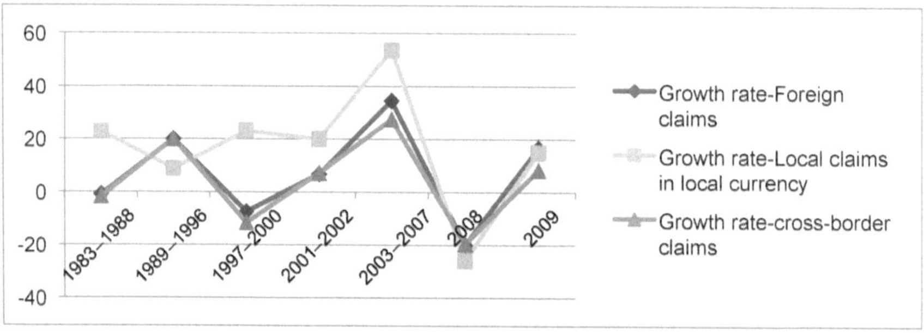

Malaysia

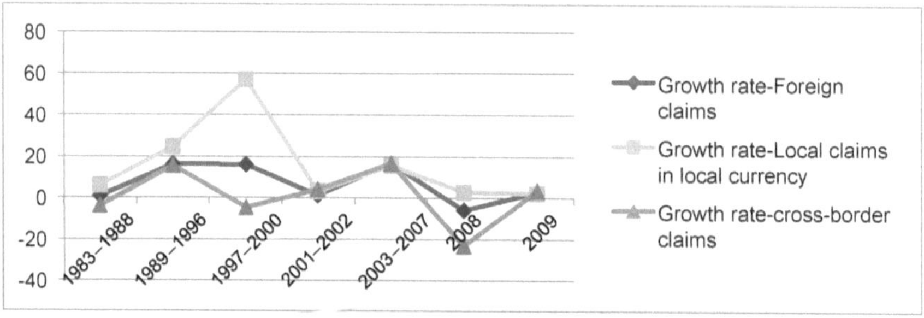

Figure 10.1 Average annual growth rate of foreign and local bank claims in major East and Southeast Asian economies

Notes: "Foreign claims" is defined as the foreign financial claims of international banks to the financial and non-financial sectors in the six Asian economies as reported in the BIS *Consolidated Banking Statistics*. These bilateral data are then comprised of the credit extended by the foreign banks headquartered overseas ("cross-border claims"), the credit extended in foreign currencies by the affiliates of foreign banks in host economies ("local claims of foreign affiliates in foreign currency"), and the credit extended in local currency by the affiliates of foreign banks in host economies ("local claims of foreign affiliates in local currency").

The Philippines

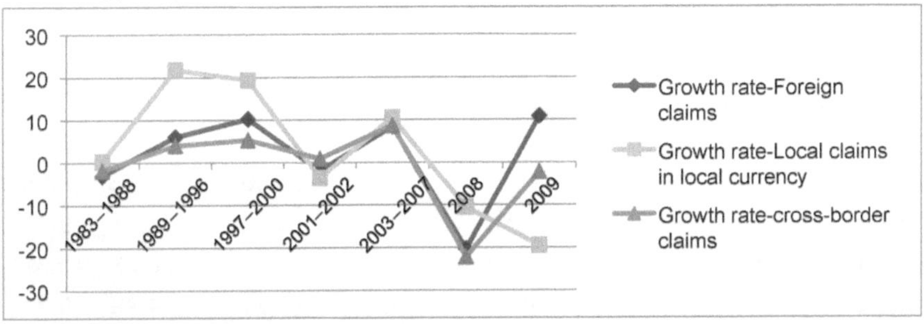

Singapore

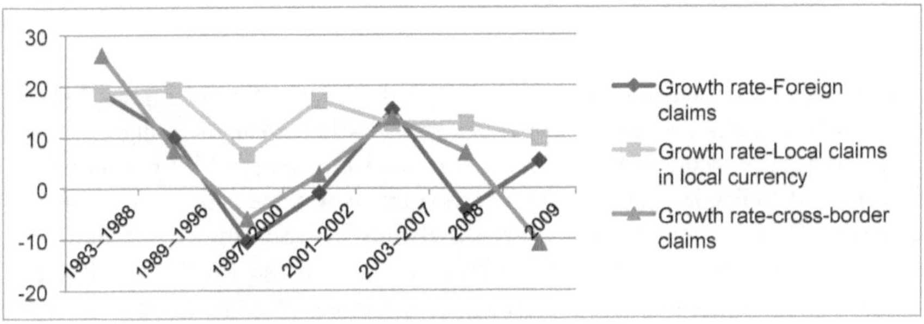

Thailand

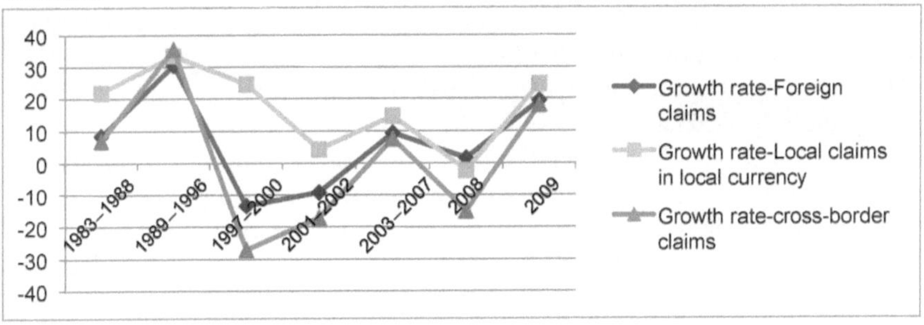

Figure 10.1 (Continued)

instance, as reported in Table 10.1, across the six Asian economies examined in this chapter, the total foreign bank claims of three major Southeast Asian economies – Indonesia, Malaysia and Thailand – grew at an annual average of 16 per cent to 30 per cent for the period 1989–96. It is unfortunate, however, that (along with Singapore) Thailand and Indonesia also experienced the most severe declines in foreign bank claims across the six economies, at about 6 per cent and 13 per cent respectively, at about the time of the most severe impact of the 1997 Asian Financial Crisis (AFC).

Table 10.1 Annual average growth of international bank claims in major East and Southeast Asian economies

Countries	*1983–88*	*1989–96*	*1997–2000*	*2001–02*	*2003–07*	*2008*	*2009*
Indonesia	8.59	16.11	–6.27	–13.33	15.16	–0.85	14.01
Korea	–0.97	20.09	–7.49	6.85	34.50	–19.98	16.76
Malaysia	0.84	16.12	15.88	1.39	16.69	–5.91	2.75
Philippines	–2.98	6.08	10.30	–2.0	8.44	–20.35	10.89
Singapore	18.79	9.98	–10.45	–0.95	15.34	–4.23	5.34
Thailand	8.45	30.65	–13.35	–9.19	9.32	1.61	19.38

Source: Bank for International Settlements (BIS) *Consolidated Banking Statistics*, for the basic data, and authors' calculations.

Moreover, about the time of the reversal of the information technology (IT) bubble in the United States in 2001–02, the drastic retreat of foreign banks' claims to these six economies was also felt to a lesser extent, with the exception of Korea and Malaysia (Table 10.1). Meanwhile, as testament to its mark as an established financial centre, Singapore was already experiencing strong double-digit inflows of international bank lending way back in the 1980s. The Philippines, on the other hand, had only experienced a reasonable size of international bank flows in the 1980s and 1990s, when compared with the other economies. Apart from Malaysia, however, which imposed capital controls during the peak of the AFC, it is the only other economy (among the four remaining Asian countries examined here) that did not experience a sudden reversal of international bank claims during the AFC (Table 10.1).

The loosening of ownership regulation, especially during the post-AFC period, also significantly facilitated the rise in the activities of international banks in Asia. Indonesia, South Korea and Thailand, for instance, have raised the allowance for foreign equity participation in local banks up to 100 per cent. Meanwhile, the Philippines has permitted 60 per cent foreign ownership. As a consequence, the significantly more liberal ownership policy, which facilitated an aura of stability and confidence in the respective economies' banking systems, has frequently been recognized as an important contributing factor to the return of sustained surges of foreign bank inflows to these economies from 2003 to 2007 – just before the outbreak of the recent sub-prime crisis in the United States (Table 10.1).

The total foreign claims of international banks, in general, continued to sustain strong momentum for some of the emerging markets of the Asian region even until the first half of 2008. Only during the weeks and months in the immediate aftermath of the Lehman Brothers debacle were countries in East and Southeast Asia engulfed in a sharp and sudden reversal of international bank claims, such that the unimaginable, sheer size of the reversals in international bank flows out of these six Asian economies saw the annual growth rate of these flows hitting negative territory by the end of 2008, with the exception only of Thailand.[2] More recent data reveal that, across the board, inflows of international bank lending to these six economies have returned (Table 10.1).

As for the nationality of the sources of these international bank flows, it is interesting that before the AFC, Japanese banks were the largest sources of funding for banks and corporations in East and Southeast Asia.[3] For example, at its peak, in the period 1989–96, Japanese lending amounted to 56 per cent and 54 per cent in the cases of Thailand and Indonesia respectively (Table 10.2).[4] Not far from these two economies are Korea and Malaysia, which recorded lending by Japanese banks of 28 and 40 per cent respectively. As presented in Table 10.2, in the aftermath of the AFC, a consistent waning in the share of lending by Japanese banks was experienced by all six economies, and this diminishing dominance in lending by Japanese banks has recently been taken on to some extent by UK banks, and consistently by US banks. As a result, such is the critical influence of banks owned by Japan, the United Kingdom and the United States, the combined lending of these three big economies accounts for about half of the combined lending by developed countries to these six Asian countries (Table 10.2).

As discussed above, while international bank lending retreated substantially in almost all of the six Asian economies in the immediate aftermath of the bankruptcy of Lehman Brothers, it could be that a key component of this international bank lending, in the form of the local claims of these foreign banks operating within the domain of these Asian economies, remained strong and was less adversely affected by the external shock that originated from the United States. As depicted in Figure 10.1, while these local claims booked by offices of foreign banks in these economies also retreated in Indonesia, Korea, the Philippines and Thailand, this was not the case for Malaysia and Singapore.

In retrospect, when we look back at previous crises, such as the AFC and the 2001–02 collapse of the IT bubble in the United States, as emphasized above, the majority of our six Asian economies experienced sharp reversals in total international bank flows for these two separate crisis periods, similar to the one that recently occurred at the end of 2008. Remarkably, these local claims have continued to register positive average annual growth rates during the past three crisis episodes – namely, the 1997 AFC, the 2001–02 IT bubble and the 2007–08 sub-prime crisis.[5] In fact, Figure 10.1 illustrates that the more volatile and crisis-sensitive component of the total claims of these foreign banks to our Asian economies has been cross-border lending. The swings and sudden reversals of cross-border lending have been the dominant drivers of the overall fluctuations in the total claims of foreign banks in these six Asian economies during the past three decades, but particularly during the past financial crisis. Indeed, the collapse in cross-border lending has proved to be a major financial channel through which stresses in the international financial system were transmitted, not only to our Asian economies, but also to the rest of the emerging market economies (Takats, 2010). As for the recent sub-prime crisis years of

Table 10.2 Average share of Japanese, UK and US banks in foreign bank lending to major East and Southeast Asian economies

Country	*Nationality of foreign banks*	*1983–88*	*1989–96*	*1997–2000*	*2001–02*	*2003–07*	*2008*	*2009*
Indonesia								
	Japanese	40.48	54.22	30.82	22.57	15.37	14.09	14.66
	UK	8.40	4.85	8.48	10.08	12.30	13.31	13.20
	US	19.06	8.96	10.56	9.08	9.32	12.75	13.27
Korea								
	Japanese	31.30	28.48	18.72	13.48	8.86	8.94	9.52
	UK	7.78	4.80	7.72	10.45	19.44	25.02	24.37
	US	29.88	18.12	18.93	22.27	23.88	18.91	25.46
Malaysia								
	Japanese	43.57	40.91	22.48	11.98	7.73	8.16	8.71
	UK	8.65	6.40	20.09	26.51	28.12	26.73	27.67
	US	19.88	24.04	19.19	15.15	14.52	11.51	13.15
Philippines								
	Japanese	21.46	19.00	13.45	13.47	10.39	12.97	13.67
	UK	10.69	8.46	9.78	11.75	12.98	14.60	16.92
	US	41.13	42.74	27.52	21.99	17.55	17.46	19.58
Singapore								
	Japanese	40.01	47.24	20.46	16.40	13.26	16.35	16.91
	UK	8.32	9.43	19.96	22.11	23.91	23.77	23.78
	US	12.40	5.51	8.11	12.42	13.18	11.25	11.44
Thailand								
	Japanese	47.33	56.39	38.70	26.62	27.17	31.15	32.39
	UK	3.18	2.79	6.58	10.95	15.26	16.38	16.50
	US	23.94	11.44	9.87	10.68	12.70	10.33	12.00

Source: BIS *Consolidated Banking Statistics*, for the basic data, and authors' calculations.

2008–09, the average growth rates of cross-border lending for the rest of the economies included in this study were significantly lower than those of the local claims, with the exception of the Philippines. In fact, the local claims of the foreign banks continued to grow positively in Indonesia, Malaysia, Singapore and Thailand during the height of the sub-prime crisis (Figure 10.1).

In summary, the cross-country experiences of our six economies highlight the seemingly indisputable evidence that global banks act as a channel of financial shock transmission from the global financial markets to the local economy. Formally testing this hypothesis, as well as significantly identifying the possible driving factors behind this cross-border lending, are therefore imperative and will be the primary objectives of the empirical work of this study.

3. Methodology and empirics

3.1 Dynamic panel generalized method of moments (GMM) technique[6]

In a pure cross-sectional regression any unobserved time-invariant country-pair specific effects would be part of the error term, leading to biased estimates of the coefficients. A panel context, however, allows us to control for these unobserved time-invariant country-pair specific effects and the problem of biased coefficient estimates is subsequently either reduced or eliminated. This is important as there is growing evidence in the literature that cultural biases and differences, for instance, have a substantial impact on a variety of financial flows: portfolio and direct investment (Ekinci *et al.*, 2008; Guiso *et al.*, 2009) as well as foreign bank lending (Giannetti and Yafeh, 2008; Mian, 2006). In addition, the GMM estimator does not require any particular distributions of the error term.

In order to estimate a certain dynamic panel model consistently and efficiently, a GMM estimator is employed. It was introduced by Holtz-Eakin *et al.* (1990) and Arellano and Bond (1991), and further developed in a series of papers including Arellano and Bover (1995) and Blundell and Bond (1998). This estimator encompasses a regression equation in both differences and levels, each one with its specific set of instrumental variables. We consider the following regression equation for the logarithmic-first differences of international bank claims

$$y_{ij,t} = \alpha y_{ij,t-1} + \beta X_{ij,t} + \eta_{ij} + \varepsilon_{ij,t}, \tag{1}$$

where y is the logarithmic-first differences of bank claims; X represents the set of explanatory variables apart from the lagged logarithmic-first differences of international bank claims; η is an unobserved, time-invariant country-pair specific effect; ε is the error term; and the subscripts i, j and t represent country pairs and the time period respectively.

We eliminate country-pair specific effects (η_{ij}) by taking first differences of equation (1)

$$y_{ij,t} - y_{ij,t-1} = \alpha(y_{ij,t-1} - y_{ij,t-2}) + \beta(X_{ij,t} - X_{ij,t-1}) + (\varepsilon_{ij,t} - \varepsilon_{ij,t-1}) \tag{2}$$

The use of own suitable lagged levels of $y_{ij,t}$ as instruments is required to deal with the problem that by differencing the lagged dependent variable, $(y_{ij,t-1} - y_{ij,t-2})$ is correlated with the error term, $\varepsilon_{ij,t} - \varepsilon_{ij,t-1}$. The same strategy is applied to form instruments for other explanatory variables that are allowed to be endogenous, in the sense that they can be affected by current and past realizations of y. This feature enables us to avoid simultaneity bias due to the endogeneity of some of our explanatory variables. Strictly speaking, under the assumption that (i) the explanatory variables, X, are weakly exogenous (no correlation with future realizations of the error term), and (ii) the error term, ε, is not serially correlated, the dynamic panel GMM estimator exploits the following moment conditions:

$$E[y_{ij,t-s}(\varepsilon_{ij,t} - \varepsilon_{ij,t-1})] = 0 \qquad \text{for } s \geq 2;\ t = 3, \dots, T \tag{3}$$

$$E[X_{ij,t-s}(\varepsilon_{ij,t} - \varepsilon_{ij,t-1})] = 0 \qquad \text{for } s \geq 2;\ t = 3, \dots, T \tag{4}$$

The resulting GMM estimator based on these conditions is known as the *difference*-GMM estimator. There is, however, an issue with the *difference*-GMM estimator. If lagged dependent variables and explanatory variables are persistent over time, the lagged levels likely represent weak instruments for the first-differenced variables. This causes finite sample bias and low accuracy, which leads to the need to complement the regression in first differences with a regression in levels. The instruments for the regression in first differences are the same as above. The instruments for the regression in levels, in turn, are the lagged *differences* of the same corresponding variables, under the assumption that although there might be a correlation between the levels of the right-hand-side variables and the country-pair specific effect in equation (1), none exists between the differences of these variables and the country-pair specific effect.

The additional moment conditions for the regression in levels are

$$E[y_{ij,t-s} - y_{ij,t-s-1})\,(\eta_{ij} + \varepsilon_{ij,t})] = 0 \qquad \text{for } s = 1 \tag{5}$$

$$E[X_{ij,t-s} - X_{ij,t-s-1})\,(\eta_{ij} + \varepsilon_{ij,t})] = 0 \qquad \text{for } s = 1 \tag{6}$$

The consistency of the GMM estimator depends on whether lagged values of the explanatory variables are valid instruments in the regression. To address this issue, we consider two specification tests: the first is the Hansen test of over-identifying restrictions, which tests the overall validity of the instruments; failure to reject the null hypothesis supports the model. The second test examines the hypothesis that the error term is not serially correlated. We test whether the differenced error term – that is, the residual of the regression in differences – is second-order serially correlated.[7] If the test fails to reject the null hypothesis of absent second-order serial correlation, we conclude that the original error term is serially uncorrelated and use the corresponding moment conditions.

3.2 Measurement and results

3.2.1 The evidence from total foreign bank claims

Our baseline general econometric model lays out the possible determinants of international bank claims represented by the following dynamic panel equation

$$\begin{aligned}\Delta\log claims_{ij,t} = {} & \alpha_0 + \alpha_1 \Delta\log Claims_{ij,t-1} + \beta_1 indiff_{ij,t} + \beta_2 VIX_t \\ & + \beta_3 Clender_{ij,t} + \beta_4 growthrate_{j,t} + \beta_5 growthrate_{i,t} \\ & + \beta_6 growth_{i,t} \times exposure_{ij,t} + \upsilon_{ij,t}\end{aligned} \tag{7}$$

where i and j represent country pairs i and j, and i = 1 to 3 denotes the major BIS-reporting home country banks of Japan, the United Kingdom and the United States, while, j = 1 to 6 denotes the East Asian host countries of Indonesia, Korea, Malaysia, the Philippines, Singapore and Thailand. The dependent variable in this section of the chapter, $\Delta\log Claims_{ij,t}$, is the logarithmic differences of total foreign bank claims[8] from banks in the home country i to host countries *j*; $\Delta \log Claims_{ij,t-1}$ is the lagged of the dependent variable. In equation (7), we assume that $v_{ij,t}$ contains the following two effects: (i) the unobserved time-invariant country-pair specific effect, η_{ij}; and (ii) a stochastic error term, $\varepsilon_{ij,t}$, varying across time and cross-section.

We follow the voluminous literature on the fundamental determinants of capital flows by accounting in our empirical model for the home or "push" and host or "pull" factors that figure prominently in this extensive literature. On this basis, we include the nominal interest differential between host country *j* and home country *i* ($intdiff_{ij,t}$), as well as the respective real GDP growth of host country *j* ($growthrate_{j,t}$) and home country *i* ($growthrate_{i,t}$). We expect a positive coefficient on the $intdiff_{ij,t}$ variable as higher interest rates in the host country or, conversely, lower interest rates in the home countries, *ceteris paribus*, should lead to an increase in international bank flows in the host economies. We also expect a positive coefficient on the real GDP growth of host countries as higher returns in these countries should then lead to a rise in international bank flows in these countries. There is, however, ambiguity as to the expected sign of the real GDP growth in home countries as, on one hand, recessionary economic conditions in home countries entail lower profit opportunities at home, which should then encourage foreign banks to seek better or higher returns abroad, in which case we expect a negative coefficient on the $growthrate_{i,t}$ variable. On the other hand, weak economic conditions in the home countries might signal a worsening of the capital position of foreign banks, which should then discourage, or worsen, retrenching their lending overseas.

Apart from considering the impact of traditional push and pull factors on international bank claims, we also take into account a measure of the state of the global financial market, the *S&P 100 Volatility Index* (VIX_t) of the Chicago Board Options Exchange, which is widely used as an indicator of the expected short-term volatility of the global financial market. A high value of the VIX indicates more volatile market expectations, and as such we expect a negative coefficient on the VIX variable as greater global volatility should lead to a reduction in international bank flows to host economies (Hermann and Mihaljek, 2010).[9] In line with the often-cited study of van Rijckeghem and Weder (2003), we also include in our empirical model a measure of the potential contagion or spillover of changes in international bank flows from one country to another, which is denoted by the $Clender_{ij,t}$ variable. More popularly known as the "common lender effect", this argues that movements in international banks' claims on one country might be transmitted to other countries that owe claims from the same international banks (Peria *et al.*, 2005). We follow Peria *et al.* (2005) in accounting for this effect and thus operationalize $Clender_{ij,t}$ as the changes in claims from home country *i* banks to all major East Asian host countries, other than that of the individual East Asian host country *j*.[10] We should then expect that if the common lender effect works, the coefficient on $Clender_{ij,t}$ would be positive and significant.

Turning finally to our main variable of interest – that is, in order to test the impact of the financial crisis on the stability of international bank lending to our respective host economies – we interact our home countries' real GDP growth rate variable, $growthrate_{i,t}$, with a measure of foreign banks' exposure to our individual host countries, $exposure_{ij,t}$ noting that we measure foreign bank exposure as the ratio of home country *i*'s international bank claims on host country *j* to the total worldwide claims of home country *i*'s banks.[11] In other words, this foreign bank exposure variable measures the level or intensity of exposure of lending by international banks to the Asian host economies examined in the chapter, relative to their global international lending. In addition, since crises coincide with deterioration in macroeconomic fundamentals such as real GDP growth rates – as happened in developed markets during the recent GFC – this interaction variable recognizes the idea that crises are basically indistinguishable from downturns in GDP.

From this perspective, this allows us to test – depending on the sign and significance of the interaction term – whether crises that coincide with deterioration in real GDP growth rates transmit across borders via the lending behaviour of international banks. To be more specific, in terms of equation (7), if the estimated coefficient of the growth rates in home countries ($growthrate_{i,t}$) come out to be negative, and if the estimated coefficient in the interaction term is positive, it then only means that a crisis in home countries *i*, which adversely affects international bank lending to host countries *j*, is mitigated when there is a higher level of exposure by international banks in host countries (stable financing). The converse of this result is then interpreted as instability in financing by international banks. In short, the interaction term can then be interpreted as measuring the degree of commitment, or lack of it, by international banks to host countries in the face of shocks in the home countries.[12] Finally, we would like to note that, in our baseline specification, regressor endogeneity is not a major concern between our left-hand-side variable and the foreign bank exposure variable. This is because the former is the change in *bilateral* foreign assets between banks, whereas the latter is measured as a proportion of the *aggregate* worldwide claims of banks.[13]

The estimation results of three alternative specifications of the dynamic panel model for the whole sample period of 2000Q1 to 2010Q3 are summarized in Table 10.3. Altogether, with the exception of the nominal interest rate differential variable (which only came out significant, but has the incorrect sign in specification [1]), all of the estimated coefficients are significant, and those variables that have clear a priori signs came out with their expected signs. Several key findings are worth highlighting. To start, we find evidence that international bank flows increase (decrease) their claims on host markets once these same economies experience stronger (adverse) macroeconomic growth performance. This result confirms the presence of a "demand factor" influencing the flows of these claims. All these Asian economies experienced slower growth, particularly during the peak of the GFC, translating into weaker demand for funding from the international banks.

Table 10.3 Dynamic panel estimation results of determinants of changes in international total bank claims, 2000Q1–2010Q3

Variables	*(1)*	*(2)*	*(3)*
$logdiffclaims_{t-1}$	–0.060 (0.081)	–0.097 (0.077)	–0.092 (0.072)
Intdiff	–0.403 (0.175)**	–0.284 (0.165)	–0.245 (0.168)
$Growthrate_J$	0.333 (0.113)***	0.222 (0.108)**	0.233 (0.101)**
$growthrate_i$	0.145 (0.116)	–0.709 (0.229)***	–0.717 (0.218)***
Vix		–0.215 (0.062)***	–0.155 (0.068)**
Clender			0.231 (0.045)***
$growthrate_i$ * exposure		0.536 (0.168)***	0.573 (0.162)***
Sargan test (*p*-value)	0.08	0.09	0.10
AB test for AR(2) (*p*-value)	0.20	0.38	0.43
No. of observations	762	764	765
No. of lags	2	2	2

Note: Standard errors in parentheses. Significance levels: *** 1%; ** 5%. Numbers in the last two rows of the table are *p*-values.

Similarly, we find a number of "supply-side factors" have also come into play here. First, the negative and significant coefficient (though insignificant and positive only in specification [1]) on the home countries' real GDP growth rate indicates that foreign banks' behaviour veers towards seeking better or higher returns abroad when domestic economic conditions are weak and fragile. The results confirm that a weaker economic outlook in the home country translates into a rise in the foreign banks' claims on the host economy.

Second, we also find evidence in support of the common lender effect in view of the positive and significant coefficient on changes in international bank claims in other countries. This seems to support the argument for the presence of a contagion effect in international banking. In particular, it demonstrates that changes in foreign bank claims on one country might spillover to other countries that hold claims from the same banks (van Rijckeghem and Weder, 2003). Third, consistent with theoretical expectations, a rise in the expected short-term volatility of the global financial market, as proxied by the widely used VIX, has indeed adversely contributed to the overall sharp decline in the total claims of the foreign banks. The overall robustness of the supply-side factors substantiates the role of the international bank claims as a key transmission channel of the impacts of a distressed banking sector in the advanced economies into the emerging markets of Asia.

Finally, the positive and significant coefficient on the main variable of interest – the interaction between home country foreign banks' real GDP growth rate and its exposure – suggest that controlling for macroeconomic conditions in developed economies – crisis episodes or shocks that originate in developed economies – do not necessarily translate into less stable financing in international bank claims to host countries in Asia. This is in contrast, however, with the earlier preliminary examination of the flows in international bank claims, wherein we observed a sharp and sudden reversal during the GFC. Perhaps one reason for this seemingly conflicting result is that the foreign bank claims data used in this section are not pure cross-border claims data. This is in view of the fact that the foreign bank claims data as consolidated by the BIS do not just comprise the cross-border claims, but also the local claims of the foreign banks' offices on residents of the country in which the foreign bank is located. Thus, it is highly likely that the local claims component in the data might be mitigating this effect since this particular component of the foreign banks' claims held up well during the GFC. To alleviate this concern, we also conduct our estimations using publicly available data on cross-border claims. The results are discussed in the following section.

3.2.2 The evidence from cross-border claims

We should emphasize at the outset that bilateral data on cross-border claims similar to those we used in the previous section are not publicly available.[14] What are publicly available are the aggregate cross-border claims of all the BIS-reporting home country banks to non-BIS-reporting countries, including the Asian economies examined here. In short, unlike what was done in the previous section, investigation of the respective bilateral claims of the three major home country banks of Japan, the United Kingdom and the United States is not permitted here.[15] Barring this limitation, we again estimated our baseline empirical dynamic panel model (equation [7]), and the results of these respective sets of dynamic panel estimations are presented in Table 10.4.

Three critical observations stand out from the results. First, only one demand-side factor is robustly significant and comes out consistently with the expected sign, and this is the case of the real GDP growth of host country *j* ($growthrate_{j,t}$).[16] This affirms our earlier results that international bank claims in general, and cross-border claims in particular, are inherently pro-cyclical – that is, these claims tend to rise during economic booms in host countries, but tend to quickly and sharply reverse during periods of economic distress. Second, we confirm the presence of a contagion effect (common lender effect) as well as the negative role of the expected short-term volatility of the global financial market as proxied by the VIX to global credit supply. Finally, and more importantly, the negative and significant coefficient in the interaction between the BIS-reporting home

Table 10.4 Dynamic panel estimation results of determinants of changes in cross-border bank claims, 2000Q1–2010Q3

Variables	*(1)*	*(2)*	*(3)*
$logdiffclaims_{t-1}$	–0.020 (0.064)	–0.095 (0.077)	–0.120 (0.061)
$Growthrate_J$	0.475 (0.121)***	0.762 (0.188)***	0.239 (0.155)
$growthrate_i$	–0.089 (0.195)	0.002 (0.171)	0.015 (0.167)
Vix		–0.137 (0.033)***	–0.073 (0.021)**
Clender			0.574 (0.163)***
$growthrate_i$ * exposure		–1.170 (0.432)***	–0.575 (0.294)**
Sargan test (*p*-value)	0.18	0.26	0.59
AB test for AR(2) (*p*-value)	0.53	0.35	0.29
No. of observations	294	294	294
No. of lags	2	2	2

Note: Standard errors in parentheses. Significance levels: *** 1%; ** 5%. Numbers in the last two rows of the table are *p*-values.

countries' real GDP growth rates and their exposure to the Asian host countries suggests that crisis episodes or shocks emanating from these developed economies lead to a further decline in cross-border claims. This is in marked contrast with the results reported in the previous section. This finding confirms the previous trend analysis, that cross-border lending in particular has been the channel of transmission of adverse shock to these Asian economies during the financial crisis. Furthermore, this is also very much suggestive of the role of the local lending or claims of foreign banks' offices in the respective countries examined here in resisting or mitigating the adverse consequences of external shocks.

4. Policy challenges going forward

The era of great moderation (low inflation) across the globe has been found to be gravely inadequate to safeguard much needed stability in the financial sector. Even during the period of sound macroeconomic conditions, the financial system was subject to various self-amplifying mechanisms in upward trends (bubbles), downward trends (busts) and phases of the credit cycle. There has been growing awareness and acceptance of the role of the central banks as a financial stability authority, in addition to a monetary authority.

New responsibility will come with new challenges. In this study, we highlight the role of the lending activities of international banks, particularly cross-border lending, as a potential source of financial instability. Going forward, a number of policy responses to manage potential risks associated with international bank lending have been tabled and debated. The following sub-sections will elaborate some of them.

4.1 Cross-border supervision

For the most part, the role of the central bank/monetary authority in managing the banking system has largely been unchallenged. Across the world – particularly in emerging markets – central banks play an important role as the lender of last resort, which has been well established and agreed to. In contrast, the supervisory role of the central bank continues to be viewed differently and debated. The 1997 AFC sparked an urgency to detach the supervisory role from the central bank/monetary authority. As discussed, the principal argument for the separation of the supervisory role from the central bank is to enhance the effectiveness of the central bank's responsibility as the monetary authority. The recent GFC, on the other hand, demonstrated the need for the central bank to play a greater part in the supervision of financial institutions.

Cross-border banking with the presence of multinational banks (including the newly emerging regional multinational banks) enhances the "interconnectedness" factor. It is now a well-known fact that globalized banks play a crucial role in the international transmission of monetary policies and economic shocks globally. In the first instance, the lack of cross-border supervisory cooperation has resulted in asymmetrical information on cross-border risk exposures, leading to an under-appreciation by supervisors and regulators of underlying systemic risks and connections (Kodres and Narain, 2009). In addition, it is rather obvious that the existence of asymmetrical information among supervisors in different jurisdictions leads to untimely and uncoordinated responses (Nijathaworn, 2010). Furthermore, adequate cross-country supervisory cooperation and coordination are necessary to overcome loopholes, such as currency substitution, or switching from domestic lending in foreign currency to direct foreign credit.

One potentially effective method to facilitate cross-border policy cooperation and coordination is through a college of supervisors.[17] The college of supervisors is defined as a "permanent, although flexible, structure for cooperation and coordination among the authorities of different jurisdictions responsible for and involved in the supervision of the different components of cross-border banking groups, specifically large group[s]" (CEBS, 2009). As a general rule, the establishment of a supervisory college should be considered for significant financial institutions in terms of size, interconnectedness with other components of the financial system and/or the roles they play in the market, which might cause systemic impacts on the country's financial system, hence affecting the region's financial stability.

A recent survey has identified a number of regional and global banks that have a strong presence in major Asian economies (Siregar and Lim, 2010). The Hong Kong Shanghai Banking Corporation (HSBC), Citibank and the Standard Chartered Bank are among the three major international banks that have wide and extensive branch networks in the Asian region (Table 10.5). In addition to these three international powerhouses, the Southeast Asian region has also witnessed the emergence of its own multinational banks. In Malaysia, banks such as the Malayan Banking Berhad (Maybank), Commerce International Merchant Bankers Berhad (CIMB) and Rashid Hussain Berhad (RHB) have expanded their networks beyond Southeast Asian countries. A number of Singaporean banks – namely, the Development Bank of Singapore (DBS), the United Overseas Bank (UOB) and the Overseas Chinese Bank Corporation (OCBC) – have achieved similar success in their efforts to become regional banks.

As of May 2010, a number of major central banks in Asia have been invited to participate in colleges of supervisors. Bank Negara Malaysia, for instance, is involved in the colleges of supervisors organized by the Financial Stability Agency of the United Kingdom for the Standard Chartered Group, the Federal Financial Supervisory Authority (BaFIN) for the Deutsche Bank Group and the Office of Superintendent of Financial Institutions (OFSI) for the Bank of Nova Scotia Group. Similarly, the Monetary Authority of Singapore (MAS) and Bangko Sentral Ng Pilipinas have also participated in a number of colleges of supervisors set-up for major European and US banks. In addition, under the foreign banking laws of a number of Southeast and East Asian economies, one of the conditions for a foreign bank to establish its subsidiary domestically is that the home supervisor of that particular foreign bank must sign a memorandum-of-understanding (MOU) with the host central banks. This MOU facilitates bilateral exchanges of data and information between the two bank supervisors. As of late 2010, however, there has not been any arrangement for supervisory colleges for Asian regional multinational banks such as the Malaysian and Singaporean banks discussed earlier.

4.2 Reducing the complexity of large cross-border banks through "subsidiarization"

An important cross-border banking issue is the relationship between the home and host supervisory agencies and central banks. If a foreign bank that is systemically important in a host country were to find itself in a crisis, it could lead to potential conflict between the home and host country authorities. These conflicts could be particularly significant if the relative size of the parent bank and its overseas affiliate is substantially different, or if the economic importance of the overseas affiliate to the parent bank is mainly marginal – for example, funding of the overseas affiliate is sourced mainly from local deposits. For instance, home country authorities will not be keen on supporting a small overseas affiliate (or the overseas affiliate will receive less attention from the parent bank or home supervisor) if the impact of such a failure of the overseas

Table 10.5 Cross-border banks in South East Asian Central Bank (SEACEN) economies

Countries	*Top 3 domestic financial institutions (FIs) in your jurisdiction that have significant presence in the region*	*Top 3 foreign FIs in your jurisdiction that originate from SEACEN member economies*	*Top 3 other foreign FIs (apart from originating in SEACEN member economies) that have significant presence in your country*
Indonesia	- Bank Mandiri - Bank BRI - BCA	- CIMB Niaga (Malaysia) - Bank International Indonesia (Maybank Malaysia controls about 43%)	- Citibank - HSBC - Standard Chartered Bank
Korea	- None	- DBS (Singapore) - UOB (Singapore) - OCBC (Singapore)	- Citibank - HSBC - Standard Chartered Bank
Malaysia	- Maybank - CIMB Group - Public Bank	- OCBC (Singapore) - UOB (Singapore) - Bangkok Bank (Thailand)	- Citibank - HSBC - Standard Chartered Bank
The Philippines	- Metropolitan Bank Corporation (Metrobank) - Philippine National Bank (PNB)	- Chinatrust (Taiwan) - Maybank (Malaysia) - Korea Exchange Bank (Korea)	- Citibank - HSBC - Standard Chartered Bank
Singapore	- DBS Bank Limited - OCBC - UOB	- Maybank (Malaysia) - Bangkok Bank (Thailand) - RHB Bank (Malaysia)	- Citibank - HSBC - Standard Chartered Bank
Chinese Taipei	- Bank of Taiwan - Taiwan Cooperative Bank - Mega International Commercial Bank	- DBS (Singapore) - OCBC (Singapore) - Bangkok Bank (Thailand)	- Citibank - HSBC - Standard Chartered Bank
Thailand	- Bangkok Bank - Kasikorn Bank - Siam Commercial Bank	- UOB (Singapore) - CIMB Thai (Malaysia) - OCBC (Singapore)	- GE Capital - ING - Standard Chartered

Source: Siregar and Lim (2010).

affiliate is relatively low or immaterial to the financial group's overall position, even if the troubled overseas affiliate is relatively systemically important for the host country. On the other hand, host country authorities could find it politically difficult to use public or taxpayer resources to support a foreign-owned bank when it gets into trouble.

One of the answers to the challenge of a systemically important foreign bank failing in a host country is to ensure local incorporation as a subsidiary rather than as a branch. All else being equal, local incorporation gives host authorities greater supervisory control over local operations, such as by making it more difficult for assets to be removed from the local operation to the parent bank – that is, "ring-fenced". Furthermore, it enables the possible imposition of specific capital-related prudential requirements that can provide some separation between the subsidiary and the parent bank, thus reducing intra-group contagion risk (Mihaljek, 2008).

4.3 Other policy considerations

4.3.1 Increasing capital levels and buffers

Introduced as part of the new capital standard under Basel III, "ample" or conservation buffers reflect the largely negatively perceived externality associated with the failure of a large cross-border bank, and as such should be available to enable banks to maintain large enough capital levels to offset losses in times of adverse financial shocks. Counter-cyclical capital buffers, on the other hand, rest on the concept that banks should accumulate extra capital in times of excessive credit growth, and as such banks can tap the buffer during periods of financial distress without having to raise new capital immediately. Implementing such types of capital buffers can improve the banking sector's resilience to financial crises, as well as mitigate its impact on the entire economy.

4.3.2 Deposit insurance scheme

Deposit insurance coverage could be lowered for large cross-border banks. There is a perception that large cross-border banks pursue scale – for example, mergers and acquisitions – in order to become "too big to fail". In order to mitigate such an incentive, a spreading or sharing of the risk in the official financial safety net (a form of co-insurance) can be introduced by reducing the deposit insurance coverage for large cross-border banks. This will also reduce the scope for free riding on the part of large cross-border banks as far as the financial safety net mechanism of the banking sector is concerned.

4.3.3 Establishment of cross-border collateral arrangements

The establishment of cross-border collateral arrangements involves the central bank in one jurisdiction providing domestic currency liquidity to eligible financial institutions against collateral placed by their offices in another jurisdiction into the liquidity-providing central bank's account at the local central bank. In essence, this is another way for central banks to provide a cross-border bridge to support funding requirements in another jurisdiction should interbank cross-border intermediation become impaired (Committee on the Global Financial System–Bank for International Settlements, 2010).

4.3.4 A systemic risk charge or a systemic risk levy on too big to fail or "systemically important" cross-border institutions

In essence, the bigger the financial institution, the higher the likelihood it will be rescued in times of financial distress. In other words, the cost of the financial rescue is directly related to the systemic relevance or size of the financial institution. One solution is a systemic risk charge that depends mainly on the size of the cross-border bank. This follows from the basic principle of the theory of externalities, which suggests that a polluter should be charged with a tax that is equivalent to the social costs of the pollution. We can then regard the systemic instability created by the cross-border bank's activities as an externality, and a systemic risk charge could be regarded as a way to "internalize" this problem of being too big to fail.

One such suggested approach is for regulators to assign systemic risk ratings to a financial institution and then assess a capital or systemic risk surcharge based on this rating. Banks with higher systemic risk ratings would receive higher capital or risk surcharges. In short, the surcharge is based on the financial institution's corresponding contribution to systemic risk. In principle, under certain assumptions, a surcharge on capital is equivalent to a levy on capital in terms of stifling the incentive for large cross-border banks to engage in systemic risk activities. An important difference between the two, however, is that a levy removes the funds from the financial institutions' balance sheets, whereas a capital surcharge leaves the funds under the control of the financial institutions (Doluca *et al.*, 2010).

In view of this difference, the advantage of the levy is that it can be used to fund a "systemic stability fund" that would act as a private safety net in the event of a financial crisis. The idea is that the accumulated levies can then be reinvested into "convertible" or liquid instruments by the systemic stability fund into the same financial institutions that paid these levies. These liquid instruments serve to fulfill the financial rescue role. In the event that a large cross-border bank gets into trouble, these same instruments can be used by the supervisory authorities to "bail-in" the weakened cross-border bank without resorting to the use of public or taxpayer resources.

5. Concluding remarks

The recent sub-prime crisis forced a rethink of the mandate of central banks in the area of financial stability. Prior to the latest financial crisis, the primary mandate for most central banks in Asia was monetary policy stability – in particular, price stability. Recent crises demonstrate that years of monetary stability during the period of great moderation did not safeguard economies from looming financial instabilities. It also clearly illustrated that the globalized banking system played a crucial role in transmitting the crisis from the advanced economies to various corners of the world, including the emerging markets of East and Southeast Asia.

For policy makers, it is no longer adequate to view domestic banking systems, in particular, and financial systems, in general, from a domestic economy perspective. The increasing interconnectedness of domestic banking liquidity to the global funding environment enhances the links between domestic financial stability and external shocks. Our study examines the role of international bank claims – in particular, cross-border lending – as a critical channel of transmission of worldwide financial shocks to local economies. We focus on the crisis period to garner greater appreciation of the exposure of local financial systems to these external shocks. In addition, we look into a number of home country indicators of economic fundamentals. The exposure and home country fundamental variables have been found to be significant factors, and confirmed the role of international bank lending as a channel of shock transmission from home countries to host economies. Furthermore, the common lender effect – whereby movements in international banks' claims on one country can be transmitted to other countries that owe claims from the same international banks – underscores the "spillover" effect that was also evident during the 1997 AFC.

Notes

1 The views expressed in this study are those of the authors alone and do not represent the official views of the SEACEN Center.
2 Though Thailand only experienced a very marginal increase in international bank inflows.
3 An exception is the Philippines, which is heavily dominated by lending from US-owned banks.
4 See, for instance, Siregar and Choy (2010), who examine the driving factors behind the total claims of seven OECD countries' banks to nine East and Southeast Asian economies.
5 The lone exception is the case of the Philippines, which, during 2001–02, also saw local claims by international banks contract along with total foreign bank claims.
6 The discussion that follows draws in part on Calderon and Chong (2001), Chong and Gradstein (2007) and Levine et al. (2000).
7 Second-order serial correlation of the differenced residual indicates that the original error term is serially correlated and follows a moving-average process at least of order one.
8 Total foreign bank claims are the sum of international claims and local claims in local currency, while international claims comprise cross-border claims in all currencies and local claims in foreign currencies.
9 It is also based on this expected relation that the VIX is construed as a factor that measures the global supply of international bank lending. Higher volatility corresponding with a high value of the VIX makes it more difficult for banks to raise additional capital (Takats, 2010).

10 As pointed out by Peria et al. (2005), in an ideal sense, the common lender effect can be equated with a portfolio allocation choice wherein changes in values of claims trigger an adjustment in other assets or claims. The limitation of working, then, with aggregated country-level data on international bank claims is that they obscure this portfolio allocation decision at the individual bank level. These major East Asian host countries are China, Indonesia, Korea, Malaysia, the Philippines, Singapore and Thailand.

11 This measure of foreign bank exposure is similar to that in Peria et al. (2005); however, based on some unique reason pertaining to the Latin American context, they measured the numerator as home country i's international bank claims on the private sector of host country j. In this chapter, we do not make this distinction between private and non-private sectors.

12 We also wish to note that the interaction term is an interaction between two continuous variables rather than the more standard approach of interacting a continuous and a binary variable. We prefer the former precisely because it allows us to capture the dynamic nature of the two variables. Although transforming a continuous variable into a binary one facilitates an easier interpretation of the coefficients, it can lead to a possible failure or limitation to capture the sensitivity of the dependent variable to this behaviour in lending by international banks – their commitment in host economies during troubled times in their own economies.

13 For a similar argument see, for instance, Peria et al. (2005) and Buch et al. (2010).

14 Added to this is the difficulty that the BIS does not disaggregate or separately report from the international claims consolidated data the "pure" cross-border claims from that of the local claims in foreign currency.

15 This then implies that the subscript i in equation (7), presented in the earlier section, is now denoted by all the BIS-reporting banks to the individual Asian host countries.

16 The interest rate differential variable was dropped altogether from the estimation as it was highly correlated with most of the variables and came out insignificant in all regressions. The real GDP growth of home country i also turned out to be consistently insignificant. This could be caused by the way we generate these data, wherein since the left-hand-side cross-border claims are the aggregate positions of all the BIS-reporting home country banks to individual Asian economies, we deem it appropriate to take a weighted average of the GDP values of all the BIS-reporting home country banks with the weights being the share of the respective BIS-reporting home country bank to the total GDP of all BIS-reporting home country banks.

17 As of September 2009, there are more than 30 colleges to supervise complex institutions.

References

Arellano, M. and Bond, S. (1991) 'Some tests of specification for panel data: Monte-Carlo evidence and an application to employment equations', *Review of Economic Studies,* 58: 277–97.

Arellano, M. and Bover, O. (1995) 'Another look at the instrumental-variable estimation of error component models', *Journal of Econometrics,* 68: 29–52.

Bank for International Settlements (BIS) (2009) 'Basel committee on banking supervision: consultative document', report and recommendations of the Cross-Border Bank Resolution Group issued for comment by 31 December 2009, (September).

Blundell, R. and Bond, S. (1998) 'Initial conditions and moments restrictions in dynamic panel data models', *Journal of Econometrics,* 87: 115–43.

Buch, C., Carstensen, K. and Schertler, A. (2010) 'Macroeconomic shocks and banks' foreign assets', *Journal of Money, Credit and Banking,* 42: 171–88.

Calderon, C. and Chong, A. (2001) 'External sector and income inequality in interdependent economies using a dynamic panel data approach', *Economics Letters,* 71: 225–31.

Cetorelli, N. and Goldberg, L. (2008) 'Globalized banks: lending to emerging markets in the crisis', *Federal Reserve Bank of New York Staff Reports.*

———. (2010) 'Global banks and international shock transmission: evidence from the crisis', (mimeo).

Chong, A. and Gradstein, M. (2007) 'Inequality and institutions', *Review of Economics and Statistics,* 89: 454–65.

Committee of European Bank Supervisors (CEBS) (2009) 'Colleges of Supervisors – 10 common principles', January. Online. Available HTTP: <http://www.c-ebs.org/getdoc/aeecaf1a-81b5-476a-95dd-599c5e967697/Clean-V3-formatted-CEBS-2008-124-CEIOPS-SEC-08-54-.aspx-2008-124-CEIOPS-SEC-08-54-.aspx>.

Committee on the Global Financial System – Bank for International Settlements (2010) 'The functioning and resilience of cross-border funding markets', *CGFS Papers,* 37.

Doluca, H., Kluh, U., Wagner, M. and Weder, B. (2010) 'Three birds with one stone: the G20 and systemic externalities', *VOX.* Online. Available HTTP: <http://www.voxeu.org>.

Ekinci, M., Kalemli-Ozcan, S. and Sörensen, B. (2008) 'Financial integration within EU countries: the role of institutions, confidence and trust', *NBER Working Paper* 13440.

Giannetti, M. and Yafeh, Y. (2008) 'Do cultural differences between contracting parties matter? Evidence from syndicated bank loans', *ECGI Finance Working Paper,* 224.

Guiso, L., Sapienza, P. and Zingales, L. (2009) 'Cultural biases in economic exchange?', *Quarterly Journal of Economics,* 124: 1095–131.

Hermann, S. and Mihaljek, D. (2010) 'The determinants of cross-border bank flows to emerging markets – new empirical evidence on the spread of financial crisis', *Discussion Paper Series 1: Economic Studies* 17/2010, Deutsche Bundesbank.

Holtz-Eakin, D., Newey, W. and Rosen, H. (1990) 'Estimating vector auto-regressions with panel data', *Econometrica,* 56: 1371–95.

Kodres, L. and Narain, A. (2009) 'What is to be done?', *Finance and Development, IMF,* 46.

Levine, R., Loayza, N. and Beck, T. (2000) 'Financial intermediation and growth', *Journal of Monetary Economics,* 46: 31–77.

Mian, A. (2006) 'Distance constraints: the limits of foreign lending in poor economies', *Journal of Finance,* 61: 1465–505.

Mihaljek, D. (2008) 'The financial stability implications of increased capital flows for emerging market economies', *BIS Papers* 44.

———. (2010) 'Domestic bank intermediation in emerging market economies during the crisis: locally owned versus foreign-owned banks', *BIS Papers* 54.

Nijathaworn, B. (2010) 'Regional financial supervision – challenges and the way forward for Asia', remarks at the Conference on Macroeconomic and Financial Stability in Asian Emerging Markets, organized by the Bank Negara Malaysia and Asian Development Bank Institute, Kuala Lumpur, 4 August.

Peria, M. S. M., Powel, A. and Vladkova-Hollar, I. (2005) 'Banking on foreigners: the behavior of international bank claims on Latin America, 1985–2000', *IMF Staff Papers*, 52: 430–61.

Siregar, R.Y. and Choy, K.M. (2010) 'Determinants of international bank lending from the developed world to East Asia', *IMF Staff Papers*, 57: 484–516.

Siregar, R.Y. and Lim, V.C.S. (2010) 'The role of central banks in sustaining economic recovery and in achieving financial stability', *Journal of Advanced Studies in Finance*, 1: 83–99.

Takats, E. (2010) 'Cross-border bank lending to emerging market economies', *BIS Papers* 54.

Van Rijckeghem, C. and Weder, B. (2003) 'Spillovers through banking centers: a panel data analysis of bank flows', *Journal of International Money and Finance*, 22: 483–509.

11 The rise of Asian-owned foreign banks and credit stability in Asia

Ying Xu

1. Introduction

There has been a surge of foreign bank entry into Asian countries since the Asian Financial Crisis (AFC) in 1997–98 that has important welfare effects. On one hand, foreign ownership has the potential for, and has started to show evidence of, improving overall banking efficiency and modernizing banking industries in Asia (Gopalan and Rajan, 2009; Jeon *et al.*, 2011; Xu, 2011); on the other hand, foreign bank entry raises serious and legitimate concerns about its implications for local credit stability, especially during crisis periods.

A certain number of empirical studies exist exploring the implications of foreign bank lending on domestic credit stability. Mixed evidence is revealed and often distinguished by differing responses to host versus home country crises. For instance, during host country crises in Argentina, Mexico and Central and Eastern Europe in the 1990s, foreign banks showed, on average, stronger credit growth compared with domestic banks. Dages *et al.* (2000) explain that parents of foreign banks in those countries have international and diversified asset portfolios and can act as the "lender of last resort", so their subsidiaries can keep lending in spite of local credit problems. In some cases, they even extend credit faster than they do during normal times, when they view local credit shortage as an opportunity to expand their presence and business activities.

However, foreign credit can be destabilizing when crises strike home countries because highly exposed parent banks are likely to downsize their business, and foreign operations are likely to be among the first to be cut-off. Therefore, host countries can easily fall victim to a sudden cut-off of credit lines – the so-called common lender effects (Masson, 1998). These common lender effects were observed in the United States in the 1990s when Japanese bank subsidiaries responded to the banking crisis in Japan by reducing lending in the United States (Peek and Rosengren, 2000). They were also observed in the recent 2007–09 Global Financial Crisis (GFC) in Eastern Europe (Ongena *et al.*, 2013), as well as globally (Cetorelli and Goldberg, 2012; De Haas and van Lelyveld 2011). There is, however, also evidence of a significant negative relationship between home country economic growth and host country credit by "greenfield" foreign banks. This is found in a panel analysis of banks in Central and Eastern Europe, where foreign banks tended to increase their lending when economic conditions in their home countries worsened in the 1990s. Worsening home country conditions led banks to seek external lending opportunities (De Haas and Van Lelyveld, 2005).

A home and host country dichotomy cannot completely account for the diversity of lending behaviour in times of economic or financial crises shown by foreign banks in different parts of the world. A model of international capital flow indicates that other factors, such as type of shocks, matter for the direction and volume of the flow of credit (Morgan and Strahan, 2004). For instance, in cases where shocks strike host countries, credit demand shocks will result in a lower rate of return on investment and, accordingly, foreign credit flowing out of the host country, while a higher interest rate arising from a credit supply shock will attract an inflow of foreign credit to offset host country credit constraints. In a nutshell, the identification of credit supply and demand shocks in host and home country crises is critical to predicting foreign bank implications for local credit stability.[1]

The origin of foreign banks has also been found to be important for understanding the overall impact of foreign bank lending, and yet it is mentioned only briefly in the literature. For instance, Clarke *et al.* (2001) suggest that diversity in foreign ownership matters for stability and that too much exposure to banks from any single country can increase instability. Spain, for instance, is in control of 30 major banks in Latin America holding almost 10 per cent of the Latin American banking sector, so it is a high-risk factor in the region if Spain's economy is subject to fluctuations. On the other hand, an increase in diversity reduces the risk of concentration and thereby improves stability. Building on this strand of the literature, my study examines how local lending by foreign banks in Asia responded to the GFC, and whether an increasingly diversified foreign bank group helped reduce instability that would have otherwise caused a potentially huge amount of turbulence in the local credit market.

A review of the literature underlines a domination of the evidence by developed countries (for example, Peek and Rosengren, 2000) and Central Europe and Latin America (Dages *et al.*, 2000; De Haas and Van Lelyveld, 2005; Goldberg *et al.*, 2002). There are few systematic analyses on this issue for Asian economies in particular, probably due to the limited presence of foreign banks in Asia and a lack of data until very recently. With the data becoming available, this study is therefore one of the first attempts to examine the Asian evidence with a focus on the features of foreign banks in Asia and their lending behaviour during the recent GFC. It employs a large, bank-level data set compiled for 10 major Asian economies covering the period 2000–09.

A number of findings from this study are informative, among which two of the major results are as follows. First, foreign banks in Asia are not a homogenous group, and their lending behaviours diverged as a result of contrasting home country conditions. In the foreign bank category, affiliates of North

American and European banks reduced credit most sharply and sizably in the Asian periphery as a result of their apparent closeness to the epicentre. Second, a set of results from different country groups confirm that the lending momentum of Asian foreign banks remained strong in spite of the crisis, compared not only to their counterparts in the foreign category, but also to local banks. Accordingly, the study highlights a distinctive and stabilizing role played by Asian-owned foreign banks in Asian credit markets during the GFC.

This chapter is structured as follows: the following section introduces a review of foreign banks in Asia, highlighting the role of Asian-owned foreign banks. Sections 3 and 4 explain the empirical framework and the data set. Section 5 presents the results, and the final section concludes with a brief discussion of policy relevance.

2. Foreign banks in Asia

Foreign banks in Asia show several rather unique features compared with other regions. Despite a gradual rise of foreign banks after the AFC, their presence remains at a moderate level in the majority of Asian countries. Among foreign banks, Asian and non-Asian foreign banks differ significantly in their presence and lending behaviour. Though non-Asian foreign banks account for a significant share of foreign bank presence in Asia, Asian-owned foreign banks start to play an increasingly important role in Asian lending markets, specifically during the GFC.

As in Latin America, foreign bank entry in Asia has been most important in the aftermath of financial crises. Asia was one of the most closed financial systems in the world. Heavy banking regulations and closed banking sectors are often cited as the main factors hampering banking development in Asia. Since the 1997–98 AFC, there has been a notable trend of financial sector deregulation in Asia and the easing of entry barriers has been one of the most prominent. For instance, Thailand, Indonesia and Korea all removed ceilings on foreign ownership of domestic banks. China, which has one of the most prohibitive banking sectors in the world, opened itself to investment from overseas financial institutions in 2001 (see Figure 11.1).

An increasing number of foreign banks have since entered the newly liberalized Asian financial markets and shares of foreign banking assets have grown substantially over the decade following the AFC, from 5.8 to 47 per cent in Indonesia, from 2.2 to 15.7 per cent in Korea, and from 7.1 to 12.6 per cent in Thailand (see Figure 11.1). Nevertheless, the average share of foreign bank assets in total banking assets in Asia remains about two-thirds that of Latin America.[2]

2.1 Asian-owned foreign banks

While mainly US and European banks dominate foreign banking in Asia, since the AFC, Asian-owned foreign banks have achieved an increasing presence and

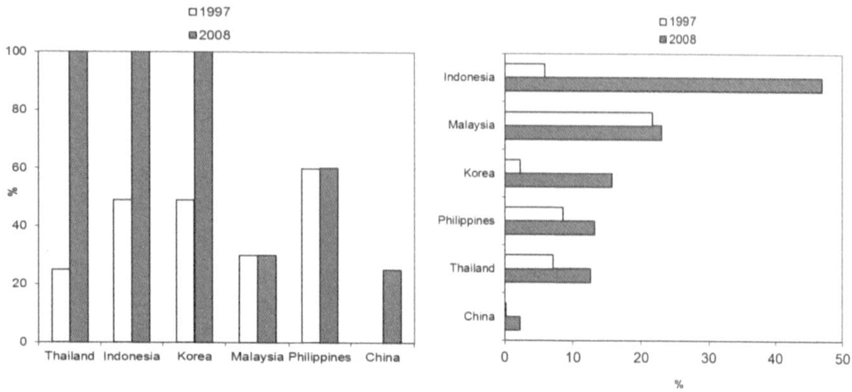

Figure 11.1 Upper limits on foreign bank ownership (left) and asset shares of foreign banks (right) in Asian countries

Source: Gopalan and Rajan (2009).

Table 11.1 Foreign banks in Asia and the Pacific

	Share in total numbers	*Share in total assets*
Domestic	0.67	0.78
Foreign	0.33	0.23
US, Europe and others	0.25	0.14
Asia and the Pacific	0.08	0.09

Source: Tanaka (2009).

Note: Asia and the Pacific region covers China, Japan, Korea, Hong Kong, Indonesia, the Philippines, Malaysia, Singapore, Thailand, Australia and New Zealand; data include both branches and subsidiaries.

become more diversified. While, in total, Asian foreign banks remain small in terms of numbers and assets compared to their global counterparts, the gap is no longer unbridgeable (Table 11.1). Historically, Japanese banks were the major sources of Asian investment in the regional financial sector. In post-AFC Asia, other Asian banks have started to invest and expand their presence in Asian countries. For example, two Singaporean banks acquired majority stakes in Thai Danu and Radanashin Bank; a Malaysian bank realized a substantial expansion in Singapore; and Hong Kong and Singaporean banks increased their asset and market shares in China. More recently, Chinese banks have also been active participants in regional financial markets owing to strong balance-sheet positions.

In the long term, these Asian banks are expected to show a competitive advantage in dealing with the institutional environment of their Asian neighbours. Regional economic integration, common language and proximity are just a few among the positive factors that predict the sustainable rising presence of Asian-owned foreign banks in Asia (Van Horen, 2007).

2.2 Foreign bank lending

Foreign bank lending increased steadily in Asia along with foreign bank assets slowly rising at the same time. Surprisingly, the share of foreign bank loans jumped in 2008 – the onset of the GFC – despite shares of total numbers and assets dropping sharply (Jeol *et al.*, 2011). Since the numbers are shares, there could be two possible scenarios for an increase in the foreign share of loans. One is an escalation of foreign bank lending and the other is a decline in foreign bank lending, albeit with a speed slower than domestic banks.

Preliminary statistical analysis seems to point to the latter and reveals further divergence in lending trends during the crisis, not only between domestic and foreign banks, but within two groups of foreign banks. A disaggregation of foreign banks into Asian-owned and global foreign banks shows that throughout the GFC both groups' loan extensions slowed, but in six Asian economies with foreign banks from the Asian region, the reduction in bank credit was sharper and faster for global than for Asian foreign banks (see Table 11.2).

The observation is likely to be related to the balance sheets of individual banks. In terms of exposure to the crisis-hit US sub-prime mortgage markets, which subsequently caused significant bank asset losses during the crisis and, as a consequence, balance-sheet adjustments, Asian-owned foreign banks certainly hold a lower average exposure than US and European banks. For instance, among 46 financial institutions involved in the sub-prime mortgage market, there are only four Asian banks.[3] In addition, the share of initial losses by these

Table 11.2 The average growth rate of foreign bank lending pre-GFC and during the GFC: Asian-owned versus global foreign banks

	Pre-GFC (01–07): a%		*During the GFC (08–09): b%*		*Change in Lending Growth: (b–a)%*	
	Global	*Regional*	*Global*	*Regional*	*Global*	*Regional*
China	0.26	0.19	0.03	0.10	–0.23	–0.09
Hong Kong	0.02	0.13	–0.13	0.07	–0.15	–0.06
Indonesia	0.10	0.15	–0.21	0.15	–0.31	0.00
Malaysia	0.01	0.14	–0.11	0.11	–0.12	–0.03
Philippines	0.23	–0.11	0.77	0.07	0.54	0.18
Thailand	0.19	0.15	0.01	0.00	–0.18	–0.15

Note: Lending data are for annual net loans and are taken from the *Bankscope* database. The sample covers all foreign (commercial) banks, except identified outliers.

Asian banks is considerably small, less than 3 per cent of the total. By contrast, the rest are all banks of US and European origin. They account for the lion's share of total loan losses and almost all of them have subsidiary presence around the globe, including in the Asian region.

Another noteworthy difference is shown on the balance sheets of the two groups. Asian-owned foreign banks have a high proportion of customer deposits in their total liabilities, whereas global foreign banks do not. Global bank subsidiaries only started to raise deposits after the crisis, probably because deposit funding has been recognized as a more stable form of funding than wholesale funding since the GFC. By then, a higher level of wholesale funding dependence by global foreign banks confirms the pattern that these banks financed a major part of their loans by wholesale borrowing. As a result, the liquidity tension created by interbank markets in the United States and Europe could be quickly transformed into credit contraction by these banks. Nevertheless, the impact of the GFC on the Asian financial system might be milder. Owing to a large and continually rising deposit pool and less dependency on wholesale funding markets, Asian banks, and specifically the liability side of Asian banks, were less affected by the crisis.

3. Empirical framework

A formal statistical analysis is employed to examine the relationship between foreign bank local lending and credit stability. Changes in loan growth are used to proxy and imply credit stability, as used in the literature. If foreign banks reduce credit supply sharply when facing economic downturns – that is procyclical lending behaviour – they cause damage to local credit stability; if foreign banks show faster credit growth or slower credit contraction than local banks in a depression, and in doing so help to alleviate business-cycle effects, they are considered to be contributing to credit stability in the host country.

The empirical models are constructed as follows. Model 1 is a baseline model: a structure form credit growth equation. Model 2 adds the interaction terms of the foreign bank dummy to all the other terms to examine whether foreign banks show different lending behaviour to domestic banks, and specifically whether they exhibit similar business-cycle responses during the GFC. In Model 3, foreign banks are disaggregated into Asian-owned foreign banks and non-Asian foreign banks. With domestic banks as a benchmark, the model tests the main hypothesis of whether Asian-owned foreign banks responded to the GFC in a manner that helped to stabilize local credit markets.

Model 1

$$rcg_{ijt} = \alpha + bank_{ijt-1}, \beta + Mac_{jt}, \gamma + \delta FB_{ijt} + \theta GFC_t + u_i + u_t + \varepsilon_{jit}$$

Model 2

$$rcg_{ijt} = \tilde{\alpha} + bank_{ijt-1}, \tilde{\beta} + Mac_{jt}, \tilde{\gamma} + \tilde{\theta} GFC_t + FB_{ijt}(\tilde{\delta} + bank_{ijt-1}, \tilde{\lambda} + Mac_{jt}, \tilde{\varphi} + \tilde{\eta} GFC_t) + \tilde{u}_i + \tilde{u}_t + \tilde{\varepsilon}_{jit}$$

Model 3

$$rcg_{ijt} = \hat{\alpha} + bank_{ijt-1}, \hat{\beta} + Mac_{jt}, \hat{\gamma} + \hat{\theta}GFC_t + aFB_{ijt}(\hat{\delta}^a + bank_{ijt-1}, \hat{\lambda}^a + Mac_{jt}, \hat{\varphi}^a + \hat{\eta}^a GFC_t) + wFB_{ijt}(\hat{\delta}^w + bank_{ijt-1}, \hat{\lambda}^w + Mac_{jt}, \hat{\varphi}^w + \hat{\eta}^w GFC_t) + \hat{u}_i + \hat{u}_t + \hat{\varepsilon}_{jit}$$

$\ln rc_{ijt} - \ln rc_{ijt-1}$ is the real credit growth of bank i in country j at year t; rc^d_{ijt} is real credit, calculated as the total amount of net loans extended by the bank divided by the consumer price index (CPI) in country j at year t. Bank variables, $bank^d_{ijt-1}$, account for a vector of bank-specific characteristics that might influence bank credit extension. They include equity to total assets as a measure of bank solvency, liquid assets to customer and short term funding as a measure of liquidity, return to average assets as a measure of profitability, and the logarithm of an individual bank's real total assets as a measure of size, following De Haas and Van Lelyveld (2005).[4] All bank variables have a one-year lag to address possible endogeneity.

Foreign banks (FB_{ijt}) are identified as banks with foreign ownership holdings of no less than 50 per cent. They are disaggregated into two key dummy variables – aFB_{ijt} and wFB_{ijt} respectively – to detect Asian and non-Asian foreign banks' varying lending behaviours.

Bank credit growth is linked closely to local business cycles and is often considered highly pro-cyclical (e.g., Bernanke and Gertler, 1989). Mac_{jt} are two macroeconomic variables commonly used in the literature to capture domestic business cycles.[5] One is the real GDP growth rate and the other is the inflation rate (CPI).

Another macroeconomic variable, and also a key variable of interest, is GFC_t, a year dummy (2008 and 2009) to capture the influence of the GFC,[6] which caused a major visible shock to Asian exports and consequently to economic growth. Credit demand was depressed subsequently, which is suspected to have caused a substantial decline in credit growth.

The key hypothesis is that Asian-owned foreign banks might have reacted less acutely to the GFC on credit extension. Two sets of interaction terms between aFB_{ijt} and wFB_{ijt}, and with other variables in the equation, are employed to put this hypothesis to the test. $\hat{\theta}$ and $\tilde{\theta}$ show specifically how Asian and non-Asian foreign banks responded differently to domestic banks and to each other regarding the GFC.

To further understand the role of the wholesale funding market in foreign bank lending in Asia, and how it might have transmitted credit turbulence from the West to Asia, the variable of money market dependence, MMD_{ijt}, is introduced into the model equation (Model 4). The variable is calculated as –log(1 + *customer_deposits/total_liabilites*) # to reduce the role of outliers following Raddatz (2010). A high value of MMD_{ijt} measures a high dependence on wholesale funds. The interaction term $G^* MMD_{ijt}$ captures the transmission effect through the money market during the GFC.

Model 4

$$rcg_{ijt} = \alpha + bank_{ijt-1},\beta + \tau MMD_{ijt} + \xi G * MMD_{ijt} + Mac_{jt},\gamma + \delta FB_{ijt} + \theta GFC_{t} + u_{i} + u_{t} + \varepsilon_{jit}$$

Two-way fixed-effects panel models are adopted as a result of the Hausman test and within-group estimators are produced. The two-way error component disturbances are: u_i, denoting the unobservable individual bank effect, such as location and age; and u_t, the unobservable time effect to catch the macro-trend. ε_{jit} is the remaining stochastic disturbance term.

4. Data

The data set employed in this study is an unbalanced panel of annual data of banks in the major Asian economies over the period 2000–09. Bank coverage varies across years as a result of frequent bank entry/exit as well as data availability, with a maximum of 417 in 2007 and a minimum of 314 in 2002. In total 129 foreign banks are covered. Not all Asian countries in the sample have Asian-owned foreign banks. Table 11.3 lists six countries that have Asian-owned foreign banks for a comparison of numbers, average assets and average loans by Asian and non-Asian foreign banks. As the scale of assets and loans varies significantly across countries, bank variables are normalized either by taking ratios or logarithms in the main analysis. Finally, major mergers and acquisitions are recorded. As merged and acquired banks often show changed lending behaviours, each acquired or merged bank is treated as a new bank to control for potential structural changes. The total number of observations is 2,774.

The main source for bank data is Bureau van Dijk's *Bankscope* database. This is a global database of bank financial statements that contains detailed and updated accounts for each bank in a universal format to compare banks globally. Data for all commercial banks in the 10 economies compiled in the database

Table 11.3 Comparing Asian-owned and non-Asian foreign banks in Asia: 2000–09

	Number		*Average assets*		*Average loans*	
	Asian-owned	*Non-Asian*	*Asian-owned*	*Non-Asian*	*Asian-owned*	*Non-Asian*
China	16	10	30.26	55.36	20.65	23.55
Hong Kong	15	12	126.01	528.15	57.58	195.81
Indonesia	19	12	25.70	5.72	12.05	2.92
Malaysia	5	8	39.44	43.16	24.48	21.07
Philippines	4	3	3.05	3.07	1.57	0.52
Thailand	4	2	26.59	43.07	18.06	20.15

Source: Bankscope database.

are extracted to construct a data set – possibly the largest in the empirical literature on Asian banking at the micro-level. The data set begins in 2001, when Asia started to show a marked increase in foreign bank presence following its region-wide regulatory reforms on foreign entry. *Bankscope* only keeps archived data in its ownership database from January 2003. The author extends the ownership data to 2001 based on other information sources, such as bank annual reports and individual banks' histories from their websites. The ultimate owners of foreign banks are specified in the data set, so the origin of foreign ownership – either in Asia or in non-Asian countries – is distinguished.

Real GDP growth and CPI data are taken from the US Department of Agriculture (USDA) *International Macroeconomic Data Set*. It has consistent and comparable macro data across economies covering Taiwan and Hong Kong, whereas most of the conventional data sources, such as the World Bank and the International Finance Corporation, do not. Table 11.4 presents a summary of variable definitions and data sources.

Table 11.4 Variable definitions and data sources

Variables	*Definitions*	*Data sources*
Dependent		
Real credit growth	Growth of real credit and real credit are the total amount of net loans divided by the CPI	Net loans data from Bankscope and CPI data from USDA^
Independent		
Solvency	Equity to total assets	Bankscope
Liquidity	Liquid assets to customer and short term funding	Bankscope
Profitability	Return on average assets	Bankscope
Size	Logarithm of bank real total assets	Bankscope
Foreign banks (FBs)	Banks with foreign ownership holding no less than 50% = 1; otherwise = 0	Bankscope^^
Asian-owned FBs	Foreign banks from Asian countries = 1; otherwise = 0	Bankscope
Non-Asian FBs	Foreign banks with Western countries (North America and Europe) = 1; otherwise = 0	Bankscope
GDP growth	Annual growth rate of real GDP	USDA^
Inflation	Percentage change in the CPI	USDA^

^: USDA International Macroeconomic Data.

^^: Bankscope keeps archived ownership data for 2003–09. The author extends the data to 2001 based on other information sources such as bank annual reports and individual banks' history from their websites.

The full sample covers 10 major economies in Asia, accounting for one-fifth of the world's total GDP. However, they by no means form a homogenous group; they are diversified by various measures: size of the economy, level of growth, social and economic institutions, etc. Japan, Singapore, Korea and Taiwan have developed sophisticated banking systems in the region, so non-Asian foreign banks are dominant in those countries and Asian-owned foreign banks merely exist. They form one group without the presence of Asian-owned foreign banks. Among the group of Asian economies that host Asian-owned foreign banks, China is unique. The state has a strong role in its banking system. Its massive fiscal stimulus package created a lending boom during the GFC. Lending from domestic, and especially state, banks remained strong despite the GFC. Hence, three samples are examined separately: China, five economies that host Asian-owned foreign banks and four economies that do not.

5. Results

5.1 China

The general insignificance of key variables is noteworthy from the Chinese sample (Table 11.5). The GFC seems to have passed the Chinese credit markets without

Table 11.5 The China sample (Dependent variable: credit growth – growth in real credit)

	Model 1	*Model 2*	*Model 3*
GFC	0.118 (0.329)	0.090 (0.474)	0.125 (0.200)
FB*GFC		–0.001 (0.998)	
aFB			4.320 (0.217)
wFB			4.834 (0.555)
aFB*GFC			–0.182 (0.459)
wFB*GFC			–1.780 (0.670)
N	478	478	478
R^2	0.173	0.264	0.323
F	14.429	76.362	.[1]
p	0.000	0.000	.

[1] There are not sufficient rankings to perform the F test for Model 3 when using the cluster-robust estimators. Key results remain when cluster-robust estimators are not used.

Notes:
1) Results are compressed to key variables to save space.
2) Regressions are estimated using two-way fixed-effects methods.
3) Robust standard errors are in parentheses. Significance levels: * 10%; ** 5%; *** 1%.

leaving a significant mark. Note that domestic banks are set as the benchmark. Both Asian-owned foreign banks and non-Asian foreign banks compare with domestic banks. As expected, aggressive lending by Chinese local banks kept credit growth strong during the GFC, which reinforced confidence in the Chinese economy. Neither Asian nor non-Asian foreign banks showed significantly varying patterns in credit growth compared with their Chinese counterparts.

5.2 Economies that have Asian-owned foreign banks

Among the five economies that host Asian-owned foreign banks, it is clear that the GFC had a significantly negative impact on credit growth (Table 11.6). Nevertheless, positive coefficients associated with *FB*GFC* and *aFB*GFC* suggest that the Asian-owned foreign banks helped alleviate the tension in the credit market and counter-balanced the negative effects of GFC stress. This pattern was not shown, however, on the part of the non-Asian foreign banks.

Table 11.6 The five economies that have Asian-owned foreign banks (Dependent variable: credit growth – growth in real credit)

	Model 1	*Model 2*	*Model 3*
FB	–0.037	0.295	
	(0.707)	(0.524)	
GFC	–0.103***	–0.145***	–0.136***
	(0.009)	(0.000)	(0.001)
FB*GFC		0.111*	
		(0.074)	
aFB			0.462
			(0.290)
wFB			0.038
			(0.968)
aFB*GFC			0.113**
			(0.028)
wFB*GFC			0.009
			(0.955)
N	901	901	901
R^2	0.088	0.103	0.138
F	6.442	17.395	64.217
p	0.000	0.000	0.000

Note: Same as Table 11.5; the five economies are Hong Kong, Indonesia, Malaysia, the Philippines and Thailand.

This has an important implication for credit stability. A fast credit contraction exacerbates a volatile credit market in crises, amplifying instability, whereas a slower credit reduction is able to enhance stability. This evidence suggests that Asian-owned foreign banks constituted a major stabilizing force in the Asian credit market during the GFC.

5.3 Economies that do not have Asian-owned foreign banks

As a counter example, the results from the sample of the four economies that do not have Asian-owned foreign banks confirm the above discussion (Table 11.7). Foreign banks – all of them non-Asian – reduced credits faster than domestic banks. They made credit conditions worse and caused deterioration in credit stability during the GFC.

The theoretical framework reviewed is useful in analyzing the results. Multiple forces seem to have been at play in response to the GFC. First, it is widely agreed that the GFC influenced Asia mainly through the trade channel, which indirectly depressed the Asian credit market. Weak consumer demand in North America and Europe resulted in a severe drop in Asian exports to these markets. Low expected returns discouraged new investment and business expansion, which led to a significant fall in credit demand, resulting in an overall reduction in credit growth in Asia.

Foreign banks, however, were subject to two additional, different types of influence: non-Asian foreign banks were around the epicentre of the GFC and were largely exposed to liquidity shocks back home. They quickly withdrew capital and credit from subsidiaries around the world including Asia.

Table 11.7 The four economies without Asian-owned foreign banks (Dependent variable: credit growth – growth in real credit)

	Model 1	*Model 2*
FB	–0.042	1.683**
	(0.268)	(0.038)
GFC	–0.027	–0.002
	(0.202)	(0.909)
FB*GFC		–0.369**
		(0.030)
N	1,466	1,463
R^2	0.341	0.377
F	21.679	29.768
p	0.000	0.000

Note: Same as Table 11.5; the four economies are Japan, Singapore, Korea and Taiwan.

Nonetheless, the reason this "common lender" effect was not explicit compared with Latin America might lie in the presence of Asian foreign banks.

Few Asian foreign banks were experiencing a credit supply shock at home – quite the opposite: the benign liquidity situation at home served as "lender of last resort". In addition, the retreat of some of the non-Asian foreign banks might have generated new opportunities for Asian foreign banks to enter the market and expand their market shares in neighbouring countries, which explains their strong lending momentum and important role in stabilizing Asian credit markets in times of stress.

5.4 Money market transmission

Lastly, it is suspected that credit contraction in non-Asian foreign banks might be a transmission effect from the global money market, which nearly collapsed during the GFC. Asian foreign banks have, on average, a lower level of money market dependence compared to non-Asian foreign banks. Table 11.8 shows that a higher level of money market dependence seems to have relentlessly distressed credit conditions in non-Asian foreign banks during the GFC, although the money market funding facilitates credit extension for foreign banks in general in the pre-crisis period. Apparently, money market funding is pro-cyclical and highly unstable, constituting a key element of the transmission of shocks and credit instability.

6. Concluding remarks

The study sets out to understand the impact of foreign bank lending on credit stability in Asia during the GFC. Employing a large (and the most recent) banking data set for 10 major Asian economies during 2000–09, the analysis provides indicative evidence that Asian-owned foreign banks played a distinctive and stabilizing role during the recent GFC compared with their non-Asian counterparts and local banks in host countries.

Non-Asian foreign banks exhibited the sharpest credit contraction in Asia during the crisis. Yet the disrupting impact remained under control and did not endanger local banking systems, largely because of the presence and lending of Asian-owned foreign banks. It is found that Asian-owned foreign banks showed the slowest credit reduction during the crisis compared to global banks and domestic banks, which helped to counterbalance the contagion effect from the GFC and stabilize credit markets in Asia.

Preliminary evidence suggests that the contagion effect of non-Asian foreign banks might have been transmitted through the money market. Non-Asian foreign banks have a relatively higher reliance on wholesale funding, whereas Asian-owned foreign banks finance their lending mainly through customer deposits. The GFC had a devastating effect on the global money market, which depressed the main funding source of non-Asian foreign banks and caused them to withdraw credit sharply. In contrast, backed by favourable liquidity positions,

Table 11.8 Money market transmission of credit instability (Dependent variable: credit growth – growth in real credit)

	Domestic banks		*Foreign banks*		*Asian-owned FBs*		*Non-Asian FBs*	
	(1)	*(2)*	*(3)*	*(4)*	*(5)*	*(6)*	*(7)*	*(8)*
MMD	0.212	0.206	0.719**	0.821***	0.907***	0.898***	0.046	0.274
	(0.246)	(0.249)	(0.023)	(0.007)	(0.000)	(0.000)	(0.946)	(0.649)
GFC	–0.017	0.036	–0.135**	–0.427**	–0.107***	–0.080	–0.202	–0.912**
	(0.519)	(0.758)	(0.037)	(0.038)	(0.015)	(0.647)	(0.283)	(0.015)
G*MMD		0.085		–0.554*		0.047		–1.502***
		(0.642)		(0.083)		(0.876)		(0.010)
N	2338	2338	487	487	274	274	208	208
R^2	0.152	0.153	0.125	0.136	0.199	0.199	0.059	0.125
F	14.506	13.100	19.573	19.884	13.615	12.211	1.510	8.451
p	0.000	0.000	0.000	0.000	0.000	0.000	0.173	0.000

Note: Same as Table 11.5; full sample.

Asian-owned foreign banks kept their lending momentum and took the opportunity to expand their presence and influence in Asia.

In brief, the study suggests that the foreign banks are a diverse group whose net effects on local credit stability are not all harmful in the Asian experience of the GFC. The reason for this is the diverse origins of foreign banks, and specifically the important stabilizing role of Asian-owned foreign banks. Since the beginning of financial deregulation after the AFC, there has always been concern about its implications for banking stability, which directly links to Asian policymakers' conservatism and uncertain policies toward foreign bank entry. This study lends support for opening up to foreign banks, and especially to Asian-owned foreign banks' participation in the local banking market. This not only benefits local banks in terms of the transfer of technology and healthy competition that many studies have demonstrated, but also reduces the risk of instability shown by this new evidence.

It is important, however, to distinguish between opening up to foreign banks' local business and cross-border lending. One of the important lessons from the AFC is that too much reliance on footloose, short term overseas borrowing and cross-border lending might provoke credit market volatility and a banking crisis. Foreign banks' local business is of a different nature. They establish local facilities and carry out banking business under local regulations, which is a much more stable and reliable source of funding.

Lastly, encouraging Asian-owned foreign banks to enter the market is not only favourable but also feasible. Many Asian countries have been favouring large international banks – most of which are non-Asian foreign banks – over regional banks due to the former's reputation and financial expertise and technology. After the GFC, however, North American and European banks have undergone extensive restructuring. Their influence in the Asian financial market has started to decline. In contrast, Asian-owned foreign banks, specifically from Singapore, Japan, Hong Kong and most recently China, have been active participants in the regional financial market owing to the strong liability side of their balance sheets. They have been a rising force and have accumulated valuable experience and expertise in foreign banking in the region. With sufficient supervision arrangements, opening up to those Asian-owned foreign banks is expected to invigorate Asian banking systems and foster financial development.

Nevertheless, a few cautions are in order. Although Asian-owned foreign banks showed slow credit reduction during the GFC, the impact of stabilization should not be overstated and might only be visible in sectors in which foreign banks were allowed to participate because their presence and areas of business are highly regulated and restricted in Asia. At the same time, non-Asian foreign banks' contagion effects were not fully captured, as the study did not take into account the effects of liquidation or the complete withdrawal from the Asian market. Those impacts on credit stability are much more severe than slower credit extension. Case studies of individual US, UK and European banks' changes in shareholdings in Asian markets during the crisis might help elucidate the situation. Lastly, slow credit contraction during economic downturns is counter to the business-cycle and beneficial to credit stability. Rapid and over-rapid credit growth in normal times is not, however, always favourable. It is legitimate to worry that over-rapid credit growth might plant the seeds of a future crisis.

Notes

1 The diagrams in Appendix A explain the inner mechanisms of the relationship between types of shocks and the flow of foreign credit.

2 Jeol *et al.* (2011) compare Latin American countries (Argentina, Bolivia, Brazil, Chile, Colombia, Mexico, Paraguay, Peru, Uruguay and Venezuela) and Asian economies (Hong Kong, Indonesia, Korea, Malaysia, the Philippines, Singapore and Thailand) and find that the share of foreign bank assets in Latin America's total banking assets in 2009 is about 50 per cent, and the share for the Asian group is around 30 per cent that year. This is largely consistent with the calculation by Tanaka (2009) of 33 per cent, an average for a group of Asian countries (refer to Note for Table 11.1).

3 A list of write-downs due to sub-prime-related losses and capital raised is available from the Bloomberg webpage (http://www.bloomberg.com/apps/news?pid=newsarchive&sid=a8sW0n1Cs1tY).

4 In De Haas and Van Lelyveld (2005), bank size is measured by the share of an individual bank's total banking assets in the total banking assets of the country in a year. However, definitions of total banking assets of the country vary significantly across the 10 Asian countries, which results in large measurement errors from cross-country comparison. Hence, the logarithm of an individual bank's total banking assets is used instead.

5 These two variables are also useful to control for the monetary policies of individual countries, as these policies might affect the supply of loans from banks if banks are the main providers of funds for households or firms, which is the case in Asia (Bernanke and Gertler, 1989).

6 The GFC is widely known as starting in July 2007 with the bursting of the US sub-prime mortgage bubble, but its effect on other financial sectors, including banking sectors, emerged mainly over the period 2008–09, which is observable from the lending data, both at an aggregate and bank-level.

References

Bernanke, B. and Gertler, M. (1989) 'Agency costs, net worth, and business fluctuations', *The American Economic Review*, 79: 14–31.

Cetorelli, N. and Goldberg, L.S. (2012) 'Follow the money: quantifying domestic effects of foreign banks shocks in the great recession', *American Economic Review*, 102: 213–18.

Clarke, G., Cull, R. and Peria, M.S.M. (2001) 'Foreign bank entry – experience, implication for developing countries, and agenda for further research', *World Bank Policy Research Working Paper Series* 2698.

Dages, B., Goldberg, L. and Kinney, D. (2000) 'Foreign and domestic bank participation in emerging markets: lessons from Mexico and Argentina', *Federal Reserve Bank of New York Economic Policy Review*, 6: 17–36.

De Haas, R. and Van Lelyveld, I. (2005) 'Foreign banks and credit stability in Central and Eastern Europe: a panel data analysis', *Journal of Banking and Finance*, 30: 1927–52.

——. (2011) 'Running for the exit: international banks and crisis transmission', *European Bank for Reconstruction and Development (EBRD) Working Paper* 124.

Goldberg, L., Dages, B.G. and Crystal, J. (2002) 'The lending cycles of banks in emerging markets: foreign and domestic owners compared', manuscript, Federal Reserve Bank of New York.

Gopalan, S. and Rajan, R.S. (2009) 'Financial sector de-regulation in emerging Asia: focus on foreign bank entry', *Institute of South Asian Studies Working Paper* 76.

Herrero, A. and Simon, D. (2006) 'Do we know why banks go to emerging countries and what is the impact for the home country? A survey', Background paper for the Working Group on Financial FDI of the BIS Committee of the Global Financial System.

Jeon, B.N., Oliver, M.P. and Wu, J. (2011) 'Do foreign banks increase competition? Evidence from emerging Asian and Latin American banking markets', *Journal of Banking and Finance*, 35: 856–75.

Masson, P. (1998) 'A rational expectations model of financial contagion', mimeo (May), IMF and Board of Governors of the Federal Reserve.

Morgan, D. and Strahan, D.E. (2004) 'Foreign bank entry and business volatility from US states and other countries', in L.A. Ahumada and J.R. Fuentes (eds), *Banking Market Structure and Money Policy*, Santiago: Central Bank of Chile.

Ongena, S., Peydro, J.L. and Van Horen, N. (2013) 'Shocks abroad, pain at home? Bank-firm level evidence on the international transmission of financial shocks', *DNB Working Papers* 385, Netherlands Central Bank, Research Department.

Peek, J. and Rosengren, E. (2000) 'The international transmission of financial shocks: the case of Japan', *American Economic Review*, 87: 495–505.

Raddatz, C. (2010) 'When the rivers run dry: liquidity and the use of wholesale funds in the transmission of the US subprime crisis', *World Bank Policy Research Working Paper* 5203.

Tanaka, M. (2009) 'Globalized banking, shock transmission, and implications on domestic and international monetary policy stances of the local economy', Speech on *Macro-Financial Links and Monetary Policy Management,* South East Asian Central Bank (SEACEN) Research and Training Centre Directors of Research Seminar, 27 October 2009.

Van Horen, N. (2007) 'Foreign banking in developing countries: origin matters', *Emerging Markets Review*, 8: 81–105.

Xu, Y. (2011) 'Towards a more accurate measure of foreign bank entry and its impact on domestic banking performance: the case of China', *Journal of Banking and Finance*, 35: 886–901.

Appendix A
The relationship between foreign bank lending and local credit stability

This conceptual framework (Table 11.A1) extends Morgan and Strahan's (2004) host country focus by adding home country shocks to cover all four possible cases. In a nutshell, identification of credit supply and demand shocks in the host and home country crises is critical to predicting the implications of foreign banks for credit stability.

As shown in Diagram 1, a reduction in credit demand as a result of credit demand shock in HOST (country) decreases return on investment. Foreign capital and credits will flow out of HOST, amplifying the decline in investment and destabilizing the credit supply ("capital fly" case). Diagram 2 illustrates the case of "lender of last resort", where a reduction in credit supply increases bank returns in HOST. Higher returns attract more credits from HOME (country) and this inflow offsets HOST credit constraints and stabilizes the credit line, as elucidated by Morgan and Strahan (2004). Similarly, the impact of home country shocks on foreign bank lending behaviour can also be interpreted by the same framework. In the case of the "common lender effect", supply shocks in HOME increase returns on investment. Foreign banks with parents in HOME will rip back funds from the periphery and invest in HOME. A sudden drop in credit destabilizes the credit market in HOST (Diagram 3). If demand shock hits HOME instead (the last case in Diagram 4), bank returns decline. Foreign banks with HOME origins look for investment opportunities abroad, with the location depending on expected returns. A promising HOST with higher expected returns will attract credit, whereas an unpromising one will not.

Although this theoretical framework applies to international banking in general, including foreign banks' cross-border lending and local lending, it is important to recognize their different natures and implications for stability. Cross-border lending implies the case where foreign banks extend credit from overseas to local borrowers. In comparison with cross-border lending, local lending tends to be retail oriented and lending decisions are made locally with consideration of the local business situation and under host country regulations. A closer connection with the host country's environment and business cycles makes local lending more likely to be affected by shocks from the host, whereas cross-border wholesale lending with decisions made overseas is inclined to reflect headquarters' conditions subject to home country influence (Herrero and Simon, 2006).

Table 11.A1 The relationship of foreign bank lending and local credit stability

	Types of shocks	*Rationale*	*Implication for credit stability*
Host country	Case 1 Credit demand shock – interest rate rises – capital flows out – foreign credit falls	Diagram 1 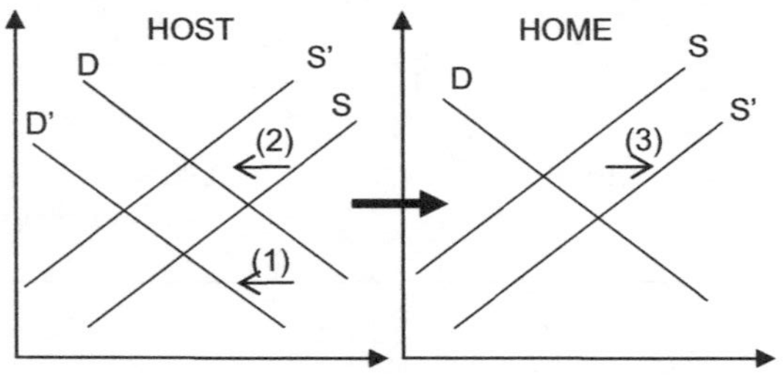	Destabilizing
	Case 2 Credit supply shock – interest rate falls – capital flows in – foreign credit rises	Diagram 2 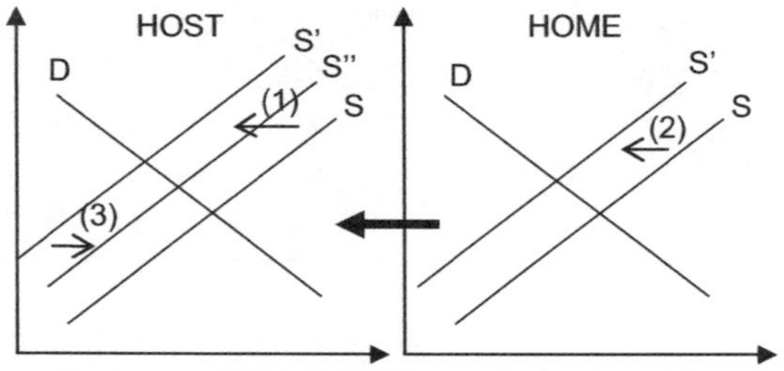	Stabilizing

	Types of shocks	Rationale	Implication for credit stability
Home country	Case 3 Credit supply shock – foreign capital withdraws – foreign credit falls	Diagram 3 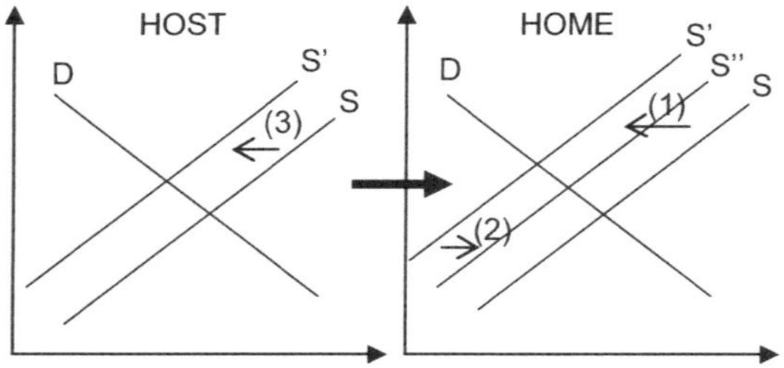	Destabilizing
	Case 4 Credit demand shock – foreign capital flows out – foreign credit might or might not increase in a particular host country	Diagram 4 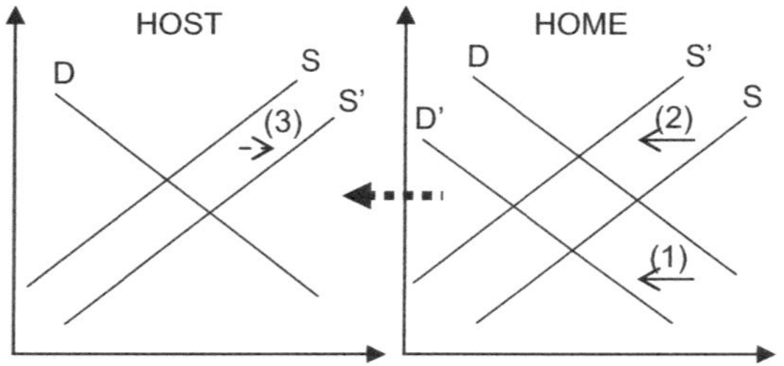	Uncertain

Index

adjustment costs of rebalancing 1–2, 4, 10, 11, 12, 23
ASEAN (Association of South-East Asian Nations) 6, 23, 146, 161, 181; exports, sensitivity to exchange rate 85, 86; modelling exchange rate regime changes 187; openness 146
ASEAN, newer countries 6, 141, 144, 146
ASEAN5 7, 136, 141, 151, 152, 153; GDP 153; level of integration 144, 146; optimal pool of countries for integration 159, 161, 166, 169; welfare gains from integration 161, 166
ASEAN+3 6, 129, 131, 132, 146
Asian Financial Crisis (AFC) 1, 2, 3, 6, 8, 10, 12, 84, 181, 197, 222, 236, 240, 242; causes of 197; crisis-affected countries 3, 4, 13, 14, 16, 17, 20, 21, 24, 152, 188, 193, 220; effect on investment 20, 21–3, 24, 27, 29, 30, 32, 34, 38, 44, 45; non-affected countries 3–4, 13, 21; production structure following 12
Asia Recovery Integration Center 135
Australia 3–4, 18; average leverage ratio 29; current account balance and components 14–16; economic integration with Asia 7; GDP 154; as an integration partner 7, 159, 161, 162, 163, 164, 166, 167; investment share of GDP 20; optimal pool of countries for integration with 160–1, 170, 177, 178, 179, 180; savings share of GDP 19

Bangko Sentral Ng Pilipinas 75, 232
Bank Indonesia 75, 86
banking system 7–8, 50, 102, 112; deregulation 218–19, 242, 254; *see also* banks; credit stability; financial integration; foreign banks
Bank Negara Malaysia 86, 232
Bank of Korea 75, 86
Bank of Nova Scotia Group 232
Bank of Thailand 75
banks: central 10, 53, 75, 76, 77, 86, 87n, 102, 104, 110, 181, 191, 198, 206, 231–2, 234–5; foreign ownership of domestic 242, 243; local bank claims 219, private 110; regionally owned 3, 8, 232, 244, 245, 254; state-owned 37, 41, 42, 43, 50, 110; transmission of financial shocks 3, 7–8, 110, 112, 217; *see also* foreign banks
Bankscope database 247–8
Bernanke "savings-glut" 20
bilateral integration, measuring 133–47; business cycle correlations (BCS) 133, 136, 137, 140, 141, 142; deviations from relative PPP (RPPD) 133, 134–6, 138, 140, 142, 146; deviations from uncovered interest parity (UIP) 131, 134–6, 138, 146; trade openness 133, 134, 136, 139, 140; *see also* economic integration; financial integration; regional integration
bonds: domestic corporate 24, 29, 32, 125; government 2
Brazil 104
Bretton Woods system of managed exchange rates 1
Brunei 137, 138, 139, 140, 141, 142, 144, 145

business cycles 3, 7, 133, 136, 137, 147n, 150, 151, 155, 163, 164, 245, 246, 252, 255, 257, 255

Cambodia 105, 132, 133, 137, 138, 139, 140, 141, 142, 144, 145
capital controls 62, 132, 221; Chinn-Ito index of capital liberalization 111, 114, 127, 132, 133
capital expenditure 4, 25, 31; effect of cash flow on 42–4; *see also* investment
capital flows 1, 3, 75, 102, 103, 108, 110, 218, 221–1; financial outflows 108, 113, 125; financial sector development and impacts on reserve accumulation 110–17; ratio to GDP, ASEAN+3 132
capital losses 2, 102, 244
capital markets *see* international capital markets
Cavoli, Tony 131, 134, 137, 138, 139, 147; openness and economic interconnection in East and Southeast Asia 6, 129–48
central banks 10, 53, 75, 76, 77, 86, 87n, 102, 104, 110, 181, 191, 198, 206, 218, 231–2, 234–5; role in financial stability 113, 123–4, 125, 230, 232, 235; *see also* liquidity provision; name of bank
Chiang Mai initiative 6, 129
China: Asian-owned and global foreign bank lending to 244; Asian-owned and non-Asian foreign bank assets and loans 247; bank expansion in Asia 243, 254; banking system 249; bank lending during the GFC 249; bilateral integration 6, 132, 136, 137, 138, 167; cash holdings 33; Chinn-Ito index 133; corporate assets 33, 34; corporate dividend payouts 35, 62; corporate finance sources 27, 28, 30; corporate retained earnings 35; corporate savings 2, 30, 39, 45, 63, 62–5; credit market 249–50; currency revaluation 2, 5, 9; current account balance and components 14–16; current account surplus 3–4, 5, 14, 57, 59–62, 65, 67, 68, 74; exchange rate 53–74; exchange rate, effect on exports 85; exchange rate, fixed 68; exchange rate, flexible, 4, 53, 86; exchange rate policy reform 76; exchange rate, real 59–62, 67; export processing trade 85; exports of labour-intensive products 85; exports within Asia 84; external debt 27–8, 30, 104, 107; financial sector deregulation 242, 243; foreign exchange reserves 104, 105, 106, 107; GDP 154; household savings 62, 65–6, 67–8; imbalance with USA 5, 10; investment share of GDP 17, 20; manufacturing growth rates 64; national savings rate 66–7; one-child policy 5, 62; optimal group of countries for integration with 162, 171, 177, 178, 179, 180; private business growth 64–5; private savings 3–4, 5, 14, 15, 16, 19, 62, 67; ratio of capital flows to GDP 132; regional integration 6, 140, 141, 142, 144, 145; renminbi, influence on asymmetrical exchange rate behaviour 5, 76–101; renminbi, LSTR2 modelling East Asian currencies against 94–6; renminbi, undervalued 59–62, 74; savings share of GDP 16, 17, 19; sex ratio imbalance 62–8; source of shocks 7, 208–10; state-owned enterprises 4, 62, 63; swap agreements 86, 88n; tax evasion 65; trade balances 97, 98, 99, 100, 101; trade openness 131, 139; trade patterns 84–6, 97–101; welfare gain from integration 165
Chinn-Ito index of capital liberalization 111, 114, 127, 132, 133
Citibank 232, 233
college(s) of supervisors, 231, 232, 237n
Commerce International Merchant Bankers Berhad 232
common-law systems 36, 40, 44, 45, 46
companies, listed: data from Compustat Global Database 49–52; *see also* corporate financial structure; corporate savings
competitiveness 5, 24, 76, 85–6, 87, 102, 109, 110, 254; competitive advantage 1, 243
Compustat Global Database 49
consumption 1, 2, 4, 9, 11, 12, 22, 39, 125, 132, 147n, 149; global 152, 154; measuring welfare gain of increased 155–7; smoothing 149, 150, 151, 152, 163, 165, 166, 167; volatility 150–1, 155–7, 161, 163,

166; welfare cost of uncertainty 150, 151; welfare gains of increased 151, 159, 161–2, 166
Corbett, Jenny 26, 31, 32, 44, 46n, 47, 147, 154, 160, 166, 167, 168; best partners for risk-sharing integration 6, 149–80; corporate savings, investment and financial structure 4, 25–52; drivers for hoarding foreign reserves 5, 102–28; macroeconomic rebalancing and financial integration 1–9
corporate financial structure 25–52; asset-accumulation 35–7; dividend payouts 4, 25, 33, 34, 35, 36, 38; finance sources 26–31; fixed assets 33, 34, 38, 45; retained earnings 33–4, 38, 45; *see also* corporate savings; financial markets; name of country
corporate savings 2, 4, 25–52; cash holdings 31–3; 25, 26; contribution to global imbalances 38–40; hoarding 9, 31, 35, 38, 40, 42, 45, 46; inclusion of depreciation amounts 45–6; reasons for and factors influencing accumulation 25–6, 40–2, 45; used for investment 38, 40, 42–4; 45, 46; withholding from investment 25, 26; *see also* corporate financial structure; name of country
corruption 36, 37, 38, 45
credit stability 8, 240–55; analysis of effect of foreign bank local lending 245–52; deterioration during GFC 251, 252; effect of home versus host country crises 240–1; importance of diversity of foreign bank ownership 241, 254; mechanism of relationship between shocks and foreign credit flows 257–9; policy responses for managing 230–5; role of central banks 231, 235–6; stabilizing role of Asian-owned foreign banks 242, 245, 246, 250, 251, 252, 254
crises: effect of home versus host country crises 240–1; effect on finance sources/flows 30–1, 112, 222, 227, 236, 249–52; *see also* Asian Financial Crisis; Global Financial Crisis
cross-border policy cooperation 8, 231
currency revaluation 2; *see also* exchange rates
current account: adjustment and exchange rate regimes 53–62, 68; persistence 55, 56, 57, 59
current account deficits 10, 16, 53; reducing 1, 21–2
current account surpluses 1, 3, 13, 14, 15–16, 53; causes 59–62, 68, 65; changing to deficits at short notice 1–2, 10, 11, 12, 23; following Asian Financial Crisis 13; means of reducing 3, 12, 22; policy responses to rebalancing 23–4, 68; *see also* name of country

debt: corporate 24, 26, 27, 38, 45; debt versus equity finance 27–9; external 110, 114; long-term debt 29, 30, 31; problem for next generation 13; short-term 29, 20, 31, 104, 108, 109, 110, 114; unsustainability of high 2, 10, 11, 23; *see also* credit stability; finance; name of country
decoupling from global business cycles 3, 6, 7, 8
Deutsche Bank Group 232
Development Bank of Singapore 232
Dungey, Mardi 181, 182, 186, 212; influences of international and domestic shocks 7, 181–216;
Dynamic Stochastic General Equilibrium (DSGE) models 181, 182

economic integration: benefits of 6–7; extent of in East and Southeast Asia 6, 129–47; methods of measuring 130–3; measuring bilateral integration 133–47; regionalism 130; regionalization 130; *see also* financial integration; openness; regional integration
economic/financial volatility i, 2, 3, 7, 8, 67, 77, 87n, 102, 103, 108, 109, 110, 112, 113, 125, 126, 149, 150, 157, 161, 163, 165–7, 188, 193, 226, 228, 229, 236n, 254; S&P Volatility Index 226
Egypt 53
emerging markets 75, 77, 87, 103, 160, 217, 218, 222
employment 3, 10, 12
Europe 6, 10, 149, 164, 232, 240, 241, 242, 243, 244, 245; European Monetary Union 183–4, 182–3

exchange market pressure index 75; 77–8
exchange rates: asymmetrical exchange rates 1, 76–101; during AFC 187, 197; effect on current account imbalances 5, 53–75; fear of currency appreciation 75–101, 110; fixed/managed 1–2, 3, 68, 69n, 110, 134, 187, 188, 197; flexible 3, 5, 53, 54, 57, 68, 75, 76, 86, 87n, 205; floating 75, 87n, 187, 188, 198; influence of regime on current account adjustment 53–7; influence on labour-intensive exports 85–6; nominal 54, 77; pre-, post, and during the GFC 79–84; real 11, 54, 59–62, 67, 68, 70–4, 112, 206, 207, 210; response to Chinese output shock 210; response to US output shock 206, 207; revaluation 2, 5, 9; sex ratio effect, China 62–8, 70–3; STAR and LSTR2 modelling 78–9, 90–6; volatility 77, 87n, 102, 108, 109, 112, 113, 125, 126, 127
exports i, 1, 2, 9, 12, 21, 22, 23, 84, 85–6, 88n, 109, 110, 197, 218; reduction during GFC 246, 251; *see also* trade

Federal Financial Supervisory Authority 232
Feng, Wei 183, 212; best partners for risk-sharing integration 6, 149–80
finance: bonds 2, 29; corporate sector sources 26–38; corporate sector uses of 31–8; corporate structure 25–52; debt/equity structure 27–9; equity 26, 27, 28–9, 30; external 26, 27, 29–30, 38, 39, 40, 45; improving private sector access to 24; long-term 29; short-term 29; *see also* debt
financial integration i, 2, 129, 147n; benefits i, 2, 6–7, 8, 9, 149–50; best partners for 3, 158–65; definition of optimal arrangements for 155–8; geographical constraints 160, 167; methods for measuring 3, 131–2; optimal pool of countries for integration 158–67, 169–75; optimal risk-sharing 150–1; quantifying welfare effects of 151–67; *see also* bilateral integration, measuring; economic integration; regional integration
financial markets 7, 8, 33, 65, 103, 150, 217, 242, 243, 254; global 8, 83, 111, 150, 217, 223, 226, 228, 229; impact of financial development of a country on capital flows and foreign exchange reserves 110–18; liberation and reform 3, 4–5, 8, 32, 39, 46, 103, 112; measuring financial development 114; underdeveloped 29, 103, 108, 110, 112, 113, 114, 117, 124, 125
financial stability 103, 109, 110, 112, 218, 230–6
Financial Stability Agency of the United Kingdom 232
foreign banks: Asian-owned 242–55, 246, 247; Asian-owned expansion 232, 240, 243, 252, 254; Asian-owned and non-Asian foreign banks in Asia compared 247; assets in Asia 7, 242, 243, 244; capital levels and buffers 234; claims to East Asian economies 217–37; collateral arrangements 234–5; common lender effects of 240–1; cross-border banks in South East Asian Central Bank economies 8, 233; cross-border loans 3, 7–8, 217–18, 219, 220, 222, 223, 227, 229–30, 254, 257; deposit insurance scheme 234; effect of origin on stability 241; equity in local banks 221; European 242, 254; Japanese bank lending 222, 223; lending prior to and during GFC 244–5; local lending behaviour 8, 240, 257; memoranda of understanding with host country banks 232; North American 242, 254; operating in SEACEN economies 233; response to crises 240, 241; separation from parent in host country 232, 234; supervision 231–2, 254; systemic risk charge 235; systemic stability fund 235; transmission of shocks 3, 8, 217, 218, 223–30; United Kingdom lending 222, 223; United States lending 222, 223, 245; wholesale funding 245, 252
foreign direct investment 6, 110, 111, 115
foreign exchange markets 2, 75, 77, 102, 110, 112, 123, 124, 125
foreign exchange reserves: causes of/reasons for accumulation 2, 5, 9, 59,

62, 77, 109–13, 117; effect on domestic economy 102; financial development of a country and the impacts of capital flows 110–17; hoarding 102–28; indicators for adequacy of 108–9; major reserve-accumulating economies 104; model of reserve demand 122–6; quantity 102; ratio of reserves to GDP 105; ratio of reserves to imports 105, 106, 108; ratio of reserves to M2 107, 109; ratio of reserves to M8; ratio of reserves to short-term debt 107, 109; reserve demand, analytical model 122–6; summary of explanatory variables for build-up 111–12; trends in accumulation 104–9; *see also* liquidity
France 164

G20 53, 68
GDP growth 23, 152–4, 157, 163, 165, 167n, 181, 227, 228, 229, 230; capital flows ratio 131, 132; foreign exchange reserves share of 104, 105, 115, 116; savings and investment shares of 16–20, 21, 23, 24; trade share of 205, 206
global banks: testing hypothesis of shock transmission to local economies 223–30
Global Financial Crisis (GFC) 2, 5, 7, 26, 44, 68, 76, 77, 181, 192, 195, 217; Asian-owned v. non-Asian-owned foreign bank behaviour 3, 8, 240, 242, 244–5, 251, 252; bank flows during 218, 251; contagion effect 218, 228, 229, 236, 252, 254; contributing factors 53, 227–9; effect on Asian economies 182; effect on currencies 83–4; liquidity shocks 251; stabilizing role of Asian-owned foreign banks 242, 245, 246, 250, 251, 252, 254
governance and reform 24, 39, 62, 63
growth rebalancing 1, 6, 9, 10–24

Heng, Dyna: drivers for hoarding foreign reserves 5, 102–28
Hong Kong: bank expansion in China 243; bank lending data 244, 247, 254; foreign exchange reserves 104, 105, 106, 107, 117
Hong Kong Monetary Authority 86
Hong Kong Shanghai Banking Corporation (HSBC) 232, 233
household savings 3–4, 5, 15, 38–9; China 62, 65–6, 67–8

imbalances i, 3, 25, 26, 46, 68; causes 1, 2, 4, 5, 9, 25, 38, 39, 53; global 12–14, 25, 38, 53, 68; loanable funds model of global 20–2; sustainability 1, 23
India: cash holdings 33; corporate dividend payouts 35; corporate finance sources 27, 28; current account balance and components 14–16; external debt 30; foreign exchange reserves 104, 105, 107; investment share of GDP 16, 17, 20; savings share of GDP 16, 17, 19; short-term debt 107
Indonesia 5, 7; bilateral integration 137, 138; cash holdings 33; Chinn-Ito index 133; corporate dividend payouts 35; corporate finance sources 27, 28; current account balance and components 14–16; corporate sources 26–38; exchange market pressure index 78; exchange rate appreciation and depreciation thresholds 79–84; exchange rate response to shocks 187, 207, 210, 215; external debt 30; foreign bank claims, 219, 221; financial sector deregulation 242; foreign bank lending sources 223; foreign exchange reserves 106, 108; GDP 154; inflation rate 189, 200, 204, 206, 215; interest rates 202, 206, 215; investment share of GDP 20; local bank claims 219; model of impact of shocks on economy 202–5; openness 131, 139, 202, 205–6, 211; optimal pool of countries for integration with 158–60; output sensitivity to Chinese output shock 208; output sensitivity to US output shock 205; output shocks, impulse responses 202–4; ratio of capital flows to GDP 132; regional integration 140, 141, 142, 144, 145; savings share of GDP 19; trade patterns 84–5, 97; welfare gain from integration 161, 162, 166
inflation 2, 188, 189, 191, 192, 194, 195–7, 197–8, 199, 200, 202, 204, 208, 209, 230; response to US

output shock 206; targeting 75, 183, 188, 198, 205; volatility 193
integration *see* bilateral integration, measuring; economic integration; financial integration; regional integration
international capital markets i, 2, 131
interest rates 4, 122, 187, 188, 189, 190, 191, 194, 198, 200, 202, 206, 208, 209, 213, 214, 215, 226; loanable funds model of global imbalances 20–2
international financial system and institutions 1, 5–6, 68; *see also* Global Financial Crisis
International Monetary Fund 12, 22, 38–9, 53, 188, 206
investment: Asia Pacific countries 14–20; constraints 4, 9, 42–4; effect of Asian Financial Crisis, 21–3, 24; effect of cash flow 42–44; effect of GFC 251; means of improving 4, 24; rate needed to sustain growth 22–3
investor protection 36, 42, 45, 46
iPhone trade 88n

Japan: banking crisis in 1990s 240; bilateral integration 6, 136, 137 138, 146, 162; bank lending to East and Southeast Asia 222, 223, 243; cash holdings 33; Chinn-Ito index 133; corporate dividend payouts 35; corporate finance sources 27, 28, 46n; cross-border bank loans 7; current account balance and components 14–16; corporate finance sources 27, 28; exchange rate, flexible 53; external debt 30; foreign exchange reserves 104, 106, 107; GDP 154; investment share of GDP 20; openness 131; optimal group of countries for integration with 162, 172, 177, 178, 179, 180; private savings 4; ratio of capital flows to GDP 132; regional integration 140, 141, 142, 144, 145; savings share of GDP 19; trade openness 131, 139; trade patterns 84–5, 97, 98, 99, 100, 101

Korea 5, 6, 7; bilateral integration 136, 137, 138; cash holdings 33; corporate dividend payouts 35; corporate finance sources 27, 28; current account balance and components 14–16; exchange market pressure index 78; exchange rate appreciation and depreciation thresholds 79–84; export processing trade with China 85; 85; external debt 30; financial sector deregulation 242; foreign bank claims 219, 221; foreign bank lending sources 223; foreign exchange reserves 104, 105, 106, 107; GDP 154; GFC effect on currency 83–4; investment share of GDP 20; local bank claims 219; optimal group of countries for integration with 162, 172, 177, 178, 179, 180; ratio of capital flows to GDP 132; regional integration with 140, 141, 142, 144, 145; savings share of GDP 19; trade openness 131, 139; trade patterns 85, 98

labour 11, 12, 24, 85, 129
Laos 132. 133, 137, 138, 139, 140, 141, 142, 143, 144, 145, 146
Latin America 241, 242, 252, 255n
Lehman Brothers 77, 79, 88n, 221, 222
liquidity 86, 103, 112, 113, 117, 245, 252; analytical model of foreign exchange reserve demand following shock 122–6; government provision 103, 112, 113, 117, 123–6; private sector provision 103, 112, 112, 117, 122–3; shocks 113, 122, 125, 251
loanable funds model of global imbalances 20–2

Maastricht conditions 149
Malayan Banking Berhad 232
Malaysia 7; bank expansion in Asia 243; bilateral integration 136, 137, 138, 144, 146; cash holdings 33; corporate dividend payouts 35; corporate finance sources 27, 28; current account balance and components 14–16; exchange rate regime 187, 205; exchange rate response to shocks 207, 210, 215; external debt 30; foreign bank claims 219, 221; foreign bank lending sources 223; foreign exchange reserves 104, 105, 106, 107, 108; GDP 154; inflation rate 189, 200, 202, 206, 215; interest rate 200, 215; investment share of GDP 20; local bank claims 219; model of

impact of shocks on economy 200–2; openness 131, 139, 205, 211; optimal group of countries for integration with 173; output sensitivity to Chinese output shock 208; output sensitivity to US output shock 200, 205; output shocks, impulse responses 200–1; ratio of capital flows to GDP 132; regional integration 140, 141, 143, 144, 145; savings share of GDP 19; short-term debt 107; welfare gain from integration 161
Maulana, Achmad 154, 160, 166, 168; best partners for risk-sharing integration 6, 149–80
mercantilism 5, 102, 109–10
Middle East 10
Monetary Authority of Singapore 75, 86, 232
monetary union, Asian 129, 146, 149, 182–3
multinational/global banks *see* foreign banks
Myanmar 132, 137, 138, 139, 140, 141, 143, 144, 145, 146

New Zealand 3–4; current account balance and components 14–16; investment share of GDP 20; savings share of GDP 19
non-performing loans 24

Office of Superintendent of Financial Institutions 232
openness 38, 43, 51, 126, 181, 182, 105, 211; financial 3, 5, 8, 9, 42, 45, 46, 50, 61, 70, 72, 111, 131, 132; measuring in East and Southeast Asia 129–48; open economy modelling 183–90; trade 38, 61, 111, 114–15, 130–1, 134, 136, 139, 147n, 205; *see also* economic integration; name of country; regional integration
Organization for Economic Cooperation and Development (OECD) 151, 217
Overseas Chinese Bank Corporation 232

Pacific Exchange Rate Service 79
People's Bank of China: policy on flexible currency 87n; swap agreements 86
Philippines 5, 7; bilateral integration 136, 137, 138; cash holdings 33; Chinn-Ito index 133; corporate finance sources 27, 28; current account balance and components 14–16; exchange market pressure index 78; exchange rate appreciation and depreciation thresholds 79–84; exchange rate response to shocks 187, 207, 210, 214; export processing trade with China 85; external debt 30; foreign bank claims 220, 221; foreign bank lending sources 223, 236n; foreign exchange reserves 105, 106, 107, 108; GDP 154; inflation rate 189, 194, 195–7, 206, 214; interest rates 214; investment share of GDP 20; local bank claims 220; model of impact of shocks on economy 193–7; openness 131, 139, 194, 205–6, 211; optimal group of countries for integration with 162, 173; output sensitivity to Chinese output shock 208; output sensitivity to US output shock 205; output shocks, impulse responses 193–5; ratio of capital flows to GDP 132; regional integration 140, 141, 142, 143, 144, 145; savings share of GDP 19; short-term debt 107; trade patterns 85, 99; welfare gain from integration 161, 162
policies: exchange rate 6–7, 84, 86, 87, 87n, 108, 124; to improve financial stability 5–6, 8, 118, 231–5; to increase investment 4, 23–4, 39–40, 45, 46; to promote regional integration 7, 147; social 62, 68; to support rebalancing 3, 167;
Pontines, Victor 87, 89, 110, 121, 124; Asian countries and fear appreciation against renminbi 5, 75–101; International bank claims on East Asian economies 7–8, 217–39

Radanashin Bank 243
Rashid Hussain Berhad 232
recessions 188, 206
regional cooperation: trade and finance 6, 8, 86, 231
regional integration 7, 9, 129, 130, 149, 244; measuring 135, 150, 141–4, normalized overall integration Top 5 145; *see also* bilateral integration; financial integration; openness

regionalism 130
regionalization 130
resource allocation 2, 6, 11–12, 23
risk-sharing integration *see* financial integration
Russia 104, 105

Saudi Arabia 104, 105
savings: Asia Pacific countries 14–20; cumulative public and private 14; excess 2, 4, 8; loanable funds model of global imbalances 20–2; shares of GDP 16, 17; *see also* corporate savings; household savings; name of country
self-insurance i, 2, 5, 102, 109
shocks 3, 6, 7, 146, 152; bank transmission i, 3, 7, 8, 112, 217, 223, 236; credit supply 257–9; exchange rate 183, 184, 187; financial 6, 7–8, 38, 110, 112, 183, 217, 218, 223; liquidity 251; modelling 181–211; money market transmission 217, 222, 252, 253; policy 62; specifications for modelling the influences of shocks on East Asia 184–7; technology 62; vulnerability to 1, 6, 9, 12, 23, 106, 111, 112, 113
Singapore 5, 7; bank expansion in Asia 243, 254; bilateral integration 132, 136, 137, 138, 144, 146; cash holdings 33; Chinn-Ito index 133; corporate dividend payouts 35; corporate finance sources 27, 28; current account balance and components 14–16; exchange market pressure index 78; exchange rate appreciation and depreciation thresholds 79–84; exchange rate regime 188; exchange rate response to shocks 207, 210, 213; export processing trade 85; external debt 30; foreign bank claims 220, 221; foreign bank lending sources 223; foreign exchange reserves 104, 105, 106, 108; GDP 154; inflation rate 189, 191, 192–3, 206, 213; interest rates 194, 206, 213; investment share of GDP 20; local bank claims 220; model of impacts of shocks on economy 190–2; openness 131, 132, 139, 191, 205, 211; optimal group of countries for integration with 174; output sensitivity to Chinese output shock 208; output sensitivity to US output shock 205; output shocks, impulse responses 190–1; ratio of capital flows to GDP 132; regional integration 140, 141, 143, 144, 145; savings share of GDP 19; trade patterns 85, 101; welfare gain from integration 161, 162, 166
Siregar, Reza 217, 232, 233, 234, 236n, 239; Asian countries fear of appreciation against the renminbi 5, 75–101; International bank claims on East Asian economies 7–8, 217–39
smooth-transition auto-regressive (STAR) model 5, 78, 79, 87n, 90–1
social policies 22, 68
social safety nets 4, 65
South East Asian Central Bank (SEACEN) economies, cross-border banks 233
South Korea *see* Korea
Spain 241
Standard Chartered Bank 232, 233
Structural Vector Auto Regression (SVAR) models 181, 182
sub-prime crisis 84, 85, 86, 182, 183, 200, 217, 221, 222–3, 235, 244; exposure of Asian banks 244; *see also* Global Financial Crisis
surplus countries i, 1, 5, 12, 53; importance of reducing imbalances 1–2; mismatch between savings and investment 2; *see also* current account surpluses

Taiwan: foreign exchange reserves 104, 105
tax evasion 37, 40, 41, 43, 44, 45, 51, 65
Thai Danu 243
Thailand 5, 7; bilateral integration 136, 137, 138, 144, 146; cash holdings 33; Chinn-Ito index 133; corporate finance sources 27, 28; currency devaluation 197; current account balance and components 14–16; exchange market pressure index 78; exchange rate appreciation and depreciation thresholds 79–84; exchange rate regime 187, 198, 205; exchange rate response to shocks 207, 210, 214; export trade 197; export processing trade with China 85; financial sector deregulation 242;

foreign bank claims 220, 221; foreign bank lending sources 223; foreign exchange reserves 105, 106, 107, 108; GDP 154; inflation rate 189, 197–8, 199, 200, 205, 206, 214; interest rates 198, 214; investment share of GDP 20; local bank claims 220; model of impact of shocks on economy 197–200; openness 131, 139, 198, 205, 211; optimal group of countries for integration with 161, 162, 174; output sensitivity to Chinese output shock 208; output sensitivity to US output shock 205; output shocks, impulse responses 197–9; ratio of capital flows to GDP 132; regional integration 6, 140, 141, 143, 144, 145; savings share of GDP 19; trade patterns 85, 101; welfare gain from integration 161, 162, 166
trade: balances 84–6, 97–101; credit 29, 31; openness/intensity 6, 38, 61, 111, 130–1, 133, 134, 136, 139, 141, 146, 147n
Twite, Garry 26, 31, 32, 44, 47; corporate savings, investment and financial structure in East Asia 4, 25–52

United Kingdom 152, 159, 161, 163, 164, 167; average leverage ratio 29; cross-border bank loans 7, 222, 223; GDP growth 154; optimal group of countries for integration 175
United Overseas Bank 232
United States 12, 151, 152, 162, 163, 208, 240; bank assets 7; business cycles 3, 8, 150, 155, 163, 164; cross-border bank loans 7, 222, 223; current account deficit 10, 21–2, 23, 53; debt to East Asian countries 10, 13, 22, 23; decoupling from 3, 7; dividend payout ratio 47n; dollar, influence on asymmetrical exchange rate behaviour 76–101; dollar, LSTR2 modelling against East Asian currencies 92–4; East Asian economic dependence on 182; GDP growth 154; imbalance with China 5, 10; information technology bubble 221, 222; intergenerational debt 13, 24n; monetary policy 75; optimal group of countries for integration 175; source of shocks 7, 182, 197, 200, 205–7; sub-prime crisis 84, 85, 86, 182, 183, 200, 217, 221, 222–3, 235, 244; trade patterns 84–5, 97, 98, 99, 100, 101, 208

Vector Error Correction Model 7, 184, 189
Vehbi, M. Tugrul 181, 212; influences of international and domestic shocks 7, 181–216
Vietnam: bilateral integration 132, 137, 138, 146; Chinn-Ito index 133; current account balance and components 14–16; foreign exchange reserves 105, 106, 107, 108; investment share of GDP 20; ratio of capital flows to GDP 132; regional integration 140, 141, 143, 144, 145, 146; savings share of GDP 19; trade openness 131, 139, 140, 141, 142

Warr, Peter: growth rebalancing and investment in Asia and the Pacific 3, 4, 10–24
Wei, Shang-Jin 39, 47, 53, 56, 57, 58, 59, 61, 62, 64, 65, 66, 67, 69, 71, 73, 74; China's exchange rates and other factors in global rebalancing 4, 5, 53–74
welfare gains from integration 1, 2, 3, 7, 8, 9, 149, 150–67, 240; definition of welfare gain 155; different models of 151; implication of different size of pool of countries 163; maximum of each country 162; measuring scale of gain 152–8; optimal pool of countries for ASEAN5, 161, 164; optimal pool of countries for non-ASEAN5 161–2, 164

Xu, Ying: macroeconomic rebalancing and financial integration 1–9; rise of Asian-owned foreign banks and credit stability 8, 240–59